Martin Guitars:
A Technical Reference

Martin Guitars:
A Technical Reference

by Richard Johnston & Dick Boak
Revised and updated from the original
by Mike Longworth

Hal Leonard Books • New York
An imprint of Hal Leonard Corporation

ISBN: 978-1-4234-3982-0

Copyright © 2009 by C.F. Martin & Co., Inc.

All rights reserved. No part of this book may be reproduced in any form
or by any electronic or mechanical means including information storage and
retrieval systems without permission in writing from the publisher, except by
a reviewer, who may quote brief passages in a review.

Published by:
Hal Leonard Corporation
7777 W. Bluemound Road
P.O. Box 13819
Milwaukee, WI 53213

Library of Congress Cataloging-in-Publication Data

Johnston, Richard, 1947-
　Martin guitars : a technical reference / by Richard Johnston & Dick Boak ;
revised and updated from the original by Mike Longworth.
　　　p. cm.
　Includes index.
　ISBN 978-1-4234-3982-0
　1. Martin guitar–History. I. Boak, Dick. II. Longworth, Mike, 1938– III.
Title.
　ML1015.G9M36 2009
　787.87'1973–dc22
　　　　　　　　　　　　　　2008051986

First Edition

Printed in China through Colorcraft Ltd., Hong Kong

Visit Hal Leonard Online at **www.halleonard.com**

CONTENTS

viii   Photo Credits
x   Acknowledgments
xi   Introductions

2   **Chapter 1: General Information on Guitars**
3   Introduction
4   Labels, Stamps, and Decals
6   The Headstock Decal
8   Early Martin Guitar Shapes and Sizes
9   Modern Martin Body Shapes
10   Cutaway Bodies
11   Appointments
11   Binding and Body Inlay
12   Herringbone
13   Backstrips or Back Purfling
15   Pearl Bordering
16   Soundholes and Rosettes
20   Internal Bracing
21   Top Bracing
23   Back Braces
23   Martin Guitar Necks
23   Early Styles and Materials
25   20th Century Martin Guitar Necks
25   12-Fret Necks Versus 14-Fret Necks
26   Headstock Shape Evolution
27   Headstock Inlay
29   Headstock Volute, or "Diamond"
30   Neck Widths and Neck Shape
31   Fretboard, or Fingerboard, Scale Length
31   Frets
32   Fretboard, or Fingerboard, Position Markers
34   Modern Neck Inlays: More Than Just Position Markers
36   Neck Reinforcement and Neck-to-Body Joints
38   Bridges and Saddles
40   Saddle Materials
40   Pickguards
42   Finishes
43   Stains and Coloring
44   Top Finish Colors
44   Woods
46   Pickups in Acoustic Guitar Models
47   Strings
48   Recorded Changes

52	**Chapter 2: Martin Guitar Models by Style**
53	Original Number Series, Styles 10–100
88	Origins and History of 20th Century Martin Guitar Shapes
88	OM (Orchestra Model)
92	Dreadnoughts
96	M Models
97	J Models
98	Martin Guitars for Specific Stringing or Playing Styles
98	Hawaiian
102	Tenor and Plectrum
104	Nylon String or Classical
110	12-String Guitar Models
114	Acoustic Bass Guitars
115	Shenandoah Models
116	Martin Guitar Series, 1993–2007
116	1 Series
117	Road Series
118	15/17 Series
119	X Series
120	16 Series Models
122	Standard Series
123	Vintage Series
125	Golden Era and Marquis Series
126	Authentic Series
128	**Chapter 3: Limited Production Martin Guitars:** Guitars of the Month, Signature Editions, Limited Editions, Special Editions, and Custom Signature Editions
166	**Chapter 4: Archtop and Electric Martin Models**
167	Acoustic Archtops
169	C Series Guitars
174	F Series Acoustic Guitars
177	R Series Guitars
179	Martin Electric Guitars
180	Flattop Electrics
181	F and GT Series Electric Guitars
184	Martin Amps
184	E-Series Electric Guitars
187	CF Series Archtops

188 Chapter 5: Mandolins, Ukuleles, and Other Small Instruments
- 189 Martin Mandolins: Young Frank Henry's Bold Move Pays Off
- 190   Bowl-Back Mandolin Styles
- 199   Flat-Back Mandolin Styles
- 204   Carved-Top Mandolins
- 207   Martin Mandolas
- 207   Mando-Cellos
- 208 Ukuleles: Martin's Unlikely Little Heroes
- 211   Descriptions of Ukulele Styles
- 215   Taro-Patch
- 216   Concert Ukulele
- 216   Tenor Ukulele
- 217   Baritone Ukulele
- 217   Martin Tiples
- 220 Martin Banjos

222 Chapter 6: Instruments Made by Martin for Other Firms
- 223 A New Way to Sell More Instruments
- 226 A List of All Known Companies
- 233 Custom-Brand Instrument Specifications
- 234 The Ditson Company
- 241 William Foden
- 243 The Paramount Guitar
- 244 Schoenberg
- 245 Southern California Music Co.
- 248 Rudolph Wurlitzer Guitars

251 Appendices
- 251   Production Totals
- 285   Price Charts and Other Appendices

304 Glossary

307 Indices
- 307   General Index
- 313   Models and Styles Index

PHOTO CREDITS

All photos are courtesy of the **Martin Guitar Archives** and the **Martin Guitar Museum** unless noted below. Unless otherwise noted, all images of Martin instruments have been photographed by John Sterling Ruth and digitally prepared by Erik Nelson, at John Sterling Ruth Studio in Bethlehem, Pennsylvania.

Chapter 1

2 photos by Robert Corwin, Frank Ford, Grant Groberg, and Ian Nansen; guitars courtesy of Robert Corwin, Boyd Delarios, and Gryphon Stringed Instruments; **4** photos at left by Ian Nansen; guitars courtesy of Gryphon; guitar on upper right from Martin Museum; **5** photos by Frank Ford and Ian Nansen; guitar and cases courtesy of Gryphon; **12** photo at left by Frank Ford, FRETS.com archives; guitar courtesy of Gryphon; photo at right by Ian Nansen; guitar courtesy of the Kelley family; **13** photos by Frank Ford and Ian Nansen; guitars courtesy of Chris Andrada, Bruce Herrmann, and Gryphon; **14** photos by Ian Nansen; guitars courtesy of Gryphon; **15** photo by Ian Nansen; guitar courtesy of Chris Andrada; **17** photos by Frank Ford and Billy Mitchell; guitars courtesy of Fred Oster, Bruce Herrmann, and Gryphon; **18** photos by Ian Nansen; guitars courtesy of Gryphon Stringed Instruments; **19** photo at left by Ian Nansen; guitar courtesy of Gryphon; photo at right by Robert Corwin, robertcorwin.com archives; guitar courtesy of Robert Corwin; **22** drawing of G Series fan bracing by Tom Culbertson; **24** upper photo by Bruce Herrmann; guitar courtesy of Bruce Herrmann; lower photo by Frank Ford, FRETS.com archives; guitar courtesy of Gryphon; **26** photos by Ian Nansen; guitars courtesy of Gryphon; **27** photo by Ian Nansen; guitar courtesy of Tony Chan; **28** photo at upper left by Robert Corwin, robertcorwin.com archives; guitar courtesy of Robert Corwin; **29** photos by Ian Nansen; guitars courtesy of Gryphon; **33** photos by Ian Nansen and Grant Groberg; guitars courtesy of Gryphon; **36** photos by Ian Nansen; **38** upper photo by Billy Mitchell; guitar courtesy of Fred Oster; other photos by Frank Ford; guitar courtesy of Richard Jones-Bamman; **39** photos by Ian Nansen; guitars courtesy of Gryphon; **41** (left to right): photo by Frank Ford, FRETS.com archives; guitar courtesy of Boyd DeLarios; photo by Ian Nansen; guitar courtesy of Chris Andrada; photo by Billy Mitchell; guitar courtesy of Fred Oster; **42** photo by Ian Nansen; guitars courtesy of Gryphon.

Chapter 2

54 photo at left by Grant Groberg; guitar courtesy of Gryphon Stringed Instruments; **55** photo by Frank Ford; guitar courtesy of Gryphon; **57** photo at left by Fred Dusel; photo at right by Grant Groberg; guitars courtesy of Gryphon; **61** photo at left by John Hamel; guitar courtesy of Fred Oster; center photo by Frank Ford, FRETS.com archives; guitar courtesy of Gryphon; **64** detail photo by Grant Groberg; guitar at right from Martin Museum; **65** photo by Robert Corwin, robertcorwin.com archives; guitar courtesy of Robert Corwin; **66** photo by Frank Ford, FRETS.com archives; guitar courtesy of Peter Overly; **68** photo at left by Grant Groberg; guitar courtesy of Tom Culbertson; **70** photo at right by Grant Groberg; guitar courtesy of Gryphon; **79** photo at right by John Hamel; guitar courtesy of the Chinery Collection; **80** photos by Robert Corwin, robertcorwin.com archives; guitar courtesy of Robert Corwin; **81** photo at left by Paul Johnson; guitar courtesy of Gruhn Guitars; **90** photo by Billy Mitchell; guitar courtesy of Fred Oster; **92** photo by Dave Machette; guitar courtesy of Elderly Instruments; **99** photo by Ian Nansen; guitar courtesy of Steve Sano; **101** photo at right by Billy Mitchell; guitar courtesy of Fred Oster; **103** photos by Ian Nansen and Grant Groberg; guitars (left to right) courtesy of Kate Ebneter, Phil Campbell, and Gryphon Stringed Instruments; **104** photo by Frank Ford, FRETS.com archives;

Chapter 2 (cont.)

guitar courtesy of Gryphon; **107** (photographer unknown) photo furnished from the Martin Archives; **111** photo at right by Grant Groberg; guitar courtesy of Gryphon; **114** photo at far left courtesy of Dick Boak.

Chapter 3

129 and **134** images courtesy of Dick Boak; **137** photo at right by Roy Kidney; **140** photo by John Sterling Ruth; **142** photo by Doug Berry; **143** photo by Fred Solomacha; **144** image courtesy of Marty Stuart; **146** photo by Paul Wilson; **147** photo courtesy of Early Morning Productions; **148** upper image courtesy of Sierra Records; lower photo by Roy Kidney; **149** photo by Rayn Barnett; **151** photo by Kenna Love; **154** photo by Lorenzo Bevilagua/CNN; **155** image courtesy of Marty Stuart; **157** image courtesy of Scott O'Malley; **158** image courtesy of Sir George Martin; **161** photo by Dick Boak; **162** photo by Mark Messner; **165** photo by Sebastian Robertson.

Chapter 4

171 photo at left by Paul Schraub; guitar courtesy of Hank Risan; **172** photo by David Burghardt; guitar courtesy of Steve Sjuggerud; **173** photo at left by Paul Schraub; guitar courtesy of Hank Risan; photo at right by Frank Ford, FRETS.com; **174** photograph by Leigh Wiener, © The Weiner Group, leighwiener.com; photo at right by Frank Ford, FRETS.com archives; guitar courtesy of Gryphon; **175** photo at left by Paul Schraub; guitar courtesy of Hank Risan; **177** photos by Grant Groberg; guitar courtesy of Gryphon; **178** photo at left by Frank Ford; guitar courtesy of Frank Ford; photo at right by Grant Groberg; guitar courtesy of Walter Jebe; **181** photo at left by Frank Ford, FRETS.com archives; guitar courtesy of Gryphon.

Chapter 5

190 photo by Billy Mitchell; **196** photos by Ian Nansen; mandolin courtesy of Leanne and Michael Simmons; **201** photo by Billy Mitchell; mandolin courtesy of Fred Oster; **203** photo by Frank Ford; mandolin courtesy of Chris Andrada; **205** photo at left by Frank Ford; mandolin courtesy of Frank Ford; photo at right by Ian Nansen; mandolin courtesy of Gary Hunt; **208** image courtesy of Michael Simmons; **211** photos by Grant Groberg and Ian Nansen; ukuleles courtesy of Gryphon Stringed Instruments; **213** photo at left by Ian Nansen; ukulele courtesy of Gryphon; **214** photo at left by Doug Youland; ukulele courtesy of Nate Westgor; **215** photo by Ian Nansen; ukulele courtesy of Gryphon; **216** photos by Grant Groberg and Ian Nansen; ukuleles courtesy of Gryphon.

Chapter 6

Thanks to John Woodland for finding many of the old letterheads from Martin's files that appear throughout this chapter. **224** image courtesy of John Woodland; **227**, image courtesy of International Guitar Research Archives (California State University at Northridge); **237** photo by John Woodland; guitar courtesy of John Woodland; **238** photos by Frank Ford and Ian Nansen; guitars courtesy of Chris Andrada; **242** photo at bottom by Kelsey Vaughn; guitar courtesy of Steve Shaw; **244** photos by Grant Groberg; guitar courtesy of Gryphon Stringed Instruments; **247** photos by Robert Corwin, robertcorwin.com archives; guitar courtesy of Robert Corwin; **248** image courtesy of John Woodland; **249** photo at right by Robert Corwin; guitar courtesy of Robert Corwin.

ACKNOWLEDGMENTS

I would like offer my sincere thanks to the following people:

- Richard Johnston, an extremely adept writer with an incredible wealth of knowledge about musical instruments in general, but especially about Martin guitars!
- Jackie Muth, for her patience and guidance during the final phases of the book design process.
- Brad Smith, for his perseverance, steadiness, and commitment to this project.
- Mike Longworth, whose initial research helped to preserve and extend Martin's rich history.
- Chris Martin, for supporting my time with the project and understanding the huge task that lay ahead of us with the book(s).
- And to the previous six generations of the Martin family: Thank you for saving nearly everything!

Dick Boak

Special thanks to Dick Boak, Frank Ford, Fred Oster, John Woodland, George Gruhn and Walter Carter, Michael Simmons, Patty Graves, and the many Martin instrument owners who graciously loaned their guitars, mandolins, and ukuleles to be photographed, or provided photos, for this volume.

I would also like to thank the following photographers who provided multiple images (in alphabetical order): Robert Corwin, Frank Ford, Grant Groberg, Billy Mitchell, Ian Nansen, and John Sterling Ruth.

All of us are indebted to six generations of the Martin family for keeping production ledgers, sales books, inventories, receipts, catalogs, and advertising materials that allowed us to study Martin instruments, and how they were promoted and sold, from 1833 to the present.

Richard Johnston

INTRODUCTIONS

Richard Johnston and I, in collaboration with Hal Leonard Corporation, are pleased to present *Martin Guitars: A Technical Reference*, a companion piece to *Martin Guitars: A History*. Both books are based upon the original text by longtime Martin employee and historian, Mike Longworth.

While our efforts in the first book primarily addressed matters of history, this second volume deals with the technical aspects of guitar specifications, the evolution of model sizes and styles, and instruments made for other firms. It also charts detailed production totals, pricing, and instrument dimensions.

In this definitive edition, we have updated and extended Mike's original efforts and have added information pertinent to the ever-expanding number of new stock model offerings, as well as the continuing evolution of custom, special edition, limited edition, and artist signature edition models.

Mike Longworth's original text included a vast amount of statistical data that has proven to be extremely useful to owners, enthusiasts, dealers, and collectors needing to determine the rarity of specific models within Martin's vast array of instruments offered. In most cases, this reference will enable the identification and precise dating of virtually all Martin instruments made since the inception of serial numbers in 1898. Though identification and precise dating of pre-1898 Martin instruments is more challenging, this text provides the researcher with the most useful tool available. This easy-to-use and fully indexed book also makes it possible to identify the significant changes in specifications that have occurred as materials and styles have evolved throughout the 175-year history of C. F. Martin & Co.

Richard Johnston's lifelong experience as a luthier, purveyor, music store co-owner, and writer have enabled him to provide unprecedented detail about the entire scope of Martin instruments and history. His knowledge of specific Martin sizes, styles, and varieties is extensive. His personal expertise thoroughly covers Martin guitars, mandolins, tiples, taropatches, tenor guitars, banjos, archtops, Hawaiian guitars, and electric guitars.

His research and writing have been no easy task. Richard has immersed himself in this book project for almost a decade. There is really no one better for such a challenge, since his familiarity with Martin guitars was already fully developed prior to writing *Martin Guitars: An Illustrated Celebration of America's Premier Guitarmaker*, published in 1997 with co-author Jim Washburn.

His depth of understanding about Martin guitars clearly exceeds my own, or for that matter, anyone else working at Martin! His writing is clear and accurate, and I am continually impressed by the insights that he derives from his knowledge. It has been an honor to work closely with him on this project.

Mike Longworth retired from Martin in 1995. By default, I was the logical person to pick up where he left off. Facilitation of book projects and the organization of company archives were first at hand. Concurrent with Richard Johnston's writing, I began digitizing Mike Longworth's production totals, originally derived from Martin's archived shop order records. With recent computer records, I extended those totals almost to the present time of publication. I quickly discovered that Martin production totals are a moving target!

Beyond the obvious need for accuracy, my goal in designing a new format for the charts in the appendix was ease of use and efficient allocation of space. I find that I am using these charts on a weekly basis to answer questions about our instruments. I think they are much more understandable now and hope you do, too.

To our readers, thanks for sharing a great interest and passion for Martin guitars.

Dick Boak

Martin Guitars: A Technical Reference follows the style of Mike Longworth's original efforts more closely than does *Martin Guitars: A History*. Following his example, I have tried to trace the technical development of Martin guitars in general, along with the evolution of specific styles, through the years. There are also summaries of how the different types of Martin instruments developed, and the origins of body shapes and how they were (and are) constructed and decorated.

Along with the updated and streamlined production totals, there are two other significant differences between this book and Mike Longworth's original. Mike relied on catalog copy when describing specific models and how they changed over time. I kept that format, but added information and placed dates in italics to reflect when changes apparently first went into effect, in advance of formal notification in a Martin catalog. A second, more important difference is an exhaustive index. (Mike's original had none.) The index allows one to gather information about specific models more quickly and effectively, but it also means readers will, in some cases, be jumping back and forth from one section to another.

If the reader is trying to research a Martin F-7 archtop, for instance, a simple glance at the index will lead them to a few pages that tell the whole story, for this model had a relatively short lifespan. However, if the reader wants to research Martin's D-18 Dreadnought, they will need to spend time in several different parts of this volume. Style 18 began to evolve in the 1850s. The Dreadnought shape has its own fascinating story, and Martin now makes about a half-dozen variants of the D-18 model alone. The only two chapters in which the D-18 does not appear are chapters 4 and 5.

There are some things about Martin guitars that are not covered in depth, but these are parts of the instrument that Martin does not manufacture. Tuning machines, pickups and electronics, and cases represent too much variety and inconsistency to be discussed with accuracy.

For a long time, the production charts have drawn Martin fans to Mike Longworth's original book. It is the edges of those pages in this new edition that will turn dark with use. Thanks to Dick Boak, those pages are now not only easier to read, but far more pleasant to browse through. Readers can look up how long a specific model was actually in production, which is often quite different than how many years it appeared in a Martin price list or catalog. For Martin historians, these production charts also tell us how the Martin Company struggled or thrived. Plain, unassuming models that get little attention have often been Martin's unsung heroes when it comes to sales, but in Dick's production charts the 0-17, the DM, and the D-45 are treated as equals and their numbers tell the real tale.

I hope readers will enjoy the story as much as I have!

Richard Johnston

CHAPTER 1
GENERAL INFORMATION ON GUITARS

INTRODUCTION

The changes in Martin guitars noted here and in the descriptions of specific styles (chapter 2) were gathered from a variety of sources. Most were taken from the catalogs and brochures issued by the company. Fortunately, the Martin Company has a quite complete collection of catalogs from 1898 to the present. Another helpful source has been *Gruhn's Guide to Vintage Guitars*, which contains valuable chronologies of changes to Martin instruments that were not noted by Mike Longworth. Much of the information in Longworth's book came from the notes of Frank Henry Martin, John Diechman, and Russell Lilly, all now deceased. Mike also had many opportunities for conversations with C. F. Martin III, who had excellent recall right up until his death in 1986. Earl Remaley and Marcellus Trach, both still living, also kept note of many of the changes that took place while they were supervisors.

Martin guitar fans and collectors are fortunate that the company had foremen and supervisors who kept such meticulous records from which many important details can be gleaned. Yet such detailed record-keeping has lulled some collectors and dealers into thinking that Martin instruments are nearly as predictable as the clock, and that all the changes are well-documented and without exception. The more we learn about Martin guitars, the clearer it becomes that this is not the case.

For example, it was often only the foremen who recorded the serial numbers of guitars to which structural changes took place, and the dates when these were made. Some of these foremen's notes have survived. The modifications, now considered important, were not noted in official Martin records at the time. The shifted position of the X-brace on Dreadnought models in the late 1930s is a good example, as is the addition of the flat brace under the fretboard on 14-fret models around the same time. (12-fret models have the flat brace; early versions of the 14-fret models do not.) Martin foremen made note of when the X-brace on Dreadnoughts was first moved closer to the bridge, but when the flat brace was first added is still unclear. In some cases where a change was noted as taking place with a certain serial number, guitars with later numbers, but with the earlier detail, have been found, and the reverse has also been noted. For instance, during the 1930s the binding on Style 18 models was switched from rosewood to black celluloid and then changed again to tortoiseshell celluloid, but later examples with black binding have been reported. Style 18 model guitars were given an ebony fretboard and bridge until at least 1940, but numerous examples from 1935 have rosewood instead, with the exception of the Dreadnoughts. More recently, the transition from tortoiseshell pattern to plain black pickguards in 1966/67 apparently took place over several months—not a few days or weeks—and there is much overlapping of the two styles. Yes, Martin was meticulous and methodical, but in some cases structural modifications or even changes in the guitars' appearance were experiments initially, so not all later guitars necessarily received the same new feature. Temporary shortages of certain materials are the most frequent cause of inconsistencies.

The first appearance or mention of a new feature in Martin's sales catalogs was usually well after the change had taken place, just as many new models were sold to dealers for a year or more before they appeared in a catalog. This delay was often because Martin simply used the same catalog for more than one year, inserting only an updated price list in the previous year's edition. Even when the catalog was reprinted, the old illustrations of the guitars themselves were often used again, so in some cases the descriptions of the model and its illustration or photo do not quite match. This is especially true from the early 1940s to the mid-1950s, when Martin relied on the same catalog, but such inconsistencies appear in later years as well. Please consider the dates given for changes, and even the introduction of some models, as approximate.

LABELS, STAMPS, AND DECALS

The earliest known American-made Martin guitars usually have paper labels glued to the inside of the guitar's back, beneath the soundhole. There is wide variation in the wording on these labels, partly because C. F. Martin Sr. had a number of short-lived partnerships during his first decade in the U.S. Due to his complex business arrangements, at least some of these labels probably appeared concurrently, and may indicate how a particular guitar was marketed rather than precisely when it was built.

The use of the familiar Martin stamped brand came very early and was evident even on most (and probably all) of the guitars containing paper labels. On these guitars the stamp can be found on the outside of the back just below the heelcap, where the neck joins the body. The stamp continues to appear in this position on all models with a black neck and cone-shaped heel until that type of neck construction was discontinued in the late 1890s. This same brand or stamp usually shows up in three places on early guitars with cedar necks: first on the center strip inside the back, second on the neck block (sometimes upside down), and last on the back of the headstock.

Early Martins usually had paper labels affixed to the inside back of the guitar, but this practice apparently was discontinued circa 1850.

The Martin stamp read "C. F. Martin, New York" from the 1830s until 1867. On many of the early guitars this mark appears to have been two separate stampings, for the alignment between the "C. F. Martin" letters in an arc, and the horizontal "New York" below it, varies, even on the same guitar. When C. F. Martin Jr. and C. F. Hartmann became partners with C. F. Martin Sr., the stamp on the inside of the back was changed to read "C. F. Martin & Co., New York." Only this stamp on the center strip can be used as a key to separating pre-1867 from post-1867 guitars, because the earlier version of the stamp (without "& Co.") was still used on the back of the headstock. In 1898, the stamped brand was changed to "C. F. Martin & Co., Nazareth, Pa." There was also at least one interim stamp still giving New York as the guitar's origin, but with "1833" between the upper and lower lines. (Evidently, this was used only for a short time.) Some guitars from this same period have only "Martin" stamped on the back of headstock. This marking was used on the company's early bowl-back mandolins as well.

These stamps are on the inside center strip, visible when looking through the soundhole. A is the pre-1867 version, B is from 1867–1898, and C is post-1898. "Made in U.S.A." was added beneath the Nazareth stamp in 1963. Stamp A appeared on the back of the headstock until the late 1890s.

Before the late 1850s, Martin did not have a model code for the different types of guitars it made. There were specific sizes, but not specific styles. Around the time the company began to describe the different styles with a two-digit number following the size designation, the black "coffin" cases were given a paper label as shown below. This would be the only indication of the model, and the paper labels often fell off, or cases were switched, so these labels are sometimes an unreliable source of information. Once the coffin cases were discontinued around 1900 in favor of leather or canvas cases, Martin guitars left the factory with no indication of the model. This oversight would not be corrected until 1930, when the model code was added to the neck block. There are several versions of these case labels, which also mention mandolins after 1895.

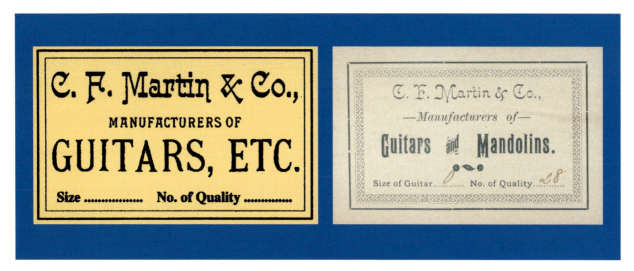

Paper labels found on the inside of the lid on Martin's wooden "coffin" cases.

It is commonly known that the use of serial numbers coincided with the change in the stamped brand. However, at least the earliest guitars with serial numbers had the New York stamp with "1833" on the back of the headstock. Although the serial number always appears on the neck block where it is visible by looking through the soundhole, until around 1902 the serial number sometimes appears on the top edge of the headstock as well. This is particularly true of the higher models.

Serial number from upper edge of the headstock on a 00-28 made in 1900.

THE HEADSTOCK DECAL

In late 1931, Martin began silk-screening the now familiar "C. F. Martin & Co." gold script logo on the headstock, starting with the new OM models. Probably because the company was nearing its centennial, "Est. 1833" was added beneath the arc of script. A nearly identical transfer, or decal, was introduced in mid-1932; by 1933 it appeared on the headstock of virtually all Martin instruments. (The silk-screened version lacked the black border around the lettering found on later decals.) This logo now represents one of the most widely recognized brands in the music industry. The second version of the logo, with black edging, soon came in two sizes. The large size was used on the solid headstock, while a smaller size was used on slotted headstocks, and also on mandolin and ukulele headstocks. (Some ukes got the large decal before the smaller size was available.) The decal also appears on the back of the headstock on some classic guitar models. The gold script Martin decal is still in use today, but there are two slightly different versions. The headstock of Vintage Series models are given a decal much like the original, but with a slightly heavier black line shadowing the gold letters. Golden Era and Authentic Series models display a decal that is virtually identical to what Martin used in the 1930s. The gold decal also appears on many Limited and Special Editions, and is often requested for Custom Shop models as well.

In 1994, gold foil lettering in the same style was introduced on the D-1, and in June 1994 was substituted for the decal on most other standard models. Another variation of the decal was used on Shenandoah models. (See chapter 2.) The different headstock decals are shown on page 26 of this chapter.

20TH CENTURY INTERNAL STAMPS, MODEL CODES, AND OTHER MARKINGS

The stamped brand disappeared from the neck block sometime before 1920, and was last used on the back of the headstock in 1935, but it continued to be stamped on the inside center strip, where it can be seen by looking through the soundhole. "Made in USA" was added below the brand in 1963. The separate caution stamp, "Use Medium or Lighter Strings Only," was added to the center strip in 1976, when Martin brought back scalloped bracing on the HD-28. (Approximately 200 guitars were given a stamp with "Medium" misspelled "Meduim" before the error was noticed.) The string gauge caution stamp appears on most models introduced after that date that were given scalloped bracing, until the caution stamp was discontinued in July 2002.

The original "Nazareth, PA" version of the stamped brand has again been used on the back of the headstock in recent years, usually on limited editions, or guitars ordered through the Martin Custom Shop. It now appears on the back of the headstock on many Golden Era, Marquis, and Authentic Series models. (If a particular Authentic Series model has been patterned on a Martin guitar made after use of the headstock stamp was discontinued, that model is not given the stamp.) Currently, the stamped brand is used on the back of the headstock whenever the headstock face does not bear a Martin logo, e.g., models with torch or tree-of-life inlays in the headplate.

In October 1930, Martin began stamping the model code on the neck block, just above the serial number, where it can be seen when looking through the soundhole. The introduction of the model code apparently wasn't consistent across Martin's wide range of models at that time, and some instruments continued to appear without it months later. The recently introduced OM models apparently were the first to get the new neck block stamps indicating the model. Flat-back mandolins were stamped on the center strip of the back, so the model code was visible through the soundhole. (Since bowl-back mandolins were discontin-

(left) Appleply laminated neck block used on all models with mortise-and-tenon neck joint. (right) Solid mahogany neck block used on models with traditional dovetail neck joint.

ued before 1930, those never had a model ID on the instrument.) The archtop guitars and mandolins that were introduced in the 1930s also have the model code stamped on the back, always where it is visible by looking through the round soundhole or the bass side *f*-hole. Martin's ukuleles were never given any model identification on the instruments themselves until the reissue of 5K models beginning in 2006. These have serial numbers and model code on the neck block.

A second type of neck block marking first appeared on the Shenandoah models, in 1983. This was a small rectangular maple plaque, affixed to the neck block, with the serial number and model designation stamped on it. A similar maple plaque is still in use on any guitars with "new technology" (mortise-and-tenon) neck joint, with the exception of some Limited Edition models, which are given a mahogany ID plate that covers the entire face of the laminated neck block. Some of the guitars with the mortise-and-tenon neck joint also have a paper label on the inside of the back, clearly visible when looking through the soundhole.

Starting in 1997, a laser-etched brand, model code, and serial number appear on the neck block of all dovetail neck joint guitars. Most Limited Edition, Signature Edition, Golden Era, Marquis, and Authentic Series models with the traditional dovetail neck joint also have a paper label on the inside of the back.

EARLY MARTIN GUITAR SHAPES AND SIZES

In old Martin sales books, the sizes of the guitars were noted by numerals as early as 1852, a system that probably was used before that date but the records have not survived. These entries were for the sizes 3, 2 1/2, 2, and 1. Although the sizes and shapes apparently were set by this time, ornamentation and appointments were still in flux.

Sales ledgers from 1854 have the first written record of guitars with the size 5 designation, and also the first entry of the size 0 guitar. Since Martin records from this period are incomplete, these sizes may have been made earlier, and a size 0 guitar has been discovered with headstock, bridge, and "screw neck" features that suggest it was made before the mid-1850s. Size 4 first appears in records from 1857. Sizes 5 and 4 were sometimes called "Terz" guitars, meaning they were tuned one-third higher than larger sizes. Although Terz guitars were mentioned at the bottom of later price lists, these smallest sizes weren't specifically listed. Sizes 2 and 2 1/2 were listed as "ladies' models," and we know women represented a significant percentage of Martin's customers throughout the 19th century. The importance and tastes of Martin's female customers can be gauged by the fact that the four highest models are shown in the price list only in size 2! Size 1 and size 0 were both considered to be full-size guitars, though they certainly do not appear so today.

The earliest mention of size 00 in Martin ledgers is a 00-28 sold August 1, 1873. This larger size was made before that date as a 00 with Style 28 appointments, but with deeper sides, has surfaced with the pre-1867 stamp on the inside center strip. Early features on this guitar suggest that it, too, may date to the 1850s, but without surviving documentation we can't be certain. Why size 00 was never mentioned in a price list, and was rarely made until Frank Henry Martin took control in 1888, will probably remain a mystery.

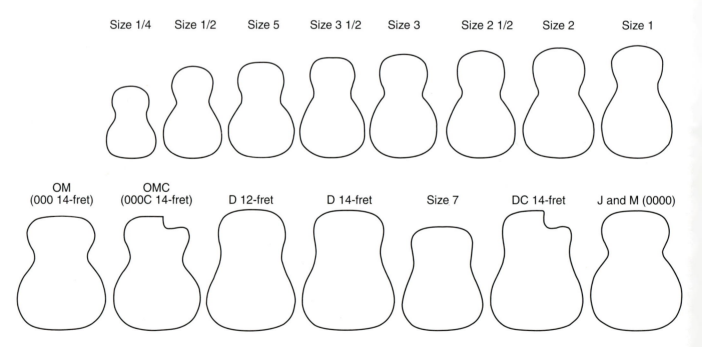

Martin makes the widest range of fretted instrument body shapes and sizes of any North American manufacturer. Almost all of the shapes it has ever made are still available, if not as stock models, at least on special order. Ironically, both its smallest shape (soprano ukulele) and one of the largest

Size 000 made its official appearance in 1902, and most of the early examples in this size were made as "harp guitars," with extra bass strings. The 000 size didn't sell very well until the 1920s, when it was offered with steel strings and quickly became more popular.

The Dreadnought, or D size, originated with the Ditson series with their style 222, Ditson serial #71, in 1916. As with the 00 and 000 sizes, the Dreadnought was not very popular initially. Even after Martin adopted the oversized model and began making them under the Martin name, the company did little to promote sales. Once the Dreadnought was modified to a 14-fret model and given a spot in the 1935 catalog, however, it began to deliver strong sales. It has since become the most widely copied steel-string acoustic guitar shape of all time. (For more information on the Martin Dreadnought, see chapter 2.)

MODERN MARTIN BODY SHAPES

The new Orchestra Model (OM) with 14 frets clear of the body, first introduced in 1929, is considered to be where modern Martin body shapes begin. The overwhelming popularity of this model with a longer neck, plus the initial popularity of Martin archtop models introduced in 1931 (also with 14-fret necks), led the company to redesign all of its flattop body shapes by 1934 to accommodate a longer and narrower neck. Around the same time, Martin began to recognize that steel-string guitarists also wanted bigger, louder guitars. This led the company finally to embrace and promote the Dreadnought, but the 14-fret 0, 00, and 000 models have continued to the present day with the same shapes that were designed between 1929 and 1932. The shapes of the smaller models, such as size 1 and size 2, were never changed.

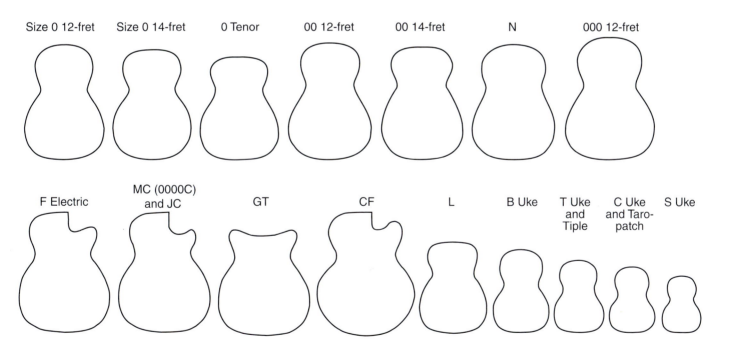

(12-fret Dreadnought) were designed at around the same time in the mid-'teens. Archtop models introduced in the 1930s were the same shape as current 14-fret flattops: R archtops were 00, C archtops were 000 (OM), and the F archtop shape was used 40 years later for the M and J. The 1/4 size guitar shape was used for the tiple and later for the tenor ukulele.

Although there were a couple of oversized D-45s made in the 1930s, the widest production Martin guitars were the F Series carved-top models that appeared in 1935. These featured shallow, 16" wide bodies. After the "F" models were discontinued in 1942, the Dreadnought reigned for many years as by far the largest guitar in the Martin line, at 15 5/8" wide and 4 7/8" deep. In 1977 the "M," a flattop version of the F models, made its appearance with the same 16" width and 4 1/8" depth. The Jumbo, or JM, with the outline of the M and the depth of the Dreadnought, was introduced in 1985. This model is now simply called a J, while the M shape was briefly renamed 0000 in 1997. Today, the shallow-bodied version is called both M and 0000, but the two designations indicate the same body shape and size.

In 1980, Martin introduced a 7/8 size Dreadnought, called a size 7. Although it was initially featured in the catalog, it has been available only through the Martin Custom Shop for several years. On the other end of the scale is the "Goliath," first built for collector Scott Chinery in 1996 with an adjustable body mold (now lost), but there are no current plans to build more of that model.

Another variant of the Dreadnought has sides the same depth as the 000. To date, these have only been available as Signature Editions. The Women and Music models, introduced in 1997, go the opposite route, with Dreadnought depth sides on a 00 size body. Over the years, there have been other variants that resulted from special orders by both individual players and Martin retailers. OM models with deeper sides, but not as deep as a Dreadnought, are but one example.

CUTAWAY BODIES

Except for the thin-body electric guitars first made in the early 1960s, Martin did not offer a cutaway model guitar until 1981, when the DC-28 and MC-28 were offered. These had Venetian (rounded) cutaways, and Martin initially gave these models a deep cutaway with 22-fret fingerboards, instead of the usual 20. These changes necessitated moving the primary top brace above the soundhole toward the bridge, which in turn required an oval soundhole. Cutaway versions of the new Jumbo body shape (J-40MC introduced in 1988, later renamed JC-40) also used the 22-fret/oval soundhole combination, and the 000-16C introduced in 1991 was a similar design. The oval soundhole was discontinued in 1996 when cutaway models were given 20 frets instead of 22, and the cutaways were made more shallow, allowing a round soundhole as on other Martin guitars. This design, most likely inspired by the Selmer guitars of Mario Maccaferri, was first introduced by Eric Schoenberg and Dana Bourgeois on Schoenberg OM models made in cooperation with Martin beginning in 1986. Cutaway versions of almost all of the company's steel-string body shapes are now available, if not as stock models, at least through the Custom Shop. This even includes a cutaway version of the 12-fret 000. For a complete chart showing all Martin's guitar body shapes and sizes, see pages 8–9.

APPOINTMENTS

BINDING AND BODY INLAY

More than any other feature, Martin styles have often been distinguished by their body binding. The easiest way to tell a Style 21 guitar from a Style 28, for instance, is to note that Style 21 has dark binding of either rosewood or plastic, while Style 28 has light-colored binding. Even on the earliest Martin guitars, ivory binding was used on the higher models; wood binding, usually rosewood, was used for medium-priced instruments. The least expensive models had rosewood binding only on the top edge, and the back was left unbound. A few instruments were made with maple or holly binding, but these aren't common.

By the late 1850s, Martin's styles became more fixed. Style 26 and higher were given ivory binding, while Styles 24 and lower were given rosewood. The ivory-bound models usually also had wood marquetry around the top edge, just inside the ivory band. The marquetry was purchased in long strips, and was not made at the Martin factory. It's important to note that Martin always referred to only the primary material on the edge of the instrument as binding, while any other contrasting lines, marquetry, or pearl within the bound edge was considered inlay. While many instrument makers would describe a modern D-28, for instance, as having three-ply white-black-white binding on the back edge, Martin refers to it as white binding with a black-white inlay because the outermost binding is a separate piece.

The ivory binding was switched to ivory-grained celluloid in early 1918, although Martin had already been using celluloid binding on some models made for other firms, and on its Style 2 and Style 3 ukuleles. The ivory in soundhole rosettes changed to celluloid at around the same time. Rosewood binding continued to be used on Styles 21 and lower until 1932, when black celluloid was used instead. (Styles 22–27 had been discontinued.) At around the same time, the black and white lines used for the soundhole rosette, and for the black-white inlaid lines on the tops and backs of most models, were switched from wood to celluloid as well. There are exceptions to this, however, such as the wood inlay bordering the pearl on Styles 42 and 45 until they were discontinued in the early 1940s. A wood inlay was also retained on the top edge of 00-21 models until many years later, proving once again that the Martin company is capable of inexplicably preserving stylistic touches from a previous era, sometimes for decades.

The color and type of plastic used for the binding continued to change. Black celluloid was replaced by tortoiseshell pattern celluloid in 1936, for instance, but the dark binding was changed back to black 30 years later. (These transitions are noted in detail in the style descriptions in chapter 2.) In response to customer demand, virtually all the materials used for binding and body inlay in the 1930s are now in use again on certain models, such as the Vintage Series, Golden Era Series, Authentic Series, Limited Editions, and Custom Shop models.

HERRINGBONE

The term herringbone is almost synonymous with Martin guitars, especially Style 28. It refers to a type of wood marquetry (sometimes called purfling) that displays an inverted V pattern of tiny dark and light stripes. It shows up on some of the earliest Martin guitars made in the U.S., but apparently was first used on the back and side edges, and not around the perimeter of the soundboard. Beginning in the 1850s, a narrow band of herringbone was used to trim the face of Martin's largest "concert model" guitar, the size 0. Within a few years this model was called the 0-28, and herringbone became one of the most consistent features of Style 28 Martin guitars for nearly a century. It was also used around the soundhole and as the backstrip of Style 21 models (and appears as the backstrip of some Style 28 models as well). Some early versions of herringbone show green or tan colors in addition to, or instead of, simply black and white, but this variant does not appear after the 1880s.

There has been much debate as to why Martin dropped the herringbone trim around the tops of Style 28 models in late 1946. The change may have been due to problems with the source of the marquetry itself, since most of it was imported from Germany at the time. It was also a difficult procedure to soak the strips of herringbone in hot water trays and work the material into the tighter bends of the guitar during the binding process. The substitution of black and white celluloid lines as previously used on the C-2 archtop models was a logical choice, with a more modern appearance that suited the times. The change occurred with a batch of D-28 models, serial numbers 98209–98233. Herringbone continued to be used as the backstrip of Style 21 models until late 1947.

The use of herringbone returned almost 30 years later with the introduction of the HD-28 in 1976, and is a standard feature on many other Martin models introduced since then. A finer pattern of herringbone, similar to that used on 19th century Martins, is also now available.

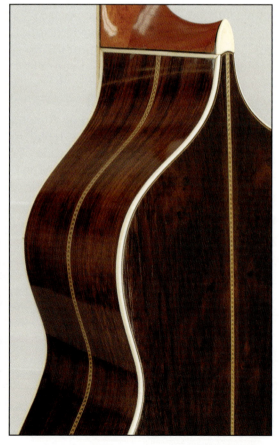

Although herringbone is now primarily thought of as a decorative border around the top of Martin guitars, it was first used around the sides on 1830s models. The guitar shown at right, presumed to be from the 1840s, has a herringbone backstrip as well as herringbone around the middle of the sides. It has a herringbone top border as well.

BACKSTRIPS OR BACK PURFLING

The decorative inlay dividing the two halves of the back on higher Martin models is commonly called the "backstrip" (sometimes "backstripe"), although the Martin Company refers to the same feature as "back purfling." This is the same type of wood marquetry used around the perimeter of its guitar tops, although pearl strips are also sometimes used. These strips of marquetry have only rarely been made in Nazareth, and today Martin relies on both foreign and domestic sources. Even during Martin's first decades in the U.S., this marquetry was imported; despite low production during the early years there was much variation. Standardization of Martin models in the 1860s notwithstanding, the marquetry used up the center of the back on Styles 21 and higher continued to vary. Except for the "zigzag" backstrip usually found on Styles 26 and 28, most of these designs relied on arrow patterns that appear like more complex and colorful versions of herringbone. Around 1916, however, when the Martin Company underwent tremendous growth and the number of guitar styles was greatly reduced, these backstrips became more standardized. By 1920, the number used was reduced to three, with only rare exceptions. Style 21 was given black and white herringbone, Style 28 received the "zigzag" pattern (sometimes called "zipper"), and Styles 42 and 45 got the more complex pattern of multicolored horizontal lines bordered on either side with diagonal lines, or "half-herringbone." This pattern is now widely known as simply a "Style 45 backstrip," or what Martin calls "Style 45 back purfling." All three of these patterns disappeared from Martin production by 1947, when Style 21 and 28 were given a black and white checkered pattern resembling chain links. All of the backstrips, or back purfling that appeared in the 1920s and '30s, are now used again at Martin. Other patterns appear on special or limited editions.

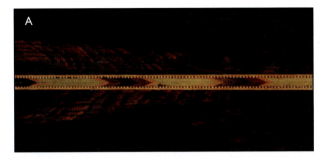

Early back purflings: (A) Pre-1867 Style 34, (B) unknown style c. 1850, (C) Late 1890s Style 42, (D) 1901 Style 34

(A) "zigzag" or "zipper" backstrip found on most post-1900 Style 28 models with herringbone around the face, (B) multicolored, sometimes called "mosaic" backstrip used on virtually all pearl-bordered Martins after 1915. By 1948, the "chain link" or "checkered" pattern (C) was the only marquetry backstrip used, and appeared on both Styles 21 and 28. All three of the above styles have been widely used by Martin since the company began reissuing its earlier models. All three of these styles were used on 19th century Martins as well.

PEARL BORDERING

The colorful pearl bordering so often found on the highest models of most modern flattop guitar brands can be traced back to Martin Style 40 and 42 guitars of the mid-19th century, intended as ladies' models. These models appeared on the earliest Martin price lists from around 1870 (see chapter 2). Martin records from before the company issued a price list indicate that these models were made at least as early as the 1850s. Bordering the soundhole and/or top of an instrument with pearl inlay wasn't a Martin innovation, of course, for many early instruments have pearl designs or engraved pearl borders, as well as elaborate pearl rosettes. Martin seemed always to strive for decoration that was more refined than gaudy, and though there are very early models with borders of a repeating pattern of small pearl shapes, C. F. Sr. apparently settled on a single narrow band of abalone bordered on either side with fine black and white lines (at least on standard models) shortly after leaving New York. Such pearl bordering was found on Martin guitars long before other American guitar companies began to use a similar style.

Pearl bordering on a turn-of-the-century 0-42 model.

In Martin's early price lists, only the small size 2 guitars (2-40 and 2-42) were offered with pearl bordering. Apparently, such decoration was considered suitable primarily for ladies' instruments, usually played in the parlor, while the larger size 1 and size 0 "concert" models were comparatively plain. By the 1890s, however, Martin's male customers frequently began ordering size 0 and 00 models in Style 42.

Except for a few special orders, Martin did not use pearl bordering around the back and sides until after 1900, when an even higher model was introduced. Abalone of a lighter color was used to border the back and sides of the newly introduced Style 45, so as to provide more contrast with the dark rosewood. The strips were even narrower, resulting in a subtle effect.

Martin discontinued the use of pearl bordering in early 1943, due to restrictions on materials, especially imports, during the war. The last of the original pearl-bordered Martins were six 000-42 models (83512–17), begun February 24, 1943. Such decoration wasn't seen on a new Martin model again until 1968, when Mike Longworth helped to initiate the return of the D-45 to the head of the price list. One major difference between the bordering on the reissued D-45, and also the less elaborate D-41 introduced shortly after it, was that the black and white purfling lines on both sides of the pearl were made of plastic instead of wood. The original style wood and wood fiber purfling adjacent to the pearl was frequently requested on Custom Shop orders beginning in the 1980s; in the 1990s they became a feature on Limited Edition "reissue" models such as the Gene Autry D-45. Wood (or wood fiber) purfling or inlay is now a standard feature on pearl-bordered models in the Golden Era, Marquis, and Authentic Series.

SOUNDHOLES AND ROSETTES

Martin relied upon the traditional round soundhole for all its guitars for nearly the first 100 years, but that doesn't mean the company took the easy route. Smaller guitars were given slightly smaller soundholes with correspondingly tighter spacing of the rosette. The Size 5 Terz guitar had a soundhole 3 1/4 inches in diameter, while the 000's soundhole was 3 7/8 inches. Every size in between those two extremes was slightly different. Martin cared enough about the aesthetic balance of its instruments to make a soundhole 1/32 of an inch different in diameter if necessary. Even today, Martin makes more soundhole sizes than most modern manufacturers, although the company isn't as fanatical about proportion as it was in the past.

Oval soundholes first appeared on Martin's bowl-back mandolins introduced in the mid-1890s, and a similar oval soundhole was used for the flat-back mandolin models that followed. Martin's first *f*-shape soundholes appeared on its carved-top guitars in 1932, barely a year after the company entered the archtop market with round soundhole models. The carved mandolins were given *f*-holes in 1936. Unlike most manufacturers, whose archtop soundholes look like an elongated letter S but with shallower curves, Martin's *f*-holes are more closely modeled on the *f*-like soundholes found on violin-family instruments. Some of the lower-priced archtop Martins, such as the R-18 and R-17 models, had tops arched by bracing, not by carving of the top itself; these models have *f*-holes with three separate segments. All Martin ukuleles have round soundholes. (Please see the respective chapters on those instruments for more details.)

Oval soundholes appeared on Martin flattop guitars with the introduction of the first cutaway models, but these were later redesigned to have round soundholes. Other soundhole variations are used in the X Series models with aluminum tops.

ROSETTES

It is unclear exactly when Martin first began using the now-familiar three-ring rosette, but since there are several examples with the Martin & Coupa paper label, it seems likely that such a rosette dates back at least to the 1840s, and probably earlier. The three-ring rosette was used on virtually all Martin models by the 1850s, although the design of the marquetry in the center ring varied. The inner and outermost rings were simple black lines on the plainest models, with higher models getting as many as five layers of black and white lines for both the inner and outermost ring. The familiar Style 28 soundhole rosette, sometimes called "5-9-5" (referring to the groupings of black and white lines), also appeared at least as early as the 1850s.

 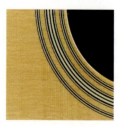 

Although Martin currently uses a variety of other rosettes for guitars in its X, Road, 15, and 16 Series, an overwhelming majority of new models with the traditional hand-fitted dovetail neck joint display one of the three rosettes shown here. On the left is a Vintage Series Style 18 rosette, in the middle, Style 28, and on the right, the Style 45 rosette. The Style 28 rosette also appears on many models with both higher and lower style numbers, while Style 45 rosettes are used on all style numbers 36 through 45, and on numerous Special, Limited, and Signature Editions.

There is much variety in early Martin soundhole rosettes: (A) 1830s model with Stauffer headstock, (B) unknown style c.1850, (C) pre-1867 Size 1 of unknown style. (Several other examples are pictured in book 1, chapter 1.)

Shortly after 1900, Frank Henry Martin reduced the number of Martin models, resulting in four different versions of the three-ring rosette. Style 18 (and early Style 17 models) were given the simplest version, with a center ring composed of nine plies of dark and light lines with a single dark line for the inner and outermost circles. Style 21 was given a rosette similar in complexity to the 5-9-5 Style 28 rosette, but with a band of herringbone in the center ring, bordered by black and white lines. (This was essentially the same rosette used since the 1850s on Styles 20 and 21.) All Martin Styles above 28 were given the pearl rosette, nearly identical to the rosette found on numerous Martins today in Styles 38 and above. (The rule about giving all models Style 30 and higher a pearl rosette no longer applies after introduction of the D-35.) When the all-mahogany version of Style 17 was added in the early 1920s, it was given a simple, single-ring rosette composed of dark and light lines.

There were exceptions to the rosettes described above, but these were found in guitars Martin made for other firms, such as Ditson, Foden, Southern California Music, and Wurlitzer. Martin archtop models, tiples, mandolins, and ukuleles, of course, displayed quite different soundhole decorations, and are not described in detail here.

By 1933, Martin began switching the black and white lines in its rosettes from wood to celluloid. The pearl rosette disappeared at the same time as pearl bordering, in early 1943. In 1946, the last of the herringbone rosettes were discontinued on Style 21, which

Soundhole rosettes and top inlay from pre-WWII Martin guitars: (A) Style 18, 1923; (B) Style 21, 1905; (C) Style 28, 1930; and (D) Style 42, 1894. The top inlay and soundhole rosette on Style 42 is the same as used on Style 45. The switch from wood purfling to celluloid in the early 1930s changed the appearance of these styles somewhat, but the number and pattern of dark and light lines remained the same.

was then given a variation of the rosette found on Style 28 or the simpler Style 18 version. The pearl rosette returned with the D-45 in 1968, and the herringbone rosette, which first reappeared on the D-76, was frequently requested once the Custom Shop was announced. The next big change regarding rosettes came in 1988, when Martin began using the Style 28 rosette on all Style 18 and 21 models, with the exception of Limited Editions and Custom Shop orders. With the introduction of the Vintage Series, however, the simpler Style 18 rosette reappeared, and with an increasing emphasis on historical reissues, Martin now offers virtually all the soundhole decorations the company has used in the last 100 years. In recent years, the most elaborate soundhole decoration is the "pearl herringbone" rosette first suggested by Marty Stuart and used on his HD-40MS Signature Model in 1996, later offered on other Limited Editions and as the stock soundhole decoration on short-lived special models such as the D-41HP.

With the introduction of the D-1, and the wide range of "new technology" models that followed using the mortise-and-tenon neck joint, numerous soundhole rosette patterns and some decal rosettes appeared. Some of these new models were given rosettes significantly different from any designs Martin had used previously. (See chapter 2 for descriptions and photos of some of these variations, such as those found on Style 16 models.)

INTERNAL BRACING

Martin was one of the first guitar companies to openly discuss the internal structure of its instruments in matter-of-fact terms. As early as the 1920s, the bracing of a Martin guitar was displayed in the catalog for all to see. The history of the internal bracing of a Martin guitar soundboard is an integral part of the story of the American flattop guitar, as Martin's bracing pattern was being widely copied over 100 years ago.

Dennis Fischl shaping top braces in Martin's body assembly area, circa 1980.

TOP BRACING

The earliest Martins had top braces horizontal to the frets, similar to European guitars of the early 19th century. Contrary to popular belief, Martin apparently began using fan-pattern top bracing around the same time the X brace was first used. The fan pattern, often referred to as "Spanish bracing" in Martin logbooks during the 1850s/60s, continued to be used on the smallest and least expensive models, such as the 2½-17, until the late 1890s. Martin seems initially to have believed that a heavier version of this pattern would be suitable for steel strings, for a fan pattern was used for the earliest Hawaiian guitars made around 1916, and also appeared on the earliest Ditson guitars. (Most of these guitars suffered considerable top distortion from string tension.) Martin abandoned the use of fan bracing for these steel-string models a few years after their introduction.

The fan-pattern top bracing reappeared on the gut-string models introduced in the mid-1930s, which were given a G suffix (for gut strings) to the model code. These classical Martin models were switched to a C suffix in 1962 and remained in regular production until the mid-1970s, available on special order until 1995. The top bracing on a mid-1950s 00-28G is very similar to the bracing on a mid-1850s 2-18, which was referred to as a "Spanish" model at the time. Martin used a more contemporary Spanish-style fan pattern for the N Series classic guitars introduced in 1968, and a quite radically different "lattice" bracing pattern for the Martin/Humphrey classical models introduced in 1997. Production of both of these variants was short-lived.

When C. F. Martin first began using the X bracing pattern for guitar tops—at least as early as 1850, and probably before that—the braces were only slightly relieved beneath the bridge. In fact, on some of the earliest X-braced Martins that have survived, the braces have no relief, or scalloping, beneath the bridge at all. In later decades, the tops of the braces were carved into small peaks and valleys like a suspension bridge. Since the early 1960s, the community of guitar technicians, vintage dealers, and collectors have called it scalloped bracing. (It is important to note that some contemporary luthiers have taken the scalloping of their X-pattern top bracing to extremes that bear no relation to Martin's style whatsoever.)

As Martin guitars were made in larger sizes, and especially when the use of steel strings became common, the braces were made heavier but the top contour, or scalloping, remained much the same. On Dreadnought models, the X-pattern was moved in late 1938. Earlier, D models had the intersection of the X about one inch below the edge of the soundhole, while on later Dreadnoughts the X was moved approximately ¾" further down, closer to the bridge. The earlier position is now called high X, or forward-shifted, bracing, and is a standard feature on most current Vintage, Golden Era, and Authentic Series Dreadnoughts, as well as on many limited editions. According to C. F. Martin III's recollections many years later, moving the X brace was an attempt to strengthen the top against the torque from heavy gauge strings. The big archtop guitars of the era were often strung with extremely heavy strings (.014 to .060, usually with a wound 2nd), and such string sets wreaked havoc when used on lightly braced flattop guitars.

The discontinuance of the scalloping in favor of a straight brace, tapered toward the outside edge of the guitar top, was not recorded in company files, but the notes kept by factory foreman John Deichman indicate the change occurred with #89926, in late 1944. It is possible that a few guitars appeared afterward with the scalloped bracing, or that a few earlier serial numbers were given top bracing with the non-scalloped profile. It should also be noted that Martin's X-bracing continued to evolve, with the tapering of the top braces being lessened until they reached

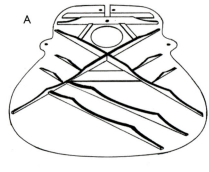
A

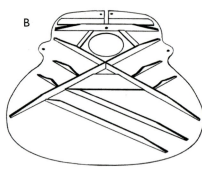
B

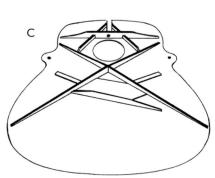
C

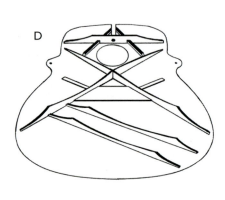
D

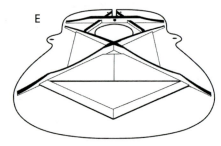
E

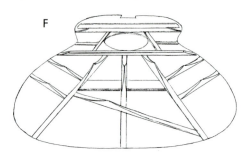
F

their heaviest form in the late 1960s and early 1970s. In 1968, Martin stiffened the soundboard even more by changing from a small maple bridgeplate to a larger and thicker one of rosewood.

Ironically, the use of heavy-gauge strings had all but disappeared in the late 1960s, when Martin top bracing reached its heaviest form. Within a few years, increased awareness of the greater volume and bass response in pre-1945 Martin guitars led the company to reconsider scalloped top bracing. The first model in which scalloped top braces reappeared was the HD-28, in 1976; Martin went back to the small maple bridgeplate for this Dreadnought as well. From 1976 until 1993, when the D-1 was introduced, most Martin models added to the line were given the combination of scalloped top bracing and the small maple bridgeplate. In 1988, Martin returned to using maple for the bridgeplate on all models, regardless of bracing.

With the introduction of the D-1 in 1993, a new version of the famous Martin X pattern appeared. The braces in the D-1 were tapered, not scalloped, and instead of two transverse braces there is only one, and it is closer to the bridgeplate. Between the soundhole and the neck block, there is also a new combination of braces forming an "A" pattern beneath the fretboard. When the mortise-and-tenon neck joint—first introduced on the D-1—began to be used on the 16 Series, another bracing pattern was introduced which combined the features of D-1 bracing with the traditional scalloped X pattern. Martin refers to this as "hybrid X bracing."

The X Series Martins with HPL (High Pressure Laminate) tops, as well as back and sides, are given yet another variation of the Martin X pattern, as shown.

Five of the most popular current bracing patterns, A–E, are shown in the order they were introduced (small tabs at the waist aid in production and are later removed): (A) scalloped X (there are several variants of this pattern for historic reissue models); (B) unscalloped X; (C) D-1 (introduced with mortise-and-tenon neck joint); (D) hybrid X; (E) X Series (HPL soundboard versions only). Pattern F (discontinued) shows the fan bracing used on G Series and C Series classical models, but it's similar to the bracing used on many small Martin models popular in the latter half of the 19th century. The fan bracing used on Ditsons and the earliest Hawaiian models has five fan braces instead of three. Martin has used other bracing patterns not shown here, and variants of these patterns are also in production.

BACK BRACES

Early Martin guitars often have five back braces, and a very few have only three, but by the early 1900s the bracing had become standardized with four back braces. The two upper back braces were always tall and narrow, while the lower two were wide and low. Martin gave its archtop models a steeper radius in the curve of the back by making the lower back braces taller and narrower, like the upper two. When the M-38, based on a converted F-7 archtop, was introduced in 1977, this type of back bracing was retained. The J-40 and other Jumbo models, being deep-bodied versions of the M Series, were also given the same back bracing pattern. In 1988, Dreadnoughts were given the taller M and J model bracing stock for the lower two back braces. This change was soon extended to other steel-string models as well. The bracing pattern with wide and low #3 and #4 back braces returned with the introduction of the Authentic Series.

MARTIN GUITAR NECKS

EARLY STYLES AND MATERIALS

The earliest Martin necks were made of light-colored hardwood, often maple, although the wood was either stained or finished black to resemble ebony. (Some were veneered with ebony or decorative patterns of ebony and ivory.) These necks were made of three separate pieces, with the headstock and the cone-shaped heel fitted to the main portion of the neck with precise joinery. The earliest examples often had the long paisley-shaped headstock used by C. F. Sr.'s former employer, Stauffer of Vienna. This design has all six tuning machines on one side, with the gear mechanisms attached to a metal plate that is mounted onto the back of the headstock. Today this is often called a "Stauffer headstock," but at the time Martin referred to as a "Vienna head." Other luthiers and guitarmaking firms have used similar shapes in recent years, most notably Paul Bigsby and also the Fender Musical Instrument Company.

Many early Martin guitars had a neck that was adjustable at the body joint, so that string action could be raised or lowered with a clock-key fitted to a screw mechanism in the neck heel. This was not a truss rod, but a floating neck joint that allowed the neck angle to be altered easily. Although not commonly seen on guitars made after the 1850s, this type of adjustable neck was still offered throughout the 19th century, and has been found on guitars made as late as 1900.

The black neck with ice-cream-cone-shaped heel appeared on the earliest Martin guitars regardless of price, but was continued on the plainest models, such as the 2 1/2-17 shown at top, until the late 1890s.

B**ecause** of the cost of the imported gears, Martin didn't use the Stauffer-style headstock on lower-priced guitar models. Even in the mid-1830s C. F. Sr. was already offering the less-expensive option of ivory or ebony friction pegs mounted in a simpler headstock, similar to what is found on a traditional flamenco guitar today. Martin continued to call this a peg head—meaning a head with pegs, as opposed to gears—until after 1900. At least by the 1840s, if not earlier, Martin was also using geared tuners that mounted on either side of a slotted headstock. This style quickly became the most popular. In Martin's short-hand descriptions, such tuners were called "two-side screw", probably because the gears came in two halves mounted on either side of the headstock, instead of one unit with internal gears mounted in the middle. Such tuners are now commonly associated with classical guitars, but because there was originally a patent for the design, Martin often referred to them as Patent pegs. It is not known when the Stauffer headstock was last used, but there are still references to its use in Martin records dating from the early 1850s.

20TH CENTURY MARTIN GUITAR NECKS

As the Stauffer headstock disappeared on Martin's higher models, Spanish cedar necks replaced the earlier style. The black neck with cone-shaped heel was still used on the smallest, least-expensive Martin models—such as the 2½-17—until the late 1890s, but with slotted headstocks. Cedar necks, given a natural finish, were in two pieces, with the headstock grafted onto the main part of the neck. This joint was reinforced with a diamond-shaped extension at the base of the headstock, behind the nut. The exceptions to the rule are Style 17 models, re-introduced around 1906 as Martin's first cataloged style with mahogany back and sides. These guitars had one-piece necks of cedar with no diamond, or volute, on the back of the headstock. Soon, Style 18 models also got the same simpler neck. These one-piece cedar necks are also the first to have the slots in the headstock rounded, instead of squared, at the top and bottom of the slots.

Martin began using mahogany for guitar necks around 1916, and at the same time eliminated the joint between the headstock and the main stem of the neck on all models. This was an era of tremendous expansion at Martin, thanks to the popularity of Hawaiian music styles, and many of the old-fashioned guitarmaking methods were being streamlined. From this period until 1999, all Martin guitars had one-piece necks of mahogany, with only a few exceptions. The use of head-stock "wings" (laminations) and experimentation with multi-piece necks has been necessitated since 2000 due to dwindling supplies of genuine mahogany.

In August 1999, cedar began to be used again for guitar necks on many models of Styles 16 and lower, although the all-mahogany Style 15 models continued to feature mahogany necks. As supply issues with genuine South American mahogany continued to worsen, Spanish cedar was introduced on many guitars in the Standard Series. The cedar necks are one-piece, or one-piece with added headstock wings, stained so that it is difficult to tell them from mahogany. It is likely that future supply issues with mahogany and cedar will necessitate two- or three-piece necks with added wings. The X Series Martins have necks made of Stratabond, a multilaminate of birch wood. The distinctive vertical orientation of the laminations makes these necks extremely strong, and easy to distinguish from other Martin guitar necks.

The use of maple for guitar necks appears on some recent models, including the American Archtop collaboration with luthier Dale Unger (CF models). Cherry appears as the neck wood on most of the recent certified or sustainable wood series guitars.

12-FRET NECKS VERSUS 14-FRET NECKS

All Martin six-string guitars were made with 12 frets clear of the body until 1929, when the Perry Bechtel-inspired OM-28 was introduced in the fall of that year. (See the section on OM models in chapter 2.) The immediate popularity of a Martin guitar with a slightly narrower neck and 14 frets clear of the body soon prompted a revolution in the necks and body shapes of Martin's entire line of flattop guitars. Although the 14-fret neck was already standard on archtop guitars like Gibson's L-5, virtually all flattop guitars were still being made with only 12 frets clear of the body.

Today, OM is understood to mean a 000 size guitar with 14-fret neck, usually 1¾ inches wide at the nut. This was not how Martin used the term in the 1930s and '40s, when OM simply meant any model redesigned in the 14-fret style, as opposed to the old Standard models with wider, 12-fret necks. Martin stopped stamping the OM designation in its new 000 models in late 1933, for by that time new 14-fret versions of almost every Martin guitar shape were being offered. A few of the old standard Martins were still being made, namely the 0 and 00 sizes in styles 21 and 42. By 1948, the 00-21 was the last remaining link to the body shape and neck style of the original Martin guitars.

By the mid-1950s, special orders for 12-fret models began to trickle in. In 1961, the 0-16NY and 00-21NY were the first reissues of the original 12-fret style Martin, and these were soon followed by 12-fret Dreadnoughts called S models. The last body shape to be reissued in its earlier, 12-fret version was the 000, which was offered as a stock model in 1994. (Many Custom Shop examples pre-date this, of course.) All of these 12-fret guitars feature a wider fretboard than their 14-fret counterparts.

Most people associate Martin's 12-fret necks with the slotted headstock, despite the fact that the company made many solid "peg head" versions with friction pegs even after 1900, and around 1930 banjo tuners were used on quite a few 12-fret guitar models given solid headstocks. The headstock style was still in flux when the OM was introduced, and a few of the earliest 14-fret Martin guitars had a slotted headstock. Despite these exceptions, during Martin's "golden era" (late-1920s through WWII) the old standard models had slotted headstocks and the new OM models had solid headstocks. Except for Limited Editions and custom orders, that distinction remained the norm until 1997, when the 00-16 DB models debuted with narrow 14-fret necks and slotted headstocks.

HEADSTOCK SHAPE EVOLUTION

As mentioned earlier, Martin offered both solid headstocks with straight-through friction pegs (peg head), and slotted headstocks with right-angle patent gears, almost from the beginning. By the mid-1930s, however, the slotted headstock was rapidly disappearing as 12-fret models lost favor and 14-fret Martins with solid headstocks ruled the catalog. The early headstock shape, with its distinctly tapered sides and crisp corners, had evolved by the 1960s to look like little more than a

(A) is a 1940 D-18 headstock, while (B) is from a D-28 made about 25 years later. (C) is a 1961 00-21NY headstock with rounded slots, (D) is a 2006 D-16GT headstock with gold foil logo.

rectangle with heavily rounded corners. Mike Longworth, who, more than anyone else working in Nazareth at that time, was aware of Martin's earlier styles, discovered that there had been no directive to alter the headstock shape. The change was merely the result of a heavily worn headstock template, but since the wear had occurred slowly over many years, the workers hadn't noticed.

Although standard Martin models now have a headstock more like those on early 14-fret models, the Vintage and Golden Era Series have the "square tapered" headstock taken directly from an original 1930s model.

HEADSTOCK INLAY

Despite building a great many guitars throughout the 19th century with elaborate pearl bordering on the body, the face of Martin guitar headstocks was left unadorned. The exception was the occasional use of small brass or silver-plated plaques fastened to the top of the headstock with tiny nails or tacks. These are often engraved with the name of the owner, although decorative themes like the one shown here were also used. Since guitars with both the pre-1867 and post-1867 stamp are found with these headstock plaques, it is assumed that they were used in the 1860s and 1870s. No later models, with dates on the underside of the top, have appeared with this unusual headstock decoration. Although they may also have been used on lower models, those that have surfaced to date have been on Styles 26 and higher.

Martin's use of pearl inlays on guitar headstocks shortly after 1900 was probably influenced by competing guitar companies, and by its own mandolins, which featured far more elaborate pearl decorations than Martin guitars. A few specially inlaid 00-42 models, with inlaid headstock, inlaid mandolin-style pickguard beneath the strings, and extra pearl bordering on the sides and back, were constructed in 1902. These were followed by the formal introduction of Style 45 in the 1904 catalog, and

Long before Martin offered pearl inlays on its guitar headstocks, some customers opted for small metal plaques like the one shown on this 1860s 1-26.

both the specially inlaid Style 42 models and the first Style 45s featured an elaborate pearl inlay on the slotted headstock, but with no binding on the edges. This inlay was soon replaced by the now-familiar torch, or flowerpot, inlay. (Martin referred to both patterns as a pearl scroll.) By this time, the headstock was also bound with a thin ivory edging. The torch pattern, which appeared at least as early as January 1905, remained Martin's stock headstock inlay for Style 45 guitars—and for custom ordered lower styles with more decoration on the neck—until the introduction of the archtop models in 1931. The C-2 and C-3 archtops were given the vertical letters MARTIN on the headstock, and the C and F were added to this inlay the following year. By sometime in 1933, this inlay also began to appear on the headstocks of Style 45 flattops with solid headstocks, although Style 45 models with 12-fret necks and slotted headstocks were given the earlier torch pattern for several more years. On many of the archtop models, the letters are pearlescent celluloid, not actual abalone or mother-of-pearl.

Pearl decorations disappeared from all Martin headstocks in 1943, when both the archtop and pearl-bordered models were discontinued. Headstock inlays did not reappear on a stock Martin model until 1968, when the D-45 returned to the lineup. Despite the often-lavish decorations that Martin workers applied to Vega banjo headstocks after that company was acquired in 1970, the C. F. Martin headstock lettering remained the only inlay on the headstocks of production model guitars until 1976 (the D-76). Since the introduction of the Custom Shop and the profusion of new models, limited editions, and later signature editions, Martin has offered a dizzying array of headstock decorations in every conceivable style, from Baroque to modern cartoon art.

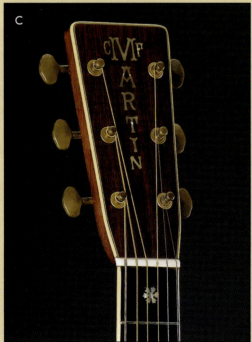

No matter how fancy the rest of the guitar, Martin headstocks were left plain until the introduction of specially inlaid Style 42 models in 1902 (later called Style 45). The first headstock inlay (A) was used only for a short time before it was replaced with what is now commonly called a torch pattern. That inlay (B), shown on a 1-45 Ditson, was joined by headstocks with the C. F. Martin letters (C) in the 1930s.

28 MARTIN GUITARS: A TECHNICAL REFERENCE

HEADSTOCK VOLUTE, OR "DIAMOND"

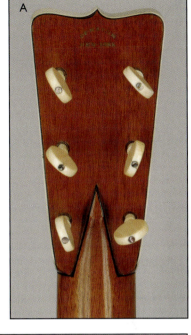

The decorative diamond, or volute, on the back of the headstock on Style 28 and higher Martin models is a holdover from the reinforcement of the complex joint formerly used to connect the headstock to the main stem of the neck. When Martin changed to using one-piece necks, only higher models were given a neck with a carved facsimile of the original joint. With typical conservatism, the company kept the appearance of the neck largely the same on the higher models, despite the effort it took to carve the diamond-shaped volute on the back of each headstock. Today, most higher Martin models retain this feature. It has been widely copied by other makers of steel-string guitars as well. Most of these builders have no idea of the origin of the headstock dart, or diamond, as it is often called, an example of how Martin styling has become absorbed into the language of the American guitar.

The D-35, introduced in 1965, was the first deluxe model to be introduced without the headstock diamond, but it wouldn't be the last. Other above-28 styles without the diamond include the M-36, D-37K, and J-40. Today, only new models that are primarily reissues of earlier Martin styles are given the headstock diamond, but it is still retained on all Style 28, 41, 42, and 45 models. Over the years, the diamond itself has changed, and it became significantly smaller between the 1930s and the 1970s. Vintage Series and Golden Era models now have a headstock diamond much like what Martin used in the 1920s and '30s.

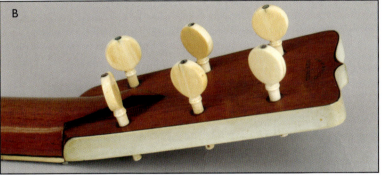

The headstock diamond on this early Martin (A and B), presumably from the 1840s, is bordered in ebony, making it easy to distinguish between the two pieces of cedar. The diamond on one-piece mahogany necks, such as the 1970 D-28 neck shown here (C), is primarily decorative. On its current Vintage and Golden Era Series necks (D), Martin has reverted to a more pronounced headstock diamond much like those found on 1930s models. Note the mahogany wings on the headstock, necessitated by dwindling supplies of South American mahogany.

NECK WIDTHS AND NECK SHAPE

Four of Martin's most popular current neck shapes (from top to bottom): low oval, low profile, modified V, and modified low oval.

Martin necks at one time had widths of 2 3/8" at the twelfth fret, and about 1 7/8" at the nut. On early models, the necks were often narrower at the nut on smaller guitars (size 2 and under) than on what were then considered full-size models, such as size 1 and 0. Necks became slightly narrower when the 14-fret necks came into fashion, resulting in a nut width of 1 3/4", and 2 5/16" spacing at the twelfth fret. (This spacing was soon reduced to 2 1/4".) The switch to the current 2 1/8" spacing occurred in 1939 with #72740, when the neck width at the nut was reduced from 1 3/4" to 1 11/16". (This neck width was first used on the archtop models a few years earlier.) The measurement at the twelfth fret is also generally used to calculate the proper spacing between the first and sixth strings at the bridge. There was a lot of variation over the years due to hand carving and shaping, so guitars that don't comply with the expected neck dimensions are common. Wood shrinkage and refretting also often reduces the fretboard width very slightly, so guitar necks that have been refretted several times may be quite different than when they left the factory.

Early Martin guitar necks have a distinct V shape. This became rounded into a D shape in the late 1930s, and from the 1940s on Martin necks rarely have a V cross section. The V shape was brought back by popular demand beginning in the 1980s, when it first appeared on limited editions and historic reissues. It is now standard on the Vintage and Golden Era Series, although the V shape is not as severe as on earlier reissues. A more modern adaptation of the V shape is the Modified V, which first saw widespread popularity on the 000-28EC (Eric Clapton) models and numerous others.

In 1985, Martin first offered a thinner neck on the new J models, when the adjustable truss rod was added. These low-profile necks quickly became the standard on most Martin models. Since not everyone felt the original Martin neck needed changing, full thickness necks are still offered through the Custom Shop and are specified on some Limited Editions.

Before the mid-1990s, the shaping on all Martin necks was done by hand, with a drawknife, although the rough outline was prepared on heavy stationary power tools. The hand work resulted in lots of variation in both neck depth and shape, although the actual width is quite consistent. Martin necks are now shaped on a CNC (computer numeric control) machine, with only the final sanding and volute carving done by hand. A wide variety of neck shapes and fretboard widths is now offered, and the end results are much more predictable than in the past.

FRETBOARD, OR FINGERBOARD, SCALE LENGTH

With few exceptions, sizes 1 and 0, Martin's largest concert models throughout most of the 19th century, had a string scale length of 24.9". (See appendix for scale lengths on all original Martin sizes.) The first stock Martins to be given the longer 25.4" scale were the early 00 models, but this was by no means universal and it wasn't mentioned in the earliest catalogs. When the 000 was introduced shortly after 1900, this new model, which Martin considered oversized, was given the longer scale, and the 00 reverted back to the shorter, 24.9" version. The 000 remained the only stock Martin to get the long scale until the arrival of the Dreadnoughts in 1931. (Ditson Dreadnoughts also had the 25.4" scale.) The OM models introduced in 1929, being derived from the 000, were also given the long scale. Shortly after the OM designation was dropped in 1933 and these models began to be stamped simply 000, they were also given the shorter 24.9" scale.

Today, most people associate OM with the long scale, and a 14-fret 000 with the shorter scale length, but this is merely coincidence, for early 1934 models stamped 000 still had the long scale. At the time, Martin seemed to reserve the long scale length for its largest model, and once the Dreadnoughts became the largest Martins, the 000 was soon given the shorter scale length. As always, there are a few exceptions to the above rules, and in late 1931 and early 1932, a few 14-fret 0-18 Specials were made with the same 25.4" scale as the OM models. These had shaded tops, large teardrop pickguards, and were the first 14-fret Martin flattops that weren't the OM size and shape. Only about a half-dozen were made before this new model was switched to the 24.9" scale that had always been the standard for 0 size Martins. The change occurred with two guitars begun on February 13, 1932, with serial number 50110 given the long scale, while 50111 got the short scale. In Martin's records at that time, these early 14-fret 0 models were called "0-18 32," because they were associated with 1932.

Today, the long scale is used on more sizes than in the past, including some 000 and 00 sizes. Because the company has responded to requests for specific models with a combination of features drawn from several earlier Martin guitar styles, many of the old rules no longer apply.

FRETS

For over 100 years Martin used fret wire with a rectangular cross section, now usually called bar stock fret wire because the frets look like tiny bars. These frets were first nicked on the bottom edge with the opposite sharp end of the fretting hammer to create burrs that helped to keep the fret seated in place, then hammered tightly into the fret slots of the fingerboard. After all the frets had been hammered into place they were filed level, followed by each fret being individually crowned on its top surface. Pre-crowned frets with a T-shaped cross section—which require far less finishing—were widely used in American fretted instrument manufacturing even before 1900, but Martin adhered to the old way decades after every other instrument maker was using T frets. One of the reasons Martin stuck with bar stock frets is that by wedging them tightly into the fret slots, the neck could be effectively stiffened against the forward curvature, or warped neck, that commonly results from string tension. Bar stock frets were, in effect, Martin's way of reinforcing the neck against string tension. Several gauges or thicknesses were employed to achieve the desired result.

Martin first used T frets in 1934, on a batch of two dozen 00-17 model guitars (serial #s 57305-329, but trial runs had been done on a few earlier models). Since the wedging effect of the T fret was not as great as with bar stock frets, Martin also began using a steel neck reinforcement beneath the fretboard, also T shaped, at the same time. Both bar stock and T-shape frets are usually of nickel-silver, but during the WWII years Martin used brass frets for a while, usually on Style 18 and lower instruments.

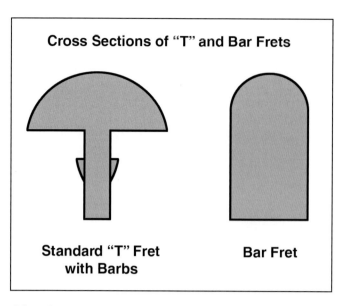

Bar stock frets are once again available (though costly) on Custom Shop orders, and are part of the specs on a few limited editions, such as the OM-45 Deluxe. The height of bar frets is typically taller, and the playing surface narrower; the feel to the player is different when compared to T frets. Needless to say, they are not for everyone, and it is more difficult to find a luthier who can work on them. Jumbo or bass fret wire, offering a wider, more gradually rounded top profile, is used on the new Martin archtop CF models, and is also available on Custom Shop orders. Jumbo frets have also been used on several limited edition offerings.

FRETBOARD, OR FINGERBOARD, POSITION MARKERS

Martin guitars did not have position markers on the neck until the late 1890s, and the addition of inlays on the face and side of the fretboard, like the later addition of headstock inlays, was probably the result of Martin's competition, such as Lyon & Healy's Washburn brand, which offered far more elaborately decorated guitar models.

Martin's first fretboard position markers were only at frets five, seven, and nine. Styles 27, 30, 34, and 42 were given single snowflake inlays of white mother-of-pearl at each of the three positions. There is no record of exactly when this change took place, but these styles are pictured with inlays in the 1898 catalog. The inlays were ordered from pearl cutters in Germany (later New York), and the size and style of these position markers initially varies from model to model and year to year. By 1899, however, Martin became more generous with pearl ornaments on the neck, and Style 42 was given the now-familiar pattern that stretched from the fifth to fifteenth frets, including the cat's eyes three-piece inlay at the twelfth fret. By 1901, the plainer Styles 28 and 21 also got fretboard position markers at frets five, seven, and nine, consisting of squares and horizontal diamond shapes of white pearl with notches cut into each side. Style 18 was given simple graduated dots for the same positions a short time later. Within a couple of years, these fretboard inlays would be of pearl from the sea snail, or light-colored abalone, instead of white mother-of-pearl. Shortly after its introduction in 1904, Style 45 was given an even more lavish helping of snowflakes and diamonds than Style 42, with inlays stretching from the first to seventeenth fret. Many of those positions were given three separate, although small, inlays.

Before 1910, the inlay patterns for all Martin guitar styles were fixed. They would remain unchanged for over 20 years—with the exception of Style 17, which was given small fretboard dots of celluloid when reintroduced as an all-mahogany model in 1923. Shortly before 1920, Martin also began putting small side dots in the edge of the fretboard. The exact date these edge dots were first used was not documented. Variations of the fretboard inlay styles found on its guitar models were also used on mandolins and ukuleles—and, later, even archtop Martin guitar models. The inlays correspond to the rest of these instruments' trimmings with remarkable consistency.

(A) Style 28 short pattern (pre-1933); (B) Style 28 long pattern, which was changed to dots in late 1944. (C) is the "short snowflake" pattern that first appeared on Style 42 in 1898, while (D) is the longer Style 45 snowflake pattern (first used circa 1909), shown here on a current model.

There were only two important changes to fretboard inlays on Martin guitar models in the 1930s. In 1932, the patterns on Styles 18, 21, and 28 were changed slightly and stretched to the fifteenth fret, with double inlays to mark the octave at the twelfth fret. The deluxe F Series archtops, introduced in 1935, had large hexagonal fretboard markers more in keeping with jazz-age guitar fashion. The hexagon inlays soon began to be requested for custom flattop models as well, and by 1939 were standard on the D-45. Some of the hexagon inlays on archtops and custom flattops during this period were made of celluloid, not pearl, but D-45 models always got genuine abalone pearl. The F Series archtops and Styles 42 and 45 were discontinued in 1942, putting an end to both hexagons and the more elaborate snowflake patterns on Martin fretboards until older styles began to be reissued. (The last Style 42 models were begun in late February 1943.)

The next change came in late 1944, when Style 28 fretboards were given graduated dots to the seventeenth fret. Style 21 got the same pattern as Style 18, which was also extended to the seventeenth fret. This change marked the last of the diamonds and squares fretboard markers, which didn't appear again until the company finally began to reissue its earlier styles decades later. Large white pearl dots, all the same size, were briefly used in 1946, but by the following year Martin returned to the graduated dot patterns on Styles 18, 21, and 28 that continue to the present. The first exception to the graduated dot sizes were the M-38 and M-36, which were given dots of a smaller size beginning at the third fret.

MODERN NECK INLAYS: MORE THAN JUST POSITION MARKERS

After 25 years of nothing but dots on its guitar necks, Martin began to bring back the earlier inlay styles, beginning with the return of the D-45 in 1968. Diamonds and squares and Style 42 and 45 snowflakes began to reappear when the Custom Shop was opened in 1980. The Guitars of the Month program begun in 1984 also introduced many variations of earlier styles, such as the hexagon outline inlays conceived by Chris Martin and first seen on the 1986 J-45M. Beginning in the 1990s, Martin began offering a wider range of fretboard inlays on Limited and Signature Editions by teaming up with a number of different inlay artists across the country. As this edition goes to press, Martin is offering a larger variety of standard fretboard inlay patterns than ever before. In addition, the Custom Shop offers customers the option of designing their own unique inlays, limited only by their imagination.

(right and opposite page) Artist models and special editions now get highly creative, and often unique, fretboard inlays. Shown at right are the "heavenly body" fret markers on the MC-40 Eric Johnson model. On the opposite page (left to right): D-45 with Celtic knot designs, an on-the-road theme for Rory Block's OM-40, and moon and stars inlays on the HD-40 Tom Petty model.

NECK REINFORCEMENT AND NECK-TO-BODY JOINTS

Martin first began reinforcing some of its guitar necks with a strip of ebony around 1920, as the company finally began to accept the growing popularity of steel strings. Before that, the wedging effect of Martin's bar stock frets had been sufficient to counteract the tension of gut strings. A steel bar with T-shaped cross-section, thought to be borrowed from blade stock for snow sleds, replaced the ebony reinforcement in 1934, at the same time Martin finally switched to modern T-shaped frets. For a time during World War II, steel was not available, so guitars from this period have only ebony neck reinforcement. This can be detected when the nut is removed, exposing the upper end of the ebony strip, though use of a strong magnet is an easier test.

The T bar was discontinued in favor of a square steel tube in 1967. In 1985, Martin started using an adjustable truss rod, a first for the company's acoustic guitars. This neck reinforcement system was an aluminum U channel with a round steel rod within it. A small piece of metal placed in the channel gives the steel rod an arch, and the unit is adjusted through the soundhole with an Allen wrench. Although not all models were given the adjustable rod at the same time, it quickly became a standard feature. The added strength of the adjustable truss rod allowed Martin to respond to demand for slimmer necks, and a low-profile neck shape was introduced, along with the adjustable rod, on the J-40M. These slimmer necks were optional on many models for a time, and were marked with a P suffix (for "profile") after the model code. By 1987, the low-profile neck was standard on most models, and the P designation was dropped. Some special orders continued to be received for Martin guitars with the non-adjustable, square steel rod. These were soon given a Q suffix after the style number. The Q designation does not appear on the neck block, only in the model code in Martin factory records. An overwhelming majority of these models were made for export, especially the highly traditional Japanese market, and were not sold in the U.S.

Neck reinforcements, shown in the order they were introduced: ebony rod, T-bar, and square steel tubing. Adjustable truss rods were first introduced in 1985; for a view of the adjustable rod in cross-section, see page 30.

Except for a very few Martins made with Spanish-style neck construction before 1867, all Martin acoustic guitars, excluding Shenandoah models, were made with a tapered dovetail joint connecting the neck to the body. With the introduction of the D-1 in 1992, this changed. The D-1 neck joint is a glued mortise-and-tenon. The bottom of the joint is clamped for gluing with a small bolt that goes through the neck block and into a threaded insert in the heel of the neck. Although not needed after gluing, this bolt is left in place, and the head concealed with a small rectangular ID plate, usually made of maple.

Shortly after the introduction of the D-1, the same neck joint technology was applied to Style 16 Martins. Following the success of these models, the new neck joint has also been used on some limited editions, such as the CEO models. It is easy to distinguish guitars with this type of neck joint, because instead of a one-piece mahogany neck block, the block is Appleply, made of multiple laminates of birch. On early mortise-and-tenon models until 2008, the block does not quite reach the inside back of the guitar. The model code and serial number are laser-etched on the maple plaque mentioned earlier, instead of directly onto the neck block itself. Some limited edition models have a larger mahogany ID plate that covers the entire face of the Appleply block, thereby giving the appearance of a traditional mahogany dovetail block.

At top is the traditional dovetail neck joint. Except for the additional routed channel for the adjustable truss rod, this neck joint is much the same as the ones used throughout Martin's history. (The threaded brass insert is for neck production purposes only.) The mortise-and-tenon neck joint (bottom) was introduced with the D-1 in 1992.

BRIDGES AND SADDLES

The bridges on the earliest Martin guitars made in America were very similar to the bridges on German and Austrian guitars of the early 19th century. These bridges were long and thin, sometimes with ornamentation at the outer points. They often had a metal fret for the saddle, and most of them used bridge pins. This type of bridge is shown in book 1, chapter 1, as seen on the oldest Martin guitar in the company's museum.

Another bridge design to appear on early Martins is shorter and wider, with rounded ends and a point in its center extending toward the bottom of the guitar (see at right). Although some have a metal fret for a saddle, most bridges of this style have an ivory saddle fitted into a narrow slot, much like that of a modern Martin guitar.

Well before 1850, Martin began using a rectangular bridge. Although some of the earliest versions had a tie block instead of bridge pins, Martin soon returned to the earlier bridge pin style of string mounting. This style of bridge had decorative points

This style of bridge appears on some Martin guitars made before C. F. Sr. left New York, but it was also used after Martin had relocated to Cherry Hill, Pennsylvania. Although it probably predates the rectangular-style bridge, both styles apparently were used concurrently in the 1840s.

on each end, and though only three of the facets are flat, it has become known as the pyramid bridge because at first glance the bridge appears to have a small pyramid at each end. The tie-block version disappeared before 1867, and from then on Martin's pyramid bridges had a saddle slot closed at both ends, with a narrow ivory saddle and ebony or ivory pins. (Martin probably used both the tie-block and the bridge-pin version during the same period.) The pyramid bridge with pins became the standard on all models from before 1867 until well after 1900, when less expensive models were given similar bridges but with flattened ends (without pyramids). The ivory saddles for pyramid bridges overlap the saddle slot at each end (see photos below), giving the appearance of a longer slot. By the 1920s, the saddle slot was open on both ends, a style now called a through-cut saddle. These saddles were always glued into the bridge, whereas saddles of the earlier style were not glued in place.

Pyramid bridge from 1890s 0-28. Note the large-headed bone bridge pins with abalone dots. Each end of the ivory saddle was notched to conceal the end of the saddle slot in the bridge. A Roman numeral was filed into the underside of the saddle (VII in this example) and a matching number scratched into the bottom of the saddle slot, so the correct saddle could be reunited with the bridge after the guitar was finished. These notched and coded saddles are typical of pre-1910 Martins.

Straight-line bridge with through-cut saddle (1961 00-21NY). This bridge shape was first used in the mid-1920s.

Belly bridge, designed in 1929 for the higher tension of steel strings (1930 0-18T shown). The saddles were glued in place.

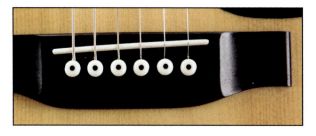

The belly bridge was given a short saddle beginning in 1965. These saddles were not glued in.

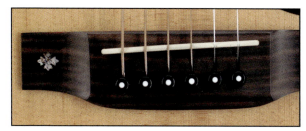

Modern bridge used on mortise-and-tenon neck joint models (SPD-16 shown). Note the bridge pins on same angle as saddle, and the string ramps between bridge pin holes and saddle.

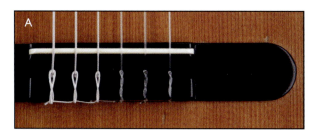

(A) Classic guitar bridge used on G suffix models, made for gut strings, beginning around 1936. Because of how the strings are tied on, Martin called this a loop bridge. It was also used on C suffix models and the N Series. (B) Bridge used on more current nylon-string acoustic/electric models.

In late 1929, Martin introduced a new, heavier bridge with a wider footing designed to provide the extra stability needed for the increased tension of steel strings. Because of the bulge in the middle portion behind the bridge pins, it has become known as a belly bridge. Except for increasing the saddle angle to improve intonation, this bridge style remained essentially unchanged until 1965, when Martin went back to the closed-end saddle slot, giving the bridge greater strength and allowing easier saddle adjustment and replacement.

With the introduction of the D-1 series, a slightly altered version of the belly bridge appeared. This has the bridge pin holes following the same angle as the saddle, with tapered string slots that provide a more consistent string angle and down-bearing pressure across the entire length of the saddle. These bridges are used on all models with the new mortise-and-tenon neck joint.

Bridges of black Micarta began to be used in 2000 on the X Series guitars, and were also specified for the Style 17 guitars introduced that same year. In 2002, black Micarta was substituted for striped ebony on the Style 16GT (Gloss Top) models. White Micarta has also been used for bridges on special projects, such as the 1902 00-45 Limited Edition Reissue and the Photo Negative models.

The pyramid bridge is now in use again on several of the reissues of pre-1930 Martin models, and the long, or through-cut, saddle is found on Martin reissues based on guitars built in the 1920s and '30s. Since the long saddle had to be glued in place, this made changing saddles to adjust string action more time consuming. Starting in 2003, most Vintage Series models that had used the long saddle were given a new saddle slot design without the saddle being glued in place, although Golden Era, Marquis, and Authentic Series models continued to use the glued-in long saddle. Beginning in October 1997, Martin added compensation to the top of drop-in style bridge saddles to improve intonation.

SADDLE MATERIALS

Martin used ivory almost exclusively for its guitar saddles until the 1960s, when it began to use white plexiglass for both the nuts and saddles on many models. Ivory was again in use on several models by 1968, but other synthetics were often substituted. White Micarta™ began to be used in the mid-1970s, and the last recorded use of ivory was on D-45 #427275 in 1980. White Micarta darkens significantly with time and exposure to UV, so many of the nuts and saddles from this period now appear tan. Other synthetics were tested and used for both nuts and saddles from the 1960s to the present, such as Tusq™ for acoustic/electric models beginning around 2000.

Starting in the early 1990s, Martin introduced both bone (from domestic cattle) and fossilized ivory for nuts and saddles, initially with Limited Editions and Signature Editions. The fossilized ivory comes from walrus, mastodon, or wooly mammoth tusks that have been buried for centuries or even tens of thousands of years. This material is not technically fully fossilized, but instead is more accurately described as "mineralized," and sometimes has dark streaks or splotches as well as the distinctive graining found in ivory. Fossil ivory saddles are found on most Golden Era models, and on many Limited, Special, and Signature Editions. The use of bone, instead of synthetics, for both nuts and saddles has steadily increased since the mid-1990s.

With the exception of most Limited, Special, and Signature Editions, plus Golden Era and Authentic models, it is not possible to determine when one saddle material was phased out and another material was used instead. Some changes were experimental, rather than permanent, and supply shortages have often resulted in substitutions.

PICKGUARDS

Pickguards were standard features on Martin's earliest mandolins, but they did not become regular features on Martin guitars until many years later. Pickguards were often installed on special order, and a variety of styles have been seen on guitars made around the turn of the century, including heavily inlaid pickguards like those found on fancy Martin bowl-back mandolins.

Although the first Martin to be cataloged with a pickguard as a standard feature was the OM pictured in the 1930 catalog, Martin had been installing pickguards quite often once the company

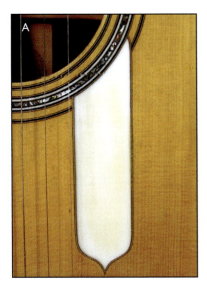  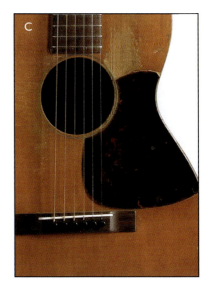

Martin's earliest pickguards were inlaid into the spruce top, as was standard practice on mandolins of the era. (A) 1904 00-42, (B) 1918 000-42 made for Hawaiian-style stringing. Around the same time the now-familiar teardrop pickguard became standard, the company also made different shapes for some retailers: (C) 1931 0-17S made for Montgomery Ward (not inlaid).

began offering steel-string models in its 1923 catalog. Even before that, the company had often been requested to add guardplates of varying sizes and shapes as a special feature. Many customers requested pickguards for Martins that hadn't been given one originally. In 1929, for instance, the company supplied Gene Autry with a pickguard of ivory-colored celluloid for his 00-42. The 1930 OM-45 Deluxe marked the first and only time Martin showed a pickguard inlaid with pearl in the catalog, until recent Limited Edition models. The short teardrop-shaped pickguard found on the 1930 OM models was replaced the next year with the larger, more elongated guard that has remained standard ever since. It is the most common acoustic guitar pickguard shape in the world today. As the company adapted its instruments for the use of steel strings and plectrum playing (with a flat pick), the larger pickguard was suggested by Martin dealers because it offered more protection from pick scratches around the upper portion of the soundhole.

Although very early examples of genuine tortoiseshell pickguards may be found, this is extremely rare. By the mid-1910s, all pickguards were of tortoiseshell-colored celluloid. This material was used until early 1967. At that time, the nitrate-base tortoiseshell-colored material was replaced with black acetate. The tortoiseshell-colored guards (acetate this time) returned when the M-38 was introduced in 1977, although the black version remained standard on most models for many years. There is considerable overlap between the use of different pickguard materials, so there is no exact date when the change from one material to another applies to all models.

Due to the disparity in shrinkage rates between the plastic pickguards and the spruce soundboard, cracks often appeared in the area between the pickguard and bridge. As a result, in 1984 Martin ceased gluing the pickguard directly to the soundboard and then finishing over it, as they had done since the earliest OM models. Instead, self-adhesive pickguards were applied on top of the finish. The tortoiseshell-colored pickguard has slowly replaced the black version on most models in recent years. Some of these pickguards are photo acetate, with the tortoiseshell image applied to the underside. Some heavily inlaid pickguards are of black Micarta, such as on the D-50. White Micarta pickguards are used for special effect, such as on the Photo Negative guitar. (See book 1, chapter 4, page 195.) Martin began using nitrate-based tortoiseshell-colored pickguards again with the introduction of the D-18 Authentic in 2005, though the nitrate is sandwiched between two layers of clear acetate to eliminate shrinkage.

FINISHES

Most pre-1900 Martin guitars have a French polish finish. Although beautiful and long-lasting, this finish is also fragile and very time-consuming to apply. Shortly after the turn of the 20th century, Martin began to use a varnish finish. Since this was French polished in the final stages of buffing, it often did not look much different than the earlier finish, although the varnish often developed a fine pattern of checking or crazing. The finishes on higher models is usually thicker and has a higher gloss than what is found on the less expensive styles.

Even as early as the 1890s, Martin offered a somewhat darker finish for the top, and numerous examples of this orange-top option have surfaced. The color is different than the somewhat browner tones found on the tops of Ditson models made a few years later.

Long before it began to offer shaded tops—Martin's version of Gibson's sunburst finishes— the company offered alternatives to a natural finish on the spruce face of its guitars. Two 0-28 models from the 1890s are shown, the one at left with the orange-top finish option, achieved by using unbleached, or orange, shellac in the French polish finish.

As the company's production increased dramatically around 1916, more changes took place in the finishing department. A note included in the company's copy of the 1918 price list states, "Beginning April 1st 1918 all Martin instruments will be finished dull." This was apparently a shellac finish, dulled by oil sanding. There were several more experiments with combinations of shellac and varnish until nitrocellulose lacquer began to be used at Martin around 1926. By 1929, this type of lacquer was in use on most models. Company records indicate a lot of experimentation with different finishes in the 1920s, and less expensive models often left the factory with very thin coatings. The finish found on a 1924 2-17, for instance, looks quite different from what is found on a 00-45 from the same year.

Lacquer gave Martin the option of using a low-gloss, or satin, finish with the sprayed final coat, which saved a lot of time compared to buffing and polishing the final coat of lacquer to a shiny, gloss finish. The Style 17 models were the first to be given the low-gloss finish. A popular misconception is that these low-gloss lacquer finishes are achieved by a "hand-rubbed" process, or that the finish is fundamentally different than gloss lacquer. The low sheen is produced by adding a flattening agent to the same type of lacquer used for glossy surfaces. The glossy surfaces on Martin guitars require more rubbing and polishing than the low-gloss finishes.

Nitrocellulose lacquer continued to be the finish of choice at Martin, and was used exclusively on necks and bodies of all models until 1992 when cross-link lacquer (a catalyzed, two-part finish) began to be used on necks that were given a low gloss, or satin, sheen. The lower-priced 1 Series then being developed also used this new finish. With the introduction of the 16GT (Gloss Top) series in 2000, and the all-gloss Style 17 the following year, cross-link lacquer has proven to be an excellent finish for gloss effects as well as satin finishes. Though the Environmental Protection

Agency continues to regulate the use of finishes with high VOCs content (volatile organic compounds, found in solvents), Martin still prefers nitrocellulose lacquer for its thinness and tone. This finish is also much easier to touch up years later, improving the odds for nearly invisible repairs. As of this writing, nitrocellulose lacquer is used on the bodies of all the guitars with a traditional hand-fitted dovetail neck joint, Styles 18 and above, as well as the full-gloss versions of Style 16. Many premium models have lacquer-finished necks as well, especially those models with a polished gloss finish on the neck as well as the body.

STAINS AND COLORING

Martin has used a variety of wood stains over the years, primarily on its mahogany models and on most mahogany necks. Part of the coloring on mahogany is the result of the pore filler used, and since stain is usually spray-applied to mahogany as well, there are two stages to the coloring process. In general, Martin often chooses a lighter-colored pore filler when the mahogany is not going to be stained, or when the stain itself will be lighter. Mahogany also darkens significantly with exposure to light, so the color we see on an older mahogany Martin guitar may be somewhat darker than when it first left the factory. The darkest stain found on Martin mahogany models was used in the 1970s, but the color had been changed numerous times before that, and is still evolving. Currently, Martin also strives to make the color of the mahogany or cedar neck compatible with the color of the different woods used in the back and sides, which results in a wide range of colors today.

With the exception of the orange-top option discussed earlier in this chapter, there was no mention of colored top finishes in Martin catalogs until its archtop models were introduced in 1931, but the company had been offering the option of a dark finish on the face for many years prior to that. Most of the Ditson models were shipped with an even (not shaded) brown color on the spruce, making these instruments look more like Hawaiian guitars with koa or mahogany tops. Dark-top or colored-top Style 18 models show up in Martin foremen's notes beginning in 1918. It seems that once Martin began offering all-koa and all-mahogany guitar models, adding color to the spruce top was a frequent request.

Colored finishes on the tops of Martin guitars became common in 1931. The C Series archtops were introduced that year, as was the 0-18 Special, a 14-fret flattop on which a dark top, only slightly lighter around the bridge, was standard. In 1932, lots of OM-18 models were sold with the same finish, and by 1934, Martin's catalog was awash in archtop guitars, including tenor models, all shown with dark tops. All Style 18 models were offered with "dark color top instead of natural finish on special order at no extra charge." By the following year, the subtle golden brown tones on Martin's dark tops were replaced by more dramatic shading from very dark brown (almost black) at the edges to a larger area in the center with very little color at all. There is much variation in the coloring throughout the late 1930s and early 1940s, when the archtop models were discontinued and the dark-top option on flattop models was rarely requested. (Several examples of these finishes can be found in chapter 2 of book 1.) Martin continued to do a few dark top finishes on its guitars by special order throughout the 1950s, but by the 1960s it was extremely rare to see one.

Martin began offering a shaded top finish again in the 1970s. Since then, a variety of shaded and sunburst finishes have been offered as extra cost options on stock models, or as quoted options on Custom Shop instruments.

TOP FINISH COLORS

In recent decades, Martin customers have also been offered subtler alternatives to a perfectly natural top finish. In 1977, the M-38, and later the M-36, were introduced with a distinctly yellow/gold tinted transparent top finish that was unique to those models. Customers have long sought the look, as well as the tone, of older Martins, especially the warm patina of naturally aged and lacquered spruce soundboards. Once the Custom Shop was in operation, Martin met this demand by offering coloring on the face of many Custom Shop models that replicated the look of older instruments. Many reissues of older models, first introduced as Guitars of the Month in the 1980s, were given a top finish with aging toner in the lacquer. This effect was supplemented in the mid-1990s with the introduction of Vintage toner on the 000-42EC, a color matched to the top of an older Martin guitar in the company's museum. Most new Martin models that are reissues of earlier guitars, as well as most Limited and Signature Editions, now have some degree of toner in the finish applied to the face.

WOODS

Martin has used a wide variety of woods over the course of the company's history. The following is an overview of the materials Martin has used, but as unusual and undocumented instruments keep turning up, it shouldn't be considered the final word.

C. F. Martin Sr. used both rosewood and maple for the backs and sides of the first Martin guitars made in New York. The soundboards were spruce. In fact, there is no record of any Martins made with other than spruce for tops until well after 1900. Many of the guitars made in the 1830s had a layer of spruce on the inside of the guitar's back, with only a thin veneer of rosewood or maple on the exterior. Spruce-lined rosewood backs continued on some models into the 1850s and perhaps later, although no Martin guitars with the post-1867 label have been reported with this feature. At least one Martin & Coupa guitar with Hawaiian koa back and sides has surfaced, presumably made circa 1850, but the company apparently didn't make use of this wood again until the Hawaiian instruments period began around 1915.

Conventional wisdom about Martin's use of mahogany has always been that it appeared in 1906, when Style 17 resurfaced, after several years' holiday, as a mahogany model. But surviving records from the early 1850s list a number of mahogany guitars, always in size 2½ or 3 and quite plain, and pre-1867 mahogany models fitting this description have been found. By the late 1850s, however, when Martin's model code was becoming more fixed, mahogany seems to have fallen out of favor. For the last third of the 19th century, it is safe to say that, with few exceptions, Martin made only rosewood guitars with spruce tops.

As Frank Henry began tweaking Martin models after 1900 in an effort to spur sales, the Martin woods story becomes more interesting. About ten years after the introduction of the mahogany Style 17 mentioned above, the Hawaiian music fad changed everything. Guitars with koa bodies, including the top, first appeared in 1916. The following year, Style 18 was given mahogany back and sides instead of rosewood. For the next several decades, most of Martin's growth was in mahogany, not rosewood, models. This was due primarily to the lower retail price of the mahogany versions. Around the same time Martin began using koa, it also made several dozen maple mandolins in the flat-back style (with a few matching guitars), although these Bitting Specials were not sold under the Martin name. Maple appeared again in the late 1920s, as the back, sides, and neck of Martin's archtop mandolins. Martin also made some maple guitars in the 1930s, but this wood was used in far greater quantities when specific maple guitar styles were introduced in 1985.

Martin's catalogs from the early 20th century give us the first public pronouncements about the company's choice of woods and their origin. The rosewood, of course, came from Brazil. In fact, there's little point in describing a pre-1960s Martin as being made with Brazilian rosewood, simply because all the rosewood used, apparently without exception, was of that species. The ebony is listed as coming from Africa, and the mahogany from British Honduras (the Central American country now known as Belize). The spruce is simply described as Eastern Mountain spruce, although this was probably what we now call red, or Adirondack, spruce. So much spruce grew in the mountains not far from the Martin factory that it was easy to acquire, and the company made little mention of it. Adirondack spruce seems to have been Martin's primary choice until 1945, when Sitka spruce tops from the Pacific Northwest first appeared. Beginning in 1968, when the D-45 was reissued, European spruce and Engelmann spruce (U.S.) were also used in very limited quantities. Until the mid-1980s, however, the company made no mention of the different spruce species used.

The success of the all-koa steel-string models, made for Hawaiian-style playing, got Martin out of the spruce-top rut. The all-mahogany 2-17 introduced in the early 1920s began a long string of all-mahogany models that lasted until the early 1960s. (Modern versions of these models were reintroduced in 1997.) Martin's original koa models disappeared in the mid-1930s, but koa returned in 1980 in the new Style 25 and Style 37 models. Although Hawaiian-style guitar playing (at least the style with elevated strings "fretted" with a steel bar) was largely forgotten by this time, koa top versions of these models proved popular with players looking for a different sound, and a more dramatic appearance. Koa has been available on numerous limited editions and short runs ever since, and as an optional wood from the Custom Shop and a few standard styles, such as the D-42K.

Beginning in 1986, Martin began to experiment with different woods for both the back and sides, and even the tops, of certain models. Most of these are clearly marked with a model code that indicates the woods used. These include, for back and sides, ash, cherry, walnut, European maple, American maple (both Eastern hard and Western), morado, ovangkol, sapele, and tulipwood. These should not be confused with the exotic woods used for the back and sides of some Shenandoah models, which were constructed of laminated veneers. The Smartwood series, introduced in 1998, utilizes a variety of woods, both inside and out, that are different from what is found on other Martin instruments.

With the rising prices and decreasing availability of Brazilian rosewood that meets C.I.T.E.S. certification, Martin has turned to alternative types of rosewood that offer similar tone and appearance. Limited runs of guitars made with Amazon rosewood have met with widespread approval, and Madagascar rosewood has been offered both as an optional wood through the Custom Shop as well as on Signature and Limited Edition models. With supplies of South American mahogany dwindling rapidly, Martin has also had to find alternative woods with which to build stable guitar necks. Spanish cedar, the same wood the company used for guitar necks prior to 1917, began to be utilized again for Martin necks in 1999.

Although spruce is the overwhelming favorite for Martin soundboards, Western red cedar and larch have also been used. At least eight different soundboard woods, including five varieties of spruce, are now available through Martin's Custom Shop. Martin is now using a wider variety of woods than in all the previous years of the company's history combined. Some of these woods are rare exotics, used to satisfy demand for unusual Martin guitars. Other woods are chosen because they offer alternatives, both in tone as well as appearance, to the standard rosewood/mahogany/spruce list of ingredients. Despite how different many of these woods look from one another, the resulting guitars always seem to sound like Martins.

PICKUPS IN ACOUSTIC GUITAR MODELS

Martin's first entry in the field of acoustic electric flattops—excluding the ill-conceived late-1950s models with magnetic pickups—came in 1975, when it made 176 D-18D and two D-28D models with FRAP pickups (Flat Response Audio Pickups). These D-suffix models were abandoned the following year, but the availability of under-the-saddle piezo pickups, and Martin's first cutaway models, led to a more successful effort a few years later. In 1983, Martin offered the option of its own Thinline brand of piezo pickups, first made by Barcus Berry and later by Fishman. The Shenandoah Series guitars, offered the same year, had Thinline pickups.

In 1987, Martin began to offer optional internal battery-powered (active) preamps, along with its Second Generation Thinline 332 pickup. The next significant change came in 1992, when the Thinline Gold Plus pickup was introduced. This active pickup system, with miniature internal preamp, offered far better tone and volume than previous under-the-saddle systems and was frequently requested on a wide variety of stock Martin guitars.

With the introduction of the D-1 in 1993, the number of pickup options was expanded further, as the laminated sides on this low-priced model invited the installation of more sophisticated onboard preamps. When the cutaway 16T (T for "technology") models arrived in 1996, Martin finally had more suitable guitars for acoustic/electric applications, and the number of pickup options was expanded further, primarily with the inclusion of Martin/Fishman options, as well as occasional offerings from other pickup manufacturers such as L. R. Baggs. Soon, cutaway models in both the 1 Series and 16 Series came standard with pickups and onboard electronics mounted in the side of the guitar. An increasing number of models with E suffixes (for electric) to their model code began to appear in Martin's catalog, especially on its more extensive price lists.

By 1997, the story of pickups in Martin acoustic guitars becomes too complex and confusing to track accurately. (That year's price list offered ten different factory-installed sound reinforcement options, which was expanded to 15 options by 2000.) Some E suffix models have been switched from one type of pickup to another mid-year, and dealers have been offered the option of upgrading the onboard electronics packages installed on their orders. In an effort to keep up with the most rapidly evolving segment of the guitar industry, Martin has also experimented with pickups from a number of different sources, although clearly having a preference for furthering the collaboration with Fishman Transducers. Because of the wide variety of pickup and onboard electronics options offered from the mid-1990s onward, Martin acoustic-electric models cannot be adequately described here.

STRINGS

Originally, all Martin guitars were made for gut strings. The company made a few steel-string guitars on special order as early as 1900, but these were few and far between. Steel-strings first appeared as a regular feature on Hawaiian models built for other firms beginning in 1916. (See chapter 6.) These guitars had a conventional neck and nut, but a metal nut extension was supplied that allowed playing with the strings raised far above the fretboard, in the Hawaiian style. Martin began to offer its own all-koa guitar models with steel strings in 1918, and ad copy mentioned that with the nut extension removed, the guitar could be used "for regular playing." The first Martin-brand model presented with steel strings specifically for conventional, or Spanish-style, playing was the little all-mahogany 2-17 model introduced in 1922 that appeared in the catalog the following year. The same 1923 catalog also lists Style 18 models with steel strings. Many other models were special ordered for steel strings in the 1916–1922 period. Martin also made a number of limited runs of all-mahogany 00 and later 000 models during the 1920s. It is safe to assume that all of these were strung with steel.

Most of the Martin guitar models made for other companies in the 1920s, and sold with their trademark (such as Wurlitzer), were intended for use with steel strings. The transition from gut to steel strings was not abrupt, and for a time Martin strung its guitars with a combination of gut and steel strings for certain large accounts. Substituting a steel high-E string in a gut string set was fairly common. In the early 1920s, Martin shipped many guitars with steel treble strings but with conventional wound bass strings from a gut-string set (i.e., bass strings that did not have a steel core).

By the end of 1926, most Martin models were being braced for either gut or light steel strings. Style 21 was cataloged as a steel-string in 1927, and most others followed in the 1928 catalog. Many guitars of the higher styles were special ordered with steel strings during this period of transition, and after 1928 many were ordered specifically for gut strings. Surviving correspondence from this period suggests that the Martin Company felt that most of its guitars could withstand steel strings, so there is no exact date when the company switched from building a particular model for gut strings to building it for steel strings. In a reply to one Martin dealer in the late 1920s, who evidently was in a hurry, Frederick mentioned that though the company didn't have in inventory guitars strung with steel, it did have a 0-28 strung with gut, and for a slight additional charge the strings could be changed and the guitar shipped immediately. The change to heavier construction for steel strings was not a single dramatic event for which we can find an exact date, but instead was evolutionary from 1916 onward.

All Martins stamped with a G or C after the model code were intended for gut or nylon classical guitar strings only. The same is true of the N Series classical guitars. Some of the NY series guitars from the 1960s were supplied with silk and steel strings, but extra light-gauge steel strings can usually be used on these models. Special orders for gut strung models were not necessarily confined to 0 and 00 models, as indicated by a 14-fret D-28 made in 1949 with wide neck, flat (no radius) fretboard, no pickguard, ultra-light X bracing, and standard Martin tie-block bridge for gut strings.

Currently, all Martin guitars are intended for use with steel strings, with the exception of occasional stock or Custom Shop nylon-string models, often offered with cutaways and onboard electronics, which are easily distinguished by a traditional classic guitar bridge with tie-block behind the saddle.

RECORDED CHANGES

1930   Style stamp added to neck block between October 1 and October 15. (Many models didn't receive a style stamp until much later.)

1934   T frets and T bar neck reinforcement first used (00-17 #57305-329, but the T fret/T bar combination was tested on a few earlier guitars)

1935   Stamp in back of headstock discontinued between #59044 and #61181

1938   First mention of X brace moved further from soundhole on D models (10/38, starting with D-28 #71358, but some D-18 models starting with #71165 from a month earlier probably have the same bracing.)

1939   Narrower neck ($1^{11}/_{16}$") #72740

1942   Ebony neck reinforcement gradually implemented #80585, steel T bar returns #90361

1944   Scalloped braces discontinued #89926

1944   Dots on fingerboard of D-28 #90021. Exact # of change not known on other Style 28 models

1947   Herringbone trim discontinued in set containing #98223

1947   Old zigzag backstrip on Style 28 was discontinued between #99992 and #100240

1963   "Made in USA" added beneath brand on inside center backstrip

1964   Last serial numbers recorded at the North Street factory 6/25/64 (196204-196228, 000-28C models). Last day of work was 6/26.

1964   First day at new Sycamore Street factory, July 6. First serial number was 196229 recorded on 7/8 (00-18E)

1964   Bridge pin holes moved back $1/_{16}$" #197207

1965   Loose, short bridge saddle #200601

1965   102C Grover machines on all "D" guitars #205251

1966   Last set of #2 ukuleles 1-4-66

1966   Boltaron (white) bindings on D-28 and D-35 #211040

1966   Boltaron (black) bindings on style 18 #212100

1966   Boltaron rosettes #213775

1966   Bridge pin holes moved to center #216736

1966   Tortoise guards discontinued after #217215 (many show up on later serial numbers)

1966   New tape strips on sides #215253

1967   Square neck bar on "D" guitars #228246, S models #231837. 24.9 twelve frets #228696, and 24.9 fourteen frets #229096

1967   Last hand stamped serial and model numbers #220467

1967   K324 Kluson machines on all style 18 guitars #224079

1967   V100 Grover machines on all 0, 00, 000, #226969

1968   Return to ivory nuts #235509

1968   Rosewood bridgeplates on all guitars #235586

1969	Rosewood bridgeplates are larger on "D" guitars #242454
1969	Heavy rosewood bridgeplates on 12-string guitars 6/69
1969	Mahogany ribbons (side reinforcements or linings, return to cedar not recorded)
1969	East Indian rosewood D-21 #254498 (some earlier trials, such as 243644-47, all D-28 models)
1971	1177-12 Kolb machines on all slotted head 12-string guitars
1973	Plastic nuts September 19
1973	Thicker headstock on D-12-28 #311837
1974	Fiber backstrips on mahogany backs on Styles 18 and below
1975	Plastic saddles on D-18 #350287, D-28 #355357
1975	Rosewood vertical side strips started between #360970 and #365831
1975	Micarta nuts on instruments below D-35
1975	Micarta saddles #370776
1975	Micarta nuts on D-35 #370976
1979	Schaller machines on some models #416625
1980	Last ivory nut on D-45 #421275
1983	Adjustable rods on #444776-781. All Shenandoahs
1984	Self-adhesive guards trial #447004
1984	Last glued-down guard in regular production #447501
1985	Adjustable rods gradually implemented #453181
1986	D-45 has scalloped braces and maple bridgeplate #467626
1986	New bracing and maple bridgeplates on 12-string guitars #446127
1986	Low profile necks on MC-28, MC-68, J-21M, J-40M, J-65, and all P Series guitars. (P means low profile) Specs start 1/28/86. This designation dropped in 1988.
1988	Maple bridgeplates on all guitars #478093
1988	D models get taller 3rd and 4th back braces like J and M models
1988	All models up to and including Style 21 get same "5-9-5"soundhole rosette as Style 28
1989	Use of white glue phased out in favor of yellow (aliphatic resin) glue
1990	Maple bridgeplates reduced in size, 6-string models only
1990	"M" suffix dropped from model code on J models
1992	First use of cross-link lacquer on necks of Standard Series models
1992	String notches no longer added in front of bridge pin holes on bridges
1991	Mandolins get serial numbers in same sequence as guitars
1992	Instruments made for export no longer stamped with "E" designation
1992	OM-28 scalloped top braces changed to $1/4$" width
1992	Double side dots added at 12th fret

1993	First necks with bottom of nut slot parallel to glue line between fretboard and neck (original "on angle" style not discontinued, however)
1994	Gold foil headstock logo replaces decal on all models except Vintage Series and many Limited and Special Edition models
1994	Custom 15 models get vintage-style tuners with "butterbean" knobs (December)
1994	First CNC shaping of necks on standard models
1994	Necks on all models above 1 Series get more pointed heel cap
1994	M-38 and M-36 top stain changed to aging toner
1995	M-38 and M-36 bridges changed from rosewood to ebony
1995	First use of Series 1 neck joint and new "hybrid" X bracing on Style 16 guitars, which get "16T" designation
1995	HD-28S headstock slots changed from rounded ends to squared ends
1996	Last cutaway models with elliptical soundholes and 22 frets
1997	First use of compensated saddles on 16 Series guitars (October)
1997	First use of laser-etched neck block markings
1998	"M" and "R" suffix dropped from model code on Vintage Series (December)
1998	Use of compensated saddles expanded to include most 6-string models with "drop-in" saddles (6/98, virtually all models included by 3/99)
1999	Spanish cedar first used for necks on DM models, Spanish cedar necks appear on 1 Series and 16 Series by October 2000
2000	15 Series models get rosewood headplate on neck
2001	Vintage style tuners (primarily used on Vintage Series) with butterbean knobs change from chrome to nickel plating
2001	Sapele (African mahogany) first appears on 15 Series models
2002	String gauge caution stamp no longer appears on back center strip
2002	First use of "drop-in through cut" saddle on Vintage Series
2004	Micarta saddles phased out, replaced with Tusq saddles (short "blind end" saddle slots only)
2004	J and M models get forward shifted X braces
2004	2-way truss rod trials begin
2004	Fret slots changed from through-cut to "pocket slots." This change began in late 2004 and continued into 2005

Note: The information in this section is unofficial. It was taken from notes made by the foremen and others. Though they may be correct in most cases, the authors, publisher, and the C. F. Martin Company ask that readers consider the above list of changes to be only a general guide as to when such changes were implemented and make no formal claims as to their correctness. Also, there are often exceptions to the dates given in the above list of changes. Mike Longworth was able to furnish exact dates and serial numbers when many changes took place, but as the Martin Guitar Company's recent production is far more complex, it is no longer possible to be certain that a particular feature first appeared, or disappeared, at a given time. This is particularly true of changes in parts added late in the production process such as bridges, pickguards, or tuners. Some Martin guitars are held back during production, and a minor change or correction may delay the completion of certain guitars for months. Such instruments might then receive the newly updated parts along with guitars with much higher serial numbers. Some of the changes listed here were the result of considerable experimentation and testing, and so there may very well be instruments with a new feature that were completed well before Martin made note of the change officially taking place. Please remember that a change listed here was not necessarily permanent, and the date when particular modifications were abandoned or superseded by yet another change in production might not have been noted.

CHAPTER 2
MARTIN GUITAR MODELS BY STYLE

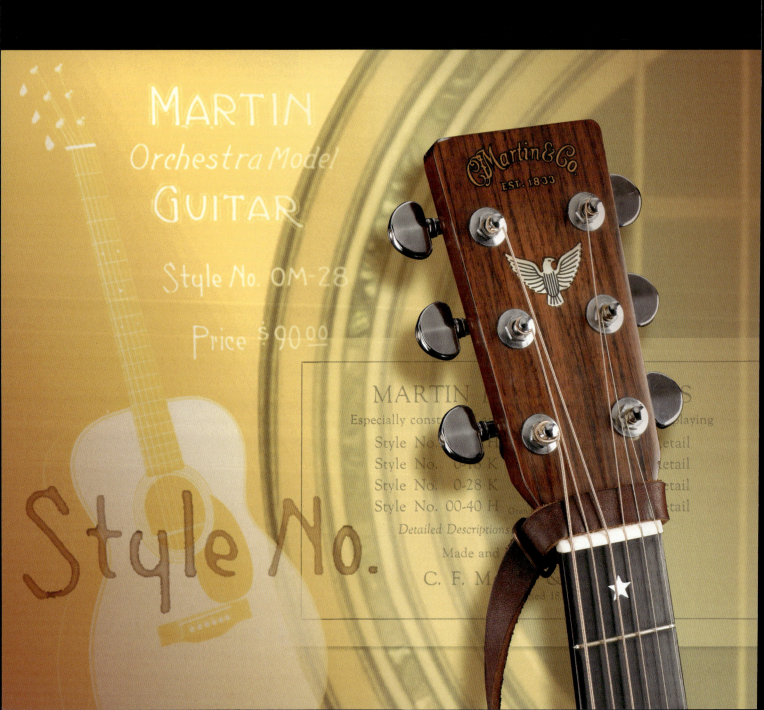

ORIGINAL NUMBER SERIES, STYLES 10–100

Until the mid-1850s, Martin recorded the appointments of each guitar it made—binding, rosette, quality of tuners, etc.—in a sales ledger, despite the fact that the company had been building mostly standardized models for several years. In the ledger, the first thing written on each line was the size, and the last was the price. Since a vast majority of the sales were to dealers, this last figure was usually the wholesale cost of the guitar. The descriptive writing between the indication of the size and the noting of the price kept getting more and more abbreviated for the most common models, until finally the two numbers were all that remained. In those days, and for the next few decades, each style number was made in only one size, although special orders were not uncommon.

Odd as it may seem, this is the origin of the now-familiar system in which the size of the guitar is followed by a two-digit number indicating the degree of ornamentation, or, as Martin called it, the "number of quality." By the time Martin got around to printing its first price list, about ten years after the abbreviations started, increases in costs meant that the style number was no longer the same as the wholesale price. (A 1-21, for instance, had gone up to $22.50.) By this time, however, the earlier style numbers were fixed, and they have been with us ever since. As Martin later added more styles, the earlier numbers served as a guide, although such numbers bore no relation to prices. A fancier version of Style 42 became Style 45, while a less expensive variant of Style 17 was called Style 15, and so on.

As stated earlier, Martin usually did not mention a change in appointments or specifications in one of its catalogs until well after the change had already taken effect. Illustrations or photographs from previous years were often used in later catalogs, adding another source of confusion. The specifications here are from the actual catalogs, but often the dates a change was first mentioned in print are clearly contrary to what has been observed by those who have handled hundreds of vintage Martin instruments. In these cases, an asterisk (*), followed by a parenthetical date in italics, indicates the date that is widely accepted as to when the change went into effect. Exceptions still occur, for instruments with earlier serial numbers were sometimes "held back" (for a variety of reasons) and sold later than other examples bearing higher numbers. Depending on when this interruption in production occurred, it might merely mean that a guitar with an earlier serial number got a later pickguard, bridge, or set of tuners. However, serial numbers were, and still are, assigned and stamped (later laser-etched) on neck blocks of Martin guitars at the earliest stage of production. This means that if a guitar, or a small batch of them, was shelved during early stages of production, such instruments might have basic structural components usually associated with guitars with later serial numbers. Another reason for later features on an earlier serial numbered instrument is that many instruments were sent back to the factory for repair or warranty service. It can be difficult to tell alterations done by Martin repair staff from original construction.

STYLE 10

The only Style 10 Martin to date is the classical N-10, introduced in 1969. Since this model does not conform to the usual Martin style formula—it's closer to Style 18 in appearance—it is covered in the section on N Series Classical models later in this chapter.

STYLE 15

For over 20 years, Style 15 represented Martin's most economical guitars. The first appearance of the style was in 1935, as Martin struggled to find new, more affordable models in response to the Great Depression. Two R-15 archtop models were made, 58652–53, and two 0-15 flattop models, 59295–96. All four were made in maple or birch. Apparently the idea was dropped, and it was not until 1940 that Style 15 finally made it into full production, and this time it was as a plainer version of Style 17, offered only in size 0 and only as a flattop. The first mahogany guitars were 74550–52. Style 15 was discontinued from 1944–47, but resumed in 1948 and continued through 1961. A tenor version, the 0-15T, was offered from 1960 to 1963.

With few exceptions, during the time the 0-15 was made, Style 17 was offered only in the 00 size, and had a glossier finish over a dark brown stain, while Style 15 was given a semi-gloss finish over a lighter (natural) mahogany color. Some batches of the 0-15 models in the first couple of years were made with tortoiseshell celluloid headstock overlays (headplates).

The specifications for the Style 15 guitars were:
1940 Mahogany top, sides, and back, rosewood fingerboard and rectangular bridge. Natural finish, semi-gloss. No bindings, black and white single ring rosette. Single position dots of plastic at the 5th, 7th, 9th, and 12th frets. (Except for the lighter finish, with less gloss, the easiest way to tell Style 15 from Style 17 is by the fretboard inlays, because Style 17 has double dots at the 7th and 12th frets.) Nickel-plated machines, plain white bridge pins and endpin.

Style 15 was re-introduced in 1997 as an all-mahogany Dreadnought in Martin's low-cost "Road Series." For details on these later Style 15 models see "Martin 15/17 Series" later in this chapter (page 118).

Please note that the "15" suffix in the Custom 15 dreadnought model code (1980–1995) is not a Style number.

(left) A 0-15, 1951. The external appearance of this model remained essentially unchanged from when it was introduced in 1940 until it was discontinued in 1961.

(right) A D-15, 1998. Later versions have rosewood headplates.

STYLE 16

Martin made some small size 2½ and size 3 guitar models in the pre-1867 era that had a wholesale price of $16. These were much like the $17 models (later called Style 17), but with mahogany back and sides. Since they never appeared on a price list, and the company was not yet using the shorthand that turned the wholesale price into a style number, we won't consider them as the earliest Style 16 models.

The Style 16 guitar was first made in 1961. Only six 0-16 models were made, 177682–87. That same year, the 0-16NY was introduced, with the first set being 178017–41. The actual differences between these versions were not documented, and the addition of NY (for New York) may simply have come after the first six were made.

The specifications are as follows:
Spruce top, with mahogany back, sides, and neck. Rosewood fretboard (no dots) with straight (rectangular) rosewood bridge. Natural semi-gloss finish, dark binding on top only. Nylon or steel strings (silk and steel, sometimes called "folk," strings recommended).

In 1962 and 1963, a size 5 version of the guitar appeared, the first set being 182104–105, and was shown in the price list for 1962 only. The 5-16 was just a simpler version of the 5-18, with no pickguard and no fingerboard inlay. The 00-16C classical model also first appeared in '62.

Starting in the mid-1980s, a number of Style 16 models were made as trade show specials and were not included in Martin catalogs or price lists. These models became so popular that they were soon shown in the price lists and were more widely available. Ten years after these new Style 16 models first appeared, there were so many variations that in some years there were more Style 16 models than all the standard Martin models combined of just a few years earlier. Unlike standard Martin styles, Style 16 models are constantly changing and often differ from one year to the next, and different sizes may have unique features. See pages 120–121 in this chapter for more on these later Style 16 models.

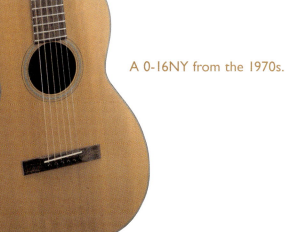

A 0-16NY from the 1970s.

STYLE D-16A

The D-16A has back and sides of ash. Except for the ash body, it is identical to the D-16M from 1987. Prototypes were #469948–950 and #474778–781. The D-16A was a trade show special for 1988.

STYLE D-16K

This was the first version of the D-16 made for dealers in the U.S. and featured Hawaiian koa back and sides.

1986 Spruce top with scalloped braces and maple bridgeplate. Style 18 soundhole rosette, tortoiseshell celluloid top binding, no black and white inlay. No back binding, thin black Style 18 backstrip. Style 18 neck, no stain, no heel cap. Rosewood fingerboard with Style 17 dots. Polished lacquer on body, toned top, tortoiseshell style pickguard.

STYLE 16M

The 1986 D-16M was made primarily for export and was not generally available in the USA. Most were sold in Canada, and a few in Europe. It was the trade-show special for the USA in 1987, 1989, and 1990, and was replaced by the D-16H in 1991. Some dealers ordered these with a gloss finish during years when the factory specifications were for satin finishes.

1986 Spruce top with scalloped braces and Style 18 rosette. Mahogany sides and back, stained. Tortoiseshell celluloid top binding without inlay, no back binding, thin black Style 18 backstrip. Style 18 neck, stained dark, no heelcap. Rosewood bridge and fingerboard, style 17 dots. Polished body with toned top, tortoiseshell style pickguard.
1987 As above, with the following changes: Top and back bound in black only, no inlay. Light maple stain on mahogany, black pickguard.
1989 Tortoiseshell celluloid binding and pickguard. 000-16M introduced.
1990 M suffix dropped, satin finish. 000-16C added, cutaway version with oval soundhole and gloss finish. (See photo book 1, chapter 3, page 163.)

STYLE D-16W

The D-16W was very much like the D-16M for 1986. The Prototype was #467576, and they were made primarily for Martin Canada. The specifications are like the D-16M except as follows:

Back and sides are walnut, top and back has black binding. Toned top, body stained in brown mahogany, black pickguard.

STYLE D-16H

Same as the D-16M, but with herringbone soundhole rosette and backstrip. Binding of tortoiseshell celluloid. The D-16H was a trade show special for 1991, and for a few years thereafter, although from 1991 on it appeared in the Martin price list as "available in limited quantities." (Previous D-16 models were never listed.) It was replaced by the D-16T in 1995.

A D-16H, circa 1994.

1992 Larger fretboard dots.
1993 Abalone dots on fretboard.
1994 Diamonds-and-squares fretboard inlays.

STYLE D-16T

1995 The D-16 and 000-16 were the first all solid wood Martins to get the new mortise-and-tenon neck joint. The "T" added to the model code stood for "(new) Technology." Along with that change came a modified X bracing pattern ("hybrid X") for the top.

The 16 Series quickly became a greatly expanded line of guitars, strategically placed between the 1 Series and traditional Style 18 Martins. Because of the numbers of models in this newer 16 Series, it has been given a separate subchapter of its own later in this chapter.

STYLE 17

Style 17 was another early Martin style that evolved from a common model of the 1850s. It was usually made only in sizes 2½ and 3, and on the first Martin price list it was the least expensive style offered. It kept that position until Style 15 was introduced almost a century later. Martin was always trying to find ways to make the Style 17 models more economically, in an effort to keep prices low. As a result, there have been more changes to this style than to any of the other original Martin styles.

(left) A 2½-17 from the 1880s. Throughout the last half of the 1800s, Martin's best-selling guitar model was the 2½-17.

(right) A 00-17, early 1950s.

1874 Price list indicates plain rosewood construction in sizes 3 and 2½. These guitars have a spruce top, with binding only on the upper edge of the body. They are almost always fan braced, with a black neck, cone-shaped heel, and brass tuners with bone buttons.
1898 Not shown.
1906 Re-introduced with mahogany back and sides.
1909 Cataloged with mahogany body, spruce top, in sizes 1, 0, and 00. Cedar neck, ebony fingerboard and bridge. Pearl position marks, three-ring rosette. Similar to Style 18, but in mahogany (18 was still rosewood). Top edge bound with rosewood.
1914 Shown with headstock with rounded corners at the top and bottom of the slots* *(1909)*. Style 17 was the first to get one-piece necks (still cedar until 1916) without a headstock diamond.
1917– Not shown in catalog, as Style 18 became a
1921 mahogany model.
1922 Cataloged as model 2-17 only. Mahogany top, mahogany body and neck, pyramid bridge, rosewood bindings, single ring rosette, natural color finish. Made for steel strings. (Martin's first regular steel string model that was not listed as a Hawaiian guitar.)
1927 2-17H Hawaiian model added. First mention of rosewood fingerboard and bridge* *(1922 or '23)*.

1929 Shown with straight bridge, no points, and straight saddle* *(1925)*. This year saw a major change in Style 17 due to the Depression. The rosewood bindings were dropped in order to make the 2-17 available for sale at $25 retail. This is the origin of the #25 guitar mentioned in production records of 1929 and 1930. The same changes applied to the larger guitars in Style 17 when they were re-introduced about this time. See book 1, chapter 2 for more photos and information.
1930 Sizes 2, 0, and 00 shown, straight bridge with slanted saddle. 0-17H Hawaiian model added.
1931 Pickguard optional.
1934 14-fret model* introduced in 0 and 00 sizes *(many made earlier starting in 1932)*.
1935 Dark finish replaces natural. Gloss finish replaces flat finish.
1959 Last listed in catalog, from 1955–'59 listed with plain white bridge pins and endpin, and available only in size 00.
1960 Last made as regular production model, although a few were made in the late 1960s and early 1970s.
1985 Returns to price list as available on special order, but few are made.
2000 Style 17 returns as a more deluxe version of Style 15. See "Martin 15/17 Series," page 118 for details.

[See page 53 for explanation of asterisks and parenthetical dates.]

STYLE 18

The first mention of Style 18 appears in the Martin sales records of 1857, but it had appeared at least a few years earlier as a small, rather plain guitar in size 2 with a wholesale price of $18. At this time it was similar to Style 17, but was offered only in the larger size 2 and had rosewood binding on both the top and the back ("double bound"). By the late 1890s it was being offered in all sizes, and it has remained one the most popular Martin styles ever since. Today almost everyone thinks of Style 18 Martins as having mahogany backs and sides, as the style was made only in mahogany after 1917. For more photos of Style 18 models see the sections on Dreadnoughts and OMs later in this chapter. Style 18 Martins are shown throughout chapters 2 and 3 of book 1.

Below are the specifications for Style 18 guitars, as per the catalogs.

1874 Price list mentions only double bindings,

1898 Rosewood sides and back, spruce top. Cedar neck replaces the black neck. Pyramid ebony bridge, ebony fingerboard. No pearl position marks (pearl dots at 5th, 7th, and 9th frets added soon after). Brass machines, ivory buttons. Binding on top only, with wood inlays. Center rosette ring had a decorative "rope" pattern of colored wood inlay. Ebony bridge pins with pearl eye.

1909 Fingerboard inlay shown* *(1901)*. Soundhole rosette has no colored inlay. By this time the cedar neck is one piece without headstock diamond.

1917 Sides and back become mahogany, top still spruce, mahogany neck replaces cedar. Flattened points shown on bridge, similar to Washburn style. (These were sample bridges and were not used for long, although they appear in catalogs for another year.)

1919 Rosewood binding front and back.

1920 Change from 19 frets to 20 frets (soundhole moved closer to bridge).

1923 Change to steel strings unless specially ordered with gut. Dark top at extra charge, shown again with regular pointed bridge. (This is possibly an older photo; flat tip bridges appear around this time.) 0-18K (koa) model first appears in catalog* *(many made starting in 1918)*.

1929 Straight bridge without points (see above), straight saddle, lacquer finish.

1930 Belly bridge with slanted saddle. 0-18T tenor guitar, modern shape, shown in catalog. OM-18 listed but not shown.

1932 Pickguard optional* *(1930)*.

1933 R-18 archtop appears (see details in chapter 4).

1934 14-fret Orchestra Models listed with all metal single unit tuners* *(1932)*, 12-fret models still available. Hawaiian stringing on special order at no charge. Shaded top (sunburst) optional. Bound in black Fiberloid plastic* *(1932)*.

1935 12-fret models dropped from catalog, except for Hawaiian versions. Dreadnought D-18 first listed (see Dreadnought section).

1937 00-18G (gut string model) introduced* *(1936)*. 00-18H Hawaiian model first shown in catalog.

1941 First mention in catalog of rosewood fretboard and bridge on 0, 00, and 000-18 models.* *(Change occurred starting in 1935, all were rosewood by 1940)*. First mention of "tortoiseshell plastic" bindings on D-18* *(1939, earlier on smaller models)*.

1956 First mention of rosewood fretboard and bridge on D-18* *(change occurred in late 1946)*.

1959 00-18E and D-18E appear on price list.

1962 00-18C replaces 00-18G as nylon-string classical model.

1966 Body bindings changed to black Boltaron at #212100.

1968 D-18S 12-fret added to catalog.

1973 D12-18 appears (12-string with 14 frets clear of body).

1984 M-18 introduced, but very few are sold and this model disappears in 1988.

1987 J-18M Jumbo first appears; shown in catalog the following year. This model has scalloped bracing, tortoiseshell celluloid binding, and diamonds-and-squares fretboard inlays. (See details in Jumbo section.)

1996 D-18VM and D-18VMS (12-fret version) become regular production models in Vintage Series, model code later shortened to D-18V and VS. See Vintage Series section for details.

1999 OM-18V added.

1999 D-18GE added as Special Edition, but continues the following year as Golden Era Series.

2003 00-18V and OM-18GE added.

2005 D-18 Authentic introduced.

2007 000-18 Authentic announced.

[See page 53 for explanation of asterisks and parenthetical dates.]

(left) A 1927 000-18 from the Martin Museum. The pickguard is probably original, but may have been added later.

(middle) Style 18 was often used for unusual or one-off instruments, such as this 1-18 with 5-string banjo neck, made in 1928.

(right) A D-18, 1937, from the Martin Museum.

STYLE 19

To date, this style has been represented by only one model, the D-19. See book 1, chapter 3, page 134 for photo.

1976   D-19 introduced. The D-19 was essentially the same as the D-18 of the same period, but with the following differences: Spruce top is stained medium brown color and has Style 28 rosette. White line inside dark binding on back.
1980   The D-19M has the same specifications as the regular D-19, with the addition of a mahogany top. The first production numbers were 420701–725. Very few were made.
1988   Last listing for D-19. Later versions would be marked "Custom."

STYLE 20

Style 20 is one of the more obscure styles of Martin guitars. It resulted from a slightly more deluxe size 2 guitar in the 1850s, with more binding and colored marquetry than Style 18, and is essentially identical to Style 21 except for being one size smaller. (A 2-20 had a wholesale cost of $20 when a 1-21 cost $21.) Like Style 21, Style 20 had a cedar neck while Style 18 had the black neck with cone-shaped heel. Some early examples of Style 20 have more colorful herringbone purfling of red, white, and green.

1896   Style 20 included in price list.
1898   Style 20 not listed in catalog.
1964   Style 20 reappears as the D12-20 12-string with mahogany body, and features identical to a Style 18 with the following exceptions:
Checkered backstrip like Style 21 and 28. White line inside back binding.
Black bridge pins with white dot. See 12-string section for details and photo.
1969   N-20 Classical model introduced. This was a rosewood guitar with appointments that did not conform to the usual Martin styles, and so it is covered in the section on N Series Classical Models.

STYLE 21

This style is another that has remained in production at Martin since before the Civil War. It has its origins in the 1850s, when it was a size 1 guitar with a wholesale cost of $21. It was the least expensive size 1 offered at the time, and sold well throughout the 19th century. Once Style 18 became a mahogany model in 1917, Style 21 represented Martin's least expensive rosewood models, and it retained that position until the mid-1990s when the company began making some Style 16 models in rosewood.

1874   Rosewood body, cedar neck.
1898   Rosewood bindings, top and back, otherwise like Style 18 of this period other than herringbone rosette and backstrip added to Style 21. Ebony bridge and fingerboard.
1901   Inlays at frets 5, 7, and 9.
1917   Catalog lists ebony bridge pins with pearl eye, but this had been standard for years.
1923   Fingerboard changed from 19 frets to 20 frets (sound hole moved closer to bridge). Mahogany neck listed* *(1916)*. Still strung with gut unless ordered with steel.
1927   Steel strings regular, but there were lots of earlier orders for Style 21 models with steel strings.

1930   Belly bridge, slanted saddle.
1932   Pickguard optional.
1934   Available as Hawaiian on special order* *(1918)* Fiberloid (black) bindings.
1935 – Style 21 still listed only in 12-fret design.
1937
1939   000-21 listed with 14 frets (first made in 1938). 12 fret 0 and 00 size models still available.
1945   Fretboard inlays changed to dots.
1947   Herringbone disappears from rosette.
1948   Herringbone backstrip changed to same pattern as Style 28.

(left) A 0-21 from 1911. (middle) Model 000-21, 1942. (right) Model OM-21, current.

1956 D-21 introduced (Six samples made in 1955, #145604–09.) Rosewood fingerboard and bridge mentioned.* *(1947 on 00 and 000).* 000-21 dropped from catalog, 00-21 still listed.

1962 00-21 NY introduced. (Made 1961–65). No pickguard, no fingerboard inlay, satin finish, rectangular bridge with flat tips. Nylon strings regular, steel on order (silk and steel recommended in 1963).

1968 Grover Rotomatic machines shown on D-21.

1969 Last year of production for D-21, the last set were #254498–522.

1985 J-21M (later just called J-21) added. Scalloped top braces, Style 28 backstrip. For details, see Jumbos section.

1990 00-21 briefly listed with solid headstock, then returns to slotted again. Since the mid-1980s, when Martin began issuing many more models, a number of other Style 21 guitars have been produced, both as regular production models and as Special Editions. The most enduring has been the OM-21.

1992 OM-21 introduced. Indian Rosewood back and sides, single black line as backstrip. Tortoiseshell colored binding on body, no BW lines. 1 3/4 inch wide neck at nut, short tortoiseshell colored pickguard.

1996 00-21 discontinued as regular model.

2007 OM-21 Special introduced, with pyramid bridge, short OM-style pickguard, herringbone rosette and backstrip, aging toner on top, other Vintage Series features.

MARTIN GUITAR MODELS BY STYLE

UNUSUAL STYLES

During the years when standard models were developed, there are a few listings in Martin's original ledgers suggesting other style numbers but with no details regarding the appointments. These are as follows:

Style 22 1858   This was probably not a style, just a listing of a guitar with a wholesale cost of $22.
Style 23 1856   Same explanation as for Style 22 above.
Style 33 1877   Though listed in the sales ledger as a style, this was actually just the wholesale price for each of two 00 size guitars special ordered by a dealer. The total wholesale cost was $66 for the two guitars. It is doubtful that there was ever an actual "Style 33" with specific features.

STYLE 24

Style 24 is one of the more obscure models, and though the details were never written down, enough of these guitars have surfaced to give the description below. One should bear in mind that with all styles, and most particularly with these unusual ones, the trimmings and specifications varied. The first mention was in the 1850s, when Style 24 was a size 2 guitar with a wholesale price of $24.

Style 24, pre-1867.

1870s Described in price list as follows:
Rosewood, with cedar neck, and "fancy inlaying." (This referred to the wood lines and marquetry around the edges and soundhole, not to pearl inlays.)

Details of trimmings for most examples are:
Rosette of colored marquetry in a wider pattern than Style 21, top trim also with colored marquetry. Rosewood bindings with a white line beneath the binding on the sides and a white line inside the binding on the back edge. Endpiece of multi-colored wood inlay (various widths and patterns), multi-colored backstrip wider and fancier than Style 21. Brass machines with oval ivory buttons.

A strip of marquetry was commonly used on the endpiece of several early Martin models, but by the 1870s this feature was only found on Style 24. The endpiece shown is from a 2-24 with the C. F. Martin & Co. (post 1867) stamp.

62   MARTIN GUITARS: A TECHNICAL REFERENCE

STYLE 25

Style 25 originated in 1980 with the return of koa models to the Martin line. Rather than make koa versions of standard Martin styles, as had been done in the past, this time the company gave its new koa models unique style numbers. Style 25 was roughly equivalent to a Style 21 of the same period.

Models 00-25K and 00-25K2, early 1980s.

1980 Introduction of Dreadnought and 00 models, D-25K and 00-25K. Spruce top, toned color, with regular (non-scalloped) top bracing. Koa sides and two-piece back, mahogany neck, no diamond on back of head, with Sperzel tuners. Rosewood fingerboard and bridge, Style 28 soundhole rosette and fretboard dots. Sides, back, and neck not stained. Black binding, with top border (inlay) of two black and two white lines. Tortoise shell (acetate) pickguard, black bridge pins and end pin with white dots. First production #421551–575.

25K2 versions of both the D and 00 models were introduced the same year, and were the same as the regular 25K but with a koa top and black pickguard. The first production numbers of D-25K2 models were 421701–725.

1990 Style 25 koa series discontinued.

STYLE 26

This style evolved from size 1 models with ivory binding that appear in the 1850s sales records with a wholesale price of $26. Many of the early listings for the 1-26 refer to it as the "de Goni" model, as this was apparently the Martin model played by Dolores Nevares de Goni, a concert guitarist who was one of Martin's early endorsers. Style 26 is nearly identical to a Style 28, except the top border is usually like one-half of a typical "herringbone" pattern. Some of the 1850s listings mention a pearl soundhole, and examples have been found, but the pearl soundhole disappeared before 1867. Some 1-26 models have herringbone trim like a Style 28, or other marquetry.

A 1-26 with dark top option (1896) from the Martin Museum.

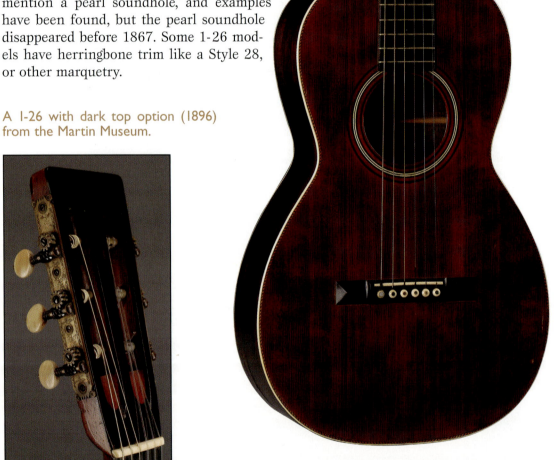

1859 Spruce top, rosewood sides and back. Ivory bindings on body, no binding on neck. Fancy wood marquetry border around top, but simpler than on Style 28. Same backstrip as used on Style 28, other details identical to 28.

Style 26 disappeared from Martin's records in 1898, but the same size 1 guitar was made and listed as a 1-28 for several years after that. With few exceptions, Style 26 models made after 1867 have identical details as Style 28, with the exception of the "half-herringbone" top trim.

STYLE 27

Style 27 had its origins in the 1850s as a deluxe guitar that cost dealers $27. It was the lowest model that came standard with ivory binding on the fretboard as well as the body, and in early listings this was described as "ivory to the nut," meaning the ivory binding extended to the nut on the neck. The 2-27 is shown in Martin's earliest price list, and also in the 1898 catalog. There has been some confusion because with a bound fretboard, pearl rosette, and elaborate colored marquetry for the backstrip and top border, it is fancier than the higher-numbered Style 28. Style 28 had a higher cost because it was originally made only in size 0, while Style 27 was made only in the much smaller size 2. Style 27 never appeared in a catalog after 1898, where it was also listed in size 1, but it was made as late as 1907. It is by far the most commonly found Martin model from the 1800s that is fancier than Style 28, so apparently it was very popular.

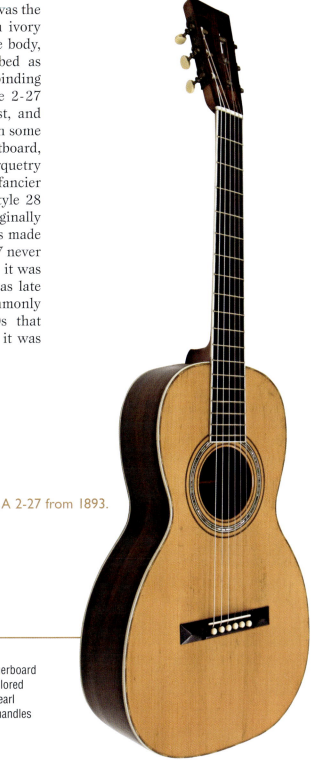

A 2-27 from 1893.

1874 Pearl inlay, ivory bindings.
1898 "Rosewood, cedar neck and head, body & fingerboard bound in ivory, pearl rosette, border of fine colored purfling, white face, ebony fingerboard with pearl ornaments... brass machine head with ivory handles finer finished than on Style 21."
Offered in size 1 and 2 only.

STYLE 28

The first entries in the sales book for a Style 28 were sometime prior to the printing of the first price list. Style 28 has its origin as a 0 size guitar, described in the sales ledgers as early as 1852 as being almost identical to a 1-26 but costing one dollar more. (One dollar was often Martin's upcharge for a model made one size larger.) Quite a number of these early 0 size guitars have surfaced in recent years, and since they are identical to the post-1867 0-28, models we can assume that the price of Martin's largest concert guitar was increased sometime in the 1860s, when the company was consistently using the wholesale cost figures to create a model code. Despite listings in the late 1850s ledgers for "0-27" models (when the cost was still $27), no 0 size Martin has ever been found with the same features as a 2-27, so it is safe to assume that an earlier 0-27 and a later 0-28 were the same model.

The 0-28 was the largest Martin guitar on its price list for decades. The model was not given much decoration, as that was considered appropriate only for the smaller "parlor" guitars usually sold to women. The appearance of pearl-bordered 0 size Martins is quite rare until the 1890s. Although Style 28 models in 00 size were recorded in the sales ledger as early as 1873 (and were made prior to 1867), these special orders were also quite rare until the 1890s.

Even after Martin began to make the larger 00 size instruments, the 0-28 was still the company's favorite. As late as the 1920s, Martin still recommended the 0-28 as its finest model for the solo guitarist using gut strings.

Model 00-28, 1900. See book 1, chapter 2, pages 76 and 83 for photos of early Style 28 models made for steel strings.

1870 Although the price list indicates "Inlaid with pearl," this was apparently an error resulting from the over-zealous use of ditto marks. (Style 2-27 listed just above it has a pearl soundhole rosette.) Even the earliest 0-28 models have the typical Style 28 soundhole with the "5-9-5" grouping of black and white lines that is still Martin's standard today. Some early examples have extra black lines bordering the herringbone top trim, and a few have green and brown herringbone. Although the "zig-zag" pattern backstrip is commonly seen even on the early Style 28 models, other backstrip patterns are often found on examples made before 1900. Also available in size 00 at least as early as the 1860s, but few made in that size. See book 1, chapter 1 for photos of the 0-28.

1898 Rosewood sides and back, spruce top, cedar neck. Ebony bridge, ebony fingerboard (no inlays) with 19 frets. Body ivory bound. Herringbone top trim (somewhat smaller pattern than on later models). Listed in sizes 1, 0 and 00.

1901 Fingerboard inlay at positions 5, 7, and 9* *(some with inlay in 1899).*

1902 000-28 first made.

1917 20-fret fingerboard first shown in catalog photo, with soundhole moved closer to bridge* *(change occurred earlier).*

1919 Celluloid bindings replace ivory* *(1917).*

1923 Mahogany neck listed* *(1917).* Gut strings still standard, steel on special order. 0-28K (koa) first listed* *(first made 1917).*

1927 Bridge pins listed as white ivory celluloid with black dot* *(circa 1920).*

1928 Steel strings regular* *(many ordered for steel earlier).*

1929 OM-28 introduced (pyramid bridge).

1930 Change to belly bridge, slanted saddle. OM models appear in catalog with small pickguard.

1931 D-28 introduced.

1932 Pickguard optional, standard on OM models, which now have larger guard* *(1931).*

1934 OM-28 dropped from listing as designation changed to 000-28. 12-fret models still available, but listed only in 0 and 00 sizes, pickguard still an option. Hawaiian stringing at no extra charge.

1935 Shown with Martin decal on head* *(1932).* Fretboard inlays extend to 15th fret* *(1934).* Shaded top optional, D-28 first cataloged (14-fret model only).

1938 00-28G for gut strings first listed* *(first made in 1936).*

1944 Last year for diamond-and-squares fingerboard inlays.

1946 Final year for herringbone trim around the top, top trim changes to black/white lines as found on the earlier C-2 archtops. (The actual change of trim occurred in the last guitar of the first set made in 1947.)

1947 The "zipper" or "zigzag" backstrip typical of the herringbone-trimmed guitars was discontinued early in the year, and replaced with a "checkered" or "chainlink" pattern.

1962 000-28C classical model introduced, 00-28G model discontinued.

1966 00-28C classical model appears. (See details in classical guitars section.)

1968 D-28S appears in catalog, many made earlier on special order.

1970 D12-28 is first stock 12-string in Style 28.

1976 HD-28 brings back many features of pre-1947 D-28 models. (See full description on page 69.)

1981 DC-28 and MC-28 added, cutaway models with oval soundhole.

1987 Low-profile neck standard on most models, but regular neck shape still available.

1988 Old-style neck available only on special order.

1990 HD-28MP (Morado back and sides) added to price list.

1991 CHD-28 offers cedar top version of HD-28.

1992 HD-282R (large soundhole) LHD-28 (larch top) added to price list.

1993 Custom 15 (HD-28 with vintage features) appears on price list as standard model.

1995 OM-28 on price list (previously available only as special order).

1996 Many Style 28 models with V-for-vintage features become stock models. All have pre-1944 features such as herringbone, old-style tuners, etc. Most had been frequent custom orders or limited editions for several years, but with different model designations. These include: OM-28VR, HD-28VR, (R suffix later dropped) HD-28VS (12-fret). 000-28EC offered as stock model, 24.9 scale and vintage features. 000-28 12-fret returns to the line, first as 000-28 Golden Era, later as 000-28VS. HJ-28 becomes first stock Jumbo in Style 28 (deleted from price list in 2000), 000-28 (14-fret) now stock model in Standard Series (previously available only as special order).

1997 HD-28LSV, "Clarence White" style D-28 replaces HD-282R. The LSV has an Adirondack top until 2000 (last LSV with Adirondack top is #737277), 0000-28H (M body shape renamed) added to price list (deleted in 2000).

1999 D-28 GE first appears on price list. See description in Golden Era Series.

2000 000-28H: short scale, 000 version with HD-28 features (deleted from price list in 2002).

2004 Marquis versions introduced (GE specs but East Indian Rosewood back and sides).

2007 First run of D-28 Authentic models produced.

Style 28 models have gone through many other changes, but since they are part of the overall evolution of Martin guitar styles in general, these changes are listed in chapter 1, General Information on Guitars. For more details and photos of early Style 28 models, see the Dreadnoughts and Orchestra Model sections of this chapter.

[See page 53 for explanation of asterisks and parenthetical dates.]

STYLE 28 (cont.)

(left) Model 000-28, 1945. See the OM and the Dreadnoughts sections in this chapter for more photos of Style 28 models.

(middle) A Standard D-28, 2005. With the exception of minor changes in tuners and headstock logo, the outward appearance of the regular D-28 has remained unchanged since 1970.

(right) A D-28S, 1973, from the Martin Museum.

STYLE HD-28

The HD-28 was introduced in 1976, and deserves special mention because it was the first model in which Martin returned to the famed "pre-war herringbone" style, making it perhaps the most important Dreadnought model of the company's modern era. Although a new model, the HD-28 incorporated important features of the older herringbone D-28 that had been discontinued in the mid-1940s. These included scalloped top bracing, a small maple bridgeplate, herringbone trim around the face, and an old-style "zipper" backstrip. The HD-28 prototypes were marked R&D #165, #166, and #167. Regular production began with #380826–850, and the HD-28 first appeared in the 1977 catalog.

CUSTOM 15 AND CUSTOM 8 (HD-28V)

The 15th custom order for 1980 was for a special guitar with more features like the earlier herringbone D-28 guitars. It was so popular as a custom model that it was added to the C. F. Martin special-order list, and appeared on the price list as a standard model in 1993. In addition to the features of the HD-28, the Custom 15 featured a "V" profile neck with a squared headstock, diamonds-and-squares fingerboard inlays, and a tortoiseshell style pickguard. This model later evolved into the HD-28VR in 1996 (later shortened to HD-28V). The Custom 8 was a similar model first made in 1980, but with Ivoroid binding instead of white Boltaron, and aging toner on the top. The Custom 8 never appeared on a price list.

Custom 15 version of HD-28 (circa 1990).

STYLE 30

Another of the earliest styles, this one has its origins as a size 2 that cost dealers $30 in the 1850s. Similar to Style 27, descriptions of Style 30 make it sound almost identical except for "German Silver" (nickel silver) tuners and a wider band of colorful wood marquetry around the face. There were frequent orders for larger sizes in this style. Throughout the 1800s, it was one of the most popular deluxe models. It did not appear in the 1898 catalog, but was reinstated in 1901, then was deleted by 1917. Examples from after 1910 often do not have the highly colorful purfling around the top, instead showing a wide and complex pattern in black and white.

A 0-30 (1916, modern tuners) from the Martin Museum.

STYLE 34

Same as Style 30 but with an ivory bridge, with similar origins in the 1850s as a size 2 that cost $34. Style 34 appeared in the 1898 catalog, listed in sizes 2, 1, 0, and 00, with retail prices from $50 to $65, going up $5 for each increase in size. It didn't appear in later editions of the catalog, but continued to be manufactured.

With its ivory bridge, pearl soundhole rosette, and colorful marquetry border around the top, Style 34 made quite a fashion statement. Shown is a 0 size model from 1901. (For a full view, see book 1, chapter 1, page 43).

1901 Spruce top, rosewood sides and back, body and fingerboard ivory bound, colored purfling border around top, pearl rosette, German silver machines. Ebony bridge, ebony fingerboard inlaid 5, 7, and 9. Offered in sizes 1, 0, and 00.

1898 "Rosewood, cedar neck and head, ivory bound body and fingerboard, pearl rosette, border of extra fine purfling, white face, ebony fingerboard with pearl positions, ivory bridge, German Silver machine head with ivory handles".

STYLE 35

Style 35 first appeared as a Dreadnought in 1965. The D-35 introduced a three-piece back with matching outside sections and a contrasting wedge in the center. This major departure in back design was the result of a shortage of Brazilian rosewood wide enough for two-piece backs on Dreadnought guitars. The D-35 was also one of the first Martins in which the features of the style number did not adhere to the company's earlier system. (Previous Martin Styles 30 and higher had a pearl rosette.) In addition to the three-piece back, the D-35 featured additional black and white inlaid lines on the sides beneath the bindings, and a bound fingerboard.

The first example was listed as X-35 #201792. Martin was concerned about the three-piece back's effect on tone, so six more sample D-35 guitars were made:

    D-35A #202219–220 had Dreadnought top braces and 000 sized back braces.

    D-35B #202121–122 had 00 top braces and D back bracing.

    D-35C #202223–224 had 00 top braces and 000 back braces.

The combination of bracing used on D-35C became the standard.

(left) A Standard Series D-35, 2005.

(right) An OM-35, 2003.

1966 D-35 first cataloged, D12-35 12-string also shown. Three-piece back with white-black-white lines between sections, white bindings on body and fingerboard, double black-white inlay on sides with matching lines beneath heelcap. Fingerboard binding mitered on ends (near soundhole). Catalog photo shows plastic buttons on Grover Rotomatic tuners.

1968 Single piece neck binding, ends of fingerboard rounded. Regular Rotomatic Grover machines with metal buttons* *(1967)*. 12-fret "S" model added to line.

1978 HD-35 introduced (see page 72). M-35 introduced, but after only one production run the model designation is changed to M-36.

2003 OM-35 added, all details the same as D-35 except $1^{3/4}"$ neck with small dots (not graduated in size), scalloped top braces, and short OM-style black pickguard (discontinued in 2006).

[See page 53 for explanation of asterisks and parenthetical dates.]

STYLE HD-35

The HD-35 is essentially a herringbone version of C. F. Martin's popular D-35 model. In addition to the standard D-35 features, it has herringbone around the edge of the top, twin zipper backstrips, and scalloped top braces. Since the HD-35 has the same $1/4$" top braces of the D-35, but scalloped, this makes it the most lightly braced Dreadnought of all Martin's production models.

An HD-35 back, current.

First production numbers were #407677–682.

1978 HD-35 introduced.
1979 Cedar top version added (CHD-35), dropped in 1996.

STYLE 36

Style 36 is another modern style that is restricted to one guitar model, the M-36. With very few exceptions, it is the same as Style 35. For more information on the M size guitars, see page 96. Twenty-six examples were made with the M-35 stamp before the designation changed to M-36. Prototype M-35 was #400851, followed by #401901–925. M-36 production began with #402151–175.

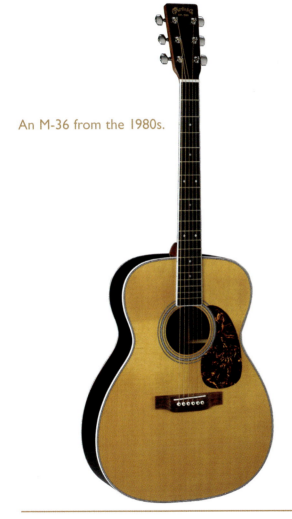

An M-36 from the 1980s.

1978 M-36 introduced. Stained spruce top, rosewood sides, and three-piece back. Mahogany neck without diamond on back of head, ebony fingerboard bound in white, dot inlays on fretboard start at the 3rd fret. Rosewood bridge, tortoise acetate pickguard, scalloped top bracing. D-35 bindings, rosette and back inlay, all other details like D-35.

2007 After years of being available only on special order, the M-36 returns to the price list.

STYLE 37

A relatively recent addition to the Martin line, Style 37K and 37K2 koa guitars were introduced in June 1980. As with the Style 25 koa models introduced the same year, the 37K models have a spruce top, and the 37K2 models have a koa top. Style 37 was more deluxe than Style 25, and the koa generally had more curly figure, or "flame."

There were three prototypes, none of which contained all the features of the final model:

424726: Single ring "Foden" rosette with abalone inlay, single white/black side inlay, koa top.
424727: Spruce top, D-41 rosette, D-35 bindings, regular style 28 fretboard dots, tortoise acetate pickguard.
424728: Same as 727, except koa top, black guard, Foden finger board inlays.
425926: First production D-37K.
426326: First production D-37K2.

A D-37K2, 1980, from the Martin Museum.

1980 Style 37 like Style 25 but with the following changes: Abalone rosette like Style 41, "Flamed" koa sides and two-piece back. Ebony fingerboard with Foden Style "D" fingerboard inlays, ebony bridge. White bindings with D-35 type body trimmings. White bridge pins with black dots. Tuners same as used on Style 28. Tortoise acetate pickguard. Offered in D and Size 7. D-37K2 also introduced; same as D-37K, but with koa top and black pickguard.

1981 MC-37K introduced, rounded cutaway, oval soundhole. Last produced in 1993. See details in section on M Series guitars.

STYLE 38

Style 38 has, to date, been represented by only the M-38, which has the distinction of being the first of the Martin M models. Style 38 is given the most elaborate body and neck binding of any model below Style 45. For more details on the M Series guitars, see page 96.

David Bromberg, long a fan of Martin guitars, prompted the company to introduce the M-38 in 1977. At that time, it was Martin's first new flattop guitar shape in over 40 years. In the days before Signature Editions, the M-38 was a rare example of a new guitar model inspired by an individual outside the Martin factory.

M-38 (1980s).

1977 Introduced and cataloged in size M only. Stained spruce top, rosewood sides and two-piece back, mahogany neck with diamond on back of head. Ebony fingerboard bound in white-black-white, headstock bound to match. Rosewood bridge, tortoise acetate pickguard. White bindings with four black and three white lines on top edge, black-white side inlay mitered at neck and end piece, binding on sides of body adjacent to neck heel, back binding with black-white inlay. Style 45 backstrip and pearl soundhole rosette. Scalloped top braces, small pearl dot inlays, all the same size, at the 3rd, 5th, 7th, 9th, 12th, 15th, and 17th frets, scale length 25.4". Prototypes marked: X38A-D 389326–329.

1997 M-38 renamed 0000-38.

1998 0000-38 deleted from price list, many still produced as special orders.

2007 M-38 returns to price list with original appointments.

STYLE 40

Style 40 originated in the 1850s as a size 2 guitar with a wholesale cost of $40. It appears on the first printed price list from the early 1870s, with a retail price of $84. The 2-40 was essentially the same as the 2-42, but without the "screw neck" and the extra pearl bordering around the end of the fretboard. Style 40 guitars in other sizes were made, though rarely, throughout the later 1800s. Although not included in the 1898–1927 catalogs, a number of Style 40 guitars were made on special order, and larger sizes from 0 to 000 are found in Martin's records beginning in 1909. Style 40 later got a second chance as a Hawaiian model. (The first was probably the 00-40K (Koa) #13245, made in 1918.) In 1928, Martin offered the 00-40H, its deluxe Hawaiian model, but a few of them show up in production records before that date.

A 2-40, 1886, from the Martin Museum.

1928 Style 00-40H introduced in a special brochure.
Same as Style 42, but with the following differences: No binding on neck, high straight saddle and nut, frets ground flush with fingerboard, no pearl border around the portion of the fingerboard that extends over the top.

1930 Belly bridge, straight saddle.
1932 Pickguard optional (listed as standard by 1935).
1941 Last catalog listing.

For photos and more information on the 00-40H, see the section of this chapter on Hawaiian guitar models.

MODERN ERA STYLE 40

In 1985, Martin introduced another version of Style 40. The first models were the J-40M and J12-40M (12-string), and were the company's first Jumbo models.

J-40M/J-40

(left) This original version of the J-40 dates from the late 1980s.

(right) An upgraded version of the J-40, from the late 1990s.

1985 Rosewood sides and back, spruce top with scalloped bracing, small maple bridgeplate. Mahogany neck with low profile and adjustable rod, no headstock diamond. Ebony bridge, ebony fingerboard, white binding with black and white inlay, fingerboard inlay $^4/_5$ size hexagons from the 1st to the 17th fret. White Boltaron binding, top with triple black and white and one wide black inlay, back with double black and white inlay. Regular Style 28 checkered backstrip, Style D-28 soundhole rosette, black pickguard, gold tuners, white bridge and endpin with Style 45 abalone dot. 25.4" scale on both 6- and 12- string versions. The J-40M was the first model to feature the low-profile neck. The first set of J-40M guitars had a Style 28 diamond on the back of the headstock. These guitars were #454401–425. The same was true of the first set of J12-40M guitars #454426–431.

1987 J-40MC cutaway added, oval soundhole.
1990 M suffix dropped, J-40MC renamed JC-40.
1996 Pearl soundhole rosette added, plus bound peghead with block vertical C. F. Martin letters in abalone, Style 45 multicolored backstrip, and tortoiseshell celluloid pickguard.
1997 D-40 introduced, matching specs to J-40

Style 40 is the starting point for several Limited and Signature Edition models. See chapter 3 and the Limited Editions chart in the appendix for details.

STYLE 41

Style 41 is another relatively recent addition to the Martin line, and when introduced it held the same position that Style 42 had occupied years earlier: a pearl-bordered Martin priced significantly below Style 45. Mike Longworth, who was responsible for bringing back the D-45, also deserves credit for what quickly became Martin's best-selling pearl-bordered model, a position the D-41 held throughout the 1970s and 1980s. In some ways, Style 41 was more elaborate than earlier Style 42 Martins, because it had a bound and inlaid headstock. However, it was given Style 40 top bordering, without the pearl border around the end of the fretboard. The prototype D-41 was made in 1969, with 48 more being made that year. Production switched to Indian rosewood with #255717. Total production with Brazilian rosewood was 31 guitars. Some D-41S (12-fret) models were made as well.

The D-41 Special, 2006.

(above) The HPD-41 was the first stock Martin model to display the herringbone pearl bordering around the top and soundhole.

(right) Factory photo of an original version of the D-41 from the 1970s.

- 1970 D-41 first cataloged. Pearl abalone border around top, no connecting link around fingerboard, pearl rosette, neck bound in white. Inlaid 3rd, 5th, 7th, 9th, 12th, and 15th frets. (Inlays were the first six pieces of the D-45 inlay set.) Bound headstock with C. F. Martin inlaid in white pearl, Style 45 backstrip.
- 1987 The D-41 gets a facelift. The first guitar with these changes was #471755, a sales sample designed by C. F. Martin IV. Changes in the production model began with #475216, with the following specs: Scalloped bracing, low profile neck, abalone Style 45 letters in polished headplate, 8 J-40 style hexagon fretboard inlays from 1st to 17th fret ($4/5$ the size of those on the D-45). Tortoise style pickguard. (For the newer D-41 neck style, see the upgraded J-40 image on page 76.)
- 1999 HPD-41 shown on price list. "HP" refers to herringbone pattern pearl bordering around the top and soundhole instead of the usual single line of pearl.
- 2004 D-41 Special added to price list. Similar to standard D-41 but with Style 45 snowflake inlays on fretboard and vintage-style tuners. Style 41 Special was also offered as a Jumbo.

STYLE 42

Style 42 appears on the earliest Martin price list from around 1870, but evolved before that as a size 2 with a wholesale price of $42. It featured an abalone pearl border around the soundhole and top like Style 40, but with the addition of a connecting link of pearl around the end of the fingerboard. The additional pearl on the face, and the adjustable "screw neck" were all that set it apart from the 2-40.

1870 "Richly inlaid with pearl, ivory bridge, screw neck." (See neck adjustment feature on the early Stauffer models shown in book 1, chapter 1.)

1898 Rosewood sides and back, cedar neck, ivory bound body and fingerboard. Pearl rosette, pearl top border, extending around fingerboard. Ivory bridge, ebony fingerboard inlaid 5th, 7th, and 9th frets. (The earliest inlays were white mother-of-pearl.), German silver machines with pearl buttons. Neck no longer listed as adjustable. Illustration shows 18 frets total, listed in size 2, 1, 0, and 00, price from $65 to $80.

1901 Five frets inlaid: 5th, 7th, 9th, 12th, 15th* *(1899-1900)*.

1918 000-42 first listed.

1919 Celluloid bindings replace ivory, ebony bridge replaces ivory.

1923 Mahogany neck*, 20-fret fingerboard, gut strings still standard, engraved nickel machines, ivory celluloid bridge pins and end pin *(change occurred circa 1918)*.

1927 Steel strings listed as standard (many made for steel earlier).

1930 Belly bridge, slanted saddle (introduced in 1929) 2 OM-42s made this year only.

1932 Pickguard optional.

1934– 12-fret 00 version listed as still available,

1937 Hawaiian style at no extra charge.

1938 000-42 listed in 14-fret "Orchestra model."

1941 Last price listing for Style 42. Last 00-42 models made.

1943 Last of original pearl bordered models are 000-42, #83512–17, begun February 24, 1943.

Style 42 was never listed in the Dreadnought size until the 1990s. Only one D-42 was made, a left-handed special order for Tex Fletcher in 1934.

1996 D-42 listed as Standard Series model. (Many custom and Limited Edition Style 42 models made earlier.) D-42 specs: Indian rosewood back and sides, scalloped "high X" bracing, tortoiseshell celluloid pickguard. Body, neck, and headstock bound in ivoroid. Vertical "C. F. Martin" abalone letters on headstock. Style 45 snowflakes on fretboard, large snowflakes on bridge tips. Gold open-back tuners with "butterbean" knobs. OM-42 listed as Standard Series model, same specs as D-42. Koa version of D-42 (D-42K) enters production.

2000 D-42K and D-42K2 shown on price list.

2006 000-42 (24.9" scale) shown on price list. Style 42 continues to be one the most popular of the pearl-bordered styles, and is often the starting point for guitars in the Artist Series or Limited Editions.

[See page 53 for explanation of asterisks and parenthetical dates.]

Model 00-42 with optional "peg head," 1902, from the Martin Museum.

STYLE 42 (cont.)

(above) The guitar that has inspired more signature edition models than any other, Eric Clapton's 1939 000-42.

(right) A D-42K2, 2001.

STYLE 44

Style 44 guitars were made to suit the aesthetic preferences of one of Martin's most prominent endorsers in the 1910s and '20s. Vahdah Olcott-Bickford had been a child prodigy on guitar, and by 1910 was a prominent concert artist. Although she had played standard Style 42 and 45 Martins, she settled upon the idea of a 42/45 quality instrument, but without the pearl inlay. Despite her prominence, Style 44 was hardly a success, and only about 32 guitars were made in this style, all between 1913 and 1938, from size 2 to 000. Many were made with ivory friction peg headstocks.

Model 2-44, 1930, with tinted top finish.

Spruce top, rosewood back and sides, ivory (Ivoroid after 1917) bindings with black, brown, and white inlaid strips (somewhat similar to current style 28). Backstrip of white and black lines, wide white in center, extra black-white lines on each side. Rosette and back border like current Style 28. Bound fingerboard and head.

More details on the origin of this style, and photos of an 0-44, can be found under Vahdah Olcott-Bickford in chapter 6, "Instruments Made for Other Firms."

MARTIN GUITAR MODELS BY STYLE **79**

STYLE 45

This style had its origin in some specially inlaid 42 models made just after the turn of the century. The first was 00-42 #9372 (1902), which had special pearl trim on the sides and back as well as on the top, along with an elaborately inlaid neck and pickguard. Two more 00-42 guitars with side and back inlay were made that same year, #9410 and #9488. Others were made in 1903. The first guitars of their respective sizes to be shown in the sales book as Styles 45 were 0-45 #9910, 00-45 #9960, and 000-45 #10201.

1904   First listed in catalog in 0 and 00 sizes. Like Style 42 with the following additional decoration: Headstock with intricate inlay, fingerboard like Style 42 with inlays at the 5th, 7th, 9th, 12th, and 15th frets. Pearl borders on top like Style 42, with additional narrow pearl bordering on sides, back, end piece, and adjoining neck on body. Pearl borders on sides and back were described as "Japan pearl."

1914   More pearl inlays in fingerboard at the 1st, 3rd, 5th, 7th, 9th, 12th, 15th, and 17th frets. "Style 45 Snowflakes" is a pattern still in use today. Bound headstock with inlay designed like torch or flowerpot. Three-piece bulb on top had slots* *(1905)*.

1917   20-fret model shown with lower soundhole. Ivory bridge still in use.

1919   Ebony "pyramid" bridge.

1923   Bindings listed as celluloid, replacing ivory* *(1919)*.

1927   Gut strings regular, steel on special order (many specially ordered for steel earlier).

1928   Steel strings on regular order.

1930   Head inlay redesigned. Similar pattern but with two-piece "bulb" at the top without slots. Belly bridge with slanted saddle. OM-45 introduced (see OM section for details), 14 OM-45 Deluxe models made.

1932   Pickguard optional (standard on OM since 1930). Gut strings optional. 12-fret model offered in Hawaiian, optional, no charge. OM-45 listed in catalog.

1934   14-fret 000-45 listed. C. F. Martin vertical inlay in headstock* *(1933)*.

1936   Chrome-plated machines.

1938   D-45 first appears in catalog. C. F. Martin inlaid head, snowflake fingerboard inlay.

1939   Gold-plated machines listed. D-45 shown with hexagon abalone inlays.

1941   Last listing for pre-war Style 45 guitars.

1968   Style 45 reissued in Dreadnought size only.

1969   D-12-45 introduced.

1972   00-45 cataloged, slotted headstock with C. F. Martin letters on head and hexagon fretboard inlays.

1983   A few D-45V models made 1983–85 with Brazilian rosewood, snowflake fretboard inlays, scalloped braces, and other features similar to later Vintage Series.

1985–1986   Effective with #460141, scalloped braces with small maple bridgeplate became standard on the modern D-45. This took effect on the D-45S with #467626.

1997   D-45VR introduced (later called D-45V). Snowflake fretboard inlays, Ivoroid binding, other features common to Vintage Series Dreadnoughts like V-shape neck, high-X bracing, toner on top, etc. Custom Shop guitars with these same features were made earlier.

2000   D-45GE and OM-45GE first listed, many Custom Shop examples made earlier.

2005   Style 45GE models deleted from price list, OM-45 first listed.

2006   D-45 Marquis first listed.

[See page 53 for explanation of asterisks and parenthetical dates.]

The pearl bordering around the sides and back of Style 45 models includes inlay bordering the neck heel and endpiece. These examples are from a 1919 0-45.

(left) Model 0-45, 1927.

(middle) Model 00-45, 1970s.

(right) Current OM-45 Marquis 1933, Martin's reissue of the 1933 OM-45 in the company's museum, shown in book 1, chapter 2, page 82.

STYLE D-45

Of all the Martin guitars produced, the D-45 is probably the most famous, so it is fitting to single out this model for special mention. The first D-45 was specially made for Gene Autry in 1933. The serial number was #53177, and it was ordered for him by Chicago Musical Instrument Company. It was a 12-fret model, with Gene's name in pearl script on the fingerboard and extra pearl bordering around the headstock.

For a long time, the rumor persisted that the first D-45 had been lost in a fire. After several years of trying to make contact with Mr. Autry, Mike Longworth was finally was able to do so with the help of Tex Fletcher (owner of the only D-42) and Mr. Roy Horton of Peer Southern Publishing Co. As a result, the rumors were laid to rest. The guitar is currently on display at Autry's Western Heritage Museum in Los Angeles. Reissues of the Gene Autry model were made in 1994.

A second D-45 of 12-fret construction, but with solid headstock, was made for Jackie "Kid" Moore of Milwaukee, Wisconsin in 1934. Two 14-fret D-45s were made in 1936 with wide bodies (16¼" at lower bout). At least one more 12-fret model was made in 1937.

By the time the D-45 was discontinued after October 9, 1942, a total of 91 had been produced. In the following list you will find references to "S" models, but that designation does not necessarily mean a 12-fret model. At the time, any special feature constituted an "S," or Special, model. Some of the features were names in fingerboards, special necks, and left hand construction.

C. F. Martin IV (Chris) with a 1942 D-45 from the Martin Museum.

A modern D-45, 2005.

82 MARTIN GUITARS: A TECHNICAL REFERENCE

The earliest D-45s had snowflake fingerboards, but this feature appeared only in the 1938 Martin catalog. The following year the catalog showed hexagon inlays, the same as used on the F-9 archtop model introduced a few years earlier. The following is a list of the original D-45 guitars compiled from Martin production and sales records:

Style	Year	Special Details	Serial Numbers	Total
D-45	1933	Gene Autry	53177	1
D-45S	1934	Jackie "Kid" Moore	56394	1
D-45S	1936	Wide Body (16 1/4")	63715	1
D-45S	1936	Wide Body	64890	1
D-45	1937	14 frets, 2 guards	65265	1
D-45S	1937	12 fret, solid head	67460	1
D-45	1938		70592–94	3
D-45	1938		71039–41	3
D-45	1938		71663–65	3
D-45	1939		72160–62	3
D-45S	1939	Special Neck	72460	1
D-45	1939		72740–42	3
D-45	1939		73126–31	6
D-45S	1939		74011	1
D-45	1940		74161–66	6
D-45	1940		75100–05	6
D-45L	1940	Left-Hand Style	75289	1
D-45	1940		75593–98	6
D-45	1941		77060–65	6
D-45	1941		78629–34	6
D-45	1941		78879–84	6
D-45	1941		79583–88	6
D-45	1942		80740–45	6
D-45S	1942	Austin	81242	1
D-45	1942	#81578 in Martin Museum	81578–83	6
D-45	1942		82567–72	6

The return of the D-45 can be attributed to Mike Longworth, who was hired in 1968 to bring that model back to the head of Martin's line. He began with two prototypes, #232933 and #236913, and regular production began in July of that year with a set of five, #236914–18. The production models had German spruce tops, whereas the prototypes had been made with Sitka spruce tops. After a time the German spruce specification was dropped, and it is not known how many were made with that wood. A total of 229 new D-45 guitars were made with Brazilian rosewood. The first D-45 to use Indian rosewood was #245237, but it did not become a regular feature of the D-45 until #256366. The change was earlier on the D-41 (225717) and D12-45 (255037).

Early D-45s of the new style had a boxed endpiece. This means a band of abalone pearl that extends around the endpiece covers all four borders, resulting in a double line of pearl between the endpiece itself and the top and bottom side borders. Russell Lilly, who had inlaid many of the old D-45s, had suggested this change. He wanted a specific alteration in inlay design to separate the new from the old. C. F. III decided to go back to the earlier design where the vertical strips bordering the endpiece intersected and were mitered into the top and bottom side borders. The change took effect with #256360, a D12-45, and extended to all Style 45 guitars.

Variations of the D-45 have been the most popular Limited and Signature Editions. Shown here are D-45 Mike Longworth and the D-45SS Stephen Stills. See chapter 3 for details on these and other special D-45 variations.

STYLE 50

Ultra-fancy Dreadnought model with lavish pearl decoration based on original one-off example inlaid by Larry Robinson. See book 1, chapter 4, page 199.

60 SERIES GUITARS

Martin made a number of flattop guitars with maple back and sides over the years, but never offered them in regular production. In 1984, the company developed a line of maple guitars that was introduced at the NAMM trade show in early 1985. Included were four M and J size models plus a Dreadnought D-62LE that was part of the Guitars of the Month program for that year. Standard 60 Series models introduced included the M-64, J-65M, J12-65M, and MC-68. Unlike other Martin styles, in the 60 Series each number was usually made in only one body shape. Although they have a higher style number than Style 45, the 60 Series guitars are not highly decorated. Martin simply chose the higher number to distinguish maple models from the other Martin styles. The maple 60 Series was discontinued in 1995—all but the J-65 had been deleted from the price list by 1994—but a few examples were still made as special orders and maple guitars are still offered in limited runs. These usually have regular style numbers, with an M suffix to indicate maple, such as the maple 16 Series models introduced in 1998.

The following features are common to all 60-65 Series guitars:
Spruce top with scalloped braces, maple back and sides. Low-profile mahogany neck without diamond on back of headstock. Tortoiseshell celluloid binding, ebony fingerboard and bridge, 25.4 string scale.

STYLE 60

This was one of the last Style 60 Series maple models to be introduced, and didn't appear until late 1989. The D-60 was essentially the same as the D-62 of the same year, with the exception of birdseye maple back and sides, matching maple headplate, and gold tuners with ebony buttons. Despite the lower style number, it was 25% more expensive than the D-62, and was the highest-priced maple model (because of the higher cost of birdseye maple). The D-60 was discontinued, along with most of the 60 Series, in 1995, although some special orders may have been produced after that date. See D-62 description below for more details.

Model D-60 from the late 1980s.

STYLE 62

Martin made the first D-62, #471925, in 1987. The original specs showed a neck width of $1\,7/8"$ at the nut and a bridge spacing of $2\,5/16"$. A nut spacing of $1\,11/16"$ and bridge spacing of $2\,1/8"$ was optional. (The wide spacing was the same as the D-62LE GOM from 1986.) This was changed to a standard narrow spacing after the first set. In the first set of #476501–525, only #476501–508 were wide spacing. Although shown in the catalog with Style 18 rosette, this was changed to Style 28 for production models.

1988 Spruce-top Dreadnought with flamed maple sides and back. Scalloped braces with X 1" from soundhole. Tortoiseshell celluloid bindings and heelcap. Style 18 dots on unbound fingerboard. Toned top, body given a light maple stain. Tortoiseshell-style guard, white pins with red dots, chrome tuners.

Model D-62, 1987.

STYLE 64

With a bit more binding and inlay, Style 64 is slightly fancier than Style 62, and almost exactly the same as Style 65, but without fingerboard binding. As it was made only in the M body, and was introduced in 1985 when the new Jumbos were getting all the attention, very few Style 64 models were produced.

1985 Introduced in M size only. Natural color spruce top with flame maple sides and back given light maple stain. Unbound fingerboard with dot inlays beginning on 3rd fret (like M-38). Tortoiseshell celluloid pickguard and body binding with five-ply black and white lines on top and two-ply on back. Style 28 soundhole rosette, D-45 style multicolored backstrip. Chrome mini tuning machines, white pins with tortoise style dots.

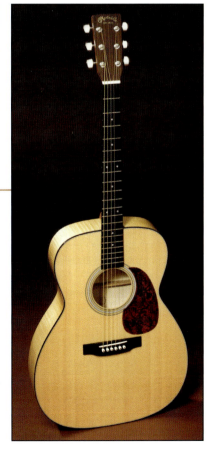

The M-64, 1986.

STYLE 65

This is a slightly more deluxe version of Style 64.

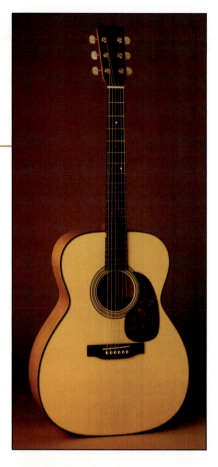

- 1985 Introduced in J size only, both 6- and 12-string models (J-65M and J12-65M). All features are the same as Style 64 described above with the exception of the following: Fingerboard has tortoiseshell celluloid binding with black and white lines. Gold enclosed tuning machines with simulated pearl buttons.
- 1990 M suffix dropped.
- 1993 CMJ-65 a frequent custom order. Sunburst finish, white binding, Style 41 fretboard and headstock, often with active electronics installed.
- 1996 J-65 dropped from price list.

A J-65M, 1986.

STYLE 68

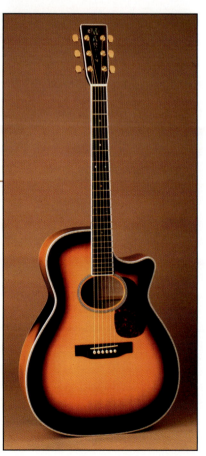

The highest 60 Series model was offered only in a cutaway M body. Unlike the other maple models, it came with white binding and was usually pictured in catalogs and ads with a sunburst finish.

- 1985 Introduced as MC-68, the prototype being #455329. White binding with five plies of black and white lines on top, and four plies on the sides (like D-35). D-28 style backstrip with added black line on each side. Oval soundhole with nine-ply rosette (like JC-40). Bound headstock with inlaid C. F. Martin letters (like D-45). Ebony bridge, 22-fret bound ebony fretboard with abalone dots. Carved diamond on back of headstock. Dropped from price list circa 1995.

The MC-68, introduced in 1985, was the first stock flattop guitar model Martin had ever offered with a full-body sunburst finish.

STYLE 76

This style is not connected to the usual Martin-style sequence because the number was chosen to coincide with America's bicentennial. The D-76 C. F. Martin guitar and the V-76 Vega banjo were Limited Editions in celebration of the 200th anniversary of the United States of America. In addition to the 1,976 guitars and 76 banjos made for retail sale, the company made 98 guitars and 16 banjos for employees. The employee models were designated D-76E and V-76E.

1976   Spruce top, East Indian rosewood sides and back, mahogany neck without diamond at back of head. Ebony bridge and unbound ebony fingerboard with 13 pearl stars, Style D-28 bindings and pins, black pickguard. Herringbone rosette, three-piece back with two herringbone backstrips. Engraved pearl eagle in headstock. Brass plate on neck block with series number and serial number. Employee model had added paper label on inside of back with signature of C. F. Martin III.

Headstock of Johnny Cash's D-76. (For a full photo of D-76, see book 1, chapter 3.)

STYLE 100

Lavishly decorated Dreadnought based on the Millionth Martin original inlaid by Larry Robinson. See book 1, chapter 4.

The D-100 featured the most elaborate inlay themes of any Martin instrument in the company's history.

ORIGINS AND HISTORY OF 20TH CENTURY MARTIN GUITAR SHAPES

OM (ORCHESTRA MODEL)

In the summer of 1929, a young bandleader, guitarist, and banjo player named Perry Bechtel visited the Martin factory requesting a flattop guitar with a longer, slimmer neck. (See book 1, chapter 2, page 76.) Like many other banjo players in dance orchestras of the 1920s and '30s, Bechtel wanted to be able to switch between banjo and guitar, but found the short, wide necks on Martins too restrictive. Martin took its largest model, the 000—the Dreadnought was still an exclusive shape made only for Ditson—and shortened the body, moving the soundhole and bridge up so the neck could be joined to the body at the 14th fret, instead of at the 12th. The neck was also made narrower and with a steeper radius to the fretboard. At Bechtel's request, a small "guardplate" (pickguard) was also added. Since the 12-fret 000 had a long scale (25.4"), the new model was given that scale length as well. The prototype made for Bechtel was #39081, listed as a "000-28 Special."

At least one other early example of the new model was made with the conventional slotted headstock, but these were the exception. Along with the change in neck length and shape, Martin opted for a solid headstock with geared straight-through tuners, the same gears as used on banjos and on Martin's highly popular tenor guitars. Ten more of the new model were completed in October and November of 1929. Though some of these appear in Martin's records as "000-28 Perry Bechtel Professional model," soon the term "Orchestra Model" was given to these new long-neck guitars. Since Perry Bechtel apparently moved on to conventional archtop guitar styles by early 1930, his name was no longer associated with what was soon called the OM-28. Today, with the exception of the banjo tuners, the result of Bechtel's request looks like an ordinary guitar. At the time, though, it was revolutionary, for necks with 12 frets clear of the body had been the standard for virtually all flattop guitars for over a century (and before that they were even shorter). Gibson's L-5 is widely heralded as the first true jazz and/or archtop guitar, but Martin's new long-necked version of the 000 was the first modern flattop by a major manufacturer.

Martin had high hopes that its new model would appeal to orchestra players like Bechtel, hence the name Orchestra Model. Although considered as primarily a fingerstyle guitar today, Martin clearly didn't have that in mind when the new model was first described in the 1930 catalog as "designed especially for plectrum playing in orchestra work." Uptown dance band guitarists paid little attention. Instead, the new OM was the instant favorite in West Coast cowboy bands, where an orchestra was more likely to consist of fiddle, accordion, and guitar. The Sons of the Pioneers (including Roy Rogers) and Mac McClintock's Haywire Orchestra were just two of the prominent cowboy groups that sported more than one OM model. The OM-28 was immediately supplemented by the OM-18 (starting with #41034–35, but "000-18 Specials" #40553–54 may have been the first OM-18 models). These less-expensive mahogany versions sold in even greater numbers than the original rosewood OM, especially as the Great Depression grew more severe.

By late 1931, Martin realized that 14-fret necks were the key to greater sales and began making similar modifications to its other guitar sizes. (C Series archtops, using the same shape as the OM, were already in production.) The first to get the longer neck was the Concert Size 0-18, and a number of "0-18 OMs" with sunburst tops were made in 1932. (A few were made in late '31.) These were called "0-18 '32 Specials" in Martin's logbook in 1933 and were pitched to dealers with a special postcard. By early 1933, 14-fret 00 models were also made in small numbers. Around the same time, the R Series archtops were introduced, using the same body shape and neck length. The popularity of these 14-fret models led Martin to revamp its entire line by early 1934, and here's where the meaning of "OM" and "Orchestra Model" gets confusing. Martin's 1934 catalog featured several new 14-fret models, including the Dreadnought. All were called Orchestra Models, and all had the slimmer necks, solid headstocks, and pickguards that signified a modern, steel-string flattop guitar. To keep the differences between these new models and the original Martin styles straight, the company divided its catalog into "Orchestra Models" and "Standard Models." Standard models had the old 12-fret neck, slotted headstock, and long body of the original 19th century Martin designs. (These included Hawaiian models.) The Orchestra Models were all 14-fret guitars with solid headstocks, guitars that looked very much like the instruments the company would rely upon in the coming decades.

But since Martin now called a group of about a dozen guitars Orchestra Models, the ones that had started the trend had to be renamed. Beginning in 1934, the original OM-18s, 28s, and 45s were stamped simply 000 instead. For the first several months of 1934, the "new" 000 models were exactly the same as when they'd been stamped "OM" the year before, but later in 1934 Martin gave the 000 the shorter (24.9") scale length. (The last long scale 000-28 models were #57544–55.) In 1939, the necks on all 14-fret models were made narrower ($1\,^{11}/_{16}$" instead of $1\,^{3}/_{4}$"),

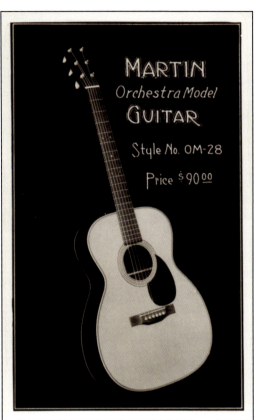

Martin wasted little time in pitching its new guitar model to retailers with this postcard. The OM-28 was the first standard 6-string model with 14 frets clear of the body.

and the conversion to the modern Martin 000 was complete. As Martin's old Standard models retreated to obscurity, the company no longer referred to its 14-fret guitars as Orchestra Models, and by the 1960s the term was widely regarded as referring only to the 000 size with wider neck and long scale. (See book 1, chapter 2 for more photos of original OM models.)

The OM returned again in 1969 with a run of six 000-28 models with $1\,^{3}/_{4}$" necks and long scale, stamped SOM-28 (S for "Special"). Similar models in Style 45 appeared in 1977. The OM-45 appeared in the late 1970s catalogs, but was available only on special order by the mid-1980s. OM-28 models were common special orders, and became more widely available with the introduction of the Custom Shop in 1979. With the exception of the brief reappearance of the OM-45—and Limited Editions beginning in 1985— the OM-21 introduced in 1993 was the first production OM model to appear on a price list in the modern era. Despite their popularity with fingerstyle guitarists, the Orchestra Models didn't get a specific heading in Martin's catalog and price list until 1995, with a vintage style version (OM-28VR) added the following year. Style 16 OMs were added to that Series in 1999.

In the new century, OM models have made more frequent appearances as Limited and Signature Editions, with the cutaway OMC Laurence Juber models issued in so many variations that they almost qualify as a Series. The OM, both as a guitar shape and as a name, has become Martin's second-most-copied model.

ORIGINAL OM STYLES

1930 OM-18, 28, and 45 first appear in catalog. Woods and appointments like regular Martin models of the same style but with the following differences: 14-fret neck, narrower than on 12-fret models. First cataloging of pickguard as standard equipment, the short tortoiseshell celluloid pickguard now widely associated with OM models only. 4:1 ratio banjo pegs with white ivory celluloid buttons.

1932 Shown with larger "teardrop" pickguard and regular right-angle guitar tuners with metal buttons* *(by late 1931).*

1933 Last use of OM designation to denote a unique body size and shape. (Beginning in 1934, Orchestra Model becomes Martin's term to indicate any flattop guitar model with a 14-fret neck.)

A 1933 OM-18 with "dark top" option. The new OM models were the first Martins made in significant numbers with what are now called "sunburst" finishes on the face. At the time, Martin referred to this option as simply "dark" or "shaded."

STYLE OM-45 DELUXE

1930 First and only appearance of Deluxe Style 45 in catalog. Has all the features of regular OM-45, plus: Snowflake inlays on bridge tips, pickguard inlaid with stylized floral design, gold-plated banjo pegs, engraved, with genuine pearl knobs.

MODERN-DAY OM MODELS

Style OM-45 was first reintroduced in 1977, on a special-order basis, and soon was added to the C. F. Martin line. Early examples were marked SOM-45 and featured custom torch headstock and snowflake fingerboard inlays. The regular OM-45 began with #406240–250. Other OM models were added as mentioned below.

1978 OM-45 appears on price list. It is shown in the 1982 catalog, but is relegated to the "available on special order" list shortly after. Same features as D-45 models of the same era (hexagon fretboard inlays and C. F. Martin letters on headstock) except OM-45 has small pickguard and scalloped top braces and small maple bridgeplate.
1990 OM-28 also shown on special order list, same as 000-28 of the same period but with wider neck and long scale.
1993 OM-21 appears on price list and in catalog.
1995 OM-28 shown on price list as a standard model.
1996 OM-28VR (later called OM-28V) listed as part of new Vintage Series.
1998 OM-45GE Golden Era (Brazilian rosewood) added as Special Edition.
1999 OM-18V added to Vintage Series, OM-1 appears in 1 Series, SPOM-16 in 16 Series, OM-42 added to Standard Series (but has many Vintage Series features).
2000 OMM added to Road Series, OM-15 and OM-16GT introduced, SmartWood SWOMGT appears as Special Edition. OM-45GE introduced (Golden Era, Brazilian/Adirondack).
2002 Cutaway OM models added to 15 and 16 Series.
2003 OM-35 added to Standard Series. OM-18GE and OM-28GE added to Special Editions column of price list.
2005 OM-28 Marquis and OM-45 Marquis added.

See the section on Limited and Special Editions for other OM models offered from 1985 to the present. The most enduring of these has been the Laurence Juber OMC models first introduced in 2002.

The OMC-28LJ shown is only one of several "LJ" OM variations Martin has issued since 2002 in collaboration with Laurence Juber. All are spec'd with Adirondack top, blank fretboard, and no pickguard.

DREADNOUGHTS

Note: Martin spelled it "Dreadnaught" until the early 1960s, and has used the "Dreadnought" spelling ever since. The second spelling is used throughout this book to avoid confusion.

It would be easy to fill an entire book with history and details regarding the Martin Dreadnought. If the company had to rely on this guitar shape alone, its reputation and influence would be secure. Below is a short summary of the development of the unique guitar shape that has become the most widely copied acoustic guitar design of modern times.

The first Dreadnoughts were part of a series of three guitar sizes, all with the same unique wide-waisted shape, made for the Oliver Ditson Company beginning in 1916. (For more information on the relationship between C. F. Martin and Ditson, see chapter 6, "Instruments Made for Other Firms.") The Ditson models were made in sizes similar to Martin's 1, 00, and the current Dreadnought "S" models, all with 12-fret necks and long bodies. The Dreadnought body outline was first drawn in 1916 by enlarging the shape of the smaller "Concert" model. These were marketed exclusively by the Ditson music stores in Boston and New York City, branded "Oliver Ditson Co., Boston, New York." Although offered in three styles, with each style available in three sizes, it was the largest size that evolved into the Martin Dreadnought. All of the early Ditson models had fan-braced tops, but Martin's own spec sheets referred to them as "Ditson Hawaiian models." The Ditson Dreadnoughts made after 1921 have standard Martin X-bracing.

The collaboration between Martin and Ditson came to an end when the Ditson Company was sold, and the last of the Ditson Dreadnoughts was made in late 1930. A few months later Martin was building Dreadnoughts for their own line. The first were designated D-1 (#47052–53) and D-2 (#47054–55), with this first batch being sent to the Chicago Musical Instrument Co. on May 22, 1931. (Two more D-2 models were made later that year.) The D-1 became the D-18 and the D-2 became the D-28. One of the D-2 models is on display at the Country Music Foundation Hall of Fame in Nashville. It belonged to the country entertainer "Arkie," who performed on the National Barn Dance over radio station WLS in Chicago. Gene Autry, who ordered the first D-45 two years later, also appeared on the same radio show around that time.

(opposite page) Today we associate the earlier 12-fret Dreadnoughts with a slotted headstock, but there were several solid headstock examples made soon after Martin adopted the Ditson Dreadnought as a regular model under its own brand. This one is from 1932.

(below) Although the herringbone top border appeared on other Style 28 models, the popularity and dominance of the Dreadnought was so pervasive that, for many years, "herringbone Martin"—or simply "herringbone"—was synonymous with "prewar D-28." (A 1941 example is shown, from the Martin Museum.)

The first Dreadnoughts given D-18 and D-28 designations also appeared in 1931, with one of each shipped in September. For another year or two, a few were made and offered to dealers with mixed results. Martin's hesitation to fully embrace the Dreadnought can be gauged by the company's reluctance to put the new model in the catalog. Unlike the OM, with four models appearing in the catalog less than a year after it was introduced, Martin essentially kept its Dreadnoughts "behind the counter." While they were sold to prominent performers and select Martin dealers, there was no sign of them in the catalogs or price lists. During this same period, Martin actively advertised and promoted both its OM models and the new archtop line, which had debuted just as Martin-branded Dreadnoughts were first shipped. Even with household-name entertainers—both Arkie and Autry were well known—playing its new model, Martin still did little to promote the Dreadnought.

The Dreadnoughts evolved from 12-fret to 14-fret models in early 1934—the first serial number specifically mentioned as a 14-fret was D-28 #55260, but there may have been earlier examples—but sales were still slow. Once the new "Orchestra Model" (Martin's term for its 14-fret flattop guitars) D-28 and D-18 appeared in the July 1935 catalog, however, Dreadnought sales increased dramatically. Ironically, the original Dreadnought shape, with longer body, 12-fret neck, and slotted headstock, first appeared in a Martin catalog as the 12-string D12-20 in 1965, almost half a century after Martin had made the first Ditson Dreadnoughts!

The new 14-fret "Orchestra Model" Dreadnoughts soon underwent another series of minor changes. The extreme string tension of heavy gauge strings prompted Martin to move the X brace down, away from the soundhole, which put the bridge closer to intersection of the X and strengthened that portion of the soundboard. This began with a batch of a dozen D-28 models (71358–69) begun on October 13, 1938. That same day a batch of 25 D-18s (71370–94) was begun with the same new top bracing. The next change came in mid-1939, when Dreadnoughts were given the same narrower neck that had first appeared on Martin archtops. This change to a neck $1^{11}/_{16}$" wide at the nut was not thoroughly documented at the time, but it's clear it quickly became the standard. For other changes to the Dreadnought, which occurred along with similar changes to Martin's other steel string models, see the "Recorded Changes" list at the end of the previous chapter. From 1947 until the late 1960s, the Martin Dreadnought underwent only minor modernizations. The D-21 was added in 1955, and the D-35 ten years later.

Considering how well Martin hid its original 12-fret Dreadnought, it's surprising that these models made the earliest comeback of any of the old style guitars. Special orders for the D-28S began in the mid-1950s, and by the early 1960s enough were ordered by the E.U. Wurlitzer store in Boston to be given a D-28SW (Special Wurlitzer) model code of their own. The S model Dreadnoughts returned to the catalog in 1968 in styles 18, 28, and 35, the same year the legendary D-45 also made a comeback. The even more widely known "herringbone D-28," in an approximate pre-WWII style, returned in 1976 with the HD-28. The return of the D-45 and the appearance of the HD-28 started a landslide of new Dreadnought models that has continued to this day, as if Martin was trying to make up for treating its chubby stepchild so shabbily after it was first adopted. And once the Custom Shop opened the door to special orders, Martin began building ever more accurate reissues of the 1930s Dreadnought styles.

Dreadnoughts have continued to reign supreme at Martin, with only a brief challenge from the Jumbo models introduced in the mid-1980s. When Martin forged into new territory with state-of-the-art manufacturing in 1993, the D-1 was the logical result. Reissues of earlier Dreadnought styles have consistently shown the way for the return of other models, such as the OM and the 12-fret 000. With the introduction of a

94 MARTIN GUITARS: A TECHNICAL REFERENCE

consistent Vintage Series in 1996, reissues of both the original 12-fret Dreadnoughts and later, but still pre-WWII, 14-fret styles have existed side by side with newer Martin D models. Martin's showpiece "over 45" models, such as the D-50 and D-100, indicate the model's continued dominance in Nazareth. To many guitar fans the world over, a Martin guitar is a Dreadnought. Period.

The list below is not a complete evolution of the Martin Dreadnought, but it does track changes in the original models and their return, as reissues, to the Martin line.

- 1916 Dreadnought body shape first designed for Ditson.
- 1931 Dreadnought shape adopted as Martin model.
- 1933 First D-45 made (12-fret, for Gene Autry).
- 1934 First 14-fret Dreadnought models are made, and first appearance of D-18 and D-28 in Martin catalog (14-fret models only).
- 1936 Two D-45 models are made with body ¼ inch wider than normal.
- 1942 Last of the original D-45 models.
- 1944 Last Dreadnought made with scalloped-top bracing.
- 1946 Last herringbone-trimmed D-28.
- 1955 D-21 introduced.
- 1964 First D12-20 12-string model, original Ditson body shape.
- 1965 D-35 introduced, first Martin model with three-piece back.
- 1968 D-45 reintroduced, first pearl-bordered Martin D since 1942, D-41 introduced the following year, 12-fret S model Dreadnoughts return to catalog.
- 1969 First set of Dreadnoughts made with East Indian rosewood, serial #s 243644–47, all D-28 models.
- 1976 HD-28 is the first reissue of herringbone D-28 with scalloped bracing.
- 1980 The 15th custom order for this year is an HD-28 with more vintage features (inlays, neck shape, high X bracing). This "Custom 15" model later becomes HD-28V.
- 1981 DC-28 is the first cutaway Martin Dreadnought.
- 1983 First reissue of Brazilian rosewood D models (D-28V, first use of V-for-Vintage suffix to model code).
- 1985 D-18V (GOM model) is first prewar Style 18 Dreadnought offered in quantity.
- 1987 D-45LE (GOM model) is first "over 45" Dreadnought offered in quantity.
- 1993 D-1 is first Martin made with "new technology." Custom 15 (later HD-28V) is finally moved from special order list and given regular model status.
- 1995 D-18 Golden Era (GOM model) with more exact mid-1930s features is first use of GE terminology.
- 1996 Vintage Series re-establishes both 14-fret and 12-fret versions of the early D-18s and D-28s as regular Martin models, D-45V added in '98.
- 1999 D-28GE "Golden Era" marks return of Brazilian rosewood/Adirondack top pre-1939 specs model. D-18GE added the same year (Special Editions category).
- 2004 D-28 Marquis brings all of the GE Series features (including Adirondack top) to a model made with East Indian Rosewood back and sides.
- 2005 Authentic Series is begun with introduction of the D-18 Authentic.
- 2007 D-28 Authentic produced in limited numbers.

See chapter 3 for more variants of the Dreadnought.

(opposite page) A 1942 D-45, from the Martin Museum. To many guitar aficionados, an original D-45 like the one shown here is the ultimate Dreadnought guitar. Mike Longworth certainly agreed with that sentiment.

M MODELS

The M Series guitars had their origin in the F Series carved-top Martins of the 1930s. (See chapter 4, "Archtops and Electrics.") These models had extremely low value in the 1960s, and a few guitar shops that specialized in vintage instruments recognized that replacing the original carved top with a new X-braced flat top would create a new and different Martin model. Since F models had sides about the same depth as the 000, the result was like a 000 model 16 inches wide at the lower bout instead of only 15 inches. Several F-7 and F-9 guitars were subsequently converted to flattop instruments by independent craftsmen such as Jon Lundberg of Berkeley, California, and Matt Umanov of New York City. One of these conversions was purchased by David Bromberg, who preferred its more balanced sound to the heavy bass and sustain of the Dreadnought models. Bromberg suggested that Martin make such a model, and the company added this style to the line in 1977. The new body shape was dubbed the "Grand Auditorium," since it was larger than the Martin 000 Auditorium size. Bromberg's example had an ebony fretboard with rosewood bridge, and this feature was included on the new models.

In the early 1980s, before the Jumbos were introduced, M models were the only large guitars Martin offered as alternatives to the Dreadnought. Shown are the M-18, MC-28, and M-38 in a catalog photo from 1984.

Original F model Martins had backs more highly arched that flattop models, with all four back braces tall and blade-shaped like the upper two back braces on flattop models. This feature was used on the new M Series, and this style of back bracing was later used on Martin's Jumbo models as well. All M Series Martins have scalloped top braces.

1977	M-38 introduced (see details in "Original Number Series" section at the beginning of this chapter, under Style 38).
1978	M-36 introduced (first called M-35).
1981	MC-28 introduced, cutaway with oval soundhole. Standard Style 28 appointments, but with a 22-fret fingerboard and single ring rosette with nine black and white lines. MC-37K koa model also appears, same soundhole and rosette as MC-28.
1984	M-18 appears but sells poorly and is discontinued in 1988.
1985	M-64 and MC-68 maple models introduced. These are fully described in the "Original Number Series" section.
1997	M-38 renamed 0000-38, but remains essentially the same guitar. 0000-28H introduced, which has the same appointments as the HD-28 in the M size.
1998	0000-38 deleted from price list.
2000	0000-1 added, first M size model in lower-priced series.
2001	In January price list no M or 0000 models are listed, but in the July 2001 list the M-16GT appears.
2002	Limited Edition versions of the M shape are listed, and a SmartWood model appears the following year, but for the most part the M models disappear from Martin's Standard Series, and don't qualify for the Vintage Series.
2007	M-38 and M-36 return to the catalog.

J MODELS

The J-for-Jumbo Martins first appeared in 1985. The shape was the same as the M, but with sides as deep as a Dreadnought. Since this new model was based on the M body shape, Martin called it a "Jumbo M" and added the M suffix to the model code to indicate its origin. This is why all the early J models have a code ending in "M," (J-40M, J-65M, etc.). In 1990 the M suffix was dropped as being redundant, as there was only one J body style and everyone knew where it came from. The late 1980s and early 1990s were the heyday of the Jumbos, and with maple models, 12-strings, and acoustic basses, Martin's catalog during this period showed more Jumbo-bodied guitars than it did Dreadnoughts. By the mid-1990s, sales slowed as fingerstyle guitarists began switching to smaller OM models and everyone else returned to Martin's original big guitar, the Dreadnought. But in the 1980s the Jumbos were widely credited with breathing new life into Martin's image and enabling it to clamber back into the music industry spotlight.

When introduced in the mid-1980s, Martin's 6-string and 12-string Jumbos were welcome alternatives to the Dreadnought.

The Martin Jumbo was introduced the same year the company began using adjustable truss rods in the neck, and subsequently making necks more slender (called "low profile"). All the new Jumbo models were given this new neck shape from the beginning. This means that a 1987 D-35P (the P standing for "low profile" neck) and a J-40M from the same year have the same neck shape. All Jumbos have a 25.4" string scale and scalloped top braces (except 12-string versions, which have the 24.9" scale and do not have scalloped braces).

Standard Jumbo model details are fully described in the "Original Number Series" section. For Guitars of the Month Jumbos and those issued as Limited Editions and Signature Editions, see chapter 3.

1985 J-40M and J-65M introduced, with companion 12-string versions (J12-40M and J12-65M). J-21M also appears but gets little notice and is deleted from price list in 1991.

1987 J-18M and J-40MC (cutaway) appear. The J-18's original specs were for a 1 3/4" neck at the nut, while the J-40MC was to have a neck 1 7/8" at the nut. Only a few examples from the first batches had the wider neck, with all other examples given a standard 1 11/16" neck. The J-18M has details similar to D-16 models of that year, namely diamonds-and-squares fretboard inlays and tortoiseshell celluloid binding.

1988 J-40MBK introduced, a J-40 M finished in black lacquer.

1990 M suffix disappears from Jumbo models (J-40M becomes J-40). At the same time, the C suffix for the cutaway J-40 is put where it belongs, and so the J-40MC becomes the JC-40.

1996 HJ-28 appears, same appointments as the HD-28. J-65 and its 12-string version are deleted.

1997 J-18, JC-40, and J-40BK are deleted from price list, leaving the J-40 and new HJ-28 as the only remaining stock Jumbo models in the Standard Series. The J-1 is introduced as the first Jumbo model in the lower-priced 1 Series guitars.

1999 JM and J-15 appear, first Jumbos in Road Series and 15 Series, JC-1E with onboard electronics also added. J12-16GT 12-string appears.

2001 HJ-28 deleted from price list, four 16 Series Jumbos are added, in both rosewood and mahogany, all have cutaways and Fishman onboard electronics. J-40 is the only original Jumbo model left on the price list.

2003 SWJGT SmartWood model added to price list. SWGT SmartWood and JC-16RGTE Premium (updated Fishman onboard electronics) added to price list.

2004 J-41 Special appears, same neck inlays as D-41 Special (see page 77).

2005 JC-16RGTE Aura replaces Premium version (another update to Fishman onboard electronics).

MARTIN GUITARS FOR SPECIFIC STRINGING OR PLAYING STYLES

Listed in the chronological order in which they were introduced.

HAWAIIAN INCLUDES K (KOA) MODELS

When the Hawaiian music fad was in full swing, the world of guitars was divided into two camps: Spanish models, a term used to describe any guitar played in the conventional upright position, and Hawaiian models, which were played lying flat on the lap and "fretted" by sliding a steel bar on the strings with the left hand (like a bluegrass Dobro). Martin's Hawaiian model guitars were almost identical to their Spanish counterparts of the same style, but with a few notable exceptions. The earliest Hawaiian models were all-koa Style 18 and 28 models that came with metal extender nuts over the regular ebony or ivory nut at the top of the fretboard, raising the strings to facilitate playing Hawaiian style. The catalog description explained that when the metal nut was removed, these guitars could be played in conventional (Spanish) style. These were the first Martin guitars shown in the catalog with steel strings. Such "convertible" Hawaiian models didn't last long, however, as more and more competitors' guitars appeared on the market that were specifically for Hawaiian playing.

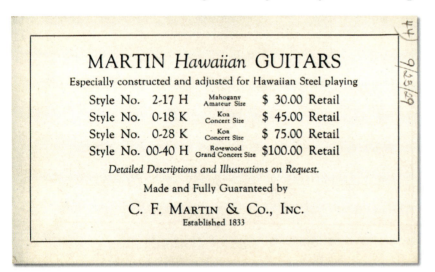

This postcard sent to Martin retailers is a reminder that the company took the Hawaiian guitar trade very seriously. Around the time this advertisement was mailed in 1929, Martin sold as many 00-40H models as it did 00-42 guitars set up for regular playing.

On later Martin Hawaiian models, the nut and saddle were left high and the frets were often ground flush with the fingerboard to facilitate Hawaiian style playing (so the steel wouldn't hit the frets). The bridge on Hawaiian models had a straight saddle even after Spanish models went to the slanted saddle required when using steel strings. Even the actual positioning of the bridge was different, because the pitch is infinitely variable when playing Hawaiian style. This means it isn't necessary to compensate the saddle to get the guitar to play in tune, and on Hawaiian models the bridge was slightly forward of the Spanish position. Unlike most other American guitar companies, however, Martin never made Hawaiian models with overly large necks or square necks. Besides models with bodies made entirely of koa, which were given a K suffix after the style number, Martin made Hawaiian guitars of mahogany or rosewood with a spruce top, and some that were all mahogany. All models made with a high nut and flush frets had an "H" after the model code, but of course this code didn't begin to appear on the instrument itself until 1931.

The popularity of Martin Hawaiian instruments covered a period from just before 1920 to 1941, when production was curtailed because of WWII, and koa was unavailable. After the war, most Hawaiian guitar players preferred the small electric "lap steel" models like the first guitars made by Leo Fender.

K (KOA) SERIES GUITARS

Martin's first Hawaiian guitar models were made of koa, and between 1917 and 1935 the company made almost 4,000 koa wood guitars from size 5 to 000. During most of those years Martin was also making a great number of koa ukuleles, so for a time the company was using far more koa than rosewood. Martin's K models evolved from similar guitars the company made for a chain of music stores in Southern California beginning in 1916. (See Southern California Music in chapter 6.) The height of popularity for Martin's koa guitars was 1927, also a peak year for ukulele production. In that year alone, Martin sold 650 0-18K and 0-28K models. Sales of conventional 0 and 00 models in Styles 18, 21, and 28 for that year totaled about 1500, which is a good indication of how important the K models were to Martin's growth at the time. Style 18K was more expensive than a regular Style 18 model of the same size ($45 for a 0-18K but only $40 for the 0-18), but Style 28K was the same price as the regular rosewood Style 28. While a number of 00 size versions of the K models were made, only size 0 was ever listed in the catalogs.

Martin began making guitars of koa again in 1980, but these models had a unique style number (either 25 or 37) and are described in the "Original Number Series" section. In 2000, koa models were added to the 16 Series, and koa versions of the D-42 were also added to the price list. In all Martin koa models made since 1980, the "K" suffix means that only the back and sides are made of koa, while a "K2" suffix means the guitar has a koa top as well.

> Martin's Style 18 models delivered stronger sales than Style 28, and the koa versions were no exception. Over 1100 0-18K models were sold in 1926-28 alone, more than all 0-28K sales combined during the 18 years the two koa models were in production. This example is from 1921.

STYLE 18K

The 0 and 00-18K models were made using plainer koa for the top, sides, and back. Except for the wood, and the changes made to accommodate Hawaiian playing, Style 18 models made of koa had the same binding and details as other Style 18 models of the period.

1918 First made.
1923 First shown in catalog. Steel strings with nut adjuster for Hawaiian playing. Suitable for regular playing with nut adjuster removed.
1925 Listed with high nut and straight bridge with straight saddle.
1926 Listed with flush frets.
1929 Optional low nut and beveled bridge for regular playing, lacquer finish.
1930 Belly bridge, straight saddle.
1934 Rosewood bindings replaced with Fiberloid* *(1932)*.
1935 Last shown on price list.

STYLE 21K

About 50 0-21K models were made between 1919 and 1929, although the model was never listed in a Martin catalog. Some were probably Style 1400 models made for Southern California Music Company.

STYLE 28K

Style 28 models were given the more highly figured, or flamed, koa. When combined with the contrasting ivory-grained celluloid binding, the result was probably the most striking looking Martin standard models, with the exception of the pearl-trimmed styles.

1918	First made.
1923	Curly koa body, including top, Listed with steel strings and nut adjuster, suitable for regular playing with nut adjuster removed.
1925	High nut and straight bridge with straight saddle.
1926	Listed with flush frets.
1929	Raised frets and low nut and saddle for regular playing optional, lacquer finish.
1930	Belly bridge, straight saddle.
1933	Last shown on price list.

Although Martin made some larger all-koa models and some with pearl bordering, the 0-28K was the highest koa Hawaiian model to appear in a catalog. This one, from the Martin Museum, dates from 1926.

STYLE 2-17H AND 0-17H

The 2-17H was much like the regular Style 17 Martin guitars, with an all-mahogany body. It was made from 1927 to 1931, and first appeared in a small brochure promoting Martin's new Hawaiian models. See the "Original Number Series" section.

1927 First appears, listed with 18 frets, ground flush. Discontinued in 1932.
1930 Style 0-17H was first shown on price list. About 60 were made that year. It was not produced again until 1935, and showed up in the 1937 price list. Production ceased in 1940. Except for the high nut, straight saddle, and flush frets it was identical to conventional (Spanish) 0-17 models in the standard, or 12-fret, style.

A 0-17H (1937) from the Martin Museum and 00-18H with dark top, (1938). The 0-17H (left) and 00-18H (right) replaced the earlier koa Hawaiian models in Martin's catalog by the mid-1930s.

STYLE 00-18H

The 00-18H was like its Spanish counterpart except for the usual changes for Hawaiian playing. It was made from 1935 to 1941. The first catalog listing was in 1937, and by this time the regular 00-18 was a 14-fret model, while the Hawaiian version was the old 12-fret style.

1937 Flat fingerboard, flush frets, available for Hawaiian style only. Most have shaded top finish.
1938 Shaded top shown in catalog.
1941 Last shown.

STYLE 00-40H

This model has the distinction of being the only pearl-trimmed guitar normally made for Hawaiian style. Other pearl-bordered models were custom ordered for Hawaiian playing, however. For a description of Style 40 in this period, see the "Original Number Series" section of this chapter.

1928 First appeared in brochure.
1929 First appears in catalog, listed "for Hawaiian playing only."
1930 Belly bridge, but saddle still straight.
1932 Pickguard optional, listed as standard by 1935.
1937 Shaded top optional.
1941 Last shown.

Model 00-40H, 1932, from the Martin Museum. This was the highest Hawaiian model shown in a catalog, but the company made lots of guitars set up for Hawaiian playing on special order, including Style 45 and Dreadnought models.

TENOR AND PLECTRUM

Tenor, or 4-string, guitars were designed to allow tenor banjo players to get the softer tone of a guitar without learning a different tuning. There was much demand for 4-string guitars by the mid-1920s, and Martin's first tenor guitar models were offered in 1927. The 5-17 and 5-21 model guitars were listed with four strings, but initially Martin did not add the "T-for-tenor" suffix to the model code, which resulted in some confusion when Mike Longworth compiled the original production charts. It's now clear that tenor production was higher than previously believed, and that the demand for tenor guitars was enough to inspire Martin to build over 1,200 of them in 1927 alone, about 20% of guitar production for that year.

Martin began with only small size tenor guitars, mostly size 5 and size 2, perhaps because the company wanted to get at least 14 frets clear of the body while still using a short string scale. Professional banjo players, however, needed far more volume than these small-bodied tenors could provide. As with many other Martin successes, it was input from key retailers and players that led to the development of the company's best-selling tenor guitar. By 1929, Martin had designed a radically shortened 0-size body, specifically for use as a tenor, at the request of the Carl Fischer Company in New York City. What began as the Carl Fischer model quickly became Martin's standard tenor guitar. The 0-18T was joined by the all-mahogany 0-17T in 1932, and the even plainer 0-15T was offered in the early 1960s. Martin's all-mahogany versions of the size 5 tenor (5-17T) continued to be popular from the 1930s through the 1940s, when it was replaced by the 5-15T. These tenors are often mistaken for baritone ukuleles.

A number of Martin's R- and C-size archtop models were also offered in tenor versions during the 1930s. The company did a number of experimental runs and special orders of tenor flattop models in almost every size and style, especially 1927–1931. Besides the size 00 and 000 models one would expect, at least two Dreadnought tenors were made in the early 1960s.

Thanks to the 0-18T's adoption by the Kingston Trio in the 1950s, and other folk groups following in their wake, this model has remained in sporadic production to the present day. Although the 0-18T was relegated to special-order status in the mid-1980s, with a very few exceptions, at least some have been made every year.

All Martin tenor models have the same woods and trim as an equivalent 6-string model of the same style. With the exception of the 0 size models, the body dimensions for tenor versions are the same as for 6-string models, the only differences being in the neck and bridge (and internal bracing for lower string tension). The various styles of tenor guitars and the years they were made can be seen in the production totals listed in the appendix.

Despite the size "0" designation, 0 size tenor body dimensions differ from the standard 6-string style. They are:
Total Length: 35 1/4"; Body Length: 17 7/8"; Width of Body: 13 1/2". Scale length is 23.2" and neck is 1 1/4" wide at the nut.

(left) Although made in 1960, this 5-15T is much the same as Style 17 models of the same size that opened Martin's tenor guitar era in 1927. The earlier examples used banjo tuners instead of right-angle gears, and were first issued without a pickguard.

(middle) Banjo players were accustomed to easy access to the upper frets, but were also used to a relatively short string scale. Trying to accommodate both requirements on a size 2 body resulted in the awkward bridge and soundhole placement of this 1928 2-28T.

(right) Except for evolutionary changes shared with all other Martin guitars, the 0-18T remained essentially the same and was in continuous production until modern times. This example is from 1930.

Martin's plectrum guitar models first appeared in 1928. Partly because there were far fewer plectrum banjo players compared to those playing tenor, the production of plectrum guitars was far more limited and lasted only about five years. The most popular model was the 1-17P, while the most interesting today are the OM-18P models made in 1930 and '31. (Many of these have been converted to 6-string models by replacing the neck.) Plectrum guitars had 15 frets clear of the body and a scale length of 27". As with tenor guitar models, the woods and trim are identical to 6-string models of the same style and period, the only difference being in the neck and bridge. The styles of plectrum guitars and the years they were made can be found in the production totals listed in the appendix. The "P" suffix for Plectrum should not be confused with the much later use of the letter P at the end of the model code to denote a low profile neck.

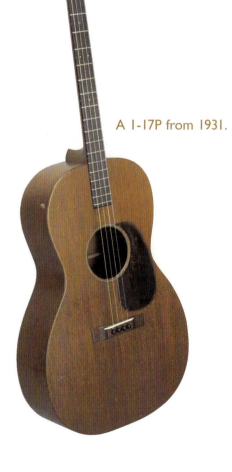

A 1-17P from 1931.

NYLON STRING OR CLASSICAL

Despite the fact that Martin had made gut-string guitars almost exclusively until the early 1920s, by the mid-1930s the company's guitar models were all made for steel strings with the exception of special orders. Most of these orders for gut-string Martins were the tried-and-true 0 and 00 models much like what the company had made almost a century earlier. But others were more modern versions with narrow necks, often 14-fret models made with extra-light bracing. Some of these had pin bridges and a few had bridges with a tie block like those used on later gut-string Martins. Although the factory order records indicate a lot of guitars with "gut" entered after the model code, the G suffix wouldn't appear until a specific gut-string model was announced. Instead, these special orders were given the catch-all "S" suffix, and many 00-28S models were made for gut strings. At least some of these had 14-fret necks and solid headstocks.

The number of special orders that Martin took for such models during the early 1930s must have convinced them that there was still demand for Martin guitars strung with gut instead of steel strings. Martin was also aware of the influence of Spanish guitars, especially among the classical guitar crowd, and wisely decided not to simply bring back its gut-string models from the past. By this time, it was clear that a classical guitar needed to have a wider neck with flat fingerboard, a tie-block bridge (which Martin called a "loop bridge"), and much lighter fan bracing. That Martin would decide to introduce such a model is not surprising, but that it would choose a hybrid that consisted of its newly redesigned 14-fret 00 body shape married to a wide, 12-fret neck seems to defy all logic. A much more attractive and logical choice would have been to use the same 12-fret 00 shape Martin was using for the 00-21. It was this body shape the company chose when replacing the G Series with the C Series about 25 years later.

Not long after the switch from the G Series to the C Series classical models, Martin introduced the N Series, which was an effort to build nylon-string models that would be more acceptable to true classical players. These new unMartin-like classics sold reasonably well for about five years before fading to obscurity. By the early 1980s, all of Martin's classical models were relegated to special-order-only status. The Shenandoah C-20, which showed up in 1989, didn't do much to fill the gap, and when the Shenandoahs were dropped Martin once again had no nylon-string guitars available except on special order. The Humphrey models, first announced in 1997, proved to be too radical a design for Martin customers and were dropped from the price list by 2003.

Martin's latest nylon-string models, announced in 2002, are cutaway versions with onboard electronics, made in the 16 Series in the 000 size, but by 2006, both models had been discontinued.

G SERIES CLASSICAL GUITARS

The 00-18G was first made in 1936, starting with prototypes #64232–34. There were 00-18 guitars made for gut that date earlier, such as #63044–46, but these probably didn't carry the G designation. This is an excellent example of the difficulty in trying to determine exact start and stop dates for some models. The 00-28G was first made in 1936, and the prototype was #65088. Some early G Series models have very light X bracing on the top, but most have a fan bracing pattern that's nearly identical to the bracing used on lower priced models (such as the 2-18) from before 1900. This fan pattern quickly became the standard for all G models.

Although these G Series classical models get little attention today, they were an important part of Martin's success, especially in the late 1950s and early '60s when a lot of folk guitarists preferred nylon-stringed guitars. Nine hundred 00-18G models were sold in 1961 alone, a year when total production of all Martin guitars was only 5,600.

The 00-28G was Martin's deluxe model for gut (later nylon) strings from 1936 until 1962. The headstock slots changed from squared to rounded, but with that exception the model remained unchanged. (Martin factory photo, late 1930s.)

STYLE 00-18G

1937 00-18G model introduced. Light construction for gut and silk strings. 14-fret 00 body but with 12-fret neck with slotted headstock, ebony fingerboard with no dots, and tie-block bridge, 25.4" scale. All other finish, wood, and binding details like 00-18 steel-string models of the same period.
1956 Catalog shows rosewood fingerboard and bridge. This change occurred shortly after 1940.
1962 00-18G discontinued in favor of 00-18C.

STYLE 00-28G

1938 00-28G first introduced in the catalog. All body and neck configuration same as 00-18G, but with Style 28 woods, binding, and details. This includes herringbone around the top until 1946.
1962 00-28G discontinued in favor of 000-28C.

C SERIES CLASSICAL GUITARS

In 1962, the C Series classic models replaced the G Series. The C Series had the old 12-fret 00 body shape, the same as the 00-21 models of the same period. The first version was done in the new, plainer Style 16, beginning with prototypes #180457–59 in 1961. Martin must have thought that a larger nylon-stringed guitar would garner more attention, and introduced the 000-28C to replace the 00-28G. Sales of the larger rosewood model were disappointing, and the 00-28C replaced the 000 in 1966. The big year for C Series Classical models was 1968, when almost 1,376 were made. Sales of Martin C Series then began to slide because emphasis was placed on the new N Series models.

For photos of an N Series and C Series model side-by-side, see page 113 of book 1, chapter 3.

A 1963 ad for the 000-28C.

STYLE 00-16C

1962 00-16C introduced. Like 00-18C described below, but with the following differences: Natural semi-gloss finish, binding only on top edge.
1970 Scale changed from 25.4" to 26 3/8" with #268173.

STYLE 00-18C

The 00-18C began with 1961 prototypes, #181104-06.

1962 00-18C introduced Standard Style 18 specifications of woods, bindings, and gloss finish, but with fan bracing and tie-block (loop) bridge.
1971 Scale changed from 25.4" to 26 3/8" with #276325.

STYLE 00-28C AND 000-28C

The prototypes of the 00-28C were #181107–09, made in 1961. This model was not added to the line until 1966, as Martin offered the 000 version instead. The 000-28C began with prototypes #181849–50. The 000 size was dropped after 1965 in favor of the smaller guitar, but a few were made later on special order.

1962 000-28C introduced. Standard Style 28 specifications of woods, bindings, and finish, but with fan bracing and tie-block (loop) bridge.
1966 00-28C added, 000-28C deleted.

N SERIES CLASSICAL MODELS

The N Series classical models were designed in 1968 and introduced in 1969 with a color catalog insert. They have a more traditional Spanish classical guitar shape than the regular Martin nylon-string models, and have fan bracing in the Spanish tradition as well. In 1970 the scale changed from 25.4" to 26 3/8" and the headstock changed from the traditional Martin style to a shape with a pointed top. Both models sold moderately well at first, but sales slowed dramatically in the mid-1970s. The N-10 was discontinued in 1993, and the N-20 followed in 1994.

Willie Nelson in the early 1970s, with his N-20.

STYLE N-10 CLASSIC

Spruce top, mahogany sides and back, rosewood fingerboard, and tie-block bridge. Typical Martin slotted headstock with squared top corners. Black bindings with black-white inlay border on top, wood marquetry rosette, white-black-white backstrip. See description of changes to scale length and headstock shape in above text.

STYLE N-20 CLASSIC

All details the same as N-10 except rosewood back and sides and ebony fretboard and bridge. The exact dates and serial numbers when the rosewood was changed from Brazilian to East Indian were not recorded, but probably took place in late 1969 or very early 1970.

MARTIN/HUMPHREY CLASSICAL MODELS

Announced in 1997 and first appearing on the 1998 price list, the CTSH and C-1R were a result of the collaboration between Martin and classical guitarmaker Thomas S. Humphrey. Both models featured a lattice-braced soundboard and elevated neck and fingerboard. The CTSH was part of the Standard Series, while the C-1R was part of the new 1 Series. They were discontinued in 2002.

CTSH

The CTSH Humphrey model classical, 1998.

Solid Indian rosewood back and sides with Engelmann spruce top. Wood mosaic soundhole rosette, Style 45 backstrip, and rosewood binding with black/white lines. Gloss finish.

C-1R

Part of 1 Series, with solid cedar top with wood mosaic rosette, laminated rosewood sides and back, black binding, rosewood fretboard, low-gloss finish.

CUTAWAY ACOUSTIC-ELECTRIC MODELS

Part of the wide-ranging 16 Series, the 000C-16SGTNE was announced in mid-2002. A rosewood version with gloss finish, the 000C-16SRNE, was added in early 2003. Both have cutaways on a 12-fret 000 body, and X-braced tops modified for the lower tension of nylon strings.

000C-16SGTNE

Cedar top, mahogany back and sides, single ring abalone rosette, dark binding. Spanish cedar neck with slotted headstock, $1\,^7/_8"$ at the nut, rosewood fretboard has 18" radius. Rosewood tie-block bridge of traditional Spanish design. Onboard Fishman electronics. 000C-16SGTNE discontinued in 2006.

The 000C-16SGTNE acoustic/electric nylon string (2003).

000C-16SRNE

Same as above but with East Indian rosewood back and sides, white binding, and gloss finish. 000C-16SRNE discontinued in 2005.

The 000C-16SRNE acoustic/electric nylon-string (2003).

MARTIN GUITAR MODELS BY STYLE

12-STRING GUITAR MODELS

Martin made a few 12-string models as special orders in the 1930s, including two C Series archtop 12-strings in 1932 and a 000-28 12-string made in 1936, but the company apparently never considered offering a regular 12-string model. (See page 172 in chapter 4 for a photo of a C-2 12-string.) During the folk music revival of the 1950s and '60s, however, there was increasing demand for 12-string guitars and Martin finally offered a mahogany model in 1964 and a rosewood version the following year. Although both models sold well, the company's decision to offer only 12-fret models with slotted headstocks didn't meet with unanimous approval, partly because changing strings was far more time-consuming than with a more conventional, and modern, solid headstock design. The D12-28, first offered in 1970, quieted most critics.

Martin's J Series 12-strings, first offered in 1985, gave players a wider range of styles, but Martin's 12-string sales did not share the revival of interest enjoyed by the 6-string models in the late 1980s and early 1990s. Since the mid-1990s, however, the company's new 12-string models from the 16 Series, 15 Series, 1 Series, and Road Series have made Martin 12-string guitars more popular and more affordable than ever before.

Following are descriptions of Martin 12-string models, listed in the order they were introduced.

The D12-20, D12-35, and D12-45—as shown in the 1970 catalog—were soon joined by the D12-41. The popularity of these 12-fret versions with slotted headstocks faded when the 14-fret versions, like the D12-28, were introduced.

STYLE D12-20

The D12-20 was the first regular Martin 12-string guitar to be added to the line. In 1964, the first one was listed as X-12 #193363. It had a slotted headstock, brass machines with white knobs, and a 12-fret style mahogany body. Later in the same year, Martin made D12-20A #195323 and D12-20B #195324. An additional 150 with the regular D12-20 designation were made that year, and the model was cataloged in 1965.

STYLE D12-35

The D12-35 first saw production in 1965, beginning with a test model called X12-35 #201943. In style and trimmings it was like the D-35 introduced the same year, but with 12-fret construction and a wide neck for 12 strings. Some of the first D12-35 guitars had a solid head with 12 Grover Rotomatic machines. These proved too heavy, and the slotted head with M-13 Waverly open-gear machines was soon substituted. Later examples of the D12-35 used imported German tuners with simulated pearl buttons.

(left) Factory photo of a D12-20, circa 1966.

(right) A 1968 D12-35.

1965 D12-20 first appears in catalog. 12-fret neck on original Dreadnought body shape (Ditson) with slotted headstock. All woods and bindings like Style 18 with the following differences: Style 28 backstrip, extra white line inside back binding, black-white strip adjacent to black endpiece, black pins with white dot.
1977 Not listed in catalog.
1982 Shown in catalog again, but few are sold. Still appears in "available on special order list" until 1994.

1965 D12-35 appears in catalog, identical binding and details as D-35 except 12-fret neck with slotted headstock on original Dreadnought body (Ditson).
1969 Transition from Brazilian to East Indian rosewood along with D-35.
1984 Listed as "Available only on special order" in price list.
1994 Disappears from price list.

STYLE D12-45 AND D12-41

The D12-45 is the same as the 6-string D-45 but with the longer body, 12-fret neck, and slotted headstock used on the D12-35 models. The first D12-45 was #252015, made in 1969, the only D12-45 made of Brazilian rosewood, with two more of Indian rosewood made that year. The model was introduced in the 1970 catalog, did not appear in the 1977 catalog, and reappears for the last time in the 1982 catalog. It was listed as "available on special order" until 1994.

The D12-41 has a similar history to that of the D12-45, but was introduced a year later. All details are like the 6-string D-41, except with the long body and 12-fret neck with slotted headstock. Very few were sold, and it last appeared in the 1982 catalog and on the 1994 special order list.

STYLE D12-28 AND D12-18

Although the D12-20 and D12-35 were popular, from the moment the 12-fret models appeared there were requests for a Martin 12-string guitar with a 14-fret neck. The D12-28 had the same body design as the D-28, but was braced to accommodate 12 strings. The neck was also in the D-28 style, but $1^{7}/_{8}$" wide at the nut. Original machines were Grover "Thinline" V-135, but M-6 mini-Schallers were later standard. Lighter bracing was introduced with #466127 in 1986.

The immediate success of the D12-28 led to the introduction of a mahogany 14-fret 12-string a few years later. The woods, binding, and details are the same as on standard Style 18 6-string models of the same period, while the extended headstock, extra bracing, and other modifications to accommodate 12 strings are identical to the D12-28. The prototype D12-18 was #322757, made in 1973. In 1984, the model was relegated to "available on special order" status, and was deleted from the special order list in 1995.

1970 D12-28 introduced. This is the only 12-string model in what is now called Martin's "Standard Series" to remain in continuous production to the present day.

(left) A D12-28, circa 2000. It is Martin's longest-running and most popular 12-string model.

(right) A D12-18, circa 1980.

J12-40M (LATER J12-40)

A 12-string version of the J-40M was introduced in 1985. Like the J-40M, the first set had the diamond on the back of the headstock (serial numbers 454426–431), but later versions did not. The J12-40 features are identical to the 6-string version, but with ebony buttons on the gold tuners. For a photo of the J12-40M, see page 97.

1985	Introduced.	1996	Gets updated appointments to neck and rosette along with J-40.
1991	M suffix dropped from model code.	1997	Deleted from price list but still made on special order.

With the exception of Signature, Limited, and Custom Editions, all Martin 12-string models introduced after 1994 have been in the 1 Series, 16 Series, 15 Series, Road Series, and X Series. (1833 Series models, introduced in 2007, are considered Custom Shop models, since they have no distinct model designation.) See those particular sections of this chapter for descriptions and a complete list. Here is a brief summary of when stock 12-string models first appeared in the price list:

1996 D12-1   1997 DM12   1999 SPD12-16R, D12XM   2000 J12-15, J12-16GT

(left) The 12-string version of the J-65M, Martin's only production maple 12-string, was introduced in 1985 and deleted from the price list ten years later.

(middle) The SPD12-16R, circa 2000. (right) A J12-15, circa 2002.

MARTIN GUITAR MODELS BY STYLE   113

ACOUSTIC BASS GUITARS

Martin's first acoustic bass guitars appeared in 1989, and were first prototyped by Dick Boak at the urging of Chris Martin and his friend, bassist Matt McFadden (see book 1, chapter 3, page 162). Although the prototype used Martin's new Jumbo body—and only Jumbo body versions made it to the price list and catalog—a few maple Dreadnought basses were also made. Both the rosewood B-40 and maple B-65 appeared on the 1989 price list, along with acoustic/electric versions with onboard preamp. Fretless models were available at no extra charge. The relatively high cost of these models limited sales—the B-40 and B-65 were more expensive than an HD-28—but Martin saw much higher sales when a bass version of the 1 Series was introduced in 1997. The B-1 was followed by bass versions of the Road Series and 15 Series.

(left) Martin's bass guitars began in 1988 with this prototype crafted by Dick Boak, who made a long 4-string neck for a Jumbo body.

A B-540 (5-string) bass, 1995 (middle), and a BC-15E from 1999 (right). For photos of the B-40 and maple B-65, see book 1, chapter 3.

1989	B-40 and B-65 introduced. See photos in book 1, chapter 3, on page 162.	1998	BM Road Series bass introduced, deleted in 2001.
1990	BC-40 cutaway added.	2002	BC-15E added, last addition to the acoustic bass line.
1992	B-540 5-string added.	2003–2006	B-1, B-1E, and BC-15E remain in price list.
1995	Only B-40 and BC-40 remain as standard models, B-540 and B-65 available only on special order.		
1997	B-1 introduced, all other previous models now available only on special order.	2007	B-1 and B-1E deleted, BC-15E only acoustic bass offered.

SHENANDOAH MODELS

Mike Longworth described the Shenandoah models: "The Shenandoah series guitars were designed as an intermediate line between the Sigma guitars and the higher priced C. F. Martin guitars. It is a sincere effort to make a C. F. Martin guitar which is more affordable… All models have the Martin Thinline pickup as a standard feature. They are made in Nazareth, Pa. from imported components." (See book 1, chapter 3 for more on the Shenandoah story.)

In retrospect, the Shenandoah guitars are as important for what they were not as for what they were. The bodies and necks were made in Japan and shipped to Nazareth, where each guitar was sanded, finished, assembled, and a pickup was installed. Partly because of where the initial construction was done, and partly because the backs and sides were laminated rather than solid, the Shenandoah models sold for about 40% less than the equivalent made-from-scratch Martin. As a result, the Shenandoahs kept the company competitive with other brands during a difficult period in the company's history.

But the Shenandoahs weren't popular with Martin's workforce, and when new woodworking technology made it possible to build a lower-priced Martin without outside help, the resulting D-1 was immediately given the role of the company's entry-level guitar and the Shenandoah models were summarily dropped from the price list in 1993.

Most Shenandoah models are nearly exact copies of regular Martin models, but with the suffix "32" after the model code and the word "Shenandoah" under the Martin logo on the headstock (replacing "Est. 1833"). All models have rosewood fretboards and bridges, usually stained black, but in 1987 there were a limited number of Custom models, with a CS prefix to the model code and extra inlay, that had ebony fretboard and bridge.

 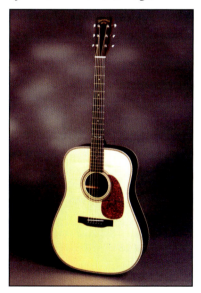 

Three late Shenandoah Series models, shortly before they were discontinued in favor of 1 Series models. SC-20E, SD-28H, and S-0028-H, circa 2000.

Below is a brief list of Shenandoah models:
- D-1832
- D-1932   Quilted mahogany, also made as 12-string.
- D-2832,   Also made as 12-string.
- HD-2832
- D-3532
- D-4132
- D-6032   Birdseye maple.
- D-3732   Quilted ash.
- 000-2832   Not the same body size and shape as Martin's 000.
- C-20   Classic model for nylon strings, no pickup.
- SE-2832 and SE-6032   (Maple) thin body acoustic electric models.

Before the entire Shenandoah Series was discontinued, the model codes were changed: an "S" prefix was added, and the "32" suffix was dropped. (For example, the HD-2832 became an SD-28H.)

MARTIN GUITAR MODELS BY STYLE   115

MARTIN GUITAR SERIES, 1993–2007

Since the mid-1990s, Martin's price lists and catalogs have been divided into several different series, usually with most models within a particular series sharing a number of basic characteristics. This is often the key to understanding what is "under the hood" of a particular model in terms of top bracing, neck-to-body joint, type of finish, etc.

1 SERIES

The D-1 was the first Martin model made with a new neck-to-body joint and assembly methods made possible by CNC (computer numeric control) woodworking technology. The original D-1 design and assembly methods were developed with the help of engineer Mike Dresdner. Introduced in 1993, the D-1's success resulted in an expanding line of similar models at prices both above and below the 1 Series. Ten years later, there weren't many 1 Series models still in production, because sales had shifted to the 16 Series GT models, and to the all-mahogany 15 Series. But the 1 Series is where the revolution in woodworking technology started at the Martin Guitar Company, and many of the most popular Martin guitars today got their start as 1 Series models. By 2007, however, the 1 Series had been deleted from Martin's catalog and price list.

The D-1 (1993) and D-3R (1997). The D-3R was a short-lived "new technology" version of the D-35, but with laminated back and sides and cross-link lacquer finish.

All 1 Series models have the following structural characteristics in common:
Mortise-and-tenon neck joint, "A-frame" modified X top bracing pattern, beveled front and rear blocks of laminated woods (neck block and tail block), and angled bridge hole pattern with string ramps. The tops of all 1 Series models are solid spruce with Style 28 rosette, while the sides are always laminated. Backs of mahogany models are solid, while the backs of rosewood versions are laminated. Other features include tortoise-shell single-layer celluloid body binding and tortoise shell-colored pickguard, a one-piece mahogany neck, rosewood fingerboard and bridge, and rosewood headstock veneer. All have a satin finish of cross-link lacquer. The D-1 was the first Martin model to get the raised gold logo on the headstock.

1993 D-1 introduced.
1994 D-1R, same as above, but with laminated rosewood back and sides.
1995 000-1 and 000-1R added.
1996 DC-1 cutaway, D12-1 12-string, and 00-1 introduced, plus D-2R and D-3R. The 2R and 3R have white binding and look similar to the D-28 and D-35, respectively.
1997 Models introduced as a Series. J-1 Jumbo, 0000-1 (M body) and B-1 bass added, plus cutaway models, some with onboard electronics.
1998 Cutaway Jumbo (JC-1E) added, Martin/Humphrey C-1R classic introduced.
1999 The 1 Series reaches its peak with 18 models. OM-1 added.
2000 No new models, 2 cutaway Dreadnoughts, the 000C-1E and 00-1, and both Jumbo models deleted.
2001–2003 1 Series reduced to D-1, DC-1E, 000-1, and two basses, the B-1 and B-1E. With the deletion of the rosewood models, all 1 Series have solid wood backs as well as tops.
2005 All 1 Series models dropped except basses.
2007 1 Series disappears from price list.

ROAD SERIES

The success of Martin's D-1 prompted the company to introduce similar models at a lower price, shaving costs by using a thinner "one-coat" matt finish. Road Series models carry the M suffix instead of a style number, and usually lack the hyphen after the body code. The primary differences between the 1 Series and M Series include the following:

Single ring herringbone rosette inlaid around the soundhole.

Thinner finish with a "dead matt" sheen.

Solid spruce top with laminated mahogany back and sides.

Black binding.

The DCM and 000M, 1997.

1996   DM introduced.
1997   DR (rosewood), DCM cutaway, DM-12 12-string, and 000M added.
1999   DCME (onboard electronics), DCRE, 000CME, 00C-MAE (acoustic/electric with thin body), JM, 000R, and the BM bass are added.
2000   OMM (wide neck version of 000) and 00M are added, DCRE deleted.
2001   Many models deleted, including the BM bass and all acoustic/electric models except the DCME.
2002   Martin's new X Series continues to expand while the Road Series shrinks. By the end of 2003, only the DM, DR, DCME, DM12, and 000M remain on the price list. This group of Road Series models continues through 2007.

15/17 SERIES

The all-mahogany 15 Series was introduced in 1997, shortly after the Road Series, starting with the D-15. While initially priced even lower than the DM, the D-15 featured solid mahogany back and sides, and a solid mahogany top. Like Martin's earlier Style 15 models, the lower price is the result of the cost savings realized by eliminating the body binding. The rosewood fretboard and bridge, top bracing, and neck-to-body joint are the same as 1 Series and Road Series models, and the 15 Series has the same one-coat matt finish as the Road Series. The soundhole rosette is a herringbone decal. A number of Martin dealers pay an up-charge to have the bodies finished in gloss, but these are still marked as Style 15 on the neck block.

Style 17 represents the deluxe all-mahogany models. These have hybrid X top bracing like Style 16, gloss finish on body, tortoiseshell celluloid binding with white line around top and back, single-ring rosette of inlaid white-black-white lines, and gold hardware. Style 17 models were the first to use black Micarta for the fingerboard and bridge.

(left) The 00-17 (2001), (middle) D-15S (2002), and (right) 5-15 (2002.)

1997 D-15 introduced.
1998 DC-15E, 000-15, and 00-15 added.
1999 J-15, 000C-15E, and BC-15E cutaway bass added.
2000 JC-15E, 00C-15AE (thin body), J12-15 (12-string), 000-15S (12-fret), and OM-15 are added. Style 17 introduced with D-17 and 00-17. Style 15 models get rosewood headplate.
2001 D-15S (12-fret) and cutaway OMC-15E added. Sapele (African mahogany) first appears on some models.
2002 5-15 introduced. D-17GT gloss top, DC-17E, 000-17S (12-fret) added to Style 17. This represents the peak year for Style 17 models,

2003 Style 15 models are all listed as "Mahogany or Sapele." (Sapele is an African hardwood, widely used in European guitars, that's often called mahogany. See Woods section in chapter 1.) Style 17 is reduced to three models, D-17, 000-17S, and 00-17, of which only the D-17 survives to the next price list.
2005 17 Series dropped from price list, but 15 Series continues with 11 models.

X SERIES

Martin's X Series utilizes the same neck-to-body joint as the 1 Series and Road Series, but is constructed with non-traditional materials. All X Series models have backs and sides of HPL, (high pressure laminate), rather than laminated veneers. On most models, the exterior is a wood-grain image photographically reproduced on the wood-fiber composite laminate, which is given a permanent mar-resistant coating serving as the semi-gloss finish. The HPL top has unique bracing incorporating solid spruce and other solid-wood panels, both for strength and to enhance tone.

Beginning in 2000, some X models were given solid spruce tops with 1 Series bracing. The following year brought the Alternative X, a model with thin aluminum top and HPL body, which was followed by other similar models.

A brief history of model introductions in the X series follows below. Like the Road Series, X Series model code does not make use of hyphens, which can make the string of letters difficult to decipher. M indicates mahogany HPL, R for rosewood, and K for koa. The numeral 1 following the X means solid spruce top with 1 Series bracing.

Just a few examples of the visual variety in the X Series: a black thinbody 00CXAE (left), an OMCXK2 (koa finish) (middle), and a D12X1 (solid spruce top) (right).

1998 DXM and DXME introduce the series.

1999 A Series is expanded with D12XM 12-string and 000XM, plus more Dreadnought models, including the cutaway DCXME. Stratabond necks first appear, replacing necks of mahogany or cedar.

2000 DX1 and 000X1 with solid spruce tops introduced, D12XM replaced by D12X1. A flurry of thin body cutaway 00 models is introduced, including several colors such as 00CXAEBLACK.

2001 More black models added, along with the DX1R.

2002 DXK2 is the first X Series with koa finish. Cowboy X introduces a 000X with Western scene on the face. (See photos in chapter 4.)

2003 LXM and LXME "Little Martin" models introduced. 00CX1AEBLACK adds a thinbody acoustic/electric cutaway with solid spruce top. X Series includes 15 models, and Alternative X models greatly expanded with graphite top, MIDI, and resonator models.

2004 The number of models with solid spruce top continues to expand, including LX1 and cutaway acoustic/electric D models with koa and rosewood HPL back and sides (DCX1KE and DCX1RE).

2005– More HPL finishes added, including four LX models
2007 in red, blue, purple, and pink.

16 SERIES MODELS

Beginning in 1995, the 16 Series became Martin's top style to utilize the new mortise-and-tenon neck joint. Unlike the 1 Series and Road (M) Series, the 16 Series represents all-solid-wood body construction and utilizes modified scalloped X bracing on the top, plus the "A frame" bracing around the soundhole common to all models using the new neck-to-body joint. This hybrid of old and new Martin guitar construction began with the D-16T (for "Technology"), first offered in 1995, which was soon followed by the rosewood D-16TR along with 000 and cutaway models. (The T suffix was dropped in 1998.) At first, there were only two price levels in the 16 Series, with the SP (for Special, introduced in 1996) as the more deluxe models with gloss finishes, gold hardware, and extra inlay. Starting in 1997, however, the 16 Series began to expand, starting with the "Women and Music" 00-16DB (deep body), which had many design elements outside Martin's usual styles. These models proved so popular that they were quickly moved from the limited editions column of the price list and became regular models in the 16 Series the following year.

In 1999, the D-16 dropped dramatically in price and became the D-16GT (gloss top). Part of the decrease in price was due to the use of Martin's new "cross-link" catalyzed lacquer finish. The following year, the 16GT model offering was greatly expanded to include 000 and cutaway models, many with pickups and onboard electronics. At the same time, the SP 16 model list grew with the addition of several different woods for the backs and sides, and with cutaway Jumbos, 12-strings, and OM models (000 models with wider necks). By mid-2000, the 16 Series column of Martin's price list included 30 models, and by 2002 fully half of the models offered were "E" versions with onboard electronics mounted in the side. Being more mindful of its heritage than in the past,

(left) The 00-16DBM, (middle) D-16, and (right) JC-16MC from the 16 Series.

Martin seemed reluctant to cut holes in the sides of its traditional models merely to satisfy the growing demand for acoustic-electric guitars. Instead, the company offered 16 Series models with similar woods and features to old favorites such as the D-28, and put the latest electronics in the newcomers instead.

By mid-2001, the number of SP 16 models was greatly reduced, and would continue shrinking. SP models were replaced by similar guitars with no specific prefix or suffix to the model code. These were usually cutaway versions with onboard electronics. Although these lack the snowflake fretboard inlays of the SP models, they retain the gloss nitrocellulose lacquer finish, while the rosette and binding vary depending on the woods and body style. The fast-changing nature of the 16 Series makes a definitive description of these models difficult, and many of the acoustic/electric cutaway models were available with more than one pickup system. Some versions didn't attract significant orders and were deleted barely a year after they were first announced. The list below is not complete, and a few 16 Series models may be missing, but most of the more popular variations are covered. When models were deleted is not always mentioned here, partly because some models were still in production a year or more after disappearing from the price list. Those 16 Series models offered as Special or Limited Editions are included in chapter 3.

Note: Because all of the models fall under the same series number, different woods are denoted with letters after the number 16: R (rosewood), M (maple), W (walnut), K (koa), etc. These sometimes have different appointment details. Most 16 Series models without a "woods letter" have mahogany back and sides.

1995 D-16T replaces the D-16H.

1996 000-16T, 000-16TR (rosewood), and 000C-16T are added (cutaway model has round soundhole, unlike earlier 000C-16). All have semi-gloss finish, herringbone soundhole rosette and backstrip, rosewood fingerboard and bridge, tortoiseshell celluloid body binding with no black/white lines, tortoiseshell-colored pickguard, and diamonds-and-squares fretboard inlays. These were offered with gloss finish for an additional charge.

1997 SP 16 models added, including SPD-16T, TR, and SP000-16T and TR. The cutaway versions are SPDC-16TR and SP000C-16TR. All SP models feature gloss-finished bodies with aging toner on the top, gold hardware, tortoiseshell celluloid binding with multi-colored backstrip (like Style 45), abalone soundhole rosette (Style 45), and "snowflake" inlays on the fretboard and bridge tips. First 00-16DB (deep body) "Women and Music" (WAM) model is announced as a limited edition.

1998 00-16DBR (deep body rosewood) is offered. These new 16 Series models feature Dreadnought-depth sides on a 00 body, with narrow 14-fret neck and slotted headstock, wide wood mosaic soundhole rosette, and gloss finish. The "T" suffix is dropped from 16 Series models. SPD-16M (maple), and W (walnut) are added, and a cutaway version of the DB series (00C-16DB, mahogany) is added to the regular 16 models (not a limited edition).

1999 GT (gloss top) models first appear. The mahogany versions have black binding, dot inlays on the neck, and a single black line for the backstrip (like Style 18), and a herringbone rosette. Rosewood versions have white binding, including a bound fretboard. All have satin finish except for the gloss top. SPOM-16 added (same as 000 but with 1 3/4 inch neck width), two 000 cutaway models are offered with onboard electronics (one SP and one GT), and the SPD12-16R is the first 16 Series 12-string. Mahogany-top 00-16DBM is added, along with the short-lived SP00-16RST (Stauffer headstock).

2000 Four cutaway Jumbo models are added, including both SP and GT versions, all with onboard electronics. The GT Jumbos have a rosette with multicolor "arrowhead" design unique to those models. The J12-16GT 12-string is added, along with SPD-16K (koa) and K2 (koa top) models. The first 12-fret 000 in the 16 Series appears, the 000-16SGT, and an OM-16GT as well.

2001 All SPD-16 models are deleted except for the koa Dreadnoughts and the rosewood 12-string. Most 16GT models now have Spanish cedar necks and black Micarta fretboards and bridges.

2002 M size (sometimes referred to as 0000) models are added, M-16GT and MC-16GTE, along with a rosewood 12-fret 000 (000-16SRGT). A new DC-16RE, JC-16WE, and OMC-16WE are similar to the earlier SP models, with gloss nitrocellulose lacquer finishes, striped ebony fretboard and bridge, small abalone fretboard dots, multicolored (Style 45) backstrip, and single-ring abalone rosette. Some of these are called "premium" after the upgraded Fishman electronics package included. (The same premium electronics are available on other 16 Series models as well.) A first for Martin is the new nylon-string model, a cutaway 12-fret 000 (000C-16SGTNE) with cedar soundboard and onboard electronics. Unlike previous Martin nylon-string models, these have a slight radius to a 1 7/8" wide fretboard and X-bracing modified for low-tension strings.

2003 The new nylon-string model is joined by a rosewood version with gloss finish (000C-16SRNE). More deluxe models with gloss finish are added, including models made with rosewood, sapele, and lyptus wood. The size 5 "mini" is added (5-16GT), along with a thinbody acoustic/electric maple cutaway finished in transparent blue that results in the tongue-twisting model code of 00C-16FMBUAE.

2004– Too many 16 Series models are added (and deleted)
2007 to make a thorough accounting possible.

STANDARD SERIES

The term "Standard Series" first appears in the 1997 price list, and is intended to provide a dividing line between the 16 Series models and the solid-wood Martin models made with the same neck joint and bracing used before the arrival of the "new technology" introduced with the D-1. The word "standard" to describe this series should not be confused with the descriptions of "standard models" in the 1930s, when "standard" referred to the older 12-fret styles, as opposed to the new Orchestra Models with 14-fret necks.

For the most part, Standard Series guitars are similar to the Martin models that made up the bulk of Martin's production in the late 1980s and early 1990s, but some examples have a host of "vintage" appointments usually associated with Vintage Series models. For instance, the Style 42 models (D and OM) and Style 21 Special models would appear to belong in the Vintage Series, but since they are not actual reissues of earlier Martin guitars, they are given Standard Series status.

The Standard Series covers a wide range, from contemporary to vintage. Shown are a DC-28E (left) and OM-21 Special (right).

VINTAGE SERIES

One could say that Martin's Vintage Series began with the 0-16NY back in 1961, for that model was the first "reissue" of an earlier guitar style to appear in the catalog. Other examples are the D-45 in 1968 and the HD-28 in 1976. But it was the opening of the Custom Shop in 1979, the first Brazilian rosewood models with prewar features introduced in 1983, and the Guitars of the Month Series begun in 1984 that mark the early stages of what became the current Vintage Series.

Besides the scalloped braces, herringbone top purfling, and zigzag backstrip of the HD-28, a number of other features were requested through the Custom Shop by customers wishing to approximate the appearance, feel, and sound of 1930s Martins. These details have become part of virtually all Vintage Series models from the mid-1980s on.

Styles 28 and higher are given ivory grained celluloid binding, Style 18 or 21 get tortoiseshell-colored celluloid binding. The finish on the top is given "aging toner" to approximate the appearance of lacquered spruce that has darkened with time.

The guitar's neck has a more V shape, rather than rounded like a C (when viewed in profile), and the headstock is "squared and tapered" like older models as well. Style 28 models get diamonds-and-squares fretboard inlays, while Style 18 gets abalone dots.

The intersection of the X pattern on Dreadnoughts is one inch from the lower edge of the soundhole, sometimes called "forward shifted" bracing. (This is actually the original position of the X brace in 14-fret D models.)

The first Martin models ordered through the Custom Shop in 1980 with the above features came to be known by their order numbers, and both the Custom 8 and Custom 15 were "upgrades" from the usual HD-28. (The Custom 8 was essentially the same as the Custom 15, but with Ivoroid binding.) The Custom 15 was ordered so frequently—almost 100 were shipped in 1980 alone—by a variety of dealers that it appeared on the special orders portion of Martin's price list a few years later. In 1993, it was made a stock model, although Martin had been treating it as such for some time.

The "V-for-Vintage" designation first appeared in 1983 on Brazilian rosewood models, although a D-18V was also introduced. These had paper labels, but not all models had the same vintage features. The D-35V marking the 20th anniversary of the D-35, for instance, had features like the original D-35 models, which didn't include Ivoroid binding, V-shaped neck, and diamonds-and-squares fretboard inlays.

In 1985, Martin also began making standard models with Brazilian rosewood. These were given a B suffix to the model code, and while not all of them had vintage features, some did (the V suffix disappears by 1986, except for GOM models). The differences between a D-28V made in 1985 and a Custom 15B made in 1986 might be insignificant, but some B models were the same as regular production guitars of the same model, except for the wood used on the back and sides. These lacked the "prewar vintage" details and were more like reissues of models made less than 20 years earlier, just before the use of Brazilian rosewood was discontinued. See the Production Totals charts in the appendix for lists of which models were made in the 1980s V and B series.

Other Vintage models were introduced as Guitars of the Month, including the 00-18V in 1984, and D-18V in 1985. (See the Limited Editions section in chapter 3 for details.) As Martin developed a firmer grasp of what customers wanted in a vintage-style guitar, some details and hardware changed, such as the switch to long "through-cut" saddles in the bridge and open-back tuners with "butterbean" knobs like those used in the 1930s.

VINTAGE SERIES (cont.)

(left) The 000-28EC (1996) and (right) HD-28V, circa 2001.

By the mid-1990s, the Vintage Series became a cohesive and predictable line of guitars that soon came to rival the Standard Series in popularity. None of these models were made of Brazilian rosewood. Here's a brief summary:

1995 Custom 15 and Custom 15S become Custom HD-28 and Custom HD-28S and are stock models. (Custom 15 has been listed as stock model since 1993.)

1996 Vintage Series gets its own subheading in the price list, and a second suffix letter indicating the wood (M or R) is added to the model code. D-18VM and D-18VMS are added, plus OM-28VR. (Custom HD-28 becomes HD-28VR, while the 12-fret version becomes HD-28VS, without the R.) By this time, Style 28 versions have Ivoroid binding. 000-28EC Eric Clapton model introduced, listed in Vintage Series and with Vintage features, but no V in model code. A black "Geib style" plywood case replaces the regular thermoplastic case included with Standard Series models.

1997 D-45VR added to Vintage Series.

1999 HD-28LSV (large soundhole) and 000-28VS added. The redundant R and M suffixes are deleted from the model code. (HD-28VR becomes HD-28V, D-18VM becomes D-18V.)

2000 OM-18V added.

2003 00-18V added.

For more photos of Vintage Series models, see book 1, chapter 4.

GOLDEN ERA AND MARQUIS SERIES

Martin first began officially using the term "Golden Era" in 1995, as part of the model code for a Limited Edition D-18. The popularity of models with vintage appointments prompted the company to go even further in recapturing the details and appearance of models made during what most guitar collectors have long considered to be Martin's Golden Era, the period from the late 1920s to the mid-1940s. In the case of the 1995 D-18 Golden Era, this meant using cloth side strips on the interior of the body and more accurately reproducing the top bracing of a 1937 D-18, along with other small details. But the most important feature was a larger $1^{3}/_{4}$" wide neck, with string spacing of $2^{5}/_{16}$" at the bridge (the dimensions Martin had used prior to 1939).

In 1996, Martin repeated the same formula with the 000-28 12-fret Golden Era. At this point, however, the Golden Era specifications did not include an Adirondack spruce top. The 1998 00-21GE Golden Era (Indian rosewood) and OM-45GE Golden Era were both given an Adirondack top, as were the D-18GE and D-28GE (Brazilian rosewood) introduced the following year. This has become a key feature of all Golden Era models ever since.

The high cost and limited availability of Brazilian rosewood for GE models in Styles 28 and higher led to the introduction of the Marquis models in 2004. These have all the same neck dimensions and exacting vintage features of the Golden Era models, including an Adirondack soundboard, but with the substitution of high-grade East Indian rosewood back and sides for the Brazilian rosewood. In 2007, Martin began offering Marquis models with Madagascar rosewood back and sides.

(left) The 000-18GE, (middle) D-45 Marquis, and (right) OM-28 Marquis Madagascar.

1998 00-21GE and OM-45GE appear in "Special & Limited Editions" section of price list.
1999 D-28GE appears in the January price list, joined by D-18GE in July.
2000 OM-45GE added, but not Deluxe version.
2001 D-45GE first appears on price list.
2003 OM-18GE and OM-28GE introduced.

2004 D-28 Marquis introduced.
2005 OM-28 Marquis and OM-45 Marquis models added.
2006 D-45 Marquis and 000-18GE models appear. Brazilian rosewood (Style 28 & Style 45) Golden Era models deleted from price list.
2007 000-42 Marquis added.

AUTHENTIC SERIES

The Authentic Series began with a D-18 model introduced in 2005, although few were shipped until 2006. Unlike Golden Era models, each Authentic model is patterned after one guitar built in the 1930s, and such features as the neck shape and top bracing contours are taken from that particular instrument rather than being more loosely based on generalized dimensions shared by most models of a given era. In the case of the D-18 Authentic, the model was a 1937 D-18 in the Martin Museum collection. Differences between Authentic and Golden Era models include the following:

Non-adjustable steel T shaped neck reinforcement instead of adjustable truss rod.

Use of hot animal-hide glue for all stages of construction instead of modern adhesives.

Tuners have antique patina finish.

The year of the Martin original being copied appears on the neck block as a suffix to the model code.

Cases have brown exterior and more closely resemble pre-WWII cases.

As with Martin's Vintage Series and Golden Era Series, there has been a trickle-down effect with features first found on Authentic models appearing on later models, particularly the Delmar nitrocellulose pickguard.

2005   D-18 Authentic unveiled at Summer NAMM show in Indianapolis.
2007   Limited run of 60 D-28 Authentics announced (Brazilian rosewood).
2008   000-18 Authentic introduced, sunburst versions of both D-18 and 000-18 Authentics are offered.

(left) A 000-18 Authentic 1937 Sunburst and (right) a D-18 Authentic 1937 from the Authentic Series.

LIMITED PRODUCTION MARTIN GUITARS:
Guitars of the Month, Signature Editions, Limited Editions, Special Editions, and Custom Signature Editions

The purpose of this chapter is to provide descriptions and specifications for Martin guitars that either do not have a standard model code or that were issued in limited numbers for a specific period. For most such models issued in the last decade (roughly 1996 on) the Martin website (www.martinguitar.com) has complete specifications, often with links to press releases and promotional descriptions offered at the time.

Martin first announced its Custom Shop in 1979, but there was no catalog of available options until several years later. Initially the Custom Shop was utilized only by Martin dealers, and a few customers, who were familiar with vintage Martins and who knew exactly what they wanted. This changed once Martin began placing magazine ads, primarily in *Guitar Player* and *Frets,* introducing the Custom Shop by showing specific custom guitars. The resulting orders were often for models identical to the guitars pictured in those advertisements. Most customers, it seemed, felt more secure ordering a custom Martin that had been designed in Nazareth.

The first customer to order a guitar through the new Custom Shop was Dick Boak, Martin's draftsman and jack-of-all-trades. Over a decade later, Boak was largely responsible for beginning the Signature Series, which essentially replaced the Guitars of the Month program with models honoring artists who had long played Martin guitars.

This led to the introduction of the Guitars of the Month program in 1984, essentially offering custom Martins in small batches. The idea of a different guitar for every month of the year was abandoned in favor of fewer models unveiled all at once, but Martin kept the plan's original name. In time the name was frequently shortened to GOM (Guitars of the Month). These instruments were announced at NAMM trade shows, but no guitar was assigned to a particular month. Prototypes were shown at NAMM, with photographs and spec sheets in special binders, prepared for Martin sales reps to show to dealers. Although in later years the number of guitars in a specific style was often pre-determined, for the first few years the number of each model sold was limited only by the number of orders received, and many Special Editions are "open-ended" even today. Each model was given a unique paper label. In 1984 and 1985, C. F. Martin III and his grandson, C. F. IV, signed the many special labels. Since C. F. III's death in 1986, C. F. Martin IV typically signs the labels (though less frequently after 2006), with additional signatures of artists and/or their surviving relative(s) on most signature editions.

Guitars offered in this program have ranged from simple Style 18 models to heavily inlaid "over 45" styles that make the original Martin Style 45s look humble. Vintage reissues patterned after Martin guitars made in the 1930s have been the most popular, and many are now stock models. (Both the Vintage Series and Golden Era Series models are good examples.) With the success of the signature editions that began in 1993 (with the Perry Bechtel OM), and especially after Martin's blockbuster hit with the Eric Clapton 000-42EC in 1995, the Guitars of the Month title was quietly retired. In 1997, the number of Limited Editions and Signature Editions was greatly expanded, and instead of about a half-dozen different models each year, the number was more than doubled, with a second batch unveiled at the Summer NAMM show. Martin currently issues about 20 Limited, Special, and Signature Edition instruments each year. To date, the company has issued over 120 signature models, with some artists—such as Eric Clapton and Laurence Juber—having several different guitars with their name on them.

Following is a list of the Guitars of the Month, Limited Editions, Special Editions, and Signature Editions issued from 1984 through 2007, followed by the list price when issued and the number of guitars sold. (When two numbers are shown, the second number was the announced maximum of the edition when issued.) The following statement from C. F. Martin & Company may shed some light on the production totals of its limited editions in general:

"As a general rule, Martin has produced between one and four prototypes of each limited edition in order to develop the model specifications. These prototypes are initially not for sale, but many prototypes have already or eventually may be sold. Prior to 1997, the Limited Edition Program produced separate labeling for the domestic and foreign editions. (e.g., the 1990 HD28BLE domestic edition had a label that read 1 of 100, 2 of 100, etc., while a separate foreign-edition label read 1 of 8, 2 of 8, etc.) Separate foreign-label editions are included in the totals given below. In 1995, Martin stopped issuing separate foreign labeling in favor of one label worldwide.

Some editions are 'fixed,' having a predetermined total, some are limited to orders taken within a predetermined time-period, and some are 'open-ended.' All numbers below are as accurate as possible, but must be viewed as approximate. Prototypes are NOT included in the 'number sold' totals given below because of the difficulty of determining if they were sold and exactly how they were marked."

Due to space restrictions, and to avoid boring repetitions, descriptions of the Guitars of the Month (GOM), Signature Editions, Limited Editions, and Special Editions are usually confined to features that differ from stock Martins of the same year that have a similar model designation. Unless otherwise stated, all the guitars listed have the same body dimensions, woods, and trim as stock models of the same model code (during the same year) and share the following features:

14 frets clear of the body, and 20 frets total unless otherwise noted (any 12-fret models are described as such).

Mahogany neck with solid headstock and a neck width of $1^{11}/_{16}$" at the nut. (All other neck measurements given here are taken at the nut as well.) String spacing at the bridge is always $2^{1}/_{8}$" for models with a $1^{11}/_{16}$" neck, so the bridge spacing is not mentioned. But for models with wider necks, string spacing at the bridge varies and that measurement is given.

After 1986, all necks have an adjustable truss rod unless otherwise noted.

Belly bridge with a short drop-in saddle (blind end saddle slot). Pyramid bridges, and the simpler "straight-line" bridges of the same size, are noted.

Pickguard is "teardrop" shape; after 1984, all pickguards are on top of the finish unless otherwise noted. The shorter OM pickguard is described as such.

Satin finish on neck, gloss finish on body: most models with pearl-inlaid headstocks have a gloss finish on the headplate. Again, differences in finish from similar stock models with the same model code are usually mentioned, but otherwise the finish is not described. Style 45 has a gloss finish on the neck, for instance, so that feature is not mentioned here on models with Style 45, or higher, specs.

Spruce top with scalloped X-bracing $1^5/_8$" from soundhole. Scalloped bracing is always accompanied by the small maple bridgeplate. Any top wood other than Sitka spruce is noted.

Fingerboard and bridge are of same wood unless noted.

Since 1993, most vintage-style GOM guitars or limited editions have been available with a dark sunburst top, at an additional charge. From 1994 forward, the total sold with sunburst top is also given.

The following abbreviations are used in this chapter:

"High X" means the X-braces on the top intersect approximately one inch below the soundhole, instead of approximately $1^5/_8$". This pattern is always scalloped.

"Long saddle" means the saddle slot is a saw kerf in the bridge, open at both ends, as found on Martins in the 1930s to 1950s. These saddles are almost always glued in place at the factory. The "long drop-in" saddle looks almost the same as the long saddle, but actually "drops in" from the top. These are not glued.

"Aging toner" (light amber color) or "vintage toner" (deeper golden color) refers to tinted lacquer coloration on the soundboard only. This is a standard feature of Martin's Vintage Series models, so if the guitar is described as having "Vintage Series appointments" the toned finish is not mentioned. Virtually all Limited and Special Editions from the early 1990s on have toned lacquer on the soundboard, so it is mentioned only on earlier GOM models.

"V-neck" refers to the neck shape when viewed in cross section: this feature is always accompanied by a squared-tapered headstock, as used in the 1930s. Martin modified its V-neck shape in the 1990s to what is now called the "modified V," but for this volume they are still simply described as a "V-neck."

"LP" stands for "Low Profile," the neck shape Martin began using on most models when the adjustable truss rod was introduced in 1985. This shape is not mentioned here unless it appears on a model that would usually get the V-shape neck, such as a guitar with Vintage Series appointments.

"Tortoise" refers to the tortoiseshell pattern celluloid (plastic) used for the pickguard or binding.

"Ivoroid binding" (often includes neck heel cap) is off-white celluloid with ivory-like graining. This is standard with "Vintage Series appointments" and is not mentioned specifically on models so described. With few exceptions, virtually all of the Limited, Special, and Signature Editions with light-colored binding have Ivoroid, not the more pure white Boltaron binding. Boltaron binding is usually noted.

"Pearl bordering" is actually abalone shell. Unless other inlays are described as "white pearl" or "MOP" (mother-of-pearl), they are also of abalone shell. "Paua" is similar to abalone but with a more intense blue color.

"Style 45 headplate," or peghead inlay, refers to the C. F. Martin letters in pearl; the earlier "torch" style is noted as such, and other headstock inlays are described.

"Backstrip" refers to the decorative center seam between the two (sometimes three) sections of the guitar's back. Although Martin has used this term in the past, it now refers to it as "back purfling" in listings of a model's specs, but we've chosen to stick with the earlier term because it is consistent with Mike Longworth's descriptions and other books' listings of Martin guitar details. (It is often spelled "backstripe" as well.)

"M & T neck joint" is an abbreviation referring to the mortise and tenon neck joint first introduced with the D-1, and later used on all 16 Series models. This new technology was first used on a Ltd Edition Martin in 1996 (MTV model).

Tuners

"Vintage-style tuners" refers to open-gear tuning machines with "butterbean knobs," or buttons, similar to the old Grover G-98 tuners used in the 1930s. "Waverly tuners" refers to similar tuners of the Waverly brand, and these also have solid brass "butterbean knobs" unless other knobs, or buttons, are mentioned (such as ebony or ivoroid, which are oval).

"Kluson-style tuners" refers to Gotoh reproductions of the enclosed Kluson tuning machines that Martin used before switching to the heavier Grover Rotomatics tuners with cast housing.

If no specific tuner style is mentioned, or if only the buttons are described, the tuners are the modern, cast housing type made by any one of several different manufacturers, but usually Schaller or Gotoh.

Woods

With a few exceptions, Martin used the same woods on these limited editions as on its regular models until the mid-1990s, when it began using a wider variety of species, or woods, with unique figure—such a bearclaw spruce and quilted mahogany. When the wood used is not what the model code would suggest, the special woods are noted. (Starting with 1996, the woods used for all models is given.) For models that do not include a number code, such as CEO models, Employee models, Concepts, etc., the woods are listed. The woods are also listed for all signature editions.

"Rosewood" is short for East Indian rosewood back, sides, and headplate (veneer on face of headstock). Other species of rosewood are described.

"Brazilian" indicates Brazilian rosewood back, sides, and headplate.*

"Spruce" refers to Sitka spruce. Other species of spruce, and other top woods, are described (Engelmann, Adirondack, Italian, etc.). All tops are spruce unless otherwise noted.

---

*Although they were not issued as Limited Editions at the time, the Brazilian rosewood Martin models offered from 1983 through 1987 are treated as such in this chapter. In a sense, these guitars were limited editions because of the limited amounts of Brazilian rosewood Martin had available. The totals for 1984–1987 follow the "Guitars of the Month" editions for those years, while the totals for 1983 are shown below. In 1983 and '84, however, these guitars were not labeled consistently, and records from this period are somewhat ambiguous as to how the early Brazilian models were marked. The "B for Brazilian" suffix was not yet in use, and some were given a standard model code with the "V" suffix (on the neckblock), but were entered in Martin's records as simply "Custom."

Models known to have been made in Brazilian rosewood in 1983, with the numbers in parentheses: D-45V Brazilian (39), 000-28V Brazilian (15), D-28V Brazilian (128), Misc. Custom Shop Brazilian (22)

1984

00-18V
Appointments similar to later Vintage Series, with ebony fingerboard and bridge, tortoise binding and pickguard, scalloped bracing, and V-neck.

List Price: $1,520.00   # Sold: 9 (0 foreign)

D-28 CUSTOM
Scalloped braces, Style 45 "torch" peghead inlay without binding, snowflake Style 45 fretboard inlay without binding, stamp on back of peghead.

List Price: $2,000.00   # Sold: 43 (0 foreign)

M-21 CUSTOM
Tortoise bindings and pickguard, scalloped braces, M-38 top stain with Style 28 rosette.

List Price: $1,600.00   # Sold: 16 (0 foreign)

M-36LE
Perhaps a prototype was made with this marking, but it was not put in production. It became the M-36B (Brazilian); see listing for 1985.

List Price: $2,140.00   # Sold: N/A

Brazilian rosewood models, totals for 1984 in parentheses, following model code. (Some may have paper labels, but they were not officially a part of the GOM program.) D-28V (25) and D-35V (10). In addition, there were 30 miscellaneous Custom Shop models made with Brazilian rosewood, but in some cases these had a standard model code on the headblock, such as HD-28V.

1985

D-18V
Pre-WWII Style D-18, similar to later Vintage Series, with ebony fingerboard and bridge, tortoise binding and pickguard, scalloped bracing, and V-neck.

List Price: $1,640.00   # Sold: 56 (0 foreign)

D-21LE
Tortoise binding and pickguard (under finish), herringbone rosette, rosewood fingerboard and bridge, nonscalloped bracing, long saddle.

List Price: $1,550.00   # Sold: 75 (0 foreign)

HD-28 LE
High X, Ivoroid binding, tortoise pickguard (under finish), aging toner on top, V-neck, diamonds-and-squares fretboard inlay.

List Price: $2,210.00   # Sold: 87 (0 foreign)

OM28LE
Appointments similar to later Vintage Series, with Ivoroid binding, scalloped bracing, tortoise pickguard (under finish), 1 3/4" V-neck, diamonds-and-squares inlay.

List Price: $2,180.00   # Sold: 39 (+ 2 foreign)

OM-28SO SINGOUT! 35TH
35th Anniversary of *Sing Out!* magazine, label signed by Pete Seeger.

List Price: N/A   # Sold: 35 (0 foreign)

Brazilian rosewood models, total for 1985 in parentheses, following model code. (Most of these do not have paper labels, as they were not part of GOM program.) 00-21B (1), 00-45B (2), 000-28B (6), 000-45 (2), D-28B (1), D-35B (1), M-36B (20), M-38B (17), N-20B (1).

1986

J-45M DELUXE
First over 45-style Martin, with the exception of custom-shop orders. Rosewood with Engelmann or European spruce, tortoise binding, Style 45 pearl bordering on body with pearl backstrip. Pearl-bordered tortoise pickguard, pearl hexagon outlines on fretboard and bridge tips, Style 45 headplate. Neck has pearl bordering on top and sides of both peghead and fretboard and on sides of heel.

List Price: $6,900.00   # Sold: 16 (+ 1 foreign)

J-21MC
First J model with cutaway. Oval soundhole with single-ring rosette, black binding, tortoise pickguard, ebony tuner buttons.

List Price: $1,750.00   # Sold: 55 (+ 1 foreign)

D-62LE
First maple Dreadnought. Flamed maple, lightly stained, tortoise bindings and pickguard, high X bracing, Style 42 snowflakes on 1 7/8" neck, 1 11/16" neck optional.

List Price: $2,100.00   # Sold: 46 (+ 2 foreign)

1986 (cont.)

HD-28SE
Similar to Custom 15, but autographed on the underside of top by C. F. Martin III, C. F. IV, and all the factory foremen. High X, Ivoroid binding, tortoise pickguard (under finish), 1¾" V-neck, diamonds-and-squares inlay, ebony tuner buttons.

List Price: $2,300.00   # Sold: 130 (+ 8 foreign)

Brazilian rosewood models, total for 1986 in parenthesis, following model code. (Most of these do not have paper labels, as they were not part of GOM program.) D-28 (11), HD-28B (47), D-35B (10), HD-35B (3), D-41B (1), Custom 15B (10), M-45B (3).

1987

D-45LE
Brazilian/spruce "over 45" D with decoration similar to J-45M of previous year. High X, Ivoroid binding, typical Style 45 pearl bordering on body, with pearl backstrip. Neck has pearl bordering on top and sides of peghead, fretboard, and on sides of heel. Pearl hexagon outlines on fretboard and bridge tips. Style 45 headplate, ebony tuner buttons.

List Price: $7,500.00   # Sold: 44 (+ 6 foreign)

HD-18LE
Similar appointments to D-18V, but with herringbone top trim, diamonds-and-squares neck inlay, and LP neck. Tortoise pickguard, 1⅞" neck standard, 1¹¹⁄₁₆" optional. Ebony tuner buttons.

List Price: $2,250.00   # Sold: 50 (+ 1 foreign)

00-21LE
14-fret 00, but with slotted headstock. Vintage appointments include tortoise binding, herringbone rosette and backstrip, and scalloped braces. Small rectangular ebony bridge, 1¾" neck, 24.9" scale, chrome 3-on-plate tuners with pearloid buttons.

List Price: $2,350.00   # Sold: 18 (+ 1 foreign)

J-40MBLE
Brazilian/spruce J-40 with Style 45 snowflakes on neck, aging toner, tortoise pickguard, pearloid tuner buttons.

List Price: $3,000.00   # Sold: 16 (+ 1 foreign)

HD-28BSE (ONE MARKED "BLE")
Brazilian/spruce, signed on the underside of the top by supervisors and C. F. Martin IV. High X, 1¾" V-neck with Style 42 inlay, Ivoroid binding, aging toner, tortoise pickguard, gold tuners with ebony buttons.

List Price: $3,300.00   # Sold: 88 (+ 5 foreign)

Brazilian rosewood models, total for 1987 in parenthesis, following model code: "Custom 15B" (2), other models probably made but only stamped "Custom."

1988

M2C-28
MC-28 with double cutaway, pearl single-ring rosette, gold self-locking tuners with small ebony buttons. Pickguard optional.

List Price: $2,700.00   # Sold: 20 (+ 2 foreign)

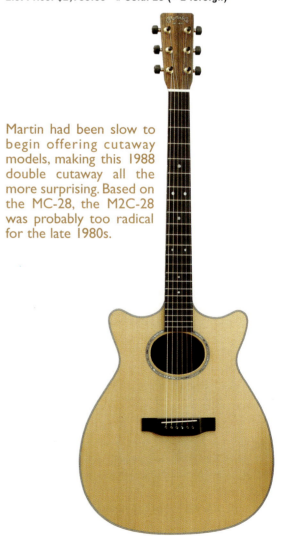

Martin had been slow to begin offering cutaway models, making this 1988 double cutaway all the more surprising. Based on the MC-28, the M2C-28 was probably too radical for the late 1980s.

HD-28M
Mahogany/spruce, high X, HD-28 binding and backstrip, Style 28 neck with diamonds-and-squares inlay, aging toner, light stain on mahogany, tortoise pickguard, gold tuners with pearloid buttons.

List Price: $2,170.00   # Sold: 77 (+ 4 foreign)

HD-28PSE
High X, Ivoroid binding, low-profile (P) neck with Style 45 snowflakes, aging toner, tortoise pickguard, Signature Edition (SE) signed by shop supervisors on underside of top, chrome gears with ebony buttons.

List Price: $2,750.00   # Sold: 93 (+ 3 foreign)

D-42LE
High X, Style 42 top bordering, J-40 neck inlay, M-38 black/white inlay lines on sides and back. Tortoise pickguard, ebony tuner buttons, signed on underside of top by shop foremen and C. F. Martin IV.

List Price: $3,300.00   # Sold: 69 (+ 6 foreign)

1989

D-41BLE
Brazilian/Engelmann, high X $1/4$" bracing, Style 45 headstock with 4/5-sized hexagons (J-40 style) on fretboard, both bordered on top edge with pearl. Aging toner, tortoise pickguard, underside of top signed by shop foremen and C. F. Martin IV, ebony tuner buttons.

List Price: $4,800.00   # Sold: 31 (+ 8 foreign)

HD-28GM
"Grand Marquis" decal on back of peghead. High X, herringbone top trim, rosette, and backstrip, tortoise binding and pickguard. Style 45 headstock inlay and snowflakes on neck and bridge. Gold tuners with engraved "M" buttons.

List Price: $3,198.00   # Sold: 112 (+ 8 foreign)

HOM-35
Brazilian/spruce, herringbone (H) OM with 3-piece back, scalloped $1/4$" braces, Ivoroid binding, zigzag backstrips, aging toner, $1 3/4$" neck, diamonds-and-squares inlay. Martin stamp on back of peghead, small tortoise OM pickguard. Vintage "Kluson-style" gold tuners.

List Price: $4,000.00   # Sold: 53 (+ 7 foreign)

D-18 SPECIAL
High X, rosewood bindings, diamonds and squares inlay, tortoise pickguard. Grover Rotomatic tuners.

List Price: $1,950.00   # Sold: 15 (+ 13 foreign)

1990

D-40BLE
Brazilian/Engelmann, Style 41 pearl bordering on high X braced top. Style 45 inlays on pearl-bordered headstock, Style 45 snowflake inlays on neck and bridge, tortoise pickguard, tuners with "M" buttons. Label signed by C. F. IV and Mike Longworth, Mark Leaf case.

List Price: $5,598.00   # Sold: 50 (+ 8 foreign)

HD-28BLE
Brazilian/spruce, herringbone top trim, rosette, and backstrip, $1/4$" high X, Ivoroid binding on body and headstock (but not on fretboard), $1 3/4$" neck, diamonds-and-squares inlay, aging toner, tortoise pickguard.

List Price: $3,900.00   # Sold: 100 (+ 8 foreign)

OMC-28
Rounded cutaway, oval soundhole with single-ring rosette. Scalloped $1/4$" bracing, C. F. Martin decal logo inlaid in MOP on headstock, $1 3/4$" neck with M-38 style inlay, no herringbone on top but with zigzag backstrip, tortoise pickguard, gold tuners with pearloid buttons.

List Price: $3,148.00   # Sold: 74 (+ 2 foreign)

D-18MB
Mahogany/Engelmann, flamed maple binding, backstrip, and headplate, shop foremens' signatures on underside of top with high X. Aging toner, Style 16 small neck dots, ebony tuner buttons.

List Price: $2,300.00   # Sold: 96 (+ 3 foreign)

1991

D3-18
Vintage Style D-18 with three-piece back. High X, herringbone backstrips, tortoise-bound ebony fretboard with MOP diamonds-and-squares, diamond inlays on bridge, Style 28 lines inside top binding, tortoise pickguard, and "M" tuner buttons.

List Price: $2,398.00   # Sold: 72 (+ 8 foreign)

D-28LSH   LARGE SOUND HOLE
High X $1/4$" bracing, $4 1/4$" diameter soundhole with two abalone rings, signed on underside of top by C. F. IV and employees. Ivoroid binding, herringbone top trim, Style 45 backstrip, Style 42 snowflakes on 22-fret neck, snowflakes on bridge and ebony tuner buttons, aging toner, tortoise pickguard. Label signed by Les Wagner, who retired after 47 years with Martin.

List Price: $4,398.00   # Sold: 200 (+ 11 foreign)

D-45KLE
Flamed koa/Engelmann with bearclaw figure, underside of top signed by employees. Ivoroid binding, Brazilian rosewood headplate with Style 45 inlay, Style 45 snowflakes on neck and bridge, aging toner, tortoise pickguard, "M" tuner buttons, Mark Leaf case.

List Price: $7,800.00   # Sold: 50 (+ 4 foreign)

OM-21 SPECIAL
Herringbone rosette and backstrip, $1/4$" top bracing, mitered white-black side inlays, tortoise binding and OM pickguard, $1 3/4$" neck, striped ebony (Macassar) fretboard, MOP diamonds-and-squares inlay MOP Martin decal logo on headstock, gold tuners with pearloid buttons.

List Price: $3,998.00   # Sold: 32 (+ 4 foreign)

000-18SO SING OUT! 40TH
40th Anniversary of *Sing Out!* magazine, label signed by Pete Seeger.

List Price: N/A   # Sold: 40 (0 foreign)

1992

D-18 VINTAGE
High X, long saddle, tortoise binding, stamp on back of headstock, Grover tuners, lower profile V-neck, other pre-WWII features similar to current D-18V.

List Price: $1,998.00   # Sold: 215 (+ 3 foreign)

HJ-28
Vintage Series Style 28 appointments on Jumbo body. High X, Ivoroid binding, diamonds-and-squares neck inlay, M tuner buttons.

List Price: $3,050.00   # Sold: 56 (+ 13 foreign)

HD-28CTB   CUSTOM TORTOISE BOUND
High X $1/4$" braces, tortoise binding with black-white side inlay, herringbone backstrip, MOP diamonds-and-squares neck inlay, Martin logo inlaid at 12th fret, headstock with enlarged Style 5K uke inlay in MOP, Martin stamp on back of peghead, gold tuners with "M" buttons.

List Price: $3,800.00   # Sold: 89 (+ 8 foreign)

D-45S DELUXE
Modified reproduction of 1937 D-45S (12-fret with solid headstock). Style 45 pearl bordering on sides and front of headstock, fretboard, and neck heel with usual 45 bordering on body. Style 45 headstock inlay and snowflakes on $1 3/4$" neck and bridge tips. Ivoroid binding, $1/4$" top bracing, 19 frets total, pearl M on ebony tuner buttons, leather cover for case.

List Price: $9,760.00   # Sold: 50 (+ 10 foreign)

1993

D-93
"93" is the year (Martin's 160th anniversary), not Style number. Mahogany/spruce D with high X $1/4$" top bracing, herringbone rosette and backstrip, white binding on body, neck, and headstock, ebony fretboard with diamonds-and-squares inlay, CFM in MOP at 3rd fret, diamond inlays in bridge tips, Brazilian headplate, tortoise pickguard, gold tuners with ebony buttons.

List Price: $3,000.00   # Sold: 148 (+ 17 foreign)

D-28 1935 SPECIAL
1³⁄₄" V-neck, long saddle in bridge with 2⁵⁄₁₆" spacing, Brazilian headplate, optional dark sunburst, other features like later HD-28V.

List Price: $3,800.00   # Sold: 217 (+ 20 foreign)

OM-28 PERRY BECHTEL
Reissue of what was then thought to be the earliest OM, appointments similar to later OM-28V. Scalloped top bracing in original pattern, wood purfling in rosette, 1³⁄₄" V-neck with diamonds-and-squares inlay, pyramid bridge with long saddle and 2¹⁄₄" spacing, Brazilian headplate, "M" tuner buttons. Label signed by Mrs. Perry Bechtel.

List Price: $4,000.00   # Sold: 77 (+ 17 foreign)

The 1993 OM-28 Perry Bechtel was Martin's first Signature Edition (at least for someone outside the Martin factory), although Mr. Bechtel died about a decade earlier. Perry was responsible for Martin's first 6-string guitar with 14 frets clear of the body. The first OM prototype was built specifically for him in 1929.

D-45 DELUXE
Brazilian/ "bearclaw" spruce, high X ¹⁄₄" bracing. "Tree of Life" inlay on neck and black pickguard, Style 45 headstock inlay, "Over-45" pearl bordering (pearl backstrip, pearl borders on all edges of neck and headstock). "Island scroll" inlay on bridge, fossilized-ivory nut and saddle, "M" tuner buttons.

List Price: $18,200.00   # Sold: 50 (+ 10 foreign)

1994

D-45 GENE AUTRY
Brazilian/spruce replica of first D-45 (12-fret with slotted headstock). Style 45 bordering with wood inlay lines, 1⁷⁄₈" neck, Martin decal on back of head, torch inlay in headstock with pearl bordering, snowflakes in bridge. Original "Gene Autry" pearl script on neck, optional with Style 45 snowflakes and small "Gene Autry" signature inlay at 19th fret. Fossilized-ivory nut and long saddle, Waverly tuners, label signed by Gene Autry, leather-trimmed case.

List Price: $22,000.00   # Sold: 50 (+ 16 foreign)

The 1994 D-45 Gene Autry was not only the first Signature Edition for a living artist, it was Martin's most deliberate effort to date that replicated both the exterior and the interior details of the first D-45 made 60 years earlier. The success of these efforts later resulted in similar turn-back-the-clock details for the Golden Era Series.

1994 (cont.)

OM-40LE (NATURAL)
Rosewood/spruce, appointments like later Vintage Series OMs but with double row of pearl bordering around top and soundhole, $1/4$" scalloped top bracing, original decal logo in abalone script on headstock, Style 45 backstrip, Style 42 snowflake neck inlay, bone nut and short saddle, ebony tuner buttons with snowflake inlay.

List Price: $7,100.00   # Sold: 45 (+ 12 foreign)

OM-40LE (SUNBURST)
As above with sunburst top.

List Price: $7,430.00   # Sold: 20 (+ 9 foreign)

HD-28 GM LSH
Rosewood/spruce, double herringbone rosette, $4 1/4$" soundhole, high X, herringbone backstrip, tortoise binding with black-white side inlay. Style 45 headstock and snowflake fretboard inlays (not bound), Grand Marquis in MOP at 12th fret, bone nut and saddle, snowflakes in bridge tips, tortoise pickguard, gold tuners with M buttons.

List Price: $4,500.00   # Sold: 106 (+ 9 foreign)

HD-28 GM LSH (SUNBURST)
As above with sunburst top.

List Price: $4,830.00   # Sold: 30 (+ 6 foreign)

HJ-28M
Mahogany/spruce, appointments found on later HD-28V but on a mahogany jumbo with LP neck. High X, Ivoroid binding, herringbone backstrip, striped (Macassar) ebony fretboard and bridge, ebony tuner buttons with M inlay.

List Price: $3,900.00   # Sold: 60 (+ 12 foreign)

The overwhelming popularity of the 000-42EC forever changed the Martin Company's policy regarding artist collaborations. Unlike many guitar manufacturers, Martin didn't have to enlist artists to use its instruments; they simply invited well-known guitarists who had always played Martins to help design a unique model.

1995

000-42EC ERIC CLAPTON (NATURAL)
Rosewood/spruce 14-fret 000, Style 45 neck with snowflake inlays, snowflakes on bridge tips, 24.9" scale, $1 3/4$" V-neck, $2 1/4$" spacing at bridge, bone nut and saddle, gold open-geared Martin tuners with butterbean knobs; other details like current Style 42 Vintage Series reissue. Signature inlay at 20th fret.

List Price: $8,100.00   # Sold: 433/461   Protos: 2

000-42EC ERIC CLAPTON (SUNBURST)
As above with dark "1935" sunburst top.

List Price: $8,320.00   # Sold: 28/461   Protos: 1

D-35 30TH ANNIVERSARY MODEL
Standard D-35 appointments except: Brazilian center wedge of three-piece back and matching headplate. Scalloped 1/4" top bracing, Ivoroid binding, mitered binding on fretboard with "1965-1995" inlaid at 20th fret, bone nut and saddle, tortoise pickguard, gold tuners with M buttons.

List Price: $4,000.00   # Sold: 207   Protos: 2

D-18 GOLDEN ERA® (NATURAL)
Many features copied directly from a 1937 D-18, including: original mahogany stain color, black binding, small abalone dot pattern on neck, Brazilian rosewood headplate with old-style decal, hot stamp burned in reinforcing center strip, cloth strips on sides, 1 3/4" V-neck, 2 5/16" spacing at bridge, long bone saddle, bone nut, chrome vintage-style tuners; other features similar to later D-18V. This first version of the D-18GE did not have an Adirondack spruce top like later GE Series models.

List Price: $3,100.00   # Sold: 272   Protos: 2

D-18 GOLDEN ERA® (SUNBURST)
Same as above, but with dark sunburst top.

List Price: $3,320.00   # Sold: 48   Protos: 2

Martin began publishing *The Sounding Board* newsletter in mid-1996, conceived and edited by Dick Boak. Published twice a year ever since (to coincide with the Winter and Summer NAMM trade shows), it contains detailed descriptions of most Limited Editions, Signature Editions, and Special Editions such as those described in this chapter. All issues of *The Sounding Board* are archived on Martin's web-site, and can be viewed online as PDF files that can be downloaded and printed.

1996

HD-40MS MARTY STUART MODEL
Rosewood/spruce, soundhole rosette of herringbone pattern pearl, regular herringbone top trim and backstrip, Ivoroid binding, high X bracing, five custom position markers on neck of Dice, Horseshoe, Steer Horns, Hearts, and Flowers. Gold vintage-style tuners.

List Price: $5,400.00   # Sold: 250/250   Protos: 2

D-45 CFM SR. (EAST INDIAN)
Rosewood/spruce 14-fret D commemorating the 200th birthday of Martin founder. Style 45 pearl bordering with pearl backstrip, Style 45 snowflake inlays on fretboard, Ivoroid binding with wood inlay beside pearl bordering, 1 3/4" neck with bone nut and saddle, snowflakes on bridge tips, gold vintage-style tuners. C. F. Sr. signature inlay at 20th fret.

List Price: $11,000.00   # Sold: 114/200   Protos: 2

D-45 DELUXE CFM SR. (BRAZILIAN)
Brazilian rosewood/spruce, all appointments of the model described above, plus Style 45 Deluxe pearl bordering on neck and peghead, fossilized-ivory nut, saddle, end pin, and bridge pins, signature inlay at 19th fret.

List Price: $19,500.00   # Sold: 91/91   Protos: 2

000-28 12-FRET GOLDEN ERA®
Rosewood/spruce (not Adirondack as on later GE Series), 5/16" scalloped X-bracing with 1/4" tone bars, fine-pattern herringbone, wood rosette, linen strips on sides, short pattern diamonds-and-squares inlay in 1 13/16" neck, 25.4" scale, pyramid bridge with 2 5/16" string spacing, fossilized-ivory nut, saddle, and bridge pins, pickguard optional; other features like current S models in Vintage Series.

List Price: $4,000.00   # Sold: 367   Protos: 2

MTV-1 SATIN FINISH
14-fret D, body is half rosewood and half mahogany (rosewood on bass side) with spruce top. Style 16 with M&T neck joint, Style 45 rosette, Style 18 tortoise binding with herringbone backstrip, ebony fretboard with letters spelling "UNPLUGGED" as position markers. MTV logo in MOP and abalone on headstock.

List Price: $2,200.00   # Sold: 73   Protos: 2

MTV-1 GLOSS FINISH
Same as above, but with gloss lacquer finish on body only.

List Price: $2,450.00   # Sold: 588   Protos: 2

HD-28SO SING OUT! 12-FRET
45th Anniversary of *Sing Out!* magazine. Rosewood/spruce 12-fret D with appointments like later Vintage Series (HD-28VS), Sing Out! inlay in fretboard, label signed by Pete Seeger.

List Price: $4,500.00   # Sold: 45/45   Protos: 1

1997

OM-42PS PAUL SIMON
Rosewood/spruce, tortoise binding on all edges, Style 42 pearl on top and soundhole, short Style 42 snowflakes pattern on neck with snowflakes on bridge tips, Style 45 backstrip. High X, bone nut and saddle, OM-style tortoise pickguard, Waverly tuners with Ivoroid buttons, signature at 20th fret. (Note: Two Protos were M size.)

**List Price: $8,000.00   # Sold: 225/500
Protos: 2 M-Size   2 OM-Size**

For the Paul Simon OM-42PS, the abalone bordering of a Style 42 was combined with the faux tortoiseshell celluloid binding usually associated with Styles 18 and 21.

000-45JR JIMMIE RODGERS
Replica of Rodgers's custom 1928 000-45: Brazilian/Adirondack 12-fret 000, Style 45 pearl bordering with wood purfling, "Blue Yodel" in headstock, MOP "Jimmie Rodgers" letters in fretboard, ebony straight-line bridge with snowflakes in tips, other GE Series appointments. Includes facsimile of original presentation label by C. F. III, available with optional "THANKS" on back. See photos in book 1, chapter 4, page 176.

List Price: $25,000.00   # Sold: 52/100   Protos: 2

KINGSTON TRIO SET OF 3
D-28KT
Rosewood/spruce, high X, standard D-28 binding in Ivoroid, checkered backstrip, Brazilian headstock veneer with old-style decal, long bone saddle, bone nut, standard Style 28 dots on neck with "The Kingston Trio" inlaid between 11th and 13th frets, "1957-1997" inlaid at 20th fret, gold vintage-style gears. Sold to dealers with 0-18T and Vega PS-5 banjo, with label signed by surviving members of the Trio.

0-18T KINGSTON TRIO
Standard 0-18T (4-string tenor guitar) but with ebony fretboard and bridge, neck inlays as on D-28KT described above, Brazilian headstock veneer with old-style decal.

VEGA 5-STRING KINGSTON TRIO
A Vega long-neck 5-string banjo (made by Deering Banjos), as played by Dave Guard (later by John Stewart) in the Kingston Trio, was marketed by the Martin Company as part of the Kingston Trio set of three instruments.

**List Price for Set: $12,500.00   # Sold: 34/40
Protos: 2 Sets**

CEO-1 CEO'S CHOICE
Mahogany/spruce SPD-16T model (M & T neck joint) with the following differences: hexagon outline inlays on ebony fretboard and bridge, C. F. IV's signature in MOP at 20th fret, N-20 black binding with herringbone top border, gold tuners with ebony buttons.

List Price: $2,600.00   # Sold: 135   Protos: 2

CEO-1R CEO'S CHOICE
Rosewood version of the above.

List Price: $2,800.00   # Sold: 191   Protos: 2

MARTIN/STAUFFER 00-40
Rosewood/spruce adaptation of early Martin 12-fret with Stauffer headstock and "ice-cream cone" neck heel shape. Current Style 40 Ivoroid binding (pearl only around soundhole), unbound 1 3/4" neck and headstock finished in black, Style 45 snowflake neck inlays, hybrid pyramid/belly bridge, 24.9" scale, wood "coffin" case included.

List Price: $7,900.00   # Sold: 35/75   Protos: 2

MARTIN/STAUFFER 00-45
Brazilian/spruce version of the 00-40 described above, but with Style 45 bordering on all body edges. Style 45 snowflakes in bound neck, unbound headstock with C. F. Martin script logo inlaid in pearl, fossilized-ivory nut, saddle, and bridge pins.

List Price: $20,000.00   # Sold: 25/25   Protos: 2

00-16DB WOMEN IN MUSIC
Mahogany/spruce 14-fret 00 body, M & T neck joint, dreadnought-depth sides, with slotted headstock and classical-style wood mosaic rosette. 1 11/16" neck, N-20 (classical model) black binding, ebony fretboard and bridge, diamonds-and-squares inlay, Style 16 top bracing with lighter transverse braces, black OM-shape pickguard.

List Price: $2,100.00   # Sold: 97/97   Protos: 2

0000-28HAG ARLO GUTHRIE (6-STR.)
Rosewood/spruce, similar to M-38, but with herringbone top trim, Ivoroid binding, unbound neck and peghead. Engraved pearl church (Alice's Restaurant in Stockbridge, MA) on headstock, circles-and-arrows inlays on fretboard with "Alice's Restaurant 30th" [anniversary] between 11th and 14th frets, signature inlay at 20th fret.

List Price: $4,750.00   # Sold: 30/30   Protos: 2

000012-28HAG ARLO GUTHRIE (12-STR.)
12-string version of the above.

List Price: $4,950.00   # Sold: 30/30   Protos: 2

Despite the popularity of Johnny Cash's music and his man-in-black persona, Martin fans continued to be lukewarm about all-black guitars; the D-42JC fell short of its projected limit. Mr. Cash, holding the first prototype, is shown here with Martin's Artist Relations director, Dick Boak at the Telluride Bluegrass Festival.

1997 (cont.)

D-42JC JOHNNY CASH (BLACK)
Rosewood/spruce with three-piece back, high X 1/4" top bracing. Gloss black lacquer on body and neck, Style 42 pearl bordering on top and rosette, Style 45 backstrips, Ivoroid binding, Style 45 headstock, bound fretboard with abalone and MOP star inlays, signature inlay at 20th fret.

List Price: $8,200.00   # Sold: 80/200   Protos: 2

00-16DBR WOMEN IN MUSIC
Rosewood/spruce version of the 00-16DB listed on page 141, but issued later in the year and kept in continuous production.

List Price: $2,400.00   # Sold: 430   Protos: 2

1998

HD-18JB JIMMY BUFFETT
Mahogany/spruce, high X bracing, Style 45 rosette, Ivoroid binding on body with herringbone top trim and backstrip. Bone nut and saddle, tortoise pickguard, short Style 42 fretboard inlays with signature inlay at 20th fret. Gold foil Martin logo on headstock with palm tree inlay.

List Price: $3,650.00   # Sold: 424/424   Protos: 2

CMSH STING CLASSICAL
Quilted mahogany/red cedar Humphrey-style classical model with squared headstock and tortoise binding. Only prototypes were completed; the model was redesigned using Certified Wood for 1999.

List Price: $4,450.00   # Sold: 0   Protos: 2
Redesigned as SWC in 1999

D-28HW HANK WILLIAMS SR.
Brazilian/spruce reissue of Hank Sr.'s 1944 D-28. Similar to HD-28V but Brazilian rosewood with GE Series bracing, signature inlay at 20th fret, Waverly tuners with Ivoroid knobs, bone nut and saddle, fossil ivory bridge and end pins.

List Price: $9,000.00   # Sold: 150/150   Protos: 2

0-45JB JOAN BAEZ

Rosewood/spruce 12-fret reissue of Joan's 1929 0-45, with Vintage Style 45 features, 1/4" bracing, belly bridge with long saddle, 1 7/8" neck, 2 5/16" spacing at bridge, Corian nut, bone saddle, tortoise pickguard, Waverly/Sloan tuners with ivoroid buttons, fossil ivory bridge and end pins, signature inlay at 19th fret, all other inlays per original.

List Price: $9,850.00 # Sold: 59/59 Protos: 2

Only 59 models were projected for the Joan Baez limited edition. (Her career began in 1959.) She was the first woman honored by a Martin Signature Edition model, and it was assumed that the small size of the guitar and the high price would restrict sales. The edition sold out so quickly that some fans wondered if producing a number reflecting all four digits of that year wouldn't have been more in keeping with her popularity.

EMP-1 EMPLOYEE MODEL

14-fret 000 with cutaway, Ovangkol/spruce with rosewood center wedge in three piece back, black binding, and black and red marquetry rosette and backstrips. M&T neck joint, Style 16 bracing, ebony fretboard/bridge, black nut/saddle, offset fretboard dots, gold tuners.

List Price: $2,450.00 # Sold: 222/262 Protos: 2

00-21GE GOLDEN ERA

Rosewood/Adirondack 12-fret 00 per 1930s (GE Series details). 1/4" bracing, tortoise binding with wood inlays throughout, herringbone rosette, neck 1 7/8" neck, 2 5/16" spacing at bridge, bone nut, belly bridge with long bone saddle, tortoise pickguard, Waverly tuners.

List Price: $3,950.00 # Sold: 163 Protos: 2

CEO-2 CEO'S CHOICE

Dreadnought, 14-fret, Macassar "striped" ebony (laminated)/spruce, toned top with Style 45 rosette, M&T neck joint/Style 16 bracing, striped ebony fretboard, ebony bridge, hexagon outline inlays on neck and bridge tips, black bindings, nut, and saddle, gold tuners.

List Price: $2,900.00 # Sold: 110 Protos: 2

CONCEPT J

Cutaway Jumbo, maple/spruce with maple neck, M&T neck joint, single ring pearl rosette, no binding, body edges radiused, all surfaces finished with holographic opalescent lacquer. Ebony fretboard and bridge with hexagon outline inlays on both. Gold tuners.

List Price: $4,100.00 # Sold: 55 Protos: 2

D-45SS STEPHEN STILLS

Brazilian/European spruce, 14-fret with GE details including neck width 1 3/4", 2 5/16" spacing at bridge, high X bracing and 5/32" binding height. Fossil ivory nut, saddle & pins, C. F. Martin letters on headstock, fretboard with Style 45 snowflakes but hexagon inlays optional, pickguard with five stars (Southern Cross) inlay. Signature inlay at 20th fret, gold Waverly tuners.

List Price: $19,000.00 # Sold: 91/91 Protos: 2

1998 (cont.)

D-40DM DON MCLEAN
Rosewood/Engelmann, white Style 40 Boltaron binding, pearl script logo on headstock with torch inlay below, hexagon fretboard inlays with "American Pie" references in red epoxy letters. Tortoise pickguard, gold Schaller tuners with pearloid buttons, Signature inlay at 20th fret.

List Price: $5,750.00   # Sold: 50/71   Protos: 2

D-28LF LESTER FLATT
Brazilian/spruce replica of Flatt's 1950 D-28. Non-scalloped bracing, checkerboard backstrip, Ivoroid binding. Bone nut and long saddle. MOP neck inlays of oversized diamonds as per Flatt's modified original. Oversized tortoise pickguard, with standard pickguard available on order. Vintage Kluson-style tuners.

List Price: $8,500.00   # Sold: 50/50   Protos: 2

Along with Lester Flatt's legendary status among the bluegrass faithful as the voice of Flatt and Scruggs, the replica of his D-28 also had another connection for Martin guitar fans: the non-standard neck inlays had been added to Flatt's guitar by a young Mike Longworth, long before he joined the Martin Company.

N-20WN WILLIE NELSON (EAST INDIAN)
Rosewood/spruce replica of Nelson's 1969 N-20 classical guitar (early version with square headstock). Per original but with bone nut and saddle, yellow toner on top, Lonestar Texas inlay on fretboard, "Trigger" at 12th fret and signature inlay at 18th. Waverly/Sloan tuners, special Fishman pickup.

List Price: $5,500.00   # Sold: 59/70   Protos: 2

N-20WN WILLIE NELSON (BRAZILIAN)
As per above, but Brazilian rosewood back and sides.

List Price: $9,800.00   # Sold: 30/30   Protos: 2

OM-45 DELUXE GOLDEN ERA
Brazilian/Adirondack replica of 1930 originals, with GE Series details throughout. 1/4" top bracing, bar frets, fossil ivory nut and saddle. Fossil ivory bridge and endpin with black pearl dots (not like original). Short OM pickguard with inlay, under the finish, engraved gold banjo tuners with MOP buttons.

List Price: $27,500.00   # Sold: 14/14   Protos: 2

1999

D12-42RM ROGER MCGUINN
Rosewood/spruce Style 42 version of D12-28 with Vintage Series appointments. Style 45 Martin letters on headstock with hexagons on fretboard, signature inlay at 20th fret.

List Price: $6,900.00   # Sold: 65   Protos: 2

00-18SH STEVE HOWE
Enhanced version of Howe's 1953 00-18 with Vintage Series appointments. Mahogany/Engelmann with 1/4" scalloped top bracing, ebony fretboard and bridge with bone nut and long saddle (short drop-in saddle optional), 24.9" scale, tortoise binding and pickguard, vintage Kluson-style Gotoh tuners, small dots on fretboard with signature at 19th fret.

List Price: $2,950.00   # Sold: 250/250   Protos: 2

SWB STING CERTIFIED WOOD AC. BASS
Jumbo body bass with B-1 construction and appointments similar to SmartWood models. Cherry/spruce body with cherry neck, katalox fretboard and bridge, gloss finish, signature inlay at 23rd fret.

List Price: $3,200.00   # Sold: 26   Protos: 2

SWC STING CERTIFIED WOOD CLASSIC
Machiche/spruce, with cherry neck, katalox fretboard and classical bridge. Neck 1 7/8" at nut, construction like Humphrey nylon-string models, but with tortoise binding, rosette, and backstrip. Interior woods as on SmartWood models, gold tuners, signature inlay at 19th fret.

List Price: $3,500.00 # Sold: 46 Protos: 2

D-28GE SPECIAL EDITION
First version of the D-28 Golden Era, Brazilian rosewood/Adirondack, a model with mid-1930s specs, including interior stamps, that was continued in following years. (See chapter 2 for details.) Neck 1 3/4" at nut, 2 5/16" spacing at bridge, fossil ivory nut, long saddle, and pins. Paper label has guitar's number in series, but no total.

List Price: $9,000.00 # Sold: 346 Protos: 2

EMP-2 EMPLOYEES MODEL
Certified Tzalam/spruce 14-fret cutaway dreadnought with shallow 000 depth sides, M&T neck joint. Ivoroid binding, wood marquetry rosette and backstrip with colored arrow pattern, large flying saucer inlays in fretboard, jumbo frets, 1920s Style 5 uke inlay in headstock.

List Price: $2,700.00 # Sold: 30/199 Protos: 2

CEO-3 CEO'S CHOICE
Laminated Brazilian rosewood/spruce version of CEO-2 from 1998, but with: Gold finish on top, Ivoroid binding, and tortoise headplate.

List Price: $3,500.00 # Sold: 56/150 Protos: 2

SIZE 5 MINI-MARTIN (DICK BOAK)
Rosewood/spruce. Vintage Style 28 features with Style 45 rosette. 21 3/8" scale, 1 5/8" at nut, 2 1/8" spacing at bridge. Paper label with guitar's number in series but no total; model continued in production.

Initial List Price: $3,250.00 # Sold: ongoing Protos: 2

Note: This model is still on the current price list as a Special Edition. List price has increased a few times since initial offering.

000-18WG WOODY GUTHRIE
Mahogany/spruce with Vintage Series features as found on later 00-18V. Signature inlay at 20th fret, paper label signed by Arlo and Nora Guthrie, numbered in sequence without total.

List Price: $3,150.00 # Sold: 140 Protos: 2

DM3MD DAVE MATTHEWS
Dreadnought, rosewood/Engelmann, three-piece back with African Padauk center wedge. M&T neck joint, Ivoroid binding with half herringbone top border, Style 45 rosette and backstrips, all black inlay lines and rosette lines replaced with red. Three-piece headplate matches back, chrome vintage-style tuners, signature inlay at 20th fret.

List Price: $3,250.00 # Sold: 234/234 Protos: 2

CONCEPT II
Maple/spruce 000 cutaway with maple neck, M&T neck joint with 1 Series bracing. Finish and edges like 1998 Concept J but magenta/gold color. Continuous abalone lightning inlay from 1st to 20th fret with matching inlays on bridge tips.

List Price: $4,100.00 # Sold: 35 Protos: 2

D-18GE GOLDEN ERA
Mahogany/Adirondack recreation of 1934 D-18. Vintage Series appointments, but with black binding, neck 1 3/4" at nut, 2 5/16" spacing at bridge, ebony fretboard and bridge with long fossil ivory saddle, fossil ivory nut, Waverly tuners. Interior features like D-28GE listed above, paper label numbered in series without total; model remained in continuous production.

List Price: $3,500.00 # Sold: 575 Protos: 2

2000

000-42ECB ERIC CLAPTON
Brazilian/Engelmann, current Style 42 binding and bordering (but with wood inlay lines), alternate torch headstock inlay, thin band of MOP around Style 45 fretboard inlays, matching inlays on bridge tips. 24.9" scale, 1 3/4" at nut, 2 1/4" spacing at bridge. Bone nut and saddle, fossil ivory pins, gold Waverly tuners, signature inlay at 20th fret.

List Price: $15,000.00 # Sold: 200/200 Protos: 3

2000 (cont.)

HDO GRAND OLE OPRY
75th Anniversary of the Opry. Rosewood/spruce 14-fret D, M&T neck joint, Style 28V binding, backstrip, and herringbone top border with Style 45 rosette. Neck 1³⁄₄", 2¹⁄₄" spacing at bridge. Ebony headplate with WSM microphone inlay, off-white Micarta fretboard with "Grand Ole Opry" in red vertical letters.

List Price: $3,350.00 **# Sold:** 574/650 **Protos:** 3

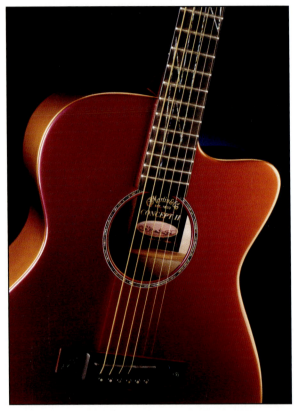

The second of Martin's Concept models featured a striking lightning bolt fretboard inlay to complement the holographic opalescent lacquer.

D-21JC JIM CROCE (INDIAN)
Rosewood/spruce late 1960s Style 21 (black binding and pickguard, Style 18 rosette, Grover Rotomatic tuners) but with ebony fretboard and bridge and high X scalloped bracing, bone nut and saddle, 1973 dime inlaid at 3rd fret, signature inlay at 20th fret.

List Price: $3,450.00 **# Sold:** 73/73 **Protos:** 2

D-21JC JIM CROCE (BRAZILIAN)
Same as D-21JC but with Brazilian rosewood.

List Price: $8,475.00 **# Sold:** 65/73 **Protos:** 2

The popularity of the D-21 has long suffered from its status as "almost a D-28," but that didn't bother Jim Croce, who relied on his D-21 throughout a prolific but tragically short career.

JLJCR JONNY LANG JUMBO
Laminated rosewood/solid spruce with cutaway, M&T neck joint, black binding, two-ring rosette, ebony bridge and fretboard with acrylic hexagon outline inlays. Bone nut and saddle, no pickguard, Fishman Prefix blender pickup panel in lower bout (just below waist), signature inlay at 20th fret.

List Price: $2,750.00 **# Sold:** 110/111 **Protos:** 3

NWD GEORGE NAKASHIMA
Claro Walnut/Italian spruce 14-fret D with two-piece maple neck, high X bracing, satin finish throughout. Single ring pearl rosette, rosewood binding, two rosewood dovetails in back joint, Nakashima family crest inlays on headstock and at 5th fret. 1 3/4" LP neck with 2 5/16" spacing at bridge, black Corian nut, black Micarta saddle, fossil ivory pins, tortoise pickguard, Waverly tuners, signature inlay at 20th fret.

List Price: $4,750.00   # Sold: 59/100   Protos: 2

OO-17SO SING OUT! 50TH
Sing Out! magazine 50th Anniversary. All-mahogany body, M&T neck joint, tortoise binding and pickguard, gloss finish. Ebony bridge and fretboard with special inlays, label signed by surviving members of the Weavers.

List Price: $2,399.00   # Sold: 50/50   Protos: 3

OOOC-16RB BABYFACE
Rosewood/European spruce cutaway, M&T neck joint, Style 28V binding, backstrip, with herringbone top border and Style 45 rosette, gloss finish, neck and scale length like Clapton models. "Baby Face" signature inlay at 20th fret.

List Price: $2,850.00   # Sold: 96/100   Protos: 4

EMP-NS EMPLOYEE MODEL
Night Shift employees model, maple/spruce 14-fret D with M&T neck joint. Black binding, transparent gloss black finish on maple, natural top, satin black on neck. Ebony bridge and fretboard with Style 18 abalone dots, black pickguard and chrome tuners.

List Price: $2,299.00   # Sold: 73   Protos: 1

D-41GJ GEORGE JONES
Rosewood/Engelmann Standard Series Style 41 but with scalloped-edge hexagon fretboard inlays, Ivoroid binding, high X bracing, 1 3/4" LP neck with 2 5/16" spacing at bridge. Bone nut and saddle, gold Waverly tuners, signature inlay at 20th fret.

List Price: $4,750.00   # Sold: 100/100   Protos: 3

D-18GL GORDON LIGHTFOOT
Quilted (figured) mahogany/Engelmann, high X bracing, Style 18V binding, finish, and inlay but with Style 45 rosette and LP neck, "Edmund Fitzgerald" freighter inlay at 12th fret, signature inlay at 20th fret, Kluson-style vintage tuners, bone nut and saddle.

List Price: $3,500.00   # Sold: 61/61   Protos: 3

As with the Joan Baez model, Martin erred on the side of caution when choosing to build only 61 Gordon Lightfoot D-18s. The edition sold out as soon as it was announced.

00-37KSM STEVE MILLER
Flamed Koa/Engelmann 12-fret 00, scalloped 1/4" top bracing. Ivoroid binding with herringbone top border, Style 45 backstrip and rosette, bound headstock with alternate torch inlay, no fretboard inlays, gloss finish on 1 3/4" LP neck, 2 5/16" spacing at belly bridge. Bone nut and saddle, ebony pins, Sloane tuners with Ivoroid buttons.

List Price: $5,750.00   # Sold: 68/68   Protos: 3

2000 (cont.)

00-37K2SM STEVE MILLER
Same as 00-37K SM, but with flamed koa top.

List Price: $6,250.00 **# Sold:** 68/68 **Protos:** 3

CEO-4 SPECIAL CEO'S CHOICE
Slope-shoulder 14-fret D, mahogany/Adirondack, M&T neck joint. White binding, single ring rosette, dark three-color sunburst top finish with black pickguard. Black Micarta fretboard and bridge.

List Price: $2,500.00 **# Sold:** 409 **Protos:** 2

COWBOY X LIMITED EDITION
000X with cowboy campfire scene on top (art by Robert Armstrong).

List Price: $999.00 **# Sold:** 250/250 **Protos:** 2

2001

000C-28SMH MERLE HAGGARD
Rosewood/spruce 12-fret 000 with rounded cutaway. 000-28V appointments but with Style 45 rosette, "Blue Yodel No. 13" headstock inlay. 1 3/4" neck, 2 1/4" spacing at belly bridge, bone nut and short saddle, Waverly tuners, signature inlay at 20th fret.

List Price: $4,799.00 **# Sold:** 122 **Protos:** 3

HD-28KM KEB MO
Flamed Koa/Engelmann, HD-28V appointments but with Style 45 rosette, LP neck, jumbo frets, ebony headplate, and gold Schaller tuners with ebony buttons. 1 3/4" neck, 2 1/4" spacing at bridge with short saddle. Bone nut and saddle, gold Schaller tuners with ebony buttons, signature inlay at 20th fret.

List Price: $3,999.00 **# Sold:** 252 **Protos:** 3

The highly figured koa on Keb Mo's Dreadnought made it a Signature Edition that was popular both with the singer's fans and with Martin guitar fans who'd been waiting for an HD-28 with koa back and sides instead of the usual rosewood.

Flatpicking legend Clarence White had long played Martin Dreadnoughts, but rights issues restricted the Martin Company from using his name for many years. Once that was resolved, Clarence White models took their rightful place in the Signature Series.

D-18CW CLARENCE WHITE
Quilted (figured) mahogany/Adirondack, non-scalloped top braces in high X pattern. Tortoise binding, single ring abalone rosette, herringbone backstrip. 1 3/4" neck with blank fretboard, 2 1/4" spacing at bridge with long saddle. Waverly tuners, signature inlay at 20th fret.

List Price: $3,999.00 **# Sold:** 292 **Protos:** 3

JC-16KWS KENNY WAYNE SHEPHERD
Jumbo cutaway, Sapele/ spruce, M&T neck joint, gloss black finish on back and sides, translucent blue toner on top with Style 45 rosette (blue Paua and blue inlay lines). Black binding, ebony bridge and fretboard with blue lapis teardrop inlays, chrome tuners w/ebony buttons, Fishman PU, signature at 20th fret.

List Price: $3,149.00 # Sold: 198 Protos: 3

00-18CTN ELIZABETH COTTEN
Mahogany/spruce, appointments like 00-18V but with $1^{11}/_{16}$" LP neck, bone nut and long saddle, Kluson-style vintage tuners. "Freight Train" inlay at 12th fret, signature inlay at 20th fret.

List Price: $3,299.00 # Sold: 76 Protos: 3

D-50 DELUXE FIRST EDITION
Brazilian rosewood/bearclaw spruce, 14-fret D with complex vine inlay on headstock, fretboard, and pickguard, plus ornate floral inlays on back and sides and over-45 Style bordering on all edges. (See page 84 of this volume, page 199 of book 1, and Dick Boak's book, *Martin Guitar Masterpieces* (Bulfinch Press), for a full description.)

List Price: $50,000.00 # Sold: 50/50 Protos: 2

COWBOY II LIMITED EDITION
000X with cowboy chuck wagon breakfast scene (Chris Martin as cook), art by Robert Armstrong. Leather textured finish on back and sides.

List Price: $999.00 # Sold: 500/500 Protos: 1

SP-NAMM100 NAMM 100TH
100th Anniversary of National Association of Music Merchants. Mahogany/spruce SP000C-16 with striped ebony fretboard and bridge, 1935 dark sunburst top, onboard Fishman Blender pickup. All other features like stock SP 16 Series.

List Price: $2,499.00 # Sold: 100/100 Protos: 0

000-40MPR PETER ROWAN
Mahogany/spruce 12-fret 000, Style 18 tortoise binding with extra inlay lines and matching binding on neck and slotted headstock. Style 45 rosette, herringbone backstrip, $1^{13}/_{16}$" neck, $2^{5}/_{16}$" spacing at pyramid bridge with long bone saddle. Phases of the moon inlays on fretboard, ebony headplate with clouds and full moon inlay, short OM-style tortoise pickguard, nickel Waverly side-mount tuners, signature inlay at 20th fret.

List Price: $4,999.00 # Sold: 87 Protos: 3

D-16BH BECK
Rosewood/spruce SPD-16 with sides 000 depth, Spanish cedar neck, tortoise binding with extra inlay lines on all edges, Style 45 rosette, unbound ebony fretboard and bridge, small dot neck inlays with signature inlay at 20th fret, tortoise pickguard, chrome tuners with ebony buttons.

List Price: $2,950.00 # Sold: 99 Protos: 3

HD-40MK MARK KNOPFLER
Rosewood/European spruce 14-fret D, high X bracing, herringbone top border and backstrip, rosette with center ring of MOP diamonds (modified version of 1840s style), Ivoroid binding, $1^{11}/_{16}$" V neck with jumbo frets and short pattern Style 42 snowflake inlays, signature inlay at 19th fret. MOP script Martin logo on headstock, bone nut and short saddle, nickel Waverly tuners.

List Price: $4,999.00 # Sold: 251 Protos: 3

As with several other artists, Mark Knopfler chose a combination of woods, decorative elements, and neck specifications resulting in a superb Martin Dreadnought that inspired many of the songs on his *Ragpicker's Dream* album.

2001 (cont.)

D-41DF DAN FOGELBERG
Rosewood/spruce, appointments like original D-41 (including standard non-scalloped bracing and gold Grover Rotomatic tuners), but with Ivoroid binding, bone nut and saddle, "winter snowflake" inlays on bridge tips, signature inlay at 20th fret.

List Price: $4,750.00   # Sold: 141   Protos: 3

COWBOY III LIMITED EDITION
000X with cowboys and bucking bronco scene on top from art by Robert Armstrong.

List Price: $1,099.00   # Sold: 750/750   Protos: 2

CEO-5 CEO'S CHOICE
Sapele/bearclaw spruce 12-fret D with M&T neck joint. Ivoroid binding, herringbone pearl rosette, herringbone top border, striped ebony bridge and fretboard with Style 18 abalone dot inlays and gold-color frets. $1^{3}/_{4}$" neck, $2^{1}/_{4}$" spacing at bridge, slotted headstock with small old-style Martin decal and gold tuners.

List Price: $2,649.00   # Sold: 366   Protos: 2

2002

000-28ECB ERIC CLAPTON
Brazilian rosewood/ spruce, appointments like 000-28EC with the following additions: herringbone pearl rosette, abalone diamonds-and-squares fretboard inlays bordered in MOP, bone nut and saddle with fossil ivory pins, Waverly tuners, signature at 20th fret.

List Price: $9,999.00   # Sold: 500/500   Protos: 3

HD-35SJC 6-STRING JUDY COLLINS
Rosewood/spruce 12-fret D with solid headstock and flamed maple center wedge in three-piece back. Ivoroid binding, Style 45 rosette, herringbone top border and backstrips, Style 45 snowflakes on bound fretboard, bound ebony headplate with wildflower inlay and signature. $1^{3}/_{4}$" LP neck with $2^{1}/_{4}$" spacing at bridge, bone nut and short saddle, black pickguard, chrome tuners with ebony buttons.

List Price: $5,149.00   # Sold: 50   Protos: 3

HD12-35SJC JUDY COLLINS 12-STRING
Rosewood/spruce 12-string version of HD-35SJC, solid headstock.

List Price: $5,349.00   # Sold: 33   Protos: 3

D-18DC DAVID CROSBY
Quilted (figured) mahogany/Engelmann with D-18V appointments, except maple stain on mahogany, black/white side inlay and tortoise heelcap, Style 45 backstrip, paua pearl Style 45 rosette, ebony headplate with MOP schooner beneath gold foil logo, bone nut and short bone saddle, Waverly tuners, signature inlay at 20th fret.

List Price: $3,799.00   # Sold: 250/250   Protos: 3

M3SC SHAWN COLVIN
Mahogany/Engelmann M (0000) body with rosewood center wedge in three-piece back and matching three-piece headplate, M&T neck joint. Tortoise binding with black/white inlays on all edges, single ring pearl rosette, ebony bridge and blank fretboard, black pins, gloss finish on body, chrome tuners with ebony buttons.

List Price: $3,199.00   # Sold: 120   Protos: 3

000CBD DION "THE WANDERER"
Mahogany/spruce 000 cutaway, M&T neck joint, gloss black finish with black binding, single ring paua rosette, Style 45 backstrip, ebony headplate with silver foil logo, "Dion" signature above pre-9/11 New York City skyline inlay. Ebony fretboard, dove inlays in bridge tips, black Corian nut, black Micarta saddle, black pins, chrome tuners with ebony buttons.

List Price: $3,299.00   # Sold: 57   Protos: 3

000-28LD LONNIE DONEGAN
Rosewood/spruce, Ivoroid binding, scalloped braces, Style 45 rosette with paua pearl, standard Style 28 checkered backstrip, 1935-style sunburst top, inlays on fretboard spell "skiffle" below crown at 3rd fret, rat inlay on headstock, signature inlay at 20th fret, gold Grover Rotomatic tuners.

List Price: $4,099.00   # Sold: 72   Protos: 3

000-28LDB LONNIE DONEGAN
Same as above, but with Brazilian rosewood back and sides.

List Price: $8,219.00   # Sold: 25/75   Protos: 3

OMC 10VLJ LAURENCE JUBER
Mahogany/Adirondack OM cutaway with GE Series appointments except: tortoise binding, no pickguard, belly bridge with short saddle and 2 1/4" spacing (neck 1 3/4"), no fretboard inlays, Waverly tuners.

List Price: $4,449.00   # Sold: 133   Protos: 3

Laurence Juber, fingerstyle's tireless ambassador, chose woods and appointments found on vintage Martin OM models from the early 1930s, combined with a rounded cutaway. The result was similar to the Soloist model guitars from the collaboration between Martin and Schoenberg several years earlier.

00-45S "1902"
Brazilian rosewood/ Adirondack recreation of 1902 "00-42 Special" model that predated the first Style 45 Martins. Differences required by modern times include Ivoroid binding, white Micarta bridge, fossil ivory nut, saddle, and pins, Waverly/Sloan tuners. Includes wooden "coffin" case.

List Price: $22,500.00   # Sold: 60/100   Protos: 2

DCRNS STEINBERGER TRANSACTION™
Rosewood/spruce Dreadnought cutaway with patented adjustable neck joint. 16 Series bracing, pearl rosette, black binding with black Corian nut, black Micarta fretboard and bridge, gloss finish.

List Price: $3,649.00   # Sold: 31/100   Protos: 2

MPFF PHILADELPHIA FOLK FESTIVAL 40TH
Rosewood/Engelmann M size (0000) with M&T neck joint. Style 45 rosette and backstrip, Ivoroid binding with herringbone top border, bound ebony headplate with alternate torch inlay. 1 3/4" bound ebony fretboard, Brazilian rosewood bridge (2 1/4" spacing). Short Style 42 snowflake neck inlays but with PFF banjo logo at 5th fret, "Philadelphia Folk Festival" at 20th fret. Gold Schaller tuners with ebony buttons.

List Price: $3,449.00   # Sold: 85   Protos: 3

000-16RGD GODFREY DANIELS 25TH
Rosewood/spruce, cedar neck w/ M&T joint, Style 45 backstrip and paua rosette, black Micarta fretboard and bridge, modified snowflake neck inlays with eighth notes and "Godfrey Daniels" at 12th fret, snowflake inlays at bridge tips, gold tuners.

List Price: $2,849.00   # Sold: 26/100   Protos: 2

HAWAIIAN X
000X with Hawaiian luau scene on face (Chris Martin enjoying the food), from art by Robert Armstrong.

List Price: $1,099.00   # Sold: 500/500   Protos: 2

ALTERNATIVE II
000X cutaway with aluminum top and headplate. Black tuners, black nut, saddle, and pins, Fishman onboard electronics.

List Price: $1,199.00   # Sold: 134   Protos: 2

ALTERNATIVE III
Dreadnought version of above.

List Price: $1,199.00   # Sold: 91   Protos: 2

CEO-4R CEO'S CHOICE
Rosewood/Adirondack version of 2000 CEO-4 slope-shoulder Dreadnought. Gold tuners, teardrop shape 1935 sunburst on top.

List Price: $2,699.00   # Sold: ongoing   Protos: 2

2002 (cont.)

DVM VETERANS' SPECIAL
Rosewood/spruce 14-fret Dreadnought, M&T neck joint, headplate with applied insignia pins of Army, Navy, Marine Corps, Air Force, and Coast Guard. Fretboard inlays include eagle, letters spelling "VETERANS," and National Defense Service Ribbon at 20th fret. Ebony fretboard and bridge, black nut and saddle, gold vintage-style tuners.

List Price: $3,199.00   # Sold: 597   Protos: 2

D-28DM DEL MCCOURY
Rosewood/Adirondack, Standard Style 28 top border, Style 18 rosette but with paua center ring, HD-28 backstrip, Ivoroid binding. High X, neck $1^{11}/_{16}$" but with $2^{1}/_{4}$" spacing at bridge. Bone nut and long saddle, lapis and MOP fretboard dots, optional inlay at 20th fret, nickel Waverly tuners.

List Price: $4,899.00   # Sold: 115   Protos: 3

HTA KITTY WELLS HONKY TONK ANGEL
Rosewood/Engelmann shallow-bodied D, M&T neck joint, Style 45 rosette and backstrip with herringbone top border. Long pattern diamonds-and-squares fretboard inlay with crown at 5th fret, ebony headplate with angel inlay (no logo), chrome enclosed tuners with pearloid knobs.

List Price: $3,299.00   # Sold: 70   Protos: 3

PS2 PAUL SIMON
Rosewood/spruce 14-fret 000, M&T neck joint, tortoise binding, Style 45 rosette and backstrip. Ebony headplate with abalone/paua "world" inlay beneath gold foil Martin logo. 24.9" scale $1^{11}/_{16}$" V neck with long pattern diamonds-and-squares inlays, signature inlay at 20th fret, bone nut and saddle, tortoise OM pickguard, nickel vintage-style tuners.

List Price: $3,499.00   # Sold: 200   Protos: 3

HDN NEGATIVE GUITAR
Rosewood/Engelmann 14-fret D, M&T neck joint, gloss black lacquer body and satin black neck, with black binding, herringbone top border, Style 45 rosette, ivory-colored Micarta bridge, pickguard, fretboard, and headplate. Torch inlay in headstock, Style 45 snowflakes in fretboard, black nut, saddle, and pins, chrome tuners with ebony buttons.

List Price: $3,699.00   # Sold: 135   Protos: 3

DSR SUGAR RAY
All-mahogany 14-fret D based on D-15. M&T neck joint, pearl rosette, body edges rounded as on Concept models, ebony fretboard and bridge, bulldog head inlay in ebony headplate, dog paws inlays on fretboard with Sugar Ray logo inlay at 20th fret. Red toner finish, gloss on body, black pickguard, bone nut and saddle, chrome tuners with ebony buttons.

List Price: $2,499.00   # Sold: 57   Protos: 3

D-28CW CLARENCE WHITE
Reissue of White's modified 1935 D-28. Rosewood/Adirondack, Golden Era Series appointments with following changes: oversized soundhole without inner rosette ring, Ivoroid bound 21 fret fretboard without position markers (side position dots only), $1^{11}/_{16}$" V neck, $2^{1}/_{8}$" spacing at bridge, light-colored "Dalmatian" tortoise pickguard, Waverly tuners.

Initial List Price: $4,899.00   # Sold: ongoing   Protos: 2

D-28CWB CLARENCE WHITE
Same as above, but with Brazilian rosewood.

List Price: $9,999.00   # Sold: 150/150   Protos: 3

2003

000-18MC MARTIN CARTHY
Mahogany/spruce, Vintage Series Style 18 appointments, but with $1/4$" top bracing not scalloped, "zero" fret in front of nut, brass bridge pins for three treble strings. $1^{3}/_{4}$" V neck, 24.9" scale, small OM pickguard, and Waverly tuners.

List Price: $3,199.00   # Sold: 67/84   Protos: 4

000-40Q2GN GRAHAM NASH
Quilted mahogany top, back, and sides. 14-fret 000 with tortoise binding on body, neck, and headstock, Style 45 paua rosette, herringbone top trim, short Style 42 snowflakes on fretboard with snowflakes on bridge tips $1^{11}/_{16}$" LP neck, 24.9" scale, "heart with wings" inlay on headstock, signature inlay at 20th fret, gold Waverly tuners.

List Price: $4,699.00   # Sold: 147   Protos: 4

D-28KTBS BOB SHANE (STANDARD PKGD)
Standard Series D-28 combined with HD-28V bracing, Ivoroid binding, aging toner, tortoise pickguard, and long saddle in bridge. Chrome Grover Rotomatic tuners, "The Kingston Trio" inlay on fretboard.

List Price: $3,799.00   # Sold: 19   Protos: 2

D-28KTBSDG BOB SHANE (DOUBLE PKGD)
Same as D-28KTBS described above, but with large black double "Josh White" pickguard.

List Price: $3,999.00 # Sold: 32 Protos: 2

000-JBP JIMMY BUFFETT "POLLYWOG"
Mahogany/spruce 12-fret 000, M&T neck joint, tortoise binding on body only, single ring paua rosette, rope pattern top border (half-herringbone pattern), ebony fretboard and straight bridge with flat tips. 1 $^{13}/_{16}$" LP neck, 2 $^{5}/_{16}$" spacing at bridge, 25.4" scale, solid headstock with gold vintage-style tuners. Ebony headplate with ship's porthole motif, ship's wheel inlaid at 5th fret, signature inlay at 20th fret.

List Price: $3,699.00 # Sold: 305 Protos: 4

000-JBS JIMMY BUFFETT "SHELLBACK"
Same as 000-JBP, but with mahogany top.

List Price: $3,699.00 # Sold: 168 Protos: 4

MTV-2 UNPLUGGED (SATIN FINISH)
14-fret 000, M&T neck joint; body is half rosewood and half flamed maple (rosewood on bass side) with spruce top. Style 45 paua rosette, tortoise binding, herringbone backstrip, ebony fretboard and bridge, MTV headstock inlay and "UNPLUGGED" fretboard inlays same as 1996 MTV model. Edition total included both satin finish and gloss finish versions.

List Price: $2,749.00 # Sold: 15 Protos: 4

MTV-2 UNPLUGGED (GLOSS FINISH)
Same as model described above, but with gloss finish on body only.

List Price: $2,999.00 # Sold: 98 Protos: 4

Note: Seven MTV models were assembled with rosewood/maple sides that were reversed in orientation to the rosewood/maple back. The resulting guitars were dubbed "harlequins" and were eventually offered for sale. There were three gloss and four satin harlequin guitars made.

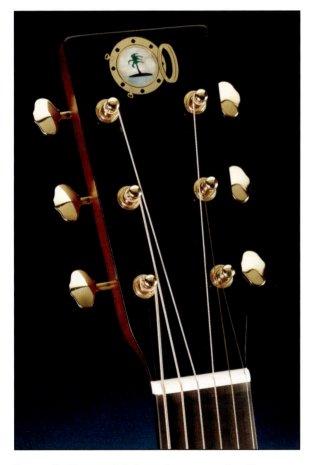

Jimmy Buffet models have been popular Signature Series editions, thanks to loyal Parrotheads (Buffet fans) and the appeal of tropical and nautical themes.

The MTV-2 continued the theme of the initial MTV model from 1996 by combining different woods on opposite sides of the guitar, this time rosewood and flamed maple on a 000 size.

2003 (cont.)

JDP DIANE PONZIO
Rosewood/spruce J-40, but with three-piece back, scalloped 1/4" top braces in high X pattern, herringbone backstrips, dark teardrop sunburst with black pickguard, black Corian nut and black Micarta saddle, black pins, gold tuners.

List Price: $3,999.00 # Sold: 101 Protos: 4

CONCEPT III
Maple/spruce 14-fret cutaway 000, M&T neck joint with 1 Series bracing, single-ring paua rosette, black Micarta fretboard, bridge, and saddle. Rounded body edges as on other Concept models, but with gold flake prismatic finish (gloss throughout), Fishman onboard blender PU, black tuners.

List Price: $3,299.00 # Sold: 18 Protos: 3

D-42AR AMAZON ROSEWOOD
Amazon Rosewood/Italian spruce, appointments and bracing like D-42 but with Vintage Series neck, long drop-in saddle, Amazon rosewood headplate. NAMM show special.

List Price: $7,999.00 # Sold: 30 Protos: 2

OM-42AR AMAZON ROSEWOOD
OM version of D-42AR described above.

List Price: $7,999.00 # Sold: 20 Protos: 2

COWBOY IV
Same as earlier Cowboy X Series 000 models, but with Chris Martin as a cowboy branding guitars.

List Price: $1,199.00 # Sold: 250/250 Protos: 4

OM-28JM JOHN MAYER
Rosewood/Engelmann with scalloped 1/4" top bracing, most appointments like Vintage Series OM, but with 1 11/16" LP neck, Style 45 rosette, aluminum line inlay around edge of bridge and headstock, triangle inlay at 12th fret, signature inlay at 20th, nickel vintage-style tuners.

List Price: $4,499.00 # Sold: 404/404 Protos: 4

Two of Martin's most popular endorsers, Eric Clapton and John Mayer, team up for a Katrina Benefit appearance on *Larry King Live*. Mayer is playing his Signature Edition OM, while Clapton is using a 000-28EC, part of the Vintage Series. Eric Clapton Signature Edition models have far outsold those by any other artist.

Andy Griffith shows off his signature edition D-18 to Marty Stuart, who was the first living country music star to get a signature edition Martin back in 1996. Andy's D-18, although comparatively plain, was an immediate sellout when introduced in 2003.

D-18 ANDY GRIFFITH
Quilted (figured) mahogany/bearclaw spruce, Brazilian headplate. Vintage Series appointments, but with 1960s headstock shape, 1 $^{11}/_{16}$" LP neck, clear pickguard, and Kluson-style tuners.

List Price: $3,699.00   # Sold: 311   Protos: 4

D-37W LUCINDA WILLIAMS
Figured walnut/Engelmann 14-fret D with herringbone top border, Style 45 rosette and backstrip, sunburst top. Due to a contract dispute, only the four prototypes were completed.

List Price: $4,999.00   Not Issued   Protos: 4

MC-40 ERIC JOHNSON
Rosewood/Engelmann M body with cutaway. Single-ring rosette, Ivoroid binding with blue fiber inlay lines, arrow-pattern backstrip, 1$^3/_4$" LP neck, 2$^1/_4$" spacing at bridge, ebony headplate with MOP angel inlay, inlays of planets on bound fretboard, top has semi-opaque adobe toner, nickel Waverly tuners.

List Price: $4,999.00   # Sold: 90   Protos: 4

D-35 ERNEST TUBB
Indian Rosewood with Brazilian rosewood center wedge on back, Italian spruce top with $^1/_4$" non-scalloped bracing, Style 45 rosette and backstrip, tortoise binding, rope pattern top border, Brazilian headplate with longhorn cattle skull inlay, Style 42 snowflakes on fretboard, State of Texas and Lone Star inlays. 1$^{11}/_{16}$" LP neck, tortoise pickguard, gold Waverly tuners.

List Price: $4,499.00   # Sold: 90   Protos: 4

D-50K KOA DELUXE
Same appointments as 2001 D-50 Deluxe First Edition described on page 149, but with highly figured (flamed) Hawaiian koa back, sides, and headplate.

List Price: $45,000.00   # Sold: 45   Protos: 2

D-50K2 KOA DELUXE
Same as above, but with highly figured koa top, number produced filled the total edition of 50.

List Price: $47,500.00   # Sold: 5   Protos: 0

OM-42 QUILTED MAPLE (SHOW SPECIAL)
Quilted Western Maple/bearclaw spruce with flamed cedar neck, Vintage Series Style 42 appointments but with LP neck, herringbone pearl backstrip, ebony headplate with alternate torch inlay, black pickguard with OM-45 Deluxe inlay, scroll inlay on bridge tips, fossil ivory nut and short saddle, gold Gotoh tuners with ebony buttons.

List Price: $6,999.00   # Sold: 30   Protos: 2

2004

FELIX THE CAT
See caption below.

List Price: $549.00
 # Sold: 756 **Protos:** 3

One of America's favorite cats made the FeLiX LX model an instant favorite. The cartoons are by Don Oriolo, son of Joe Oriolo, creator of the original *Felix the Cat* cartoons.

HD-40 TOM PETTY 6-STRING
Rosewood/Italian spruce Style 40 with Ivoroid binding, alternative torch inlay in ebony headplate, and moon and stars fretboard inlays.

List Price: $4,999.00 **# Sold:** 274 **Protos:** 4

HD12-40 TOM PETTY 12-STRING
12-string version of above.

List Price: $5,199.00 **# Sold:** 90 **Protos:** 4

OMC-28 LAURENCE JUBER
Rosewood/Adirondack cutaway OM with Style 28 GE Series appointments, otherwise like OMC-18VLJ of 2002.

List Price: $4,999.00 **# Sold:** 133 **Protos:** 4

OMC-28B LAURENCE JUBER
Brazilian rosewood version of above.

List Price: $9,999.00 **# Sold:** 50/capped **Protos:** 4

0-28 IAN ANDERSON "CHAMELEON"
Rosewood/Adirondack 12-fret 0, GE Series Style 28 appointments but with MOP triangles rosette, Waverly Sloane tuners, and convertible bridge saddle allowing use with either nylon or steel strings.

List Price: $5,499.00 **# Sold:** 07 **Protos:** 4

Ian Anderson of Jethro Tull opted for a modern version of an early 0-28. It can be converted from use with nylon (classical) strings to light-gauge steel strings, utilizing an innovative tri-angular saddle slot in the bridge, with two different saddles, ensuring accurate intonation with either type of guitar string.

Long known for using vintage Martin guitars, Norman Blake chose to create a vintage-like model that the company had never made for his Signature Edition. The 12-fret neck on a 14-fret 000 body puts the bridge lower on the soundboard, resulting in a sound that's different from either the original 12-fret models or the more modern 14-fret versions.

000-28 NORMAN BLAKE
Rosewood/Adirondack, 12-fret neck with slotted headstock on 14-fret 000 body shape, 00 size soundhole, 24.9" scale, 1 $^{13}/_{16}$" at nut, belly bridge with long drop-in saddle. GE Series Style 28 appointments, but no diamond at base of headstock.

List Price: $4,999.00 Special Ed./Open Protos: 4

000-28B NORMAN BLAKE
Same as above, but with Brazilian rosewood.

List Price: $9,999.00 # Sold: 52/capped Protos: 4

OM NIGHT DIVE
Brazilian rosewood/bearclaw spruce OM with elaborate pearl inlay scene on neck, based on original design by Grit Laskin. See photos in book 1, chapter 4.

**List Price: $19,999.00 13/20 combined maximum
Protos: 1**

D NIGHT DIVE
Dreadnought version of above, edition of 20 includes both D and OM versions.

List Price: $19,999.00 7/20 combined maximum Protos: 0

D-45 CELTIC KNOT (PRE-50)
Brazilian rosewood/Adirondack D with GE Series Style 45 appointments, plus Celtic knot inlay designs in fretboard and bridge tips.

List Price: $35,000.00 # Sold: 30 Protos: 0

Note: 50 serial numbers prior to #1,000,000 were reserved for the Celtic Knot Limited Edition.

2004 (cont.)

D-100 (POST-50)
A slightly less elaborate version of the Millionth Martin, inlays by Pearl Works from original designs by Larry Robinson. See book 1, chapter 4.

List Price: $10,000.00 # Sold: Pending/50 Protos: 0

Note: 50 serial numbers following #1,000,000 were reserved for the D-100 Limited Edition.

CONCEPT IV
Cutaway Jumbo version of 2003's Concept III, but with Fire Mist Blue metallic lacquer.

List Price: $3,999.00 # Sold: 15 Protos: 3

HD-40LSH TOM PAXTON
Rosewood/bearclaw spruce D with Style 40 appointments, plus oversized soundhole and stylized portrait of Paxton in MOP on ebony headplate.

List Price: $4,899.00 # Sold: 30 Protos: 4

OM-40 RORY BLOCK
Rosewood/Engelmann OM, Style 40 appointments but with Ivoroid binding, ebony headplate with MOP script Martin logo, road theme inlays on headstock and fretboard, hardened nickel silver frets.

List Price: $5,199.00 # Sold: 38 Protos: 4

000-ECHF (Eric Clapton / Hiroshi Fujiwara) BELLEZZA NERA
Rosewood/Italian spruce with gloss black finish on body and neck, 24.9" scale, herringbone top border and backstrip with soundhole rosette of MOP slotted squares. Silver-plated tuners, Style 45 snowflake fretboard inlays with alternative torch headstock inlay, "Bellezza Nera" script inlay at 20th fret, no pickguard.

List Price: $5,999.00 # Sold: 476 Protos: 4

TATTOO
X Series 000 model with old-fashioned tattoo designs on face and headstock.

List Price: $1,299.00 # Sold: 100 Protos: 2

OM-42QM2 (SHOW SPECIAL)
Quilted Western maple/Italian spruce (NAMM show special), appointments like the OM-42QM described on page 155, but with the following differences: "British tan" stain to maple, pyramid Stauffer-style bridge, tortoiseshell-pattern OM pickguard without inlay, ebony tuner buttons with "M" inlay.

List Price: $7,499.00 # Sold: 30/30 Protos: 2

2005

D-45 MIKE LONGWORTH
Rosewood/Adirondack, appointments like D-45 GE, but with boxed pearl bordering at endpiece, MOP Martin script logo on headplate above torch inlay, Style 45 snowflake fretboard inlays with "L" at 20th fret, fossilized ivory nut, saddle, bridge and end pins.

List Price: $13,999.00 # Sold: 91/91 Protos: 4

000-45S STEPHEN STILLS
Rosewood/Adirondack 12-fret 000, Golden Era Style 45 appointments with C. F. Martin block letters on slotted headstock, Style 45 snowflakes on fretboard, fossilized ivory nut, saddle, bridge and end pins, Waverly Sloane tuners, signature inlay at 20th fret.

List Price: $12,999.00 # Sold: 91/91 Protos: 4

000C STEVE MILLER
Mahogany (light quilting figure)/Engelmann, M&T neck joint, 24.9" scale, Ivoroid-bound body with fine-pattern herringbone, bound neck and headstock with alternative torch inlay, Style 45 rosette, no fretboard inlays, black pickguard, Fishman Ellipse Blend pickup system.

List Price: $4,499.00 # Sold: 383 Protos: 4

HD-7 ROGER MCGUINN
Rosewood/spruce Style 40 D with Ivoroid binding and herringbone top border, octave G string added for 7th string.

List Price: $5,499.00 Special Ed./Open Protos: 4

D FIGURED KOA
ANAHEIM SHOW SPECIAL
Figured koa/Adirondack with flamed cedar neck. Vintage Series Style 45 appointments but no pearl bordering on sides, 1/4" top bracing, Tree-of-Life fretboard inlays.

List Price: $14,999.00 # Sold: 25/25 Protos: 2

DC TREY ANASTASIO
Rosewood/Italian spruce with three-piece back, flamed koa in center wedge. Cutaway D with overall appointments like Style 40, but with M&T neck joint, black C. F. Martin letters on koa headstock, Wurlitzer Style 42 snowflakes on neck with signature at 20th fret.

List Price: $5,199.00 # Sold: 141 combined Protos: 4

DCE TREY ANASTASIO
Same as above, with Fishman onboard Ellipse Blend electronics.

List Price: $5,499.00 # Sold: 141 combined Protos: 0

M3M GEORGE MARTIN
Mahogany/Italian spruce M with three-piece back (figured mahogany center wedge), 1 3/4" neck. Style 40 appointments, but with Ivoroid binding, three-piece headplate (matching three-piece back), short Style 42 snowflake fretboard inlays, signature inlay at 20th fret.

List Price: $5,699.00 # Sold: 127 Protos: 4

George Martin chose an M model for his Signature Edition, a body shape that has long been favored by recording engineers. The "M" initial was skillfully worked into both the headstock and the three-piece back.

LIMITED PRODUCTION MARTIN GUITARS

2005 (cont.)

STING: MINI
Soloman padauk/Western Red Cedar Size 5 made with 77% sustainable woods. Katalox fretboard (1 3/4" at nut) and bridge, tortoise binding, herringbone top border with pearl rosette, signature at 18th fret.
List Price: $3,999.00   # Sold: 100/100   Protos: 4

CLAIRE'S GUITAR
Brazilian rosewood/spruce Size 5 with Style 41 top and soundhole bordered with Awabi pearl, Ivoroid binding on body only. Special headplate and fretboard inlays commemorate the September 13, 2004 birth of Claire Francis Martin.
List Price: $6,999.00   # Sold: 100/100   Protos: 3

D-18 AUTHENTIC 1937
Mahogany/Adirondack, D-18 Golden Era appointments, but a replica of a specific 1937 D-18 in the Martin Museum. Compared to a D-18GE, differences include: constructed with hot animal hide glue, steel T-bar neck reinforcement with old-style neck block, original shape (low and wide) third and fourth back braces, aged finish on vintage-style tuners with small oval buttons, celluloid pickguard.
List Price: $7,999.00   # Sold: ongoing   Protos: 1

OMC FINGERSTYLE 1
Spanish cedar/Adirondack with Spanish cedar neck, single ring pearl rosette, became a standard model.
List Price: $3,799.00   # Sold: ongoing   Protos: 3

OM-45 TASMANIAN BLACKWOOD
Flamed Tasmanian Blackwood/figured Engelmann spruce, Vintage Series appointments with 1/4" scalloped top bracing. Style 45 pearl bordering with MOP C. F. Martin script logo above torch inlay on headstock, fossil ivory bridge and end pins, engraved gold Waverly tuners. Carbon fiber Accord case.
List Price: $13,999.00   # Sold: 29   Protos: 1

CUSTOM SIGNATURE EDITIONS

Beginning in 2005, Martin began to issue Custom Signature Editions for specific artists, with signed and numbered labels. Unlike the regular Signature Edition models, Custom Signature Editions are built in the Custom Shop and do not have a specific cut-off date for ordering, or a specified edition total. The early models listed below had prototypes, though subsequent Custom Edition models typically are built in production lots of seven with no prototypes.

000C DAVID GRAY
Mahogany/Italian spruce 000 cutaway, M&T neck joint. Black binding and pickguard, herringbone top border, zig-zag backstrip, Style 18 rosette with blue paua center ring. 24.9" scale, 1 3/4" mahogany neck.
List Price: $3,799.00   Protos: 4

M3H CATHY FINK
Rosewood/Adirondack M (0000), three-piece back with flamed koa center wedge, M&T neck joint. Ivoroid binding, herringbone top border, Style 45 rosette and backstrips. Bound ebony headplate with torch inlay, short Style 42 snowflakes on 1 11/16" mahogany neck with two hands inlay at 12th fret, gold Schaller tuners with ebony buttons.
List Price: $4,399.00   Protos: 3

MC3H MARCY MARXER
Cutaway version of M3H described above.
List Price: $4,799.00   Protos: 3

2006

ARTS & CRAFTS
Flamed mahogany/bearclaw Sitka spruce D with ginko leaf neck inlays, herringbone rosette, leather-like pickguard, belly bridge with pyramid tips, and "bow tie" dovetails in center of back.
List Price: $5,799.00   # Sold: 100/100   Protos: 4

OMC-41 RICHIE SAMBURA
Madagascar rosewood/Italian spruce Style 41 OM with light tobacco sunburst, belly bridge with pyramid tips, modified hexagon fretboard inlays and special torch headstock inlay. 1 11/16" neck, gold enclosed tuners.
List Price: $6,999.00   Pending (200 combined)   Protos: 4

MC12-41 RICHIE SAMBURA
Cutaway M body 12-string to match model described above.
List Price: $7,199.00 Pending (200 combined) Protos: 4

000-ECHF (Eric Clapton / Hiroshi Fujiwara) BELLEZZA BIANCA
Western maple/Engelmann version of the Bellezza Nera from 2004 described above, but with opaque white finish instead of black.
List Price: $5,999.00 # Sold: 410 Protos: 4

000C-28 ANDY SUMMERS
Rosewood/Italian spruce 000 cutaway, black/white chevron checkered top binding, herringbone rosette, pyramid-tipped belly bridge, Buddhist-themed inlays on headstock and fretboard. Waverly tuners, 24.9" scale, 1³⁄₄" neck with signature at 20th fret.

Many Signature Editions have unique fretboard and headstock inlays with special significance to the artist, but Andy Summers, lead guitarist of Police, also requested checkered top binding composed of black and white chevrons. This type of binding was common on early Hawaiian-made instruments, but it was a first for a Martin guitar.

List Price: $5,999.00 # Sold: 87 Protos:

OM-45 ROY ROGERS
East Indian Rosewood/Adirondack reissue of original 1930 OM-45 Deluxe as described in chapter 2. Golden Era specs throughout, signature at 20th fret.
List Price: $14,999.00 # Sold: 84 Protos: 4

OM-45B ROY ROGERS
Brazilian rosewood version of the above.
List Price: $29,999.00 # Sold: 14 Protos: 4

FELIX II
Same size and materials as 2004 FeLiX model, but with different art.
List Price: $599.00 # Sold: 625 Protos: 10

POW/MIA
Mahogany/spruce D, M&T neck joint, finished in gloss black, honoring Barry Rinker, Marine Corps sergeant and Vietnam War veteran who died in 2002 after working 35 years at Martin's factory.
List Price: $5,699.00 # Sold: ongoing Protos: 4

OMJM JOHN MAYER
Rosewood/Engelmann OM with cedar neck, M&T neck joint. Style 45 rosette, herringbone top border, zig-zag backstrip, simple dot fretboard inlays. 1¹¹⁄₁₆" neck with signature at 20th fret.
List Price: $3,999.00 # Sold: ongoing Protos: 4

5-K UKULELE
Flamed koa reissue of 5K soprano uke described in chapter 5.
List Price: $5,199.00 # Sold: ongoing Protos: 4

D-42 FLAMED MAHOGANY
Figured mahogany/Adirondack, Vintage Series appointments. Style 42 pearl trim to top and soundhole, Vine of Harmonics fretboard inlay on 1³⁄₄" neck. Winter NAMM show special.
List Price: $9,999.00 # Sold: 30/30 Protos: 2

D-42 PETER FRAMPTON
Rosewood/Adirondack, Vintage Series appointments but with short Style 42 fretboard inlays, 1¹¹⁄₁₆" neck, gold Waverly tuners, ebony headplate with camel inlay, signature at 20th fret.
List Price: $7,799.00 # Sold: 76 Protos: 4

HD-35 NANCY WILSON
Rosewood/Engelmann, three-piece back with bubinga center wedge. HD-35 appointments but with Ivoroid binding and Style 45 rosette, ebony headplate with special inlay, signature at 20th fret.
List Price: $4,399.00 # Sold: 101 Protos: 4

2006 (cont.)

JC BUDDY GUY
Rosewood/spruce cutaway Jumbo with three-piece back, M&T neck joint. Ivoroid binding with muli-layered black/white purfling on all edges. Turquoise-colored polka-dot inlay theme on neck, bridge, and rosette, matching C. F. Martin letters on ebony headstock. 1 11/16" neck, Fishman electronics with tone and volume knobs mounted in top.

List Price: $6,399.00 **# Sold:** 36 **Protos:** 4

One doesn't usually associate polka dots with the blues, but Martin wisely gave blues legend Buddy Guy exactly what he wanted: lots of turquoise polka dots all over his cutaway Jumbo Signature Edition.

000-40S MARK KNOPFLER
Rosewood/Italian spruce 12-fret 000 with Vintage Series appointments. Herringbone top trim and backstrip, diamond-shape pearl inlay in rosette, short pattern Style 42 neck inlays, binding on neck and ebony headstock with MOP Martin script logo. 1 13/16" neck, signature at 20th fret. (Dubbed "Ragpicker's Dream" Model)

List Price: $6,999.00 **# Sold:** 155 **Protos:** 4

COWBOY V LITTLE MARTIN
Same as earlier Cowboy X Series models, but this time on LX body with Chris Martin and family on horseback at sunset.

List Price: $599.00 **# Sold:** 500 **Protos:** 4

M-42 DAVID BROMBERG
Rosewood/Italian spruce, appointments like Vintage Series Style 42 but with white-black-white stripes on fretboard (like on F-9 archtop), gold enclosed tuners, signature at 20th fret.

List Price: $6,999.00 **# Sold:** 83 **Protos:** 4

SW00DB MACHICHE
Sustainable woods machiche/spruce deep body 00 with cherry neck, wide wood rosette, half-herringbone top border, Ivoroid binding, copper-toned frets and tuners.

List Price: $2,999.00 **# Sold:** 125 **Protos:** 4

D-35 JOHNNY CASH
Rosewood/Engelmann, appointments and bracing like HD-35 with the following exceptions: gloss black finish, Ivoroid binding with bound headstock, Style 45 rosette, Grover Rotomatic tuners, small stars inlays on fretboard with signature at 20th fret.

List Price: $5,499.00 **# Sold:** ongoing **Protos:** 0

OM-42 FLAMED MAHOGANY
Summer NAMM show OM with same woods and appointments as D-42 issued earlier in the same year.

List Price: $9,999.00 **# Sold:** 30/30 **Protos:** 2

CUSTOM SIGNATURE EDITIONS

OMC-28M LAURENCE JUBER
Madagascar rosewood version of 2004 OMC-28 Laurence Juber.

List Price: $5,599.00 **Protos:** 0

00-18H GEOFF MULDAUR
Mahogany/Adirondack 12-fret 00 with Vintage Series Style 18 appointments, 1 13/16" short-scale neck (2 5/16" spacing at bridge), Waverly/Sloane tuners with Ivoroid knobs on slotted headstock with small Martin decal, dark 1935 sunburst top. Despite H model code suffix, not set up for Hawaiian (slide) playing.

List Price: $4,999.00 **Protos:** 0

HD ELLIOT EASTON
Mahogany (light quilting figure)/Adirondack with Vintage Series Style 28 appointments (specs nearly identical to HD-28V), but fine pattern herringbone rosette and top border, and gold Waverly tuners. HDE version includes Fishman Ellipse Aura electronics.

List Price: $4,899.00   Protos: 0

2007

DOOBIE-42 TOM JOHNSTON
Rosewood/Engelmann D-42 with Vintage Series appointments. Herringbone pattern pearl bordering on top and rosette, plus winged insignia on headstock and special inlays on 12th fret and bridge tips.

List Price: $8,499.00   # Sold: 35   Protos: 4

FELIX III
Tie-dye theme LX with Felix the Cat art by Don Oriolo, same materials as earlier FeLiX editions.

List Price: $649.00   # Sold: pending/1000   Protos: 5

CLAIRE 2
Maple/spruce size 5 with Awabi-pearl bordering and rosette, Style 45 snowflakes on fretboard and Alternate Torch (early Style 45) inlay on headplate.

List Price: $6,799.00   # Sold: pending/100   Protos: 4

DITSON DREADAUGHT III
Mahogany/Adirondack reissue of 1924 X-braced Ditson D (12-fret) with single-ring rosette and large cellulose nitrate pickguard (see chapter 6). GE Series appointments, including rosewood binding, pyramid bridge, $1^{7}/_{8}$" neck.

List Price: $6,499.00   # Sold: ongoing   Protos: 4

CSN GERRY TOLMAN TRIBUTE
Rosewood/Engelmann D-40 with Vintage Series appointments, plus Crosby, Stills, Nash, & Young logos on fretboard and headstock and pyramid-tipped belly bridge.

List Price: $4,999.00   # Sold: ongoing   Protos: 7

While it bears the familiar logos of David Crosby, Stephen Stills, and Graham Nash (plus Neil Young), the CSN Dreadnought was actually a tribute to Gerry Tolman, the manager of the group who worked tirelessly behind the scenes before his tragic death in a car accident on New Year's Eve, 2005. A portion of the proceeds from sales of this model went to a special fund for Tolman's two children.

2007 (cont.)

D-7 ROGER MCGUINN
Rosewood/spruce (cedar neck) M&T neck joint version of the 2005 HD-7. Single ring herringbone rosette and backstrip, Ivoroid binding on body, ebony bridge and fretboard with SP-16 Series snowflakes inlay pattern.

List Price: $2,999.00   # Sold: ongoing   Protos: 4

OMC ARTINGER I
Rosewood/spruce cutaway OM, designed in collaboration with luthier Matt Artinger. Koa binding, arm bevel on bass side lower bout, sound port in side, unique bridge design, tipped elliptical soundhole and 22-fret neck.

List Price: $4,499.00   # Sold: ongoing   Protos: 4

The collaboration between C. F. Martin and luthier Matt Artinger resulted in an OM with both visual and structural features normally found only on guitars by independent builders. Even if you didn't notice the arm bevel on the lower bout or the bass side "sound port," there's no mistaking the OMC Artinger for any other Martin model.

DAISY UKE
Flamed mahogany version of 5-K soprano uke. This is a copy of the uke in the Martin Museum, made circa 1940 for C. F. Martin III's wife, Daisy Allen Martin.

List Price: $5,449.00   # Sold: pending/100   Protos: 3

D-28 AUTHENTIC 2007 EDITION
Brazilian/Adirondack recreation of mid-1930s D-28. See 2005 D-18 Authentic for construction and appointments details; otherwise, like GE Series.

List Price: $39,999.00   # Sold: 50   Protos: 4

OMC RED BIRCH
Red Birch/spruce Sustainable Woods model with back center wedge and neck of cherry.

List Price: $2,999.00   # Sold: 175   Protos: 3

D-42 AMAZON ROSEWOOD
Amazon Rosewood/Adirondack Vintage Series D-42 with scroll inlay at base of fretboard and on bridge tips (not the same model as 2003 D-42 AR). Other appointments like D-42. NAMM show special.

List Price: $9,999.00   # Sold: 35/35   Protos: 2

OM NEGATIVE LIMITED EDITION
Rosewood/Engelmann OM version of 2002 HDN. (See description of that model for details.)

List Price: $5,599.00   # Sold: 60   Protos: 4

HDC-40 TRAVIS TRITT
Rosewood/Adirondack cutaway D with 000 depth body, Vintage Series appointments, Style 45 headplate, rosette and backstrip, herringbone top border, black pickguard with floral inlay, scroll inlay on bridge tips, Vine of Harmonics fretboard inlay with signature at 19th fret.

List Price: $8,999.00   # Sold: 40   Protos: 4

D-42 CAMBODIAN ROSEWOOD
Cambodian rosewood/Adirondack spruce, GE Series appointments, 1 3/4" neck with short Style 42 snowflakes, 2 5/16" spacing at bridge, gold vintage style tuners, otherwise like D-42. (NAMM Show Special)

List Price: $9,999.00   # Sold: 19   Protos: 2

000-X HIPPIE LIMITED EDITION
Summer of '67 hippie theme, art by Don Oriolo.

List Price: $1,249.00   # Sold: 200/200   Protos: 4

000-18 NORMAN BLAKE
Mahogany/Italian spruce Vintage Style 18 version of 2004 000-28 Norman Blake model, but with the following differences: solid headstock with Waverly tuners, pyramid bridge, cellulose nitrate tortoise pickguard.

List Price: $4,599.00   # Sold: ongoing   Protos: 4

0-45S STEPHEN STILLS
Madagascar/Adirondack 12-fret, Golden Era Series Style 45 appointments, C. F. Martin block letters on slotted headstock, 1 7/8" neck with Style 45 snowflake fretboard inlays and signature at 19th fret, pyramid bridge w/ 2 5/16" spacing, Waverly Sloan tuners.

List Price: $15,999.00   # Sold: pending/91   Protos: 4

00-21 KINGSTON TRIO
Rosewood/Italian spruce 12-fret, Vintage Series Style 21 details but with Style 28 rosette, checkered Style 28 backstrip, ebony belly bridge and fretboard with 1930s Style 21 inlays. 1 7/8" neck (2 3/8" spacing at bridge), Waverly Sloan tuners.

List Price: $6,299.00   # Sold: pending/100   Protos: 4

00-42K ROBBIE ROBERTSON
Flamed koa/Italian spruce 12-fret, Vintage Style 42 appointments plus torch inlay on Madagascar rosewood headplate, 1 13/16" neck, 2 5/16" spacing on pyramid bridge, 24.9" scale, Waverly Sloan tuners on slotted headstock.

List Price: $8,799.00   # Sold: pending/100   Protos: 4

00-42K2 ROBBIE ROBERTSON
Koa top version of the above.

List Price: $8,999.00   # Sold: pending/100   Protos: 4

Robbie Robertson, leader and songwriter of The Band, was happy to have his favorite Martin guitar, a unique 1919 00-45K, recreated for today's players. Along with the all-koa reissue of the original, a spruce top version was also offered.

CUSTOM SIGNATURE EDITIONS

OMC JACQUES STOTZEM
Rosewood/spruce cutaway OM with Vintage Series Style 18 appointments, plus additional black/white inlay lines on sides, headstock diamond, Style 35 backstrip, extra tall frets in blank fretboard, and a 1 11/16" neck.

List Price: $3,399.00   Protos: 0

000-18 KENNY SULTAN
Figured mahogany/Adirondack with Vintage Series appointments plus single-ring herringbone pearl rosette, cellulose nitrate tortoise pickguard, herringbone backstrip, C. F. Martin pearl script logo on headstock, short Style 28 diamonds-and-squares fretboard inlay, 1/4" top bracing, 1 3/4" neck, Waverly tuners. Dark sunburst with coloring confined to a more narrow band around the perimeter of the top.

List Price: $4,899.00   Protos: 0

CHAPTER 4
ARCHTOP AND ELECTRIC MARTIN MODELS

ACOUSTIC ARCHTOPS

Martin made a serious effort to join the archtop guitar revolution during that style's tremendous popularity in the 1930s, and the company had every reason to be looking for another instrument to bolster sales. The ukulele craze had virtually disappeared overnight, mandolin sales were drastically slowed, and the Great Depression had Frank Henry and C. F. III deeply worried about Martin's future. After a heady 15 years of tremendous growth, the father and son team was not about to lay off a majority of its 70-odd workers and wait for the good times to return.

But even without the influence of such economic forces, Martin had other reasons to reconsider building only flattop models: namely, pressure from its dealers to offer something for customers wanting the latest style in steel string guitars. Martin's new Orchestra Model, it seems, did not go far enough; longer, narrower necks were not all that was required. Today, we think of archtop guitars as having been popular with players of early versions of jazz or swing. In 1930, though, dark-faced archtop guitars were also being requested by guitarists of all kinds who simply wanted their next instrument to be in the modern style. Martin responded quickly to this new demand and wasn't too late to the archtop party, enjoying considerable success with its less expensive archtop styles. The later, more deluxe models, however, essentially flopped, and today Martin archtops are considered little more than a curious footnote in the company's history. (Martin returned to the archtop guitar market in 2004 in cooperation with Dale Unger, but these 17 inch "CF" models are in no way related to its 1930s archtop models.)

Unlike Gibson, which practically invented the archtop style, and Epiphone, which successfully fielded similar designs, Martin never put both feet into the archtop guitar arena, refusing to stray very far from its familiar flattop style. Martin carved the spruce top, but relied on only minor variations to the rest of its time-honored methods of constructing the back, sides, and neck. The back was arched with braces, rather than being carved, and the upper portion of the fretboard was still glued to the top. As a result, Martin's archtops were more like hybrid flattop guitars with a steeply pitched neck and a carved soundboard replacing the usual X-braced flat top. With only a few exceptions, the back and sides on all Martin archtops were mahogany or rosewood, not maple, which was the preferred wood for archtop bodies. This refusal to make a fully carved archtop model, with maple back and sides, is curious, because in 1929 Martin had introduced a fully carved maple and spruce mandolin, the Style 20.

The first Martin archtops were the C-1 and C-2, which were essentially an OM-18 and an OM-28 with carved tops and round soundholes. Ironically, both were first constructed in June 1931, less than a month after the first Martin-branded Dreadnoughts were begun. In early August of the same year, Martin made its first C-3 model, which had more binding and inlays on the neck. The extra time required to carve the top can be gauged by the price: the C-3 debuted at $200, while an OM-45 made the same year was priced at $180. The R Series came next, in 1933, and these were less expensive versions based on the 00-size mahogany body. Martin's deluxe archtop entries came in 1935, the larger-than-000 F Series. By this time, all Martin archtops had two *f*-scroll soundholes instead of the antiquated round soundhole design. Martin struggled to find the right formula with a flurry of new models, constantly tinkering with the tops, but sales continued to slide from acceptable to forgettable, despite putting archtop models front and center in the Martin catalog.

(opposite page) This 1938 window display in Dayton, Ohio, gave Martin's archtops top billing. There are three flattop guitars shown—one a Hawaiian model—but there's not a Dreadnought in sight.

Part of the problem was the size of Martin's archtops. Its F Series, the largest Martin model, was still only as large as Gibson's first L-5 models of a decade earlier. Gibson went on to build 17- and even 18-inch wide archtops by 1934. Epiphone did the same, leaving Martin's models sounding severely underpowered. This is part of the reason why Martin's best archtop sales were from 1932 to 1935, and why, by 1936, when rival companies where hitting their stride, Martin's sales hit the skids. After building 28 F-9 models for its debut in 1935, sales quickly sank to barely a half-dozen per year. Wartime restrictions on the use of brass and steel gave the company a good reason to cancel all archtop production shortly after the U.S. entered WWII, but Martin's archtops were already headed for cancellation anyway.

the same numbers. In summary, the C-1 and R-18 models have nearly identical appointments, while the C-3 and F-9 also share a similar list of features.

Although its archtops may not have been a success, they still had a lasting impact on the Martin guitar and helped usher in the more modern 14-fret style. Several Style 28 000 and Dreadnought models were special-ordered in the 1930s with the same neck binding and inlay found on archtop models like the C-3 and F-7, and other archtop models shared decorative elements with later flattop Martins. The black and white celluloid lines around the top of the C-2, for instance, became the top border of all Style 28 guitars in 1947, and the hexagon fretboard inlays of the F-7 and F-9 were Martin's first step away from the

Although its archtops may not have been a success, they still had a lasting impact on the Martin guitar.

The model designations for Martin archtops seem almost calculated to create confusion, making it difficult to compare similar models in different sizes. The C Series models are numbered in much the same fashion as Martin ukuleles: C-1, C-2, and the deluxe C-3. (A similar number code was used for bowl-back mandolins introduced in the 1890s.) The smaller and plainer R Series archtops have a two-digit style code identical to flattop guitar models with the same woods, binding, and decoration, making it easy to guess what an R-17 and R-18 look like. The F Series archtops were introduced with the F-7 and F-9 in 1935, but Martin added the plainer F-1 and F-2 in 1940, which closely matched the appointments of earlier C Series models given

old-fashioned "snowflake" inlay style and toward more modern designs. The same can be said of the vertical Martin letters on the headstock, which actually predate the now-familiar decal. The body outline of the F Series, of course, would later be used for the flattop M models introduced in the late 1970s, and a deeper version of that same shape became the Martin J-40 Jumbo a few years later.

Today, most guitarists feel that the early, round soundhole models, like the C-2, were Martin's best archtops. While they don't sound like a Gibson L-5, they have a powerful sound all their own.

Note: Some variation in tailpieces occurred on all Martin archtop guitars.

C SERIES GUITARS

Martin had high hopes for its new line of archtops, and wasted no time in announcing the C Series models with this small flyer.

STYLE C-1

Original factory photos of C-1 archtops showing the original round soundhole model and the *f*-hole version that followed.

1931 First made (#47365–70, 6/20/31).
1932 C-1 introduced in catalog.
   Carved spruce top with round soundhole. Mahogany neck, rosewood fretboard with Style 18 dots, plain elevated pickguard, nickel-plated metal parts. Dark mahogany finish, black Fiberloid bindings, back arched by braces, not carved. Solid headstock with individual tuning machines, trapeze tailpiece. Early examples had MARTIN inlaid vertically in the head, without C. and F.

[See page 53 for explanation of asterisks and parenthetical dates.]

1934 *f*-holes replace round soundhole*
   (first f-holes in late 1932).
   Ebony fingerboard replaces rosewood, headstock shown with C. F. Martin & Co. decal instead of pearl letters* *(1933).*
1935 Bindings listed as white Ivoroid.
1941 Last shown in catalog, last produced in 1943.

Model C-1 was also available in tenor and plectrum (4-string) versions. (See advertising flyer on page 169.) In 1932 Martin made three mando-cellos on the C-1 body, #51458–60. There was also one 12-string made in 1932, #50803, presumably with round soundhole.

170 MARTIN GUITARS: A TECHNICAL REFERENCE

STYLE C-2

(left) The C-2 was in production for 12 years. It was Martin's longest running and best-selling rosewood archtop by far. (This example is from 1932.)

(right) Although the *f*-scroll soundholes weren't mentioned in Martin's catalogs until later, the new soundholes appeared on C Series archtops barely a year after those models were first introduced. (1932 C-2, from the Martin Museum.)

1931 First made (see advertisement pictured on page 169).
1932 First cataloged.
      Same as C-1 described on page 170, but with the following differences: Rosewood sides and back, unbound neck with ebony fretboard and bridge, body bound in Ivoroid. Neck inlays and backstrip like Style 28 guitars, C. F. Martin pearl head veneer (usually pearloid letters).
1934 *f*-holes replace round soundhole* *(first made in 1932)*.
1935 Fingerboard and guard bound in white.
1939 Fingerboard inlay upgraded to hexagons like F-7 (pearloid).
1941 Last listed.

ARCHTOP AND ELECTRIC MARTIN MODELS **171**

STYLE C-2

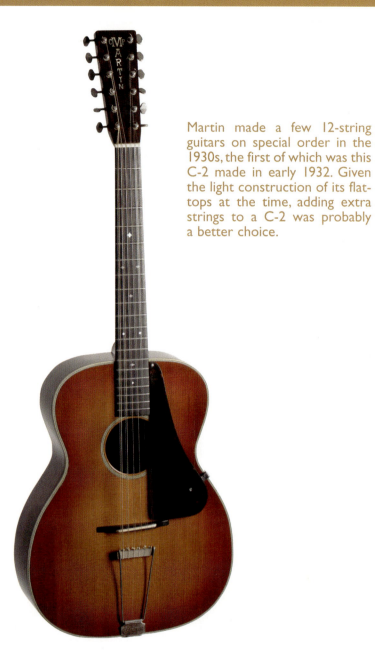

Martin made a few 12-string guitars on special order in the 1930s, the first of which was this C-2 made in early 1932. Given the light construction of its flat-tops at the time, adding extra strings to a C-2 was probably a better choice.

This same year Martin made two mando-cellos on the C-2 body, #50668 and #51151. The C-2 was also available in tenor and plectrum 4-string models.

STYLE C-3

(left) A 1932 C-3, the most expensive guitar in Martin's catalog at the time.

(right) A 1933 C-3 with f-scroll soundholes. The C-3 sold poorly and was discontinued the following year. (Original factory photo.)

The C-3 was also introduced in 1931 with a round soundhole prototype, #47839. This was a C-2, but with fancier trimmings and gold-plated parts. In 1932 Martin made a curly maple C-3 with maple neck, #51805. The first C-3 specified with f-hole top construction was #52833 in 1933. The C-3 was also available as a tenor guitar.

1932 C-3 introduced, same as C-2 but with the following differences: Gold tuners and tailpiece, pickguard inlaid at the edge with W/B/W lines, Ivoroid bound fretboard inlaid with style 45 snowflakes, multi-colored style 45 backstrip.
1934 f-holes replace round soundhole* *(1933)*.
1935 C-3 discontinued.

F SERIES ACOUSTIC GUITARS

All have a body 16 inches wide and 20 inches long, similar in shape to the 14-fret Martin 000 but about an inch wider, and with the same depth.

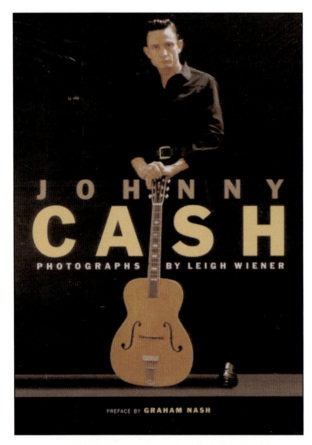

Johnny Cash, long a fan of Martin guitars, lends a rare touch of star power to an F Series archtop. But with its top refinished blond and no pickguard, the F-7 John is holding bears scant resemblance to the examples shown decades earlier in Martin's catalog.

STYLE F-2

An F-2 model from 1942, the last year of Martin's archtop production.

STYLE F-1

The F-1 had the same appointments as C-1 models of the same period, and was made only from 1940–42. In 1941, a single 12-string version #78016 was made.

The F-2, with features like the late versions of the C-2, was also made only from 1940–42. In 1941 a single example was made in maple, #78042.

STYLE F-5

STYLE F-7

(left) A 1940 F-5. Why Martin made only a few archtop guitars with maple back and sides is still a mystery.

(right) A 1937 F-7 from the Martin Museum. Original pickguard was bound, like the one shown at left.

This was essentially a blond maple version of the F-7, and only two were made, #74815–16.

The F-7 was first designed and produced in 1935.
One F-7S with a round soundhole was made, #65138.
All others had *f*-hole tops.
1935 Carved spruce top, rosewood sides and back, Ivoroid binding on body, neck, and pickguard. Ebony fingerboard with pearloid hexagon inlays at the 3rd, 5th, 7th, 9th, 12th, and 15th frets and inlaid white line $1/4"$ from edge. Bound head with C. F. Martin pearl veneer (usually pearloid letters), top shaded golden brown, chrome metal parts, Style 45 multi-colored backstrip.
1941 Last cataloged.

ARCHTOP AND ELECTRIC MARTIN MODELS **175**

STYLE F-9

1935 F-9 from the Martin Museum, shown with the 1935 catalog page introducing the highest arch-top model the company produced.

The F-9, a deluxe carved-top guitar with the same body as the F-7, was also introduced in 1935. The prototype was #58756. This was the most expensive guitar in Martin's catalog.

1935 The F-9 shared many features with the F-7, but with the following differences: gold tuners and tailpiece, additional pearl hexagon inlays at the 1st and 17th frets, plus white-black-white lines about 1/4" from edge of fretboard. Center backstrip has added black-white lines on each side, pickguard has double inlaid border. Additional binding lines on some edges, headstock with C. F. Martin letters in real pearl (not pearloid).

1941 Last cataloged.

R SERIES GUITARS

The Style R guitar was a less expensive 00-size archtop that debuted shortly after the introduction of the C models. The first one made was #52010, with the designation 00-18S. If all the 00-18S guitars made about the same time were archtops, we can assume a total of nine were made in 1932. The R-18 model code was used for the first set made in 1933. Early examples of the R-18 had round soundholes, but the tops were soon switched to *f*-holes. Samples of two other models show up in the records of 1934, the R-17, #58575–76, followed by Style R-15, #58652–53.

Of the two models regularly produced, the R-18 was more popular. At first, both the R-18 and the R-17 had arched tops, rather than carved tops. The tops were from the same flat stock used on the regular flattop guitars, but the soundboards were shaped in molds and fitted with arched bracing to approximate the appearance of the carved-top models.

As with flattop Style 18 and Style 17 models, the R-18 was given a spruce top while the R-17 had an all-mahogany body, with binding only on the top edge. The arched top of the R-18 was later changed to a carved top due to problems in molding the spruce, but the R-17's mahogany top was always pressed, not carved. The first carved-top R-18 was #63844. All pressed-top R Series guitars have three piece *f*-holes, instead of the more elegant one-piece *f*-holes found on carved models.

See book 1, page 89, for a photo of an unusual R model in Style 21 with wide neck and slotted headstock.

STYLE R-15

The R-15 never saw regular production. The samples 58652–53 in 1934 were the only two made, and the model never showed up in a catalog. The R-15 had a pressed (not carved) spruce top with shaded finish, with maple or birch sides and back, all shaded around outer edges.

STYLE R-17

1935 First cataloged and shown on price list. Same as R-18 except with mahogany top, less inlay and plainer trimmings.
1941 Last appearance in catalog and price list.

STYLE R-18

They weren't glamorous, but R-18 models like the 1933 and 1934 examples shown here far outsold Martin's 0 and 00 size flattops at the time.

1933 First made and priced.
1934 First appears in catalog: Dark mahogany finish, spruce top arched with shaded finish, black Fiberloid binding with black and white inlay around top. Rosewood fingerboard and adjustable bridge, plain elevated pickguard, nickel-plated hardware.

1937 Carved-top replaces pressed top.
1941 Last cataloged.

MARTIN ELECTRIC GUITARS

The Martin Guitar Company's first official electric guitar was a D-18E prototype in 1958. In 1959, that model entered production, along with the 00-18E and D-28E. All were regular flattop models with DeArmond pickups mounted in the top, with the pickguard cut out to accommodate the chrome mounting hardware surrounding the pickup. Both Dreadnought models saw their X-bracing sacrificed to ladder bracing to accommodate the second pickup near the bridge, while the single pickup 00-18E retained a conventional X-braced top. ("Ladder bracing" simply means horizontal braces similar to the braces on the guitar's back.) The D-18E was discontinued after 1959, with the other two E models continuing through 1964. Other models made on special order were 0-28E, 0-18TE, 000-28E, and D12-20E.

In 1961, Martin introduced a line of thin, hollow-body electric models with arched tops and backs. These *f*-hole models were made with laminated woods, in the shape of the F Style archtops of the 1930s, but with cutaways. The first regular archtop electrics were the F-50, F-55, and F-65. These were phased out of production in 1965 and replaced by two new designs, the GT-70 and GT-75, which were Martin's first guitars with an adjustable truss rod in the neck. The GT-70 was discontinued after 1966, and the GT-75 followed after 1967. Despite their rather outdated pickups (again by DeArmond), the F Series sold reasonably well at the time; over 500 of each of the three versions were built. The G Series, with their oversized and more stylish headstock, looked less like Martins; more than 500 of the double-cutaway GT-75 were sold in 1966. Though they probably wouldn't have enjoyed long-term success, the reason they were discontinued at the time was simply the rapidly growing demand for regular acoustic Martin models.

Earl Remaley inspecting F-50 and F-55 models circa 1964.

In 1975, Martin introduced an early version of what would later become the standard type of acoustic/electric flattop. This was the D-18D, a D-18 guitar with addition of a FRAP (Flat Response Audio Pickup) transducer on the underside of the top. One-hundred seventy-six guitars were made that year, with two additional instruments in style D-28D, before the style was discontinued.

With acoustic sales slowing, the company re-entered the electric guitar market in 1978 with the E Series solid-body line. Development took about a year, and production began in April 1979 with serial number 1000. (Martin's solid-body guitars got their own serial number sequence.) The models were the E-18 and EM-18 six-string guitars and the EB-18 electric bass. These were followed by the E-28 guitar and EB-28 bass, which featured carved tops and active circuitry. All solid-body models were discontinued in 1983. Despite up-to-date components, the solid-body models suffered from a confused identity, because rock guitarists didn't think of Martin as an electric guitar company.

Martin re-entered the flattop acoustic/electric guitar market in 1983 with an under-the-saddle pickup, and a succession of different pickup options have been offered ever since. For more details see page 46 in chapter 1.

FLATTOP ELECTRICS

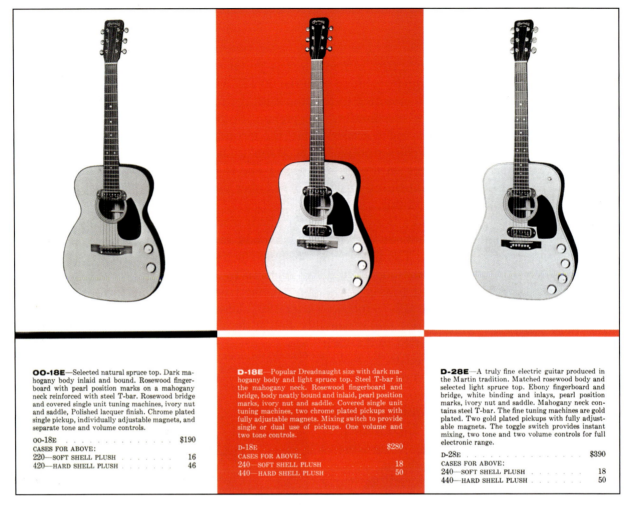

00-18E—Selected natural spruce top. Dark mahogany body inlaid and bound. Rosewood fingerboard with pearl position marks on a mahogany neck reinforced with steel T-bar. Rosewood bridge and covered single unit tuning machines, ivory nut and saddle, Polished lacquer finish. Chrome plated single pickup, individually adjustable magnets, and separate tone and volume controls.

00-18E	$190
CASES FOR ABOVE:	
220—SOFT SHELL PLUSH	16
420—HARD SHELL PLUSH	46

D-18E—Popular Dreadnaught size with dark mahogany body and light spruce top. Steel T-bar in the mahogany neck. Rosewood fingerboard and bridge, body neatly bound and inlaid, pearl position marks, ivory nut and saddle. Covered single unit tuning machines, two chrome plated pickups with fully adjustable magnets. Mixing switch to provide single or dual use of pickups. One volume and two tone controls.

D-18E	$280
CASES FOR ABOVE:	
240—SOFT SHELL PLUSH	18
440—HARD SHELL PLUSH	50

D-28E—A truly fine electric guitar produced in the Martin tradition. Matched rosewood body and selected light spruce top. Ebony fingerboard and bridge, white binding and inlays, pearl position marks, ivory nut and saddle. Mahogany neck contains steel T-bar. The fine tuning machines are gold plated. Two gold plated pickups with fully adjustable magnets. The toggle switch provides instant mixing, two tone and two volume controls for full electronic range.

D-28E	$390
CASES FOR ABOVE:	
240—SOFT SHELL PLUSH	18
440—HARD SHELL PLUSH	50

Today the sight of a D-18 or D-28 with magnetic pickups screwed into the soundboard sends shudders down the spine, but in 1959 it probably seemed like a logical way to enable a fan of Martin guitars to plug in and get loud. The cover of this 1959 mini-catalog is shown in book 1, page 100.

STYLE 00-18E

Style 00-18E was a regular 00-18 guitar with a single DeArmond pickup at the end of the fretboard, and with one tone control and one volume control mounted in the top along the lower bout (where they would have the greatest negative impact on the acoustic tone). It was first produced in 1959 and discontinued in 1964. Versions of the 00-18E with two pickups were also made around the same time.

STYLE D-18E

The D-18E was a regular D-18 with two pickups, a mixing switch, one volume control and two tone controls mounted in the top. Three-hundred-one were made in 1959, and they were never made again. Since they appeared in the catalog after that date, it is assumed that the initial production sold slowly. The D-18E's most visible moment came over 30 years later, when Kurt Cobain of Nirvana played a D-18E on a 1993 *MTV Unplugged* segment.

STYLE D-28E

The D-28E was a regular D-28 with two pickups installed. The pickups were the same as on D-18, but all hardware was gold, including gold Grover Rotomatic tuners. It was last made in 1964. See book 1, chapter 2, page 100 for a photo.

F AND GT SERIES ELECTRIC GUITARS

STYLE F-50

The F-50 was the least expensive of the F Series electrics introduced in 1962. Fifteen had been built in 1961. The prototypes were #179828–30.

1962 First shown in catalog and price list.
Single cutaway, two-inch deep body of laminated woods, adjustable single pickup, one volume control, one tone control, adjustable plexiglass bridge, shaded honey maple top. Last shown in 1965.

F-50 model and catalog page are shown on page 101 of book 1.

STYLE F-55 / STYLE F-65

(left) An F-55 from 1963.

(right) The F-65 (original factory photo from 1962).

The F-55 was a two-pickup version of the F-50. Fifteen were made in 1961; it was introduced in 1962 and last shown in 1965. The prototypes were 79831–33.

The F-65 had the same components as the F-55, but it was a double cutaway model. Like the others, it was first made in 1961. The prototypes were #179834–36. It was introduced in the 1962 catalog and price list, and last shown in the 1965 catalog.

The GT models featured more modern finishes, a spikey headstock, and a companion solid-state amp—with racing stripes—loud enough to annoy the neighbors.

STYLE GT-70

The GT-70 was first made in 1965. There were three prototypes. These were called XTE-70 #203803–05. GT models superseded the F Series electrics. The GT-70 is shown in the above ad, upper right corner.

1966 Introduced in catalog.
Single cutaway, adjustable truss rod in neck, two pickups, two volume, two tone controls, with selector switch. Burgundy or black finish with white pickguard.
1968 Dropped from line.

STYLE GT-75

(left) Original factory photo of GT-75-12, Martin's first electric 12-string model.

(right) Along with the more radical headstock design of the GT Series, one of the color options for the new electrics was an unMartin-like bright red, as seen on this 1967 GT-75 from the Martin Museum.

The GT-75 was identical to the GT-70, except that it was a double cutaway version. The first samples were called XTE-75, #204108–10.

Note: At least three GT-75 guitars were equipped with 12-string necks, #218391, 405, and 411.

MARTIN AMPS

Martin offered a limited line of amplifiers with both the F Series and GT Series electrics, ranging in size from the small portable #700 to the giant SS-140. (See page 101 in book 1 for a photo of an early Martin amp.) Most, if not all, were made by the Allen Organ Company in Macungie, Pennsylvania, a company that collaborated with Martin on the amp project.

E-SERIES ELECTRIC GUITARS

STYLE E-18

1979 Body of hard maple with rosewood or walnut laminates, mahogany neck with 25.4" scale 22-fret rosewood fingerboard, modified Viennese headstock with Sperzel tuners and brass nut. DiMarzio pickups, PAF in rhythm position, super distortion in treble position, two volume controls and two tone controls, passive circuitry, three-position selector switch plus phase switch. Leo Quan "Badass" bridge/tailpiece, weight 8½ lbs.

Martin's E Series electrics shown here were introduced in 1979 and were joined by carved-top mahogany models a year later. All were discontinued in 1983.

1979 Exactly like E-18 with following exceptions: Pickups are Mighty Mite or DiMarzio, three-position coil selector switch added.

EB-18, also introduced in 1979, was the bass version of the E-18, with one DiMarzio pickup, a 33.825" scale, and weighing 9 1/4 lbs.

| STYLE E-28 | STYLE EB-28 |

An E-28 6-string and EB-28 bass from 1980.

The E-28 and EB-28 were the second generation of C. F. Martin solid-body electrics, introduced in June 1980. Series 28 were lighter in weight and featured active electronics, mahogany bodies with carved tops, and neck-through-body construction. Both were discontinued in 1983.

E-28
1980 Mahogany body and neck, shaded finish, ebony finger board, 24 frets, 24.9" scale. Seymour Duncan pickups designed for C. F. Martin, active tone circuit with master bass and treble controls. Schaller bridge/tailpiece, Schaller tuners, weight 7¼ lbs.

EB-28 Electric Bass, also introduced in 1980, was the bass version of the E-28, with two DiMarzio pickups.

CF SERIES ARCHTOPS

(left) Chris Martin with Dale Unger in 2004, introducing the new CF Series archtop.

Martin returned to the archtop field in 2004 with the introduction of the CF Series. These were designed in collaboration with archtop guitar luthier Dale Unger, who had studied with archtop pioneer Bob Benedetto. The result is a line of modern archtop guitars available in two distinctly different models. Both models feature a 17-inch-wide cutaway body with three-ply Alpine spruce top, solid European flamed maple sides, and a laminated maple back with flamed European maple veneer. The necks are flamed maple, with 21-fret ebony fretboard of 25" scale (1¾" wide at the nut). The ebony bridge is adjustable, above a floating ebony tailpiece. Both the CF-1 and CF-2 are available in a natural, sunburst, or gloss black finish. The differences between the two models are as follows:

CF-1 3-inch deep body, X-braced top with single Kent Armstrong floating pickup and ebony finger rest with discreet volume pot attached.

CF-2 2½-inch deep body, parallel top bracing with two Seymour Duncan pickups mounted in the top, plus tone and volume controls with pickup selector switch. No finger rest (pickguard).

A CF1 (top) and CF2 (bottom), 2005.

CHAPTER 5
MANDOLINS, UKULELES, AND OTHER SMALL INSTRUMENTS

MARTIN MANDOLINS: YOUNG FRANK HENRY'S BOLD MOVE PAYS OFF

Martin's mandolins are given little notice today, partly because the company no longer makes them, but also because even the best Martin mandolins are not as highly favored by modern musicians as are the company's flattop guitars and ukuleles. But for almost three decades, beginning in the late 1890s, mandolins were a significant part of the company's success. Production totals from 1898 to 1916 suggest that before the Hawaiian music craze of the late 1910s and '20s finally swept the company into a period of dramatic growth, mandolins were as critical to Martin's survival as guitars.

It's hard for modern Americans to fully comprehend their country's mania for the mandolin a century ago. From an almost chance introduction to the instrument in 1880 by a touring group of musicians from Spain (who actually played bandurrias, not mandolins), the country quickly developed an unquenchable passion for tremoloed melodies on double strings. America's extensive population of Italian mandolinists was suddenly in demand, and soon people, from servants to railroad magnates, were playing the mandolin. This new musical fashion was just what the guitar needed. As accompaniment for the mandolin, the guitar came out of stuffy parlors, where it had been stuck for decades, and was swept into mainstream popularity at last.

Frank Henry Martin was a young man when the mandolin fad struck. Although he wasn't a musician, he couldn't help but notice the trend as mandolins trickled, and then streamed, into his company's shop for repair. The company he inherited upon his father's death in 1888 had been looking at only minor swells in an essentially flat line of sales totals for over 40 years. By the early 1890s, companies like Lyon & Healy of Chicago had gone from start-up to full-blown success by following America's musical trends, while Martin stuck with the guitar and went nowhere. Was building mandolins an opportunity to get back into the game?

The young F. H. Martin must have thought so, for he began taking extensive measurements and notes on the mandolins that Martin was repairing, and he also borrowed mandolins from friends and business contacts for further study. The Martin Company began building a line of Italian style (bowl-back) mandolins in 1895, the first instruments stamped as originating in Nazareth, PA. Martin mandolins were introduced in the company's first catalog the following year, and by 1899 Martin was selling two-thirds as many mandolins as guitars. That was an impressive start considering that Martin guitars already had a 60-year tradition and an established reputation throughout the country, whereas Martin mandolins were only in their fifth year. Judging by the number of instructors who began ordering high-grade examples of Martin's new instrument, Frank Henry's homework paid off.

By 1898, if not earlier, Martin was once again distributing its own guitars, rather than relying on C. A. Zoebisch in New York. The company's first complete catalog showed both guitars and mandolins. (The 1896 catalog showed only mandolins.) Such features as mahogany necks, serial numbers, and pearl fretboard inlays first appeared on Martin's mandolins, and the simpler mandolin styles were the first low-priced instruments Martin made in large batches. Martin's most successful mandolins were the flat-back style, introduced in 1914. Of these, the plain Style A, which shared similar appointments with Style 18 guitars, was by far the most successful. This simple mahogany model was quite popular until the 1930s, when mandolin sales plummeted for all manufacturers. It's hard to imagine today, but in the late 1910s and early 1920s Martin's Style A mandolin often outsold all its Style 18 guitar models combined! But the Style A was Martin's only real success in the later years of the mandolin era, for its mandolins with carved top and back, like its archtop guitars, never competed successfully with similar instruments from Gibson. The exception to this rule was the 2-15, with over 1300 sold in the ten years following its post-WW II revival.

Today Gibson-style mandolins rule the American mandolin market, while Martin's versions are not highly valued by players or collectors except as companions to the company's guitars. Despite being largely ignored by modern players, all Martin's mandolins are well-made instruments, and each of the three types has a pleasing sound of its own. More importantly, mandolins mark the Martin Company's first tentative step toward producing instruments aimed at America's changing musical tastes. The decision to build a new type of instrument was key to the company's survival in the early years of the 20th century. Mandolins paved the way for Martin's tremendous success with the ukulele, a move that changed the company forever.

BOWL-BACK MANDOLIN STYLES

In identifying Martin's bowl-back mandolins, it is important to connect the features with the date of manufacture indicated by the serial number. Each style became less fancy in the period after 1900, so the pickguard of an early Style 4, for instance, is considerably more ornate than the pickguard of a Style 6 from 15 years later. Some styles showed a different pickguard inlay in each successive catalog, and before 1910 other pickguard designs were used that were never shown in a catalog at all. Several different patterns of purfling were used around the top edge of the same style, again depending on the year. Features shared by all Martin bowl-back instruments: Spruce top with oval soundhole. Mahogany neck. Bent top, with a crease just behind the bridge. All have ebony fretboard and bridge unless otherwise specified.

Shown here are original tools and fixtures used to build Martin bowl-back mandolins. At left is an original mold used for holding the rosewood ribs after they had been steamed and bent. At right is a completed Style 6 or Style 7 rosewood "bowl" showing the fluted ribs with narrow strips of ivory between each rib. In the center is a fixture used for cutting the fret slots in mandolin fingerboards. From the Martin Museum.

STYLE G MANDOLINS

Little is known about the G Series mandolins. They were introduced in a small catalog issued about 1896 when F. H. Martin was making his first entry into the mandolin market. Sales records from this period have been lost, and since the surviving sales book begins in mid 1898, no other information is available except for the mandolin serial number chart shown in the appendix, page 296. Since the mandolins pictured in the 1898 catalog are quite different, and those instruments must have been built well in advance of when the catalog was issued, the total production of all Martin G Series mandolins with serial numbers was probably around 100 instruments. The 1896 catalog shows only four models: G-1, G-2, G-3, and G-5.

MARTIN MANDOLINS

THE manufacturers ask attention to some special points of excellence in the Martin Mandolin.

Only a few styles are here pictured, but the same principles are observed in all. The framework is built up by a system at once neater and more durable than any other in use; the tone is superior because of careful work on the sound-board, which is the life of the instrument; the neck and head are shaped to fit the hand for easy and rapid execution, and the strings are regulated with the same end in view. In the ornamentation artistic simplicity has been observed, and in brief, the methods which have made and kept the Martin Guitar without a peer, have been applied to the Martin Mandolin throughout.

Other and finer styles will be made to order. The prices quoted are net cash.

. . MANDOLINS . .

OUR MANDOLINS are meant to supply the demand for something better than the market now affords—something, in short, to go with Martin guitars. Several years of experiment and research have gone towards the work and we hope to show in the succeeding pages that the effort has been successful. The most critical examination is invited.

The model is a well tested one. No novelty is claimed for it, as we believe that by adding to the good qualities of standard Italian makes the finish for which our work is known, and the safety from warping which this climate affords, we gain a degree of perfection unknown before. The ornamentation is in a variety of styles to suit different tastes, but chaste in all and perfectly worked.

Only choice materials are used. Rosewood is taken for the body or shell except where otherwise ordered; it is true pretty effects may be obtained by using other woods alternately, as birdseye maple, but there is nothing quite so fine as well selected and properly matched rosewood; also our manner of polishing with only a thin coat serves to bring out the markings and never obscures, as is the case where colored varnish is used or a heavy coat laid on. All wood is matched on opposite sides, thus working out designs of unrivalled beauty which can be obtained in no other way. The face is finished white and the mahogany neck and head also in natural color, to admit of the rich shading which time brings. For guardplates we use tortoise shell and for bindings ivory. Celluloid is commonly taken and at much less expense but we cannot believe that it is acceptable to players and for ourselves we prefer to use only genuine articles. The machine heads are the best made and will not give constant trouble.

The tone of our mandolins has the quality so much sought after, mellow and ringing, with great clearness in the upper register. There is a richness in it which comes only from finish of interior work—a degree of refinement not even attempted by many and which finds its best expression here. Balance is obtained by proper bracing and careful graduation.

These, briefly stated, are our claims but over and above them is the painstaking accuracy which pervades every part of the work and gives it when finished a character of its own. The difficulties to be overcome when perfection is aimed at are many and various; haste is forbidden and the ratio of cost is increased; nevertheless there is resulting a sense of completeness which repays the effort and which, we are confident, will be a source of pleasure to the purchaser far beyond the price. We present our catalogue in the hope that, although it cannot reproduce the infinite care expended, it may receive more than a passing glance and lead to further examination.

The simple prose in the 1896 catalog (above) that introduced Martin mandolins gave way to a more competitive challenge two years later (right). Frank Henry's statement that "several years of experiment and research" had gone into the development of the company's mandolins was no idle sales pitch: his handwritten notes from this period show that he measured and tested dozens of bowl-back mandolins from both American and Italian makers, making notes about their construction and tone.

STYLE G-1

A G1 mandolin, circa 1895, from the Martin Museum. This instrument has no serial number, so it probably is from the first year's production.

STYLE G-5

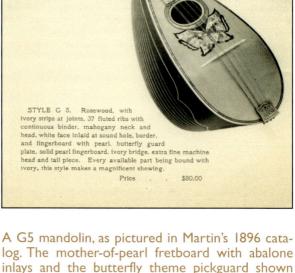

A G5 mandolin, as pictured in Martin's 1896 catalog. The mother-of-pearl fretboard with abalone inlays and the butterfly theme pickguard shown here are not unique to Martin, with both features appearing on other brands around the same time. Martin's mandolins from 1898 on were more uniquely their own.

STYLE 1

(left) A Style 1, as pictured in the 1898 catalog.

(right) Style 1 was not only Martin's longest-running bowl-back mandolin, it was also the only style ever made as a mando-cello (roughly the same dimensions as a full-size guitar). This one was made in 1909. From the Martin Museum.

This style lost most of its inlays by 1904 and became a very plain model, one step up from the Style 0. Style 1 was also offered as a mandola.

1898 First cataloged.
Rosewood bowl with 18 ribs, tortoiseshell guard inlaid with pearl, purfling around soundhole, German silver machines, engraved German silver tailpiece, cutout in top of headstock.

1901 Not priced or cataloged. 1904: No pickguard inlay, 20 ribs, pearl position dots. 1909: 22 ribs. 1917: Shown with pickguard on treble side.

1923 Last shown in catalog, last made in 1924.

| STYLE 2 | STYLE 3 |

(left) A Style 2 mandolin, as pictured in the 1898 catalog.

(right) A Style 3 mandolin, as pictured in the 1898 catalog.

1898 First cataloged.
Rosewood bowl with 26 ribs, inlaid tortoiseshell guard, German silver machines with pearl knobs, engraved tailpiece.
1901 Design of guard inlay changed, bound with rosewood, colored purfling on top and around soundhole. (Guard inlay changed again in 1904.)
1917 Shown with pickguard on treble side.
1918 Dropped from catalog, but some made as late as 1924.

1898 First cataloged.
26 rib rosewood bowl, ivory binding with fine colored purfling, soundhole border of pearl and ivory, inlaid tortoiseshell guard and German silver machines w/pearl knobs (fancier than Style 2), same tailpiece as Style 2.
1901 Guard inlay design changed, ivory tuning knobs.
1904 Black and white border, guard inlay design changed, fingerboard inlays similar to style 42 guitar.
1919 Dropped from catalog but some made as late as 1922.

| STYLE 4 | STYLE 5 |

(left) A Style 4 mandolin, as pictured in the 1898 catalog.

(right) A Style 5 mandolin, from 1901.

1898 First cataloged.
Rosewood bowl, 34 ribs, ivory-bound fretboard and body with pearl border on top. Soundhole border of pearl and ivory. Tortoise guard, richly inlaid, fine position ornaments in frets, 5, 7, 10, 12, and 15. Single plate German machine head, pearl knobs, engraved German silver tailpiece.
1901 Guard inlay changed, 30 ribs, ivory knobs.
1904 Guard inlay changed again.
1919 Dropped from catalog, but some made as late as 1921.

1898 First cataloged.
Rosewood bowl, 34 ribs, with pearl border on top and corded white pearl and tortoiseshell binding (alternating diagonal pieces of pearl and tortoiseshell, sometimes also referred to as "in the Italian style"). Soundhole inlay of pearl and ivory, #4 type guardplate, ebony fingerboard inlaid with vine, same machines and tailpiece as #4.
1901 Ivory knobs, catalog shows addition of head inlay. Last cataloged, guard inlay is plainer, "snowflake" inlays on fretboard similar to Style 45 guitar.
1920 Last made.

STYLE 6

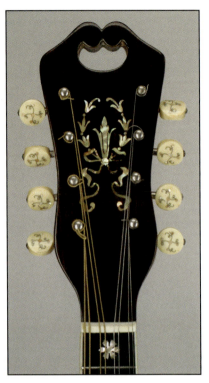

Except for the inlaid pickguard, this 1913 Style 6 exhibits the same decoration as the flat-back Style E mandolin first offered the following year.

1898 First cataloged.
Rosewood bowl, 42 ribs, fluted and joined with ivory. Ivory-bound body and fretboard, pearl border on top, extended around end of fretboard. Tortoise guardplate with extra fine inlaying, ivory bridge, ebony fretboard with inlaid vine, guardplate inlay to match. Extra fine German machines, German silver tailpiece.
1901 Catalog shows addition of headstock inlay, inlay around end of fretboard deleted.
1904 Inlay changed on head, fingerboard, and guard. Cap (the scalloped side border) bound with ivory.
1914 Photo in catalog shows fretboard inlays similar to Style 45 guitar.
1919 Dropped from catalog, last made in 1921.

STYLE 6A (NOT SHOWN)

This was a minor variation of Style 6 and was never cataloged. They were made primarily for Joseph A. Handley of Lowell, Massachusetts, who is known to have suggested moving the pickguard to the treble side instead of centering it beneath the strings.

STYLE 7

"Style 7 Special" mandolins, like this one from 1902, were the most elaborately inlaid instruments Martin produced in the 20th century, and highly decorated Style 42 guitars were also made that year. In recent times, even this high level of decoration has been surpassed by the D-100 guitars.

(left) Style 7 mandolins were the most ornate stock instruments the Martin Company produced until after the turn of the next century. Note the double row of pearl bordering around the soundhole and the perimeter of the top on this example from 1908.

Style 7 features the same fluted ribs and neck inlays as Style 6, but with a double row of pearl bordering around the top and soundhole, and pearl bordering around the cap (upper side) as well. Even more highly decorated versions with engraved pearl bordering were also made.

1904 First cataloged.
1914 Top border shown in standard width.
1917 Last cataloged and last made.

STYLE 0, 00, AND 000 MANDOLINS

All have solid headstocks without decorative cutout, rosewood bindings, nickel-plated tuners and tailpiece, and plain celluloid pickguards. Pickguards were changed around 1915 to the same shape as used on the earliest flat-back mandolins. Style 000 was the least expensive bowl-back mandolin Martin produced.

STYLE 00

A Style 00 mandolin, as pictured in the 1914 catalog.

1907 First made.
1909 First cataloged. Rosewood bowl, nine ribs.
1919 Not shown in catalog, but still in production.
1923 Model reinstated in catalog for this year only, with 14-rib mahogany bowl. Last made in 1925.

STYLE 0

1905 First made.
1908 First shown in price list, more expensive than 00 and 000.
1909 Rosewood bowl, 18 ribs.
1919 Not cataloged, but still in production.
1923 Catalog listing reinstated, last made in 1925.

STYLE 000

1909 First made.
1914 First cataloged. Natural finished mahogany bowl with nine ribs.

HARP MANDOLIN

This unusual harp mandolin was made in 1901 for C. H. Gaskins & Co. of Shamokin, Pennsylvania in accordance with Mr. Gaskin's U.S. patent dated December 1895. It predates Martin's simpler flat-back mandolin styles by almost 15 years. From the Martin Museum.

FLAT-BACK MANDOLIN STYLES

American mandolinists began to abandon the bowl-back style instruments around 1910. This probably suited Martin just fine, as the newly popular flat-back style was far easier to construct. Martin's flat-backs were introduced in 1914, with five models that roughly corresponded to the company's guitar styles. All shared the bent-top construction and soundboard bracing of the bowl-back style, but with the back and sides constructed like a guitar. This is the mandolin style that survived the longest at Martin, with the mahogany Style A still in production in the 1980s.

In 1915, Martin's flat-back mandolins were featured in a small catalog devoted to their introduction. The opening pages are shown in full in book 1, pages 56–57.

In the early 1980s, Martin made a very few flat-back mandolins in both rosewood and koa, but gave them different model designations than used previously. Style A-3 was a modern version of Style B (see page 201), while Style A-3K2 (later called AK2) was a modern version of the AK (see page 200).

STYLE A	STYLE AK
MARTIN MANDOLIN STYLE A PRICE.... $24.00	**MARTIN MANDOLIN** STYLE A KOA
MAHOGANY NATURAL COLOR NECK AND BODY. SPRUCE TOP, EBONY FINGERBOARD AND BRIDGE. BUILT FOR BALANCED TONE. A FIRST CLASS INSTRUMENT IN PLAIN FORM.	THIS IS EXCELLENT VALUE. THE BEAUTIFUL HAWAIIAN KOA SUITS WELL FOR NATURAL FINISH AND HAS REMARKABLE TONE QUALITY. THE DESIGN IS PLAIN, THE WORKMANSHIP FINE; DURABILITY, CORRECTNESS, AND BALANCE ARE BUILT IN AND WARRANTED. RETAIL PRICE $26.00 STOCK IT FOR CHRISTMAS TRADE. STYLE B KOA $36.00

Martin frequently advertised its Style A mandolin in the late 1910s and early 1920s. It was one of the most popular instruments in the catalog at that time.

1914 First made. Rosewood sides and back.
1915 First shown in catalog and price list.
1917 Mahogany sides and back, spruce top, rosewood binding on front only. Ebony bridge and fretboard with small position dots, nickel trimmings. Regular guard beside soundhole, squared headstock, similar to guitar, without cutout.
1919 Bound front and back with rosewood.
1935 Bound with Fiberloid (black).
1937 Shaded top on regular order.
1955 Rosewood fingerboard and bridge* *(late 1940s).* Dark plastic (tortoiseshell) bindings* *(late 1930s).*
1995 Available only on special order, all production ceased in 2000.

Style A and AA mandolas were made from 1915 to 1935.
AA was simply the early designation for the Style A mandola.

1920 First shown in catalog.
       Same as A, but with top, sides, and back of koa wood.
1935 Bound with Fiberloid (black).
1936 Last shown on price list, discontinued in 1937.
1980 Reintroduced in price list as A-3K2, but none were made with that designation.
1981 A-3K2 renamed AK2 in accordance with the current practice of using a 2 suffix to designate instruments having koa tops.

[See page 53 for explanation of asterisks and parenthetical dates.]

STYLE B

A 1931 Style B with optional dark top, now called sunburst.

1915 First shown in catalog (introduced in 1914). Shown with early pickguard variant, woods and all details of binding and trim like Style 21 guitar of same period. Headstock with decorative cutout (same as bowl-back models).
1917 Regular pickguard.
1946 Dropped from line.
1980 Reintroduced as A-3, but did not enter production with that designation.
1981 Renamed Style B. Very few made.

STYLE BK (NOT SHOWN)

Only a few Style BK mandolins were made: 51 in 1921 and 6 in 1925. These would have conformed to the same specifications as Style B, but with koa tops, sides, and backs.

Style B and BB mandolas were available from 1917 to 1939. BB was simply the early designation for the Style B mandola.

STYLE C

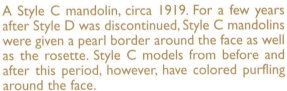

A Style C mandolin, circa 1919. For a few years after Style D was discontinued, Style C mandolins were given a pearl border around the face as well as the rosette. Style C models from before and after this period, however, have colored purfling around the face.

1915 First shown in catalog (introduced in 1914). Same woods as Style B, but with ivory binding on front and back. Top border of colored purfling, pearl rosette, fancy pearl position marks (similar to Style 42 guitar), tortoiseshell celluloid side guard, engraved German silver trimmings. Fancy headstock shape with decorative cutout, no inlay.

1917 Top border of abalone pearl. (This may have been changed because Style D had been dropped.)

1919 Celluloid (Ivoroid) bindings.

Note: Mandolins #8241–58 had pearl borders on at least some examples in 1920. By #9610–21 in 1921, Martin had returned to the border of colored marquetry.

1923 Soundhole still pearl-trimmed.
1925 Colored wood (purfling) in top and back* (1920), embossed tailpiece.
1934 Last made, the only C mandolin made this year was done in maple.

STYLE D

1915 First shown in catalog (introduced in 1914). Same woods as Style C, body and fingerboard ivory bound, fine position markers (similar to Style 45 guitar). Engraved German silver trimmings, abalone pearl border on top and rosette, fine purfling on sides, shown with same inlay on headstock as Style E.
1917 Last made.

STYLE E

A 1923 Style E, Martin's top mandolin model at the time.

1915 First shown in catalog (introduced in 1914). Rosewood sides and back, spruce top, ivory bridge, ebony fingerboard with fancy position marks (similar to Style 45 guitar). Body and neck ivory bound. Pearl borders of top, sides, back, and soundhole, German silver trimmings, inlaid knobs on tuning machines. Inlaid headstock (same inlay as late Style 6 bowl-back mandolin).

1917 Pickguard changed.
1923 First mention of celluloid trim* *(1918)*.
1937 Dropped from line.

CARVED-TOP MANDOLINS

STYLE 15

Surviving correspondence between the Martins and some of their mandolin retailers suggests that the company thought mandolin sales would pick up again once the ukulele craze began to fade in the late 1920s. This was a serious misreading of America's musical trends, and it meant that Martin invested much time and effort developing a line of carved-top mandolins after the mandolin craze had been in serious decline for nearly a decade. Instead of a rebound, mandolin sales continued to fade as the 1930s wore on. Martin's oval soundhole models, Styles 15 and 20, already out of date when introduced in 1929, were replaced in 1935 with *f*-soundhole models. These were given a numeral 2 prefix before the same Style number, so a Style 20 with *f*-holes was a 2-20. Except for a few special orders, only the comparatively plain Style 2-15 was revived after World War II.

These instruments were the only ones Martin ever made with a fully carved back. Though they arrived too late to enjoy the mandolin's glory years, they were still beautifully constructed and finished in the Martin tradition. Martin's carved mandolins were fashioned more like the carved mandolins of Lyon & Healy (Washburn) rather than like Gibson's models. Martin's carved mandolins do not have the volume needed for bluegrass music, but these instruments have a sweet tone that was popular with many highly regarded performers, most notably Carlos DeFelipis.

All have carved spruce top with carved maple back. The sides and neck are also maple. All have ebony fretboard and bridge and a lacquer finish.

An original factory photo, hand-colored, of the Style 15 mandolin at the time it was introduced.

1930 First shown in catalog (introduced in 1929). Natural color spruce top with oval soundhole, dark celluloid bindings. Elevated fingerrest (pickguard), nickel-plated hardware. Maple stained antique brown, neck joined to body at 10th fret, 13" scale, solid headstock without cutout.
1941 Last made, but still appeared on 1942 price list.

STYLE 20

STYLE 2-15

(left) A Style 20 mandolin from 1929.

(right) The Style 2-15 mandolin, circa 1948.

1929 First made, cataloged, and priced.
Same features as Style 15, with the addition of the following: Body bound with ivory-colored celluloid, with two symmetrical points, cutout in headstock, engraved tailpiece.
1930 Neck also bound.
1935 Shown with decal on headstock* *(circa 1933)*
1940 Last shown in catalog, last made in 1942.
1949–52 20S style made for students of Carlos DeFilipis.

STYLE 30 (NOT SHOWN)

There were only two mandolins made in Style 30 with oval soundholes. One was made in 1932, the other in 1941. See Style 2-30 for appointments.

1936 First made, cataloged, and priced. Same shape as Style 15, but with shaded top with f-holes. Back, sides, and neck stained golden brown, no cutout in headstock, white Ivoroid bindings, neck joins body at 12th fret, 13 3/4" scale.
Three prototype 2-15 mandolins were made, #15894–96, marked 15F.
1964 Last made, but still shown in 1965 catalog.

| STYLE 2-20 | STYLE 2-30 |

(left) Martin experimented, at least briefly, with a wide-body carved-top mandolin in 1936, as evidenced by this oversized 2-20. It looks like a mandola, but the string scale is the same as the 2-30 (Gibson also made wide-body A models around this same time.) From the Martin Museum.

(right) A 1940 2-30 mandolin from the Martin Museum.

1936	First made, cataloged, and priced. Same as Style 2-15 with the addition of the following: Headstock has cutout, "two-point" body same shape as Style 20, fretboard bound, engraved tailpiece.
1941	Last made, but shown in 1942 price list.
1949–1957	Some special 2-20S models made.

A 1940 Style 2-20 mandolin is shown in book 1, chapter 2, page 87.

1937	Introduced in catalog (first made in 1936). Same as 2-20 with the addition of the following: Finely bound and inlaid on all edges, including pickguard (extra black and white lines), fretboard has extended frets on treble side with diamonds-and-squares inlay, chrome fittings.
1942	Discontinued.

MARTIN MANDOLAS

Martin began making mandolas in the bowl-back style as early as 1900. Beginning in 1915, the flat-back mandolas began to appear in styles A and B. These were sometimes referred to as AA or BB styles. Production totals for mandola styles 1, 2, AA, and BB are given in the appendix. The last flat mandolas were made in 1941. To the best of our knowledge, no carved Martin mandolin styles were made as mandolas.

MANDO-CELLOS

The baritone voice in the mandolin family is the mando-cello. Martin never seemed to pursue this style, but a few were made. The first evidence of a Martin bowl model mando-cello was in 1909, when a total of four were made. (See photo at the beginning of this chapter.)

The mando-cello shows up in the records again in 1932. There were two made using C-2 archtop guitar bodies, called C-2 mando-cellos. The same year, three instruments called MC-1 models were made. These had C-1 guitar bodies and this model was cataloged from 1933 to 1940. However, only two more were made, in 1935. All of these C model mando-cellos are identical to regular carved-top guitars except they have a longer headstock and eight strings.

Original factory photo of an MC-1 mando-cello.

UKULELES: MARTIN'S UNLIKELY LITTLE HEROES

Among musicians as well as collectors, Martin ukuleles are given the same high marks as the company's flattop guitars. During the ukulele's heyday in the 1920s, Martin ukes were considered among the best—if not the best—available, and even today vintage Martin ukes are played by many of the instrument's top musicians. The company only recently began making ukuleles again, for the simple reason that so many were sold between 1916 and the mid-1960s that, with a few exceptions, most vintage Martin ukes sell for less than what the company has to charge for a new one.

Buster Keaton taking a break from filming by strumming his Style 3 Martin uke. Martin's archives contain a letter from one of Martin's dealers inquiring about a taropatch with Keaton's name on the neck, but we don't know if the order was filled.

The ukulele looms large in Martin's history, even if isn't a critical part of the company's current offerings. Despite its reputation as a company of guitarmakers, in the late 1910s the little ukulele was Martin's ticket out of the economic stagnation that had plagued it for decades. The uke was young Frank Henry Martin's most successful effort to keep his company relevant to the new century in America.

Perhaps buoyed by his company's moderate success with mandolins, F. H. Martin first decided to try building ukuleles in late 1907, when the instrument was still rarely seen in the continental United States. The first attempts were not successful, because the instruments were too heavy for the light tension of gut strings and typical ukulele tuning. Frank Henry must have realized that making miniature Martin guitars with spruce tops and lots of internal bracing was not the formula for good sounding ukuleles, and the project was dropped.

A few years later, however, the Hawaiian craze was sweeping the country. *Bird of Paradise*, the first Hawaiian Broadway show, had stunned New York in 1912 with exotic scenery, dazzling costumes, and the authentic music of five Hawaiian musicians. The show went on the road throughout the U.S. and Canada, playing to packed houses everywhere. An even bigger boost came from the opposite coast, where the Hawaiian Pavilion at the 1915 Pan-Pacific Exposition in San Francisco staged Hawaiian music shows several times a day, drawing the highest attendance of the exposition and lots of favorable press. Soon Hawaiian bands were criss-crossing the continent and images of palm trees and surf-swept beaches appeared on everything from napkins and lemonade glasses to carpets and sofa cushions. America sought refuge from the news of a depressing war in Europe with the bright, bubbling sound of an instrument almost anyone could play—the ukulele.

Martin had ample opportunity to inspect genuine Hawaiian ukuleles in the early 1910s, and the company's second attempt at building a ukulele was far more successful. In late 1915, Martin built a few ukes using thinner woods, an all-mahogany body (including top), and a minimum of very light bracing. The result was a good-sounding ukulele, and before the summer of 1916 the orders were pouring in. The first Martin ukes of this period were serially numbered, with the first number recorded on January 15, 1916. Martin must have decided that numbering ukuleles was too much effort, because starting in mid-July of the same year the numbers were dropped. (For a photo of serial number 105, see book 1, chapter 2, page 61).

The first Martin ukuleles were offered in Styles 1, 2, and 3, along with larger, 8-stringed taro-patch versions. Koa models followed in 1920, and these are the Martin ukes most sought after by collectors today, especially the higher models. At the time, the most popular were the plain mahogany models like the Style 1, which had a minimum of binding and decoration. In 1925 Martin added the Concert model, which had the taro-patch body and scale but only four strings.

The ukulele brought a little extra publicity to the Martin Company in 1926. Richard Konter, a volunteer member of Commander Byrd's historic first flight over the North Pole, smuggled his Martin 1K uke aboard the plane. After the landing, Konter and other members of the expedition signed the instrument. He later gave the first musical instrument to cross the North Pole back to its makers, and the Konter uke became the first ukulele in the small collection of instruments that later grew to become the Martin Museum.

(above) Richard Konter at the White House, strumming the Martin uke he carried with him on the first flight over the North Pole on May 9, 1926.

(left) The Konter uke, now in the Martin Museum, was later signed by members of Commander Byrd's expedition and the Ammunson expedition that followed it. Signers include Calvin Coolidge, Thomas A. Edison, and Charles Lindburgh, as well as many senators, congressmen, and dignitaries of the day.

MANDOLINS, UKULELES, AND OTHER SMALL INSTRUMENTS

Martin's greatest success with ukuleles was the Style 0, introduced in 1922. This was even simpler than the Style 1, a mahogany soprano model without any binding, offered for a mere $10. This model allowed Martin to compete more effectively with the cheaper mail-order ukes offered by companies like Sears and Montgomery Ward. Of all the Martin instruments that turn up in the corner of an attic or the top shelf of a closet, an overwhelming majority are Style 0 ukes. There wasn't much profit in a $10 ukulele, but it kept Martin's uke line in stores and catalogs that wouldn't have bothered if all Martin had offered was higher-priced instruments. A decade later, the company repeated this success with the Style 17 guitars during the Great Depression.

By the time the 1927 catalog appeared, Martin's stable of ukes reached its zenith, with nine ukuleles, six taro-patches, and three tiples. The only other significant uke models to appear were the tenor (1-T) that debuted in 1928, and the baritone model introduced in 1960. Demand for ukuleles overshadowed guitar sales in the approximately 15 years of the initial uke craze. The main building of the North Street factory had been doubled in size around the time the Hawaiian fad began, and growing uke sales then prompted Martin to add a whole new wing in 1925. Production peaked in 1926 when Martin made over 14,000 ukuleles in that year alone, allowing the funding of a second story to the new wing of the factory in 1927. Uke sales slowed in 1928 to less than a third of what they'd been earlier, before plummeting as the Depression deepened in the early 1930s. Part of the initial decline in sales in 1928 may have been due to the untimely death in 1927 of Herbert Keller Martin, C. F. III's younger brother, who had readily taken to the role of traveling salesman for the family business.

Although the ukulele had allowed capital improvements and cash reserves, the company's preoccupation with meeting the demand for ukuleles had left them little time for anything else. Martin's files contain numerous requests made in the mid-1920s for larger guitars or other special orders, all politely turned down with the explanation that the company was too back-ordered to take on new projects. Although Martin guitars were gradually being made stronger to withstand the tension of steel strings, the company made no other efforts to modernize its by-now-ancient designs during the uke-rush of the mid-1920s.

The ukulele had another run of popularity in the years following WWII. In 1950 almost 12,000 were sold, making that year second only to 1926 in ukulele sales. Even with such a strong showing, Martin did not revive the koa models. As demand for Martin guitars grew in the 1950s, resulting in long delays for musicians who wanted the increasingly popular Dreadnoughts, the company still fielded an extensive uke line that showed impressive sales totals hovering around 4,500 annually. The baritone model, which sold well in the 1960s, served almost the same role as the tenor guitar, but with easier-to-play nylon strings. But as folk music soared, Hawaiian music soured, and by the late 1960s Martin ukuleles were no longer pulling their own weight.

C. F. III kept Martin's ukuleles in production despite low demand, because he remembered what the little instrument had done for the company. Frederick knew that the updated factory and secure financial footing, which allowed Martin to survive the Depression, had not come from building its now-famous steel-string guitars, but instead from the phenomenal sales of Martin ukuleles between 1916 and 1930.

Until late 2005, Martin ukuleles were represented only by all-mahogany S-O models built in the Navojoa, Mexico facility where the Backpacker guitars are made. But in a repeat from almost 40 years earlier—when rising prices and increased demand prompted Martin to bring back the D-45 guitar—the 5K ukulele was revived and made its official debut, or we should say, reappearance, in January 2006. Despite the price tag, strong sales of a fancy made-in-Nazareth uke resulted in the announcement of a limited edition of 100 figured mahogany "Daisy Ukulele" models in 2007. (The original from the Martin Museum is shown in book 1, chapter 3, page 158.) Other models, including Style 3, were introduced in January 2008.

DESCRIPTIONS OF UKULELE STYLES

Note: Because some models were unchanged for decades, dating Martin ukuleles is not an exact science. Peghead decals first appeared between 1932 and '34, and the Martin stamp on the back of the headstock disappeared in 1935. Bar stock frets were replaced by "T" frets shortly after the headstock stamp was deleted. Some dealers apparently ordered ukes with friction pegs long after Martin had begun using patent pegs on stock models, so combinations of earlier and later features are not unusual. The "Made in U.S.A." stamp appeared on the inside center strip of the back, just under the regular Martin stamp, around 1963. Unlike Martin guitars, there isn't much difference in value between the plainer 1920s mahogany ukes and the same model made 30 years later, nor is there much difference in their tone.

STYLE 0 | STYLE 1

(left) Martin's Style 0 was the company's best-selling ukulele by a huge margin—from shortly after it was introduced to dealers with this postcard in 1922, right up until it was relegated to special-order status 60 years later. This Style 0 dates from circa 1950.

(right) A 1K model with wooden friction pegs from the early 1920s.

1923 First shown in catalog (first made in 1922). Plain mahogany, natural finish, with no body binding, hardwood fingerboard, hardwood friction pegs, small position dots.
1927 Rosewood fingerboard* *(1922)* ebony nut and bridge saddle, nickel patent pegs.
1982 Still shown in catalog.
1984 Available only on special order but still pictured in catalogs.
1993 Dropped from catalog, a few still made on special order.
2000 Production ceases in Nazareth.

1917 Introduced in special ukulele mini-catalog (first made in 1916).
1919 First shown in main catalog (appears in main price list in 1918), Mahogany body, front bound with rosewood, small position dots.
1920 Koa model, 1K, introduced.
1923 Dark finish specified on mahogany models. Wood friction pegs* *(1918)*, Koa version cataloged.
1927 Rosewood fingerboard* *(1918)*, patent pegs.
1942 Last listing of 1K.
1965 Last cataloged and priced.

The exact period when celluloid bindings replaced wood bindings was not recorded, but was probably circa 1932. First the binding was black, then became tortoiseshell color around 1935.

STYLE 2

Throughout the 1920s, Martin continued to issue small catalogs showing only its ukes.

- 1917 Introduced in special ukulele mini-catalog (first made in 1916).
- 1919 First shown in main catalog (appears in main price list in 1918).
  Same as Style 1 but with ivory celluloid binding on front and back.
- 1920 Koa model, 2K, introduced.
- 1923 Dark finish specified on mahogany models, patent pegs, koa version cataloged.
- 1933 Last listing of 2K.
- 1965 Last priced and cataloged.

212 MARTIN GUITARS: A TECHNICAL REFERENCE

| STYLE 3 | STYLE 3K |

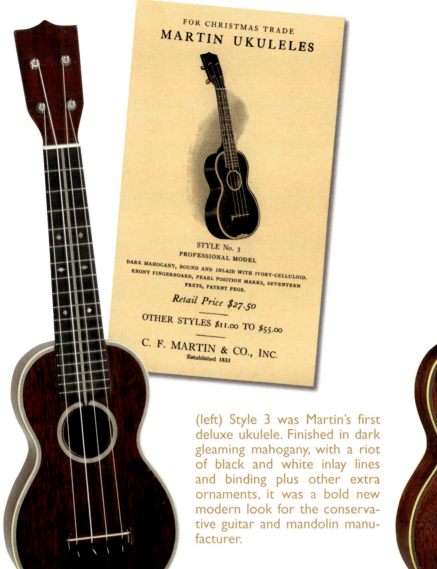

(left) Style 3 was Martin's first deluxe ukulele. Finished in dark gleaming mahogany, with a riot of black and white inlay lines and binding plus other extra ornaments, it was a bold new modern look for the conservative guitar and mandolin manufacturer.

(right) A 3K soprano uke, circa 1934, from the Martin Museum.

1917 Introduced in special ukulele mini-catalog (first made in 1916).

1919 First shown in main catalog (appears in main price list in 1918).
Same as Style 2 with the following additions: Body binding has extra black and white lines, ebony fretboard with diamond position marks with celluloid lines running down center of fretboard. Celluloid ornament at base of top, and four-point celluloid ornament on headstock. 17-fret fingerboard, friction pegs.

1920 Koa model, 3K, introduced, mahogany Style 3 still offered. Appointments on both models are identical.

2008 3 ukulele reintroduced.
3 cherry ukulele reintroduced.

1923 Patent pegs, headstock ornament dropped, koa version cataloged. 7th-fret inlays no longer join at center of fretboard.

1948 Last listing of 3K version.
Slotted diamonds on fretboard changed to dots circa 1945. Celluloid ornament at base of soundboard disappears in late 1940s, dates not documented.

1982 Still shown in catalog.

1984 Available only on special order but still pictured in catalog.

1993 Dropped from catalog, all production ceased in 2000.

2008 3K ukuleles reintroduced.

STYLE 5

(left) Although only the 5K soprano was shown in the catalogs and price lists, Martin made a number of concert-size koa ukes in Style 5, and even a few tenor models like the one shown here (circa 1930).

(right) The 5K uke returned to Martin's line of deluxe instruments in 2006.

1922 5K priced.
1923 Style 5K described:
Figured koa body, ivory celluloid binding on body and ebony fretboard. Koa bridge, patent pegs, koa head veneer with pearl inlaid scroll, pearl soundhole ring. Pearl trimmed top and back, elaborate position markers on fretboard.
1925 Pearl on sides of 5K, in addition to top and back.
1927 Pearl on sides dropped from specs.
1940 Last pricing for 5K.
1941 Curly mahogany Style 5 uke listed.
1942 Mahogany Style 5 uke dropped.
2006 5K ukulele reintroduced.

TARO-PATCH (NOW USUALLY SPELLED "TAROPATCH")

Shortly after Martin made its first ukuleles, the taro-patch was added to the line. This instrument had eight strings arranged in four pairs, and used gut strings like the uke. In early Martin advertisements they were called "taro-patch fiddles." The first Martin taro-patches were sold in August 1916, but they didn't appear in the price lists until 1918.

The taro-patch body was larger and the scale was longer than the standard ukulele, but the strings were still tuned like a soprano uke. While offering greater volume, the taro-patch was harder to play than a uke, much harder to keep in tune, and proved to be much less popular. No accurate production figures are available, but based on the number that appear today, taro-patch sales represented a very small percentage of Martin's ukulele production.

Around 1925, Martin had brought out the concert uke, which was the same size as the taro-patch, but with four strings. This was simply making an official model out of what had been an option, as in earlier catalogs Martin had suggested that customers could order a taro-patch with only four strings. The concert model proved to be far more popular than the taro-patch, which was finally discontinued after 1931.

A Style 1 taro-patch from the 1920s. Although Style 2 and 3 versions were offered, an overwhelming percentage of the taro-patches sold were Style 1.

1918 First priced in styles 1, 2, and 3.
1919 First shown in main catalog.
      Larger than regular ukulele, regularly made with eight strings, four strings on special order (later to become concert uke).
1923 Available also in koa wood styles 1K, 2K, and 3K, 4-string variation not listed (renamed concert uke).
1929 Last pricing of Style 3K.
1930 Available only in Styles 1 and 2K.
1931 Last prices for Styles 1 and 2K.
1932 Taro-patch dropped from Martin line.

CONCERT UKULELE

STYLE 1-C

TENOR UKULELE

STYLE 1-T

(left) An original factory photo from the 1920s, showing the 1-C concert uke.

(right) The 1-T tenor uke on the left is from the 1930s, while the one on the right, with a longer neck, is from the 1950s.

1924 First cataloged and priced.
Taro-patch body and scale, narrow neck for 4 strings, materials and trimmings like Style 1 ukulele.
1965 Last priced and cataloged.

1929 First shown in catalog (appears in 1928 price list). Mahogany body and neck, rosewood fingerboard and pin bridge. White position dots and side dots, ebony nut, ivory saddle, rosewood-bound, inlaid with black and white wood. Nickel-plated patent pegs with black buttons.
1936 Binding has changed to tortoiseshell celluloid.
1982 Still shown in catalog.
1984 Available only on special order but still pictured in catalog.
1993 Dropped from catalog. All production ceases in 2000.

Note: At some point not recorded, the 12-fret neck was changed to a neck with 14 frets clear of the body. Apparently this change was made in the 1940s, but the catalog illustrations were not changed until the early 1960s. When the binding changed from rosewood to celluloid was also not recorded, but probably took place before 1935.

BARITONE UKULELE

STYLE 51

Martin's catalogs in the 1970s and '80s showed the Style 0 and Style 3 soprano ukes, plus the 1-T tenor and Style 51 baritone.

1960 First priced and cataloged.
Same materials and trim as 1-T tenor, but in a larger size. 14-fret neck, 20" scale, strings tuned D, G, B, E.
1984 Available only on special order, but still pictured in catalog.
1991 Dropped from catalog. All production ceases in 2000.

MARTIN TIPLES

HISTORY OF THE MARTIN TIPLE
FROM AN ARTICLE BY C. F. MARTIN, III, 1972

The Martin Tiple was designed about 1920 from a somewhat larger prototype imported from Argentina by Mr. William J. Smith of William J. Smith Music Co., New York City. As a folk instrument in Argentina (tiple is a Spanish word meaning "small guitar") it was strung with ten gut strings, tuned to guitar pitch. Mr. Smith suggested the use of steel strings, and we used our obsolete quarter-size guitar patterns, smaller than the Argentine instrument, with ten steel strings tuned to ukulele pitch A, D, F♯, B. The first and fourth strings are double, like a mandolin, while the second and third are triple with the center string tuned an octave below the outer strings in each group. The firsts are tuned in unison. A felt or plastic pick is used for strumming like a ukulele.

Note: Although Martin tiples were considered part of the company's ukulele family, they were given guitar serial numbers, possibly because the body was an old quarter-size guitar pattern.

STYLE T-15

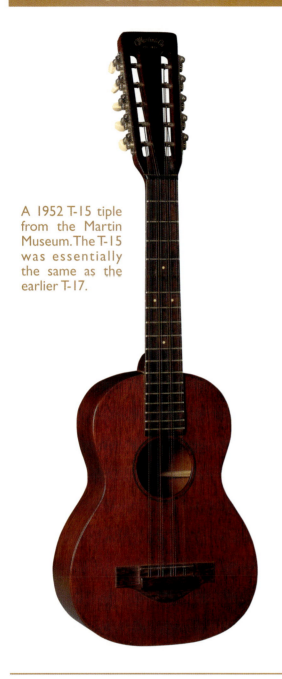

A 1952 T-15 tiple from the Martin Museum. The T-15 was essentially the same as the earlier T-17.

STYLE T-17

1949 First shown on price list.
(No new additions to catalogs from 1942 to 1955.)
1956 First cataloged.
Mahogany body, including top, no binding, natural finish. Rosewood fingerboard and bridge, white position marks and side dots. Ring of white and black lines around soundhole. Mahogany neck, nickel machines, Ivoroid buttons.
1966 Shown on June 1966 price list, omitted from September 1966 price list.

1926 First priced.
1927 First cataloged. Same specs as T-15, but finish has deeper luster.
1946 Omitted from price list.
1949 Priced for the last time. Dropped in favor of T-15.

| STYLE T-18 | STYLE T-28 |

Tiples—shown here alongside the trusty A mandolin—continued to hold their own in Martin's catalogs, even in the 1970s,. The changes to binding and inlay on T-18 and T-28 tiples always followed the changes to Martin Style 18 and Style 28 guitars.

1923 First cataloged and priced. Materials same as used on Style 18 guitar, rosewood bindings.
1956 Still listed as rosewood bound* (but binding switched to tortoiseshell celluloid 20 years earlier).
1984 Available only on special order, but still pictured in catalog.
1993 Dropped from catalog. All production ceases in 2000.

For a photo of a 1920s T-18, see page 188.

1925 First shown in catalog, first made in 1924. Materials same as Style 28 guitars. Features change simultaneously with Style 28 guitar.
1984 Available only on special order, but still pictured in catalog.
1993 Dropped from catalog. All production ceases in 2000.

MARTIN BANJOS

Martin made a brief effort to break into the tenor banjo market in the early 1920s, but demand for its ukuleles was so great that the company didn't put much effort into the project. Martin's banjo, pictured on page 72 in book 1, was a typical 17-fret tenor with maple neck and rim, constructed much like the Weymann banjos built in nearby Philadelphia. All metal parts were from A. D. Grover of New York—which some years later became Grover Musical Products in Cleveland, Ohio—and provided Martin with a wide range of tuners for its guitars.

According to the sales records in Martin's archives, only 96 banjos were sold, all between March 1923 and July 1926. The tenor banjo was evolving very rapidly at this time, and heavier and more advanced tenor models from companies like Paramount, Bacon & Day, and Vega far exceeded the tone and volume of Martin's lightweight model. Martin's tenor banjo appeared only in the 1924 price list.

Martin returned to the banjo market in 1970 when it purchased Vega of Boston. This venture is described in book 1, chapter 3, with Martin-made Vega banjo models pictured on page 120. More details on the production numbers of Martin-made Vega models can be found on page 271 of the appendix.

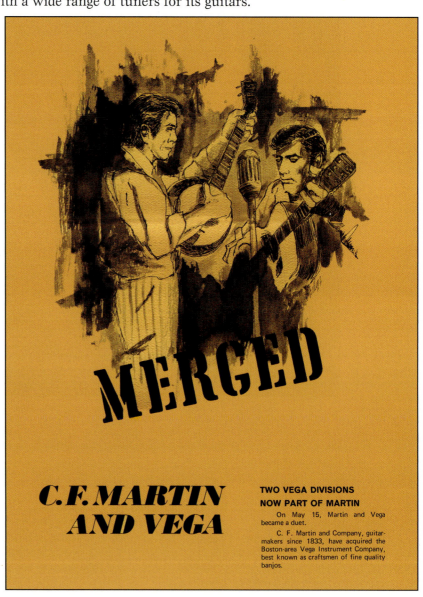

CHAPTER 6
INSTRUMENTS MADE BY MARTIN FOR OTHER FIRMS

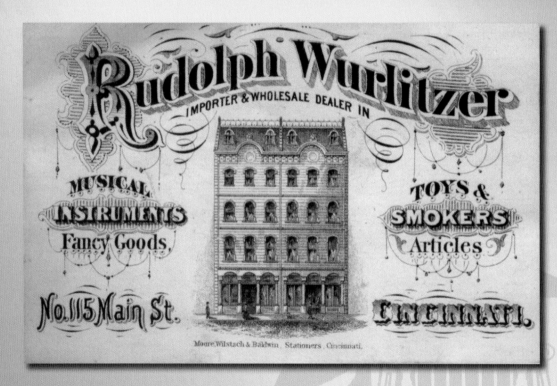

A NEW WAY TO SELL MORE INSTRUMENTS

Selling instruments labeled with the name of a retailer or distributor, rather than with markings indicating who actually made the instrument, is part of a long tradition in American stringed-instrument manufacturing. James Ashborn, one of Martin's competitors in the 1850s, rarely put his own name on the thousands of guitars his small Connecticut company made for major New York wholesale and retail outlets. Years later, the Larson Brothers of Chicago, contemporaries of Frank Henry Martin, built high-quality guitars and mandolins for a number of different firms, usually with no label indicating where they were made or who made them. During the same time period, the big instrument building factories of Chicago, especially Regal, produced dozens of guitar and mandolin models, some of very high quality, with labels and brands that gave no hint of the instruments' actual source.

Despite a number of early partnerships that had ended by the 1850s, there is no indication that C. F. Martin Sr. ever subscribed to this practice, and instruments made by Martin, but sold by partners C. Bruno, John Coupa, and others, were still clearly marked with Martin's name. Even after these partnerships ended, Martin sometimes agreed to build instruments with special features for certain accounts, but such guitars still carried the Martin brand. This practice is part of the reason that the Martin name and reputation were so well known, while other builders often were forgotten once their primary distributor went out of business or switched to another manufacturer.

Frank Henry must have felt that this long-standing "we stamp our name on everything we make" rule was hampering business, though, because in 1915 he began an ambitious campaign to build custom-brand instruments for a number of the big accounts that had been buying regular Martin models for many years. The obvious reason for this uncharacteristic way of selling Martin instruments was that Frank Henry was desperate to increase his factory's production since, despite his best efforts, Martin sales hadn't increased much in years. In fact, 1915, the year Martin embarked on the custom-branding venture on a large scale, was one of the lowest periods in the company's annual guitar production since 1850, with barely 150 guitars sold.

Another reason for the new policy on branding was Martin's venture into building steel-string guitars, especially steel-string models intended for Hawaiian-style playing. There was considerable animosity among proponents of the long-established conventional style of guitar playing—which was essentially classical style (fingerstyle) played on gut strings—toward the new fad for playing guitar

with a metal slide, or "steel," while holding the guitar flat on the lap. This may account for Martin's willingness to build hundreds of guitars for Ditson and for Southern California Music, marketed by those firms for Hawaiian-style playing, which had no markings indicating they were made by Martin. Once Frank Henry had more confidence in the Hawaiian-music trend, and the Martin Company had such models in its own catalog, the Martin brand, in its usual interior location, again appears in virtually all "custom brand" instruments, including those for Ditson and Southern California Music. The Martin stamp on the back of the headstock, however, often was still replaced by that of the company for whom the instrument was made. These markings were applied at the Martin factory, and many of the steel stamps have survived.

This Ditson ad from March of 1917 indicates that store's commitment to instruments for playing Hawaiian music. The higher priced ukuleles and steel guitars were undoubtedly those made by Martin but sold with the Ditson brand.

The importance of this brief flurry of custom branding to Martin's evolution into a successful business, rather than just a small workshop that made excellent guitars, has been largely overlooked. Ditson and Southern California Music, in particular, were responsible for many changes that allowed Frank Henry's small company finally to emerge as a modern, 20th-century American instrument manufacturer. The earliest production guitars for steel strings were made for Ditson and Southern California Music, and the Ditson stores sold a majority of Martin's uke production in the first years after they were introduced. The first use of koa for guitars was for Southern California Music, which also aided Martin in procuring the wood from Hawaii. Introduction of the deluxe 5K uke was prompted by Ditson's Harry Hunt, and it was Hunt's insistence on an extra-large Ditson Hawaiian guitar that resulted in the Dreadnought, the model that later made Martin's reputation. Other custom brand accounts, such as Wurlitzer, were the first to order large numbers of more typical Martin models strung with steel strings.

Custom branding allowed Martin to dramatically increase its share of the guitar, mandolin, and ukulele market, because it allowed Frank Henry to sell to stores competing in the same city. He could sell Wurlitzer brand guitars to the E. U. Wurlitzer store in Boston, for instance, and sell Martins with the Ditson brand to the Oliver Ditson store in the same city. In the past, Martin often had to choose one retailer in a given market and grant them an exclusive on selling Martin instruments in that territory. As cities like New York and Los Angeles grew much larger, and as Martin's list of instruments became more diverse, such exclusive selling arrangements had seriously hampered Martin's sales in an increasingly complex market.

The effects of Martin's venture into building instruments for Hawaiian music styles, often with custom brands, were immediate. In less than five years, its guitar production had jumped to over 1,000 instruments annually, over a fourth of which were sold as Hawaiian guitars, and the company sold three times as many ukuleles as it did guitars. Martin mandolin sales also increased, but not as dramatically. Although what is widely regarded as Martin's "Golden Era" of steel-string guitar design did not begin for several more years, it is clear that the leap into building steel-string guitars for Hawaiian-style playing was an important intermediate step for a company that had focused on gut-string guitars for nearly a century. It would have been impossible for Martin to make the transition from building gut-strung guitar models to building the OM-28, for instance, if it hadn't first learned about steel-string guitar construction by making Hawaiian guitar models, and then applied that knowledge as it slowly adapted its earlier designs to the different playing styles, and added tension, that came with steel strings.

Initially, Frank Henry entered into these custom brand contracts partly because they allowed him to increase production by building instruments that long-established, and often stodgy, Martin retailers probably didn't want. More importantly, the custom brand contracts guaranteed the sale of such instruments, at least at the wholesale level, so Martin would not be stuck with unsold inventory as it sometimes had been in the past. These special models with other names on them allowed Martin to grow very rapidly, but prices it received for many such instruments were often significantly below the wholesale price of an equivalent Martin-brand model. As demand for Martin ukuleles and steel-string Martin-brand guitars grew in the 1920s, custom brand contracts became a lower priority. It simply didn't make sense to keep dealers waiting for Martin guitars and ukes while filling orders for equivalent instruments, and at lower prices, that had another name stamped on the back of the headstock.

For the most part, Martin's change of heart about branding lasted less than a decade, and most instruments made in Nazareth after the mid-1920s have some markings indicating their source, even if another brand name is present. Regular Martin serial numbers were apparently stamped in all guitars and tiples, regardless of brand, by 1923. (Since ukuleles were not given serial numbers, it is more difficult to track changes in Martin's policy regarding those instruments.) Despite the hard times that Martin suffered during the Great Depression, with a few rare exceptions the company did not return to building instruments to be marketed under other names. Martin did build slight variations of its standard models for specific accounts, however, giving these instruments a model code outside

Although most of Martin's custom brand business was for large distributors or music store chains, it also made special models for a few specific stores such as Rudick's of Akron, Ohio.

the usual Martin system. The 00-55 model in the Martin Museum—made for Rudick's, a music store in Akron, Ohio—is such an example. Since this guitar was made after the introduction of model codes stamped on the neckblock, its model identity isn't questionable, as with similar special runs of instruments made earlier.

A LIST OF ALL KNOWN COMPANIES

Some of the instruments made for the companies or individuals listed below were marked as made by Martin, while others were not. This list of special-brand customers is complete as far as Martin's written records are concerned, and it is doubtful that the company made instruments under any names other than those listed here. Readers should remember that many of these companies and instructors also had instruments made for them by other manufacturers. Attributing a Bacon or Stetson guitar to Martin, for instance, is usually an error, because an overwhelming majority of the guitars with these brands were not made by Martin. Although Martin often made minor changes in the outward appearance of instruments made to be sold under other names, the interior construction remained the same. The characteristic neck and end blocks, linings, and braces make it easy to identify an instrument made in Nazareth.

The earliest instruments made for Ditson and Southern California Music Company were given a separate series of serial numbers, but this was soon abandoned, and later versions of the same models used regular Martin numbers. A few of the earliest guitars made for Wurlitzer and others did not contain serial numbers. To make it even more confusing, most of the companies for whom Martin made special models also ordered and sold regular Martin-brand instruments during the same period. This means there is a high probability for error in any estimates of how many special brand instruments were actually sold. There are also detailed descriptions in Martin's records for special models that apparently never went into production. Since most of this activity was in the 1920s, before Martin stamped the model code on the neckblock, some firms simply gave a standard Martin model a different name or number in their own catalogs. The original stampings used at Martin for the names or brands below are shown when available. The stamps for some brands may have been lost, but some of the firms below may have opted for applying their own paper labels instead.

BACON

A few guitars without Martin stamps were made for the Bacon Banjo Company in Groton, Connecticut about 1924. Bacon had guitars made for them by other manufacturers as well.

BELLTONE

Perlburg and Halpin, a wholesale firm in New York City, used the Belltone trademark. Martin made only a few instruments under this name, 15 guitars, 10 mandolins, and 12 ukuleles in Style 3K.

VAHDAH OLCOTT-BICKFORD

This famous concert artist, composer, and teacher was the primary founder of the American Guitar Society, actively promoting the use of guitar in musical ensembles. She had a close relationship, primarily through correspondence, with C. F. Martin III, who was only nine years her junior. The young Martin's preference for simple but elegant guitar decorations, rather than fancy pearl inlay, probably was the result of her influence. Vahdah Olcott-Bickford was the Martin Company's last and most active link to the classical guitar community.

Beginning in 1913 Vahdah had a few guitars specially made by Martin, both for herself and for her pupils. Most were sold through Ditson's retail store. They were known as Style 44 "Soloist" models, but there was also a model #450 Ditson. Style 44, which Mike Longworth described as "severely plain" despite its high price, never appeared in a Martin catalog or price list. See book 1, page 50–51, for more on Vahdah Olcott-Bickford, and Style 44 in chapter 2 of this volume for more details. Production numbers for the different sizes made in Style 44 can be found in the production charts.

Vahdah Olcott-Bickford was an important endorser of Martin guitars, but her Style 44 "Soloist" models never sold in significant numbers. Only about three dozen were made in all, in four sizes.

BITTING SPECIAL

Both mandolins and guitars were made for Mr. Bitting, a well-known teacher in Bethlehem, Pennsylvania, which is just a few miles from Nazareth. (See details on page 233.)

BRIGGS SPECIAL

A slight variation on Martin's flat-back A Style mandolin was made for Briggs Music in Utica, New York. (See details on page 234.)

INSTRUMENTS MADE BY MARTIN FOR OTHER FIRMS

BRUNO

C. F. Martin Sr. had a short partnership with Charles Bruno from May 1, 1838 to November 29 of the same year. (Bruno apparently had worked for Martin earlier as an accountant.) At least some of the guitars made during this period had paper labels reading "C. F. Martin & Bruno." Later guitars marked "C. Bruno" were not made by Martin, for by that time Martin's New York distributor, C. A. Zoebisch, was C. Bruno's competitor.

CABLE PIANO COMPANY

There is a stamp in Martin's archives that reads "Made Especially for Cable Piano Co." Cable Piano Company was a large music retailer in Atlanta, Georgia. Cable carried Martin guitars, and the initial order for the first 14-fret model, made for then-Cable salesman Perry Bechtel, was through the Atlanta store. That guitar model, first called a "000-28 Special," later became the OM-28. Since the original prototype has never surfaced, we don't know if the stamp was used in that instrument. The stamp was later employed for at least one Hawaiian guitar model, but it was not significantly different from the regular Martin style. The Cable store burned in 1935.

CHICAGO MUSICAL INSTRUMENT COMPANY

Chicago Musical Instrument Company was a prominent Windy City retailer that sold the first Dreadnought models Martin made after the Ditson stores had closed. Frank Henry may have been considering having CMI replace Ditson as the sole distributor of the Dreadnoughts, because the stamp inside the first non-Ditson Dreadnoughts reads, "Dreadnaught Model made exclusively for Chicago Musical Instrument Co. by C. F. Martin & Co." All D models recorded as D-1 or D-2 apparently were sold through CMI. Martin then must have had a change of heart, for the Dreadnoughts were given regular style numbers of 18 or 28 and were also made available to other dealers. CMI went on to become a music industry powerhouse and later owned the Gibson Company.

OLIVER DITSON

Ditson had stores in Boston and New York City. This was one of Martin's most extensive and influential accounts, and Frank Henry Martin had a long and involved history with Ditson, until it closed in 1930. Martin made many instruments for Ditson including guitars, bowl and flat mandolins, ukes, tiples, and taro-patches. (See details on pages 234–240.)

228 MARTIN GUITARS: A TECHNICAL REFERENCE

CARL FISCHER

This New York City wholesaler and music publishing firm ordered the first 14-fret Size 0 tenor models in early 1929. These guitars, first called the "Carl Fischer Model" in Martin's records, became the 0-18T. There is no indication that these instruments had special labels or markings.

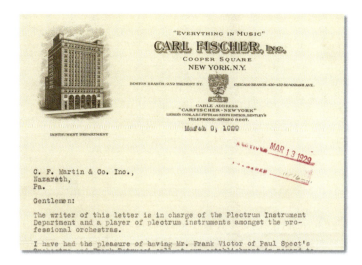

WILLIAM FODEN

Mr. Foden was a well-known concert guitarist and instructor, and one of Martin's foremost endorsers during the period from 1900–1920. He had his own series of Martin guitars, known as Foden Specials, which were sold primarily to his pupils. (See details on page 241.)

GRINNELL BROTHERS

This Detroit music store chain had Martin make "Wolverine" brand guitars, mandolins, and ukuleles for them. These instruments had regular Martin serial numbers. Along with the stamp shown to the right was one that read simply, "Wolverine."

MADE ESPECIALLY FOR GRINNELL BROS. AT NAZARETH PA.

J. A. HANDLEY

Mr. Handley was a mandolin teacher in Lowell, Massachusetts, around 1900. Details are not available, but we do know the treble-side pickguard was his idea. The 6a mandolins made for him were probably Martin's #6 with pickguard on the treble side, instead of centered beneath the strings.

JENKINS

Jenkins was a Kansas City, Missouri retailer. They purchased Martin Style #1 and #2 ukes, and used their numbers #35 and #40, respectively.

KEALAKAI

Major Kealakai was a famous Hawaiian musician and bandleader. The name "Kealakai" shows up as a guitar model on Martin spec sheets from 1917 and again from 1923. Although the dimensions given are the same as for a Ditson Dreadnought, the listing is with standard Martin models rather than with instruments made for Ditson. A paper template found among old records at the factory, and labeled "Kealakai," is also slightly different than the shape of a Ditson Dreadnought. (It is essentially an enlarged 12-fret 000 shape.) Serial #12210 was an "extra large 17" model made for Major Kealakai in March 1916, and another extra large Style 17 without serial number was made in June 1917. There was also a large and ornate Kealakai bridge shape that was quite unlike any standard Martin bridge. Factory foreman John Deichman used this same bridge design for an all-mahogany Dreadnought that he made for his own use in 1917.

The unique oversized bridge design for Kealakai models was designed to reduce the excessive bulging of the soundboard as a result of the high tension from heavy-gauge steel strings. Martin installed such a bridge on at least one older standard guitar model in 1916, as shown here, apparently to correct damage to the top from Hawaiian stringing. (Photo from Martin archives.)

MONTGOMERY WARD

About 1932, Montgomery Ward sold several different styles of instruments made by Martin—guitars, flat mandolins, and ukes—all made of mahogany. No sales figures are available, and the arrangement evidently lasted only a short while. Montgomery Ward had an overwhelming majority of its instruments made by the much larger, and cheaper, instrument factories in Chicago.

PARAMOUNT

The famous New York City banjo firm, headed by William Lange, ordered a few special resonator guitars with their head inlay and name. (See details on page 243.)

ROLANDO

See Southern California Music Company, pages 245–247.

RUDICK'S

In 1934–35, this Akron, Ohio firm ordered several 00-17 guitars (14-fret versions), requesting that the number 00-55 be stamped in them. Martin records show only about two dozen with the 00-55 stamp, but more may have been produced. The model in the Martin Museum has rosette and binding like Style 18, but with mahogany top. All were given regular Martin serial numbers.

A 00-55 (1935) made for Rudick's of Akron, Ohio, from the Martin Museum.

SCHOENBERG

In 1986, C. F. Martin entered into an agreement with Eric Schoenberg to produce a line of Schoenberg guitar models, although Schoenberg luthiers Dana Bourgeois and T. J. Thompson performed certain key stages of construction. (See details on page 244.) Almost identical Schoenberg guitars made after 1994, however, were not constructed at Martin.

H & A SELMER, INC.

The Selmer stamp has survived, but records regarding specific models made for them are incomplete. Mike Longworth's notes indicate that some 2-17 models and T-18 tiples were made for Selmer in 1923. Selmer had a large retail showroom in New York City at the time.

WILLIAM J. SMITH

William J. Smith was another New York City music publishing company and retailer that featured Martin-made ukes, taro-patches, and tiples in its line, starting around 1917. Smith apparently was responsible for Martin making tiples, and for a short time had an exclusive claim on that instrument.

The Kamiki paper label was added by the William J. Smith firm, but their Kamiki tiples also had the "Wm. J. Smith & Co." die stamp on the back of the headstock, which was done at the Martin factory.

SOUTHERN CALIFORNIA MUSIC COMPANY

From roughly 1917–1920, Martin made a line of all-koa Hawaiian guitars for this retail chain. The earliest versions, starting in 1917, had paper labels and a headstock decal indicating they were made by "M. Nunes," but later versions were marked Rolando. (See details on page 245.) Old letters in Martin's archives suggest that Martin may also have made special ukuleles for the Southern California Music stores, but no specifications have survived.

STETSON

Three guitars were made under this label for W. J. Dyer & Bro., St. Paul, Minnesota, in 1922.

S. S. STEWART

Buegeleisen and Jacobson (B & J) of New York City had Martin make ukuleles and related instruments with the S. S. Stewart label from about 1923–1925. Other manufacturers also made similar instruments for B & J.

JOHN WANAMAKER

The Wanamaker's department stores in New York and Philadelphia had Martin make a few special models for them about 1909. There were at least two stamps, only one of which is shown here.

H. A. WEYMANN & SON

Weymann made its own guitars, mandolins, and banjos in Philadelphia, but Martin made some ukuleles and taro-patches for them about 1925.

WOLVERINE

See Grinnell Brothers on page 229.

RUDOLPH WURLITZER

Wurlitzer was one of the largest music store chains in the country and Martin made several special models for them in the early 1920s. (See details on page 248.) The company also ordered regular Martin models with Martin stamps on the inside, but with a large Wurlitzer stamp (shown at right) on the back of the headstock.

CUSTOM-BRAND INSTRUMENT SPECIFICATIONS

BITTING SPECIAL MANDOLIN

About 40 special flat-back model mandolins were made from 1916–1918. No production figures are available for the guitars, and presumably only a few were made.

1917 Sides and back of curly maple, rich red color. Spruce top, rich brown color, binding like #2 uke (Ivoroid), otherwise like Martin A mandolin.
1918 Bridge, tailpiece, and position markers changed to be same as Martin B mandolin.

BITTING SPECIAL GUITAR

1917 Size 0, with woods, color, and bindings like Bitting Special Mandolin. Style 18 rosette, Style 21 fretboard inlays, brass machines, gut strings.

BRIGGS SPECIAL MANDOLIN

A 1915 Briggs Special mandolin, from the Martin Museum.

Sixty-five of these mandolins were made between 1915 and 1919.

1917 Regular Style A Martin, but with the headstock scalloped at the top like Ditson (bowl-back) pattern. Fretboard markers, bridge, and tailpiece vary slightly from Style A. The Briggs stamp was used on some standard Martin mandolin models as well.

THE DITSON COMPANY

The Ditson Company was an important music-publishing house and retail music store chain selling a wide range of musical goods. With headquarters in Boston, its store in that city carried the name Oliver Ditson & Co., while the New York branch was Charles H. Ditson & Co. (The J. E. Ditson branch in Philadelphia closed around 1910.) Martin had been selling its instruments to Ditson since the 1860s, so there was a long history of intertwined business and personal relationships between the two companies. Martin's primary competitor from 1890 through the early 1920s was Lyon & Healy of Chicago, a company that started out as a Ditson branch and Martin retailer.

Beginning in 1916, Martin made a special line of guitars and ukuleles for Ditson, stamped with the name of the parent Oliver Ditson store. (Martin had already been making some bowl-back mandolins with special appointments that were sold with the Ditson brand.) There were three guitar styles in three sizes, all with a shallow curve at the waist. The guitar nomenclature was different from Martin's in that there was no prefix indicating the size. Style 1 was the plainest and smallest. Style 11 was a larger version of the same model, and Style 111 had the same features, but in Dreadnought size. Styles 2, 22, and 222 had white celluloid binding but were still relatively plain. Styles 3, 33, and 333 were the highest models. All of these were mahogany with spruce tops, and the tops were usually stained a light brown. The specifications written out by Martin in 1916 called them "Ditson Hawaiian Guitars," so it is likely that all were strung with steel strings, regardless of size. Unlike later Martin Hawaiian models, the Ditsons had conventional raised frets. At least one of the Ditson Dreadnoughts had an octa-chorda bridge.

Harry L. Hunt, the manager of the New York Ditson branch, suggested the unique Ditson shape, probably derived from a baroque guitar outline. Hunt had a long history in the New York City music scene, and Frank Henry consulted him often, both by letter and in person. Hunt's influence was by no means limited to the Dreadnought, although that is certainly his most important contribution by today's standards. The deluxe 5K ukulele was introduced at his suggestion, and he helped promote Martin's little all-mahogany 2-17, its first steel-string guitar that wasn't pitched as a Hawaiian model. Although Hunt suggested the need for an extra-large model in the Ditson shape, the actual drawings of what later became Martin's famous Dreadnought were done at Martin, by John Deichman, who simply expanded the outline for the smaller Ditson model. The original paper templates and wooden forms for these models are now in the Martin Museum. It is interesting to note that the original Dreadnought design was an afterthought, one not considered particularly important either by Hunt or by Martin. By the mid-1920s, however, it was the only Ditson guitar shape that Harry Hunt bothered to have Martin continue building. By this time, the brown stain on the top was rarely used.

Ditson Building

The name, originally spelled "Dreadnaught," was borrowed from a large English battleship of the period that had been launched with the phrase, "Trust in God and dread not." Martin continued to use its original "Dreadnaught" spelling until the early 1960s, when it was changed to the current "Dreadnought." (The later spelling is used throughout this book to avoid confusion.)

Ditson-brand Martins were not limited to the styles described here. Over the years, Martin made several other styles for them that utilized standard Martin features. For instance, Martin made small guitars with the Ditson stamp that had rosewood bodies and trimmings like Style 21, Style 28, Style 30, and Style 45 guitars, but with Ditson's unique shape.

> Ditson had two large retail stores and carried a wide range of instruments, but music publishing was the most profitable part of its business.

At first, the Ditson guitars and ukuleles carried only the Ditson stamp. Later ones had both the Martin and Ditson identification. (The Martin stamp was on the inside centerstrip of the back, with the Ditson stamp on the back of the headstock.) Early Ditsons also had their own serial number series, but this was discontinued after #571 in 1921. Martin serial numbers were used thereafter.

DITSON GUITARS

STYLE 1-45

A Ditson style 1-45 (called Baby D-45), one of four made. Style 45 models in the larger Ditson body shapes were never manufactured. The ivory bridge shown here is slightly larger than the original. From the Martin Museum.

Along with the distinctive shape, the special Ditson models were given a single ring rosette and light brown stain (optional) to the spruce top that more closely matched the mahogany back and sides.

STYLE 1, 11, 111

1917   Style 1 Standard
        Style 11 Concert
        Style 111 Extra Large (Dreadnought)

Specs: (Martin's sheet of specifications listed them as "Ditson Hawaiian Guitars.")

Stained mahogany body, spruce top stained brown, 19 frets. Rosette has single ring like Foden Style A. "Spanish bracing"(fan braced). Front edge inlay of single black-white, back not bound, rosewood centerstrip, rosewood endpiece. Position marks like Martin Style 18 guitar, ivory nut, brass machines, and plain ebony pins.

Note: Back bound as of March 10, 1920.

STYLE 2, 22, 222

1917   Style 2 Standard
        Style 22 Concert
        Style 222 Extra Large (Dreadnought)

Same specs as Style 1, except for bindings and pins. Celluloid bindings like Style 2 Martin ukulele, celluloid heel cap, inlaid ebony pins.

STYLE 3, 33, 333

1917   Style 3 Standard
        Style 33 Concert
        Style 333 Extra Large (Dreadnought)

Specs: Same as Style 2, except ebony endpiece, single ring rosette, of 20 ga. and 40 ga. Celluloid. Front edge bound like Style 3 uke, back edge bound like Style 3 uke, fingerboard Celluloid bound. Position marks 3, 5, 7, 9, and 12, like #3000 series mandolins. German silver machines, white pins, pearl inlaid bridge, edge of soundhole bound in 65 ga. Celluloid.

Note: The earliest Style 3 and 33 Ditsons had a more elaborate engraved mother-of-pearl fretboard inlay pattern quite unlike anything seen from Martin. Lyon & Healy supplied the pearl inlaid bridges mentioned above.

The Ditson Concert guitar was similar in size to Martin's regular Size 0, except for the characteristic shallow waist. The example shown is a Ditson 33, the most ornate of the three special styles made at the request of Harry Hunt.

PRODUCTION TOTALS: JANUARY 31, 1916 TO JANUARY 3, 1921

Style 1	116	Style 2	60	Style 3	23
Style 11	71	Style 22	31	Style 33	24
Style 111	7	Style 222	7	Style 333	None

DS-18 (1-18)	65	2-17	12	1-45	4	
DS-21 (1-21)	26	1-30	12			
DS-28 (1-28)	13	1-42	12			

Note: The size 1 guitars in this list do not correspond to regular Martin size 1 instruments. Instead, they have the same body shape as the Ditson Style 1 model.

The numbers above give some idea of production, but they should not be treated as conclusive because some may be missing from the list. There may have been one or more guitars made in Style 333, for instance, but to date none have surfaced.

In addition, there were two guitars made with the specification Olcott-Bickford Artist Model #450 in 1929, sold through Ditson and with Ditson's unique wide-waisted shape. The numbers were #38721 and #39235. With the exception of these two guitars, the Martin-made Ditsons apparently were strung with steel strings. Although there is no specific mention of the string type in Martin's records, the Ditsons were listed as Hawaiian models, and the fan bracing of the top is nearly identical to the fan bracing Martin used on the all-koa Hawaiian models made for Southern California Music at the same time. This same fan-bracing pattern was also used on the early 0-18K and 0-28K Martin models.

The smaller Ditson guitars did not sell particularly well and production of most Ditson guitar models ceased after January 1921, although uke orders continued. A letter from Harry L. Hunt dated June 1, 1923 asked Martin to make Style 111 guitars again. This was the plain style in Dreadnought size. Between 1923 and 1930, Martin made

Early Ditson Style 33 concert size on left, with a Style 1 standard. The headstock inlay on the 33 model is not original.

19 more of this type, including #19734 for Roy Smeck. These had standard Martin X-bracing, and the later ones had the plain flat-tipped rectangular Martin bridge instead of the pyramid bridge found on earlier examples. The last Ditson Dreadnoughts were #44997 and #44998, begun November 22, 1930. Shortly after they were delivered, the Ditson Company was sold and the store stock liquidated. It is interesting to note that exactly six months later, on May 22, 1931, Martin began building four Dreadnoughts, two in mahogany and two in rosewood, which would be the first sold under its own brand.

Ditson wrote letters to Martin in 1925 requesting special 8-string bridges "for a new style of guitar that has been invented, called the Octa-Chorda." A Ditson 111 Dreadnought with special 8-string bridge was ordered in early 1930 and this 000-28 version of the octa-chorda was started the same year. It was intended to be played in the Hawaiian style. From the Martin Museum.

This early 1929 guitar is one of the last Ditson 111 models. Except for the sound-hole rosette, bridge, and lack of a pick-guard, it is much the same as the first D-18 models that Martin made a short time later. From the Martin Museum.

In 1916, Martin also began making ukuleles for Ditson. The first few were serially numbered, #1–167, between January and May of that year. These were in several styles, similar to Martin ukes, but with the unique Ditson shape. A letter from Harry Hunt in early 1925 asked for 24 Style 0 ukes, 24 Style 1 ukes, and a dozen other Ditson uke models, including two Style 5s, to be delivered each month during the summer. Martin also made a total of 45 Ditson Empire Series mandolins from July 13, 1915 to June 27, 1916. These were of many models, a few of which are described below.

Harry Hunt ordered a full line of Martin ukes in the distinctive shape we now associate with Dreadnought guitars. Shown here is a Style 1, with newer tuning pegs.

DITSON MARTIN MANDOLINS

Martin made several styles of mandolins for Ditson. No production totals are available except for a single Style R sample, serial #1235, in 1903. There were no specs available and the model doesn't show up again in Martin records. Martin also made flat-back mandolin models for Ditson that were identical to regular Martin models, but with the Ditson stamp.

All of the mandolins styles listed below are bowl-back styles, with Ditson stamp and serial number. Not many were made because the bowl-back style was losing favor by 1915, when these models were first described in Martin records.

Style # 1517: Virtually identical to Martin Style 00.

Style #2250: Like Martin Style 0, except for a different black-and-white rosette.

Style #2538: Similar to Martin #1, but with different rosette and top binding, and with a simpler cap (scalloped side border).

Style #3035: Similar to Martin #2, except for minor differences in rosette and binding, and simpler cap.

Style #3540: Similar to Martin #3, with differences as listed above.

WILLIAM FODEN

William Foden (1860–1947) was a well-known concert guitarist, composer, and instructor who endorsed Martin guitars from 1900 to 1920. After briefly endorsing Washburn guitars in the late 1890s, he began ordering Martins for his pupils, and eventually persuaded Martin to modify some of their standard designs and call them Foden Specials. The construction was exactly the same as regular Martin guitars, but with minor changes to the fretboard inlays and other details. One particular feature used on Foden models, and later used on guitars made for other firms, was the single-ring rosette.

The Foden Specials were built at the height of Foden's career, although he had long been considered America's first native-born guitar virtuoso. He was known for his mastery of the tremolo, and his two-part "Grand Method for Guitar" was already in wide use when he teamed up with Frederick Bacon on banjo and Giuseppe Pettine on mandolin to form a trio that was soon billed as The Big Three. They toured North America to wide acclaim in 1910–11, which was just prior to the construction of the first Foden Specials.

Production information on the Foden models is very limited. The totals below indicate those sales recorded in the sales books 1912–17 and may not be complete. All styles listed below were offered in both 0 and 00 sizes.

Style A	None	Style D	10*
Style B	5	Style E	9
Style C	3		

*(Inc. one with 7 strings)

William Foden was a highly influential endorser of Martin's gut-string models. He ordered Style 42 guitars with ebony bridges instead of ivory, as shown in this photo.

Mr. Foden was responsible for suggesting the 20-fret fingerboard (instead of 19 frets) to Martin, a feature that quickly became standard on most models.

FODEN SPECIAL GUITARS

STYLE A

Similar to Martin Style 18, none were made.

STYLE B

1917: Corresponds to Martin Style 21 guitar, but with single-ring rosette with Style 21 purfling (herringbone).

STYLE C

1917: Corresponds to Martin Style 28 guitars. Front edge trimmed with thin veneer strips, five black and five white, back same as Style 28, single ring rosette, three strips of ivory bordered with black and white lines. Position marks 5, 7, and 9, special design.

STYLE D

1917: Corresponds to Martin Style 30 guitars. Single-ring rosette like center ring of Style 30, single black-and-white lines added. Position marks 5, 7, and 9, special design, fingerboard not bound. German silver machines, white pins, scale 24.9 inches. Martin stamp sometimes appears on back of neck.

The special fretboard inlays used on Foden Style C and Style D models were revived for the D-37 koa models in 1980. This inlay has been used on a few Limited Editions as well.

STYLE E

The 1917 features combined from Martin Styles 40 and 45. Front Style 40 (like 42, but without bordering around fretboard), back Style 45, sides Style 45, but without vertical strips of pearl at heel and endpiece. Three-ring rosette, Style 42, fingerboard bound but headstock plain, not inlaid. Position marks of special design in 3, 5, 7, 9, 12, and 15. German silver machines, ebony bridge, white pins.

Foden Style E, circa 1917 (there's no serial number). Style E had a combination of elements from Styles 40 and 45.

THE PARAMOUNT GUITAR

In 1930, William Lange of the Paramount Banjo Company asked Martin to make a special guitar for them. The guitar had a resonator, somewhat like the one on the back of a banjo, which was intended to produce extra volume. (Paramount also made some banjos with spruce tops around the same time.) There were about 36 of these guitars made, some with four strings and some with six. Some tops were shaded, and the engraved headstock inlays read "Model L" on some examples and "Style L" on others.

PARAMOUNT GUITAR SPECIFICATIONS

May 22, 1930

Body: Size #2, 14-fret neck. Spruce top, rosewood sides and back, top braced for loose bridge and tailpiece like mandolin, no soundhole (some models were made with soundholes.) Total height: back, 4 $9/32$"; front, 3 $7/16$"; waist, 3 $7/8$".

Resonator: Depth 1 $3/8$", extension of 1 $1/8$" on each side, rosewood construction. Back braced like 000-size guitar, but all flat braces, $1/4$" thick, with special end blocks.

Neck: Orchestra model, Style 18, geared banjo pegs. Rosewood fingerboard, 20 frets, 14 clear of body, position marks 5, 7, 10, 12, and 15, ivory nut. No side position dots.

A 1930 Paramount L from the Martin Museum. Paramount supplied the pearl-inlaid headstock veneer.

INSTRUMENTS MADE BY MARTIN FOR OTHER FIRMS

SCHOENBERG

In 1986, C. F. Martin entered into an arrangement with Schoenberg Guitars to cooperate in the production of a special guitar designed by Eric Schoenberg and Dana Bourgeois with some operations performed by Bourgeois (and later, T. J. Thompson), and marketed under the Schoenberg label. These guitars were made expressly for, and warranted by, Schoenberg Guitars, but were given Martin serial numbers. Schoenberg supplied a variety of woods that were unavailable from Martin at the time. The prototypes were #467821–22.

After the two prototypes, production of approximately 195 guitars followed, including:

- 160 Soloists, cutaway and non-cutaway
- 9 OM-45 Deluxe
- 7 Concert Models (1929 OM-28 specs)
- 6 Concert Model Vintage (bar-stock frets and ebony neck reinforcement)

  A few 12-fret 000 models were also made.

A Schoenberg Soloist from 1994, the last year of Schoenberg's contract with C. F. Martin.

Dana Bourgeois was the luthier for Schoenberg from 1987–1990, with T. J. Thompson taking over in 1990 and continuing until Martin production of Schoenberg guitars ended in 1994. The change from Dana to T. J. occurred around serial number 500,000, and Schoenberg production is nearly equally divided between them. Unlike Martin cutaway models at the time, Schoenberg Soloist cutaway models had 20-fret fingerboards and a round soundhole. Martin later abandoned its oval soundhole cutaway models and adopted the round soundhole and Schoenberg cutaway shape as well.

SOUTHERN CALIFORNIA MUSIC CO.

Southern California Music Company was a large retail music store chain, with branches in Los Angeles, Pasadena, Riverside, and San Diego. It was a major Martin account for many years. Martin began making special models for them in 1916. At that time, they were especially interested in instruments made of Hawaiian koa wood. Although called Hawaiian models, the guitars had raised frets and were often played as regular guitars with steel strings, with a metal "nut adjuster" used to convert the guitar for Hawaiian-style playing. For the first two years, these models were fan-braced, a pattern nearly identical to that used on the early Ditson models. The success of the Southern California Music all-koa models led Martin to introduce its own koa wood guitars two years later.

Martin first sent Southern California Music six sample guitars, two in each of the three styles listed below, although the details on the two higher models were later changed somewhat. These first six had koa backs and sides, but spruce tops. The manager of the project then requested that future batches have koa tops as well. At least through 1917, and possibly later, Southern California Music sold these guitars with the "M. Nunes & Sons Royal Hawaiian" paper label inside the soundhole, and the "M. Nunes" decal with the Hawaiian royal crest on the headstock. (M. Nunes & Sons was making ukuleles for them at the time.) Once Martin returned to putting its own stamp on the inside centerstrip, and the models sent to Los Angeles were the same as Martin 18K and 28K models, the only marking regarding Southern California Music was the stamp on the back of the headstock. Many, but not all, of these later koa guitars also have the paper "Rolando" label shown on page 246 inside the soundhole.

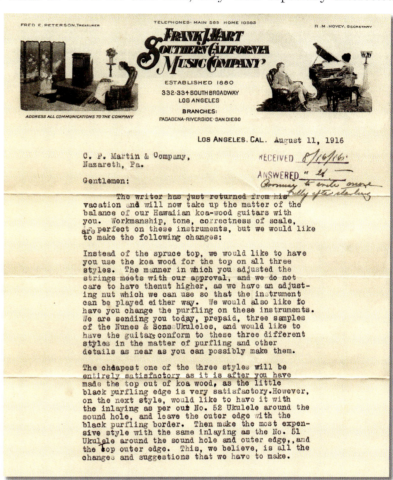

As indicated by their letterhead, Southern California Music was a full-line retailer of everything pertaining to music.

GUITARS

STYLE 1350 (0-18K)

1917 1-17 bracing pattern (fan-braced), rosette and border like Foden A, other details like Style 18.

1919 Neck not stained, rosette and border like Style 18, regular braces (X-braced).

STYLE 1400 (0-21K)

1917 Neck stained, special rosette with first and third rings of single white holly, second ring of black and white purfling. 1-17 bracing pattern (fan-braced), other details like Style 21.

1919 Neck not stained, regular Style 21 rosette, regular bracing (X-braced).

STYLE 1500 (00-28K)

1917 Neck stained dark, special rosette, like #1400, but Celluloid binding (white) on body and fingerboard. Top binding same as rosette with thin black veneer added against binding. Colored backstrip like Style C mandolin, position marks like Foden Style C. German silver machines, inlaid ebony pins, other details like Style 28.

1919 Neck not stained, rosette, border and positions like the regular style 28 guitar. (This model was also switched to regular X bracing, but the change occurred after the decorative trim was changed to match Style 28 features.)

The following totals are for guitars produced for Southern California Music from November 17, 1916 to June 29, 1918. After that time they were still made, but were mixed in production lots with Martin instruments and given Martin serial numbers. Those below were consecutively numbered from #1.

Style 1350   (0-18K)   138   Style 1400   (0-21K)   76   Style 1500   (00-28K)   47

The Rolando label was used on later Style 18K and 28K models made for Southern California Music Company. Unlike earlier koa models made for this firm, those with the Rolando label are identical to Martins, and have the Martin stamp on the interior with regular serial numbers.

The decal on the headstock, and the paper label inside this Style 1400 model, suggest that the guitar was made by M. Nunes & Sons. The Nunes firm made ukuleles for Southern California Music Company, but the koa wood guitars like this one were made in Nazareth.

RUDOLPH WURLITZER GUITARS

For a short time between 1922 and 1924, Martin made a special line of guitars for Wurlitzer. These had the Wurlitzer stamp on the back of the head and utilized the single ring rosette like the Foden models. Their model numbers, corresponding Martin style where known, and the production totals for the period are:

Wurlitzer Style	Martin Style	Total Made
2075	2-17	99
2076	0-18K	21
2077	0-28K	28
2082		3
2085	0-18	66
2086	00-18	15
2087	000-18	18
2088	0-21	13
2089	00-21	5
2090	0-28	11
2091	00-28	5
2092	0-42	11
	00-42	1
	1-28	1

Early Wurlitzer models were not serially numbered. Beginning February 28, 1923, Martin serial numbers were used. (We can't be sure that all of the above Wurlitzer styles were given the single-ring rosette.) The last ones with Wurlitzer designations were made March 22, 1924. Both before and after that date, Wurlitzer stores were also sent regular Martin models that had the prominent Wurlitzer stamp on the back of the headstock. Sometimes the Wurlitzer stamp replaced the typical Martin headstock stamp, but other times it appeared above the Martin name.

Wurlitzer numbers for other Martin-made instruments were as follows:

835 = Style 0 Martin uke
836 = Style 1 Martin uke
837 = Style 1K Martin uke
838 = Style 2K Martin uke
839 = Style 3K Martin uke
841 = 2K Martin Taro-patch
851 = T-18 Martin tiple

There were numerous Wurlitzer music stores, and the parent company provided ready-made ads that could easily be used in local newspapers to promote sales of Martin guitars.

(above) Since Wurlitzer was a chain of music stores with several locations, their stamp did not mention a specific city.

(left) Wurlitzer model 2092, 1922, from the Martin Museum. Note that this 0 size guitar displays a mixture of features from Style 40 to Style 45, and has a single-ring rosette similar to earlier Foden Special models.

INSTRUMENTS MADE BY MARTIN FOR OTHER FIRMS

Appendices
PRODUCTION TOTALS

The charts on the following pages combine Mike Longworth's tremendous early efforts in consolidating Martin production log books with Dick Boak's more recent work in extending and updating Martin production totals by model to current time for this book project. With the tremendous growth of the company, the great proliferation of models, and the many transitions from hand-kept records to several differing methods of computerized recordkeeping, tracking or making sense of these totals is, as anyone can imagine, a tedious, time-consuming, and often imperfect task. Such a challenge has required several years of work and focused concentration. If inaccuracies are discovered, we apologize and accept responsibility, but ask your assistance in reporting errors or inaccuracies to us so that future corrections can be made.

The company's amazing archives remain one of the richest collections in America, thanks mostly to the available attic space at North Street and a Martin family aversion to throwing anything away. It needs to be stated, however, that the company's first and primary purpose is to make guitars and that the task of historical record keeping is sometimes an afterthought. With the construction of the Martin Museum and Visitors Center, the company made the important commitment to provide space for archives, enabling all of the important records and artifacts to be consolidated and organized into one area for the first time. The task of archiving will be ongoing and the initial phases will take many years, if not decades.

For the greater part of the company's history, guitars were initiated and recorded in logs by quantity and lot number based upon the day that the serial number was stamped onto the front block. In more recent times, it seems that a second method of totaling models emerged with the counting of completed instruments as they pass through final inspection. This fact became apparent when comparing limited edition sales totals with final assembly computer records. Though the numbers often matched, occasionally they didn't and the anomaly can only be attributed to the change in methodology of production total tracking. Mike Longworth stated this and we state it once again. We have tried to the best of our ability to present accurate statistics, but the numbers, especially more current totals, must be viewed as approximate.

Though a few charts are updated to 2007 or 2008, most are complete through the close of 2005. We have thorough computer records after that date, but a cutoff was needed in order to compile and transfer all the information into a concise format and layout.

To make the charts efficient and useful, obscure models that have very low production totals have been moved into the footnotes or to the Rare Model section. This eliminates a tremendous waste of chart columns and page space. If you are looking for extremely low production or odd models, look in these locations. The index will be helpful in locating specific model information throughout the book.

Speaking of indexes, the original Longworth book did not have one. This was perhaps the greatest shortcoming of the book, as it was very difficult to look up any model or topic without a degree of luck or frustration. We hope we have provided the reader with a reasonable means for locating information.

FINDING PRODUCTION TOTALS

Acoustic Bass Totals	261
Alternative, Concept and Graphite Totals	281
Archtop Model Totals	256
Backpacker Totals	261
Classical Totals	266
Custom Shop, Prototype, Test Model Totals	284
Dreadnought Totals	262
Electric Guitar and Bass Totals	284
GOM, Special and Limited Edition Quick Reference	282
Guitar of the Month Totals	278
J Size Jumbo Totals	267
Limited and Special Edition Totals	279
M Size (0000) Totals	261
Mandolin Totals	268
N, P, Q, and R Designation Totals	274
OM Orchestra Model Totals	257
Size 0 Totals	252
Size 00 Totals	254
Size 000 Totals	258
Size 1 Totals	270
Size 2 Totals	271
Size 2 1/2 Totals	270
Size 3 Totals	270
Size 5 Totals	272
Tiple Totals	276
12-String Totals	275
Ukulele Totals	276
Unusual Size Totals	277
Shenandoah and Sigma Martin Totals	281
Vega Banjo Totals	271

0 SIZE PRODUCTION TOTALS (PART ONE)[b]

	0-15	0-15H	0-15T	0-16	0-16NY	0-17	0-17H	0-17T	0-18	0-18K	0-18P	0-18T	0-18TE	0-18TB	0-21 (12-fret)	0-21 (14-fret)	0-21K	0-21T	0-28	0-28H	0-28K	0-28NY	0-28T	0-30	0-34	0-40	0-42	0-44 Soloist	0-45	0-55 (00-175)
TOTALS	10705	12	476	6	6140	10430	369	2238	23553	3132	2	3834	2	5	2048	3	66	6	1354	2	641	2	74	162	19	6	392	17	158	12
1898						55			21						17				36					3	7		7			
1899						79			40						44				49					18	11		17			
1900						41			37						58				71					2			17			
1901									1						37				28					17			3			
1902															7				17					7			20			
1903									2						33				62					16			18		2	
1904						45									14				24					7			5		1	
1905						26			48						35				40					14			3		1	
1906						26			65						24				23					17			3		3	
1907						33			24						28				45								3		5	
1908						41			30						33				14											
1909						12			46						12				16					7	1		12			
1910						21			28						14				18					6			2		1	
1911						41			30						14				9					6						
1912									35						12				6					3			5			
1913									33						20				13					5			4		3	
1914									33						24				7					3			6			
1915									25						7		1		16					5			6			
1916									149						11		6		2					5			4		2	
1917									210						30		6		28					14			5		3	
1918									355						35		4		17					5			2			
1919									165						53		11		45					4			4			
1920									151	8					92		4		86		6						5	8		
1921									342	29					104				88					1			11			
1922									350	270					51				23		5						10			
1923									375	165					77				25		13						24	2		
1924									900	75					100		4		78		25						11	2	2	
1925						1			375	249					135		4		59		65						12		11	
1926						328			700	200					195		25		112		50						39		13	
1927						353	60		475	200					155	3			124		175						52	1	19	
1928						343			401	330		34[a]			76		3		50	2	75		26				34	1	42	
1929						881	7		306	475		358			150		2	3	50		100		45				25	1	1	
1930						1100	127	4	283	302		201			103			1	54		51			1			10		20	
1931						954	75	140	350	201		151	31		75				12		25							1	1	
1932						861	50	50	506	125																				
1933						651	25	51	175	150								1												
1934			2			451	25	75	227	100	2	12			1						1						1			12
1935						402		50	150	50		30			24															
1936						226		25	175	103		12			27				6											
1937						327		50	227	100		24		1	12								1							
1938						325		87	151			12																		
1939						475		36	200			24			19															
1940	578	12				500		60	250			12															1			
1941	475					575		48	275			60			6															
1942	506					575		84	475			36																		
1943	365					600		134	425			72			30															
1944						75		109	400			133			48															
1945								110	500			97			6												1			
1946								99	450			72		2																
1947	450							125	525			72																		
1948	750							150	475			72																		
1949	700							100	551			60																		
1950	575							76	575			72																		
1951	550							75	625			72															1		1	
1952	375								650			74																		
1953	825								750			50																		
1954	925								526			24															1			
1955	626								601																					

[a] footnote marker.
[b] footnote marker.

0 SIZE PRODUCTION TOTALS (CONTINUED)[b]

	0-15	0-15H	0-15T	0-16	0-16NY	0-17	0-17H	0-17T	0-18	0-18K	0-18P	0-18T	0-18TE	0-18H	0-21 (12-fret)	0-21 (14-fret)	0-21K	0-21T	0-28	0-28H	0-28K	0-28NY	0-28T	0-30	0-34	0-40	0-42	0-44 Soloist	0-45	0-55 (00-17S)
TOTALS	10705	12	476	6	6140	10430	369	2238	23553	3132	2	3834	2	5	2048	3	66	6	1354	2	641	2	74	162	19	6	392	17	158	12
1957	625							37	600			63																		
1958	876							101	600			50	1																	
1959	701							125	500			127																		
1960	526			6				51	276			175	1																	
1961	275		175		476				626			151						1					1							
1962			76		425				500			251																		
1963			150		525				502			202											1							
1964			75		775				550			150																		
1965					375	1			500			250																		
1966					251				450			125																		
1967					400				577			50																		
1968					650				452			27										1								
1969					302	6			326			49		2					1			1								
1970					425				376			48		3																
1971					500				400			61																		
1972					325				175			18																		
1973					151				51			43																		
1974					128				50			12																		
1975					136				88			23																		
1976					112				22			35																		
1977					17				3			24																		
1978												13																		
1979					23				15			14																		
1980					11				5			12																		
1981					16				11			2																		
1982									6			13																		
1983					5				6			8																		
1984					4							12																		
1985					4				3			16																		
1986					11							1																		
1987					10				1			3																		
1988					12				3			16																		
1989					16				4			4																		
1990					20				4			4																		
1991					16				4			4																		
1992					17				2																					
1993									19																					
1994					2				9			2																		

Footnotes for SIZE 0 Production Totals

a The first 0-18T models made in 1929 were made for Carl Fischer, a Martin dealership, though they had identical specifications to the 0-18T models that followed.

b The following one-of-a-kind Size 0 Model guitars **are not** included in the production tally above:

Model	Quantity	Year	Type
0-18H	1	1920	Hawaiian with Raised Nut
0-18TD	1	1976	Tenor (Exact Meaning of "D" Designation Unknown)
0-18TK2	1	1980	Tenor with Koa Top
0-21H	1	1918	Hawaiian with Raised Nut
0-21P	1	1929	Plectrum
0-28E	1	1963	With Pickups
0-28P	1	1930	Plectrum

0-44 – 1923

APPENDICES 253

00 SIZE PRODUCTION TOTALS (PART ONE)

NOTE: FOR 00 CLASSICAL, NYLON STRING AND GUT, SEE CLASSICAL CHART

Year	00-17	00-17H	00-17P Plectrum	00-18	00-18G	00-18H	00-18K	00-18T Tenor	00-21	00-21G	00-21H	00-21NY	00-21T Tenor	00-28	00-28G	00-28K	00-28T Tenor	00-30	00-34	00-40	00-40H	00-40K	00-42	00-42K	00-44	00-45	00-45K
TOTALS	13936	20	1	22004	5138	255	61	6	4334	3	5	906	2	758	1531	40	2	101	6	4	244	6	503	1	7	288	1
1898				4					6					11				4	5				3				1
1899				34					31					22				5	1				11				
1900				26					42					35				7					5				
1901				1					29					18				7					9				
1902									12					14				7					40				
1903				3					11					19				17					11				
1904	3								10					10				6					11				
1905									7					4									5				
1906				4					5									2								1	
1907				12					9					21				18					7				3
1908	4			14														1								1	
1909	8			6										4				2					1			3	
1910				1					12					16				3					5			3	
1911				2					7					7				1									
1912	16			6					10					5				2					2			3	
1913				7					8					6				7					4		2	1	
1914	11			12					10					8									2			3	
1915				15																			1			1	
1916	4			11					6			1		3		21		12		3ᵃ			5			3	
1917	8			28					18					16		3		2					3	1	1	1	
1918				26				4	14					4		10		3					11			9	
1919				58				7	19					24				1					14			16	
1920				101				11	38					34									12		2	6	
1921				21				1	34					32									25			7	
1922				50					25					24							40		6			6	
1923				97				16	25					12	1	1					44		34		1	14	
1924				150				18	36					32	4	1					30		8				
1925				96				3	30					23	11	1					25		12				
1926				325					100	1				64	19	1					28		46		1	19	
1927				375					120	2				74	18		1				11		27			32	
1928				202					76					75	18						12		65			12	
1929				227					101					51	12						24			1		10	
1930	161			76					85					16	24						12		30				
1931	151			201			1		110					55	12						12	5					
1932	75			50					50		2		2		6						6		1			1	
1933	150			25					1					5									1				
1934	237	19		53					37					6	4								12		1	2	
1935	175	1		257	3	2		1	77	1					11	1							24				
1936	227			275	19	128			26	2				1	19	1		1					24				
1937	300			353	12	75		2	41					2	18	1		1									
1938	300			201	24			1	15					1	18								1			1	
1939	202			176	12	25			24						12								6			1	
1940	350		1	251	18	25			25						24								12			2	
1941	375			350	24				24						12												
1942	475			450	6				24						6								6				
1943	525			425	12				36						30												
1944	525			425	18				27						54												
1945	600			575	24				36						30												
1946	600			600	66				87						36												
1947	676			575	36				18						66												
1948	650			501	60				6						53												
1949	650			525	109				26						60												
1950	776			551	158				12		1				48												
1951	750			651	171				24						97											1	
1952	850			701	237				36						108										1ᵇ		
1953	575			800	350				12																		
1954				450	425				12		1																

00 SIZE PRODUCTION TOTALS (PART TWO)

NOTE: FOR 00 CLASSICAL, NYLON STRING AND GUT, SEE CLASSICAL CHART

Year	00-16	00-17	00-17H	00-17P Plectrum	00-18	00-18G	00-18H	00-18K	00-18T Tenor	00-21	00-21G	00-21H	00-21NY	00-21T Tenor	00-28	00-28G	00-28K	00-28T Tenor	00-30	00-34	00-40	00-40H	00-40K	00-42	00-42K	00-44	00-45	00-45K
TOTALS	8	13936	20	1	22004	5138	255	61	6	4334	3	3	906	2	758	1531	40	2	101	6	4	244	6	503	1	6	288	1
1956		625			651	200				12																		
1957		600			677	375				24																		
1958		601			575	375				15																		
1959		277			504	725				62						74												
1960		50			427	703				51						112												
1961					630	900				66						125												
1962					475	76				78			103			125												
1963					603					126			126			176												
1964					551					76			176			177												
1965					575					150			275			35												
1966					550					200			226															
1967					650					213																		
1968					776					153					1													
1969					402					179																		
1970					602					152																		
1971					751					175																		
1972					403					126																	3	
1973					202					101														1			5	
1974					152					114																	1	
1975					181					137																	20	
1976					128					93																	9	
1977					1					10																	13	
1978																											22	
1979															1												11	
1980		12			22					30																	9	
1981		23			10					20																	2	
1982					4					24																	4	
1983					4					11																		
1984										10					2												1	
1985					2					10																	2	
1986		4			4					8																	1	
1987		4			4c					22																		
1988		4			4					24																	2	
1989					18					20																		
1990					16					20																		
1991					4					29																	6	
1992										20																	5	
1993	8				8					20																		
1994					16					1																	3	
1995					6					6																	3	
2000		135																										
2001		322																										
2002		6																										
2003		12																										

Footnotes for 00 SIZE Production Totals — Parts One and Two

a. These three were made with Hawaiian koa back and sides. (See 00 SIZE Chart Part One.)
b. One 00-44 noted as 00-44G was made in 1938.
c. One was made with East Indian rosewood back and sides. (See 00 SIZE Chart Part Two.)

00-40H – 1932

CF-1 American Archtop – 2004

00 SIZE PRODUCTION TOTALS (PART THREE – RECENT 00 MODELS)
NOTE: FOR 00 CLASSICAL, NYLON STRING AND GUT, SEE CLASSICAL CHART

	Totals	1996	1997	1998	1999	2000	2001	2002	2003	2004	2005
00M	163					156	7				
00CMAE	411			169	132	110					
00CXAE Black	5859					233	1496	1535	1479	610	506
00CXAE Navy	120					44	76				
00CXAE Red	94					29	65				
00CXMAE	99					36	63				
00CXRAE	150					77	72	1			
00CX1AE Black	520							146	222	152	
00-1	482	60[a]	135	126	81	67		13			
00-1R	131	46	25	59	1						
00-15	3284				498	912	457	388	272	337	420
00C-15AE	272					129	141	2			
00-16DB	99		97		2						
00-16DBM	472					270	48	50	44	52	8
00-16DBFM	104						48	27	29		
00-16DR	407				395	10	2				
00-16DBM	166				96	59	7	4			
00C-16DBRE	69								69		
00C-16FMBUAE	58					41	17				
00C-16GTAE	115					107	8				
00-16RST Stauffer	0										
00-18V	591					239	186	166			
00-21GE	165				123	41	1				
00-40ST Stauffer	35				34	1					
00-45ST Stauffer	25				21	4					
SP00-16RST Stauffer	76					49	26	1			
SP00C-16AE	50					27	19	3	1		

Footnotes for 00 SIZE Production Totals – Part Three

a. One designated as 00-1G (Gloss).

ARCHTOP GUITAR PRODUCTION TOTALS[c]

	Totals	1931	1932	1933	1934	1935	1936	1937	1938	1939	1940	1941	1942
Round C-1	449	139	285	25									
F-Hole C-1	786	2	78	262	156	127	26	50	25		36	24	
Plectrum C-1P	10	3	5	1					1				
Round C-1T	71	26	37	8									
F-Hole C-1T	83		10	42		12	12	7					
12-String C-1	1			1									
Round C-2	269	104	153	12									
F-Hole C-2	439	2	40	163	90	36	60	12	12	12	12		
Plectrum C-2P	2	2											
Round C-2T	15	1	11	2	1								
F-Hole C-2T	2			1	1								
12-String C-2	1	1		1									
Maple C-2	1				1								
Mando-Cello C-2	2	2											
Round C-3	53	21	26	6									
F-Hole C-3	58		27	31									
Tenor C-3T	1	1											
F-1	91				54	25	12						
12-String F-1	1			1	1								
F-2	46				22	12	12						
Maple F-2	1			1	1								
F-5	2			2									
F-7	187				91	36	36	12	6	6			
Round F-7	1			1									
F-9	72				28	19	6	6	7	6			
R-15	2				2								
R-17	940				2	331	106	176	100	25	100	50	50
R-18	1937				9[a]	481	486	304	192	250	125	6	12	72
R-21	1									1			
Tenor R-18T	133					60	24	24		7	12	6	
Plectrum R-18P	4					1	2	1					

MARTIN/AMERICAN ARCHTOP[b] PRODUCTION TOTALS

	Totals	CF-1 Natural	CF-1 Sunburst	CF-2 Natural	CF-2 Sunburst	CF-1 Black	CF-2 Black
		186	25	36	26	8	2
2004		91	9	1	5		
2005		95	16	35	21	8	2

Footnotes for ARCHTOP GUITAR and MARTIN/AMERICAN ARCHTOP Production Totals

a. Marked as 00-18S.
b. Martin Collaboration with Dale Unger, American Archtop Guitars.
c. Introduced in 2004. Production is ongoing.
   Two rare DC-1 Dreadnought-shaped archtops were prototyped in 1934 and are not shown on this chart.

256 MARTIN GUITARS: A TECHNICAL REFERENCE

OM (Orchestra Model) Production Totals — Later Models 1977–2005

TOTALS	MMO	OM-1	OM-15	OMC-15E	OM-16GT	OMC-16E	OMC-16E Premium	OMC-16E Koa	OMC-16E Maple	OMC-16RE	OMC-16RE Premium	OMC-16RE Aura	OMC-16WE	OMC Aura	OM-18GE	OM-18V	OM-21	OM-28	OM-28GE	OM-28 Marquis	OM-28V (OM-28VR)	OM-35	OM-41 Special	OM-42	OM-42K (Koa)	OM-45	OM-45GE	OM-45 Marquis	SWOM	SPOM-16	SWOMGT
	686	569	459	1096	1201	68	176	267	254	90	292	163	254	130	231	787	2373	440	127	196	3100	494	124	1210	93	195	123	53	90	233	620
1977																															
1978																															
1979																															
1980																															
1981																															
1982																															
1983																															
1984																															
1985																										56 e					
1986																										11					
1987																										63					
1988																										11					
1989																										12					
1990																										3					
1991																										2					
1992																										1					
1993																															
1994		182																								1					
1995		197																													
1996																										5					
1997																						177		121		3					
1998	175		333	10	422		79				84		219		181	111	340 a	20			238		131		3	16				
1999	334	181	117	605	339		41				96		35		16	137	192 b	21			252		162		5	41		89	46	90
2000	170	9	9	190	75	68	56	267	254	90	112	163		129	34	54	102 c	100	32		388 d	219	124	226		3	35	53	1	123	171
2001				99	150									1		176	136	38	46		361	117		160		5 f	24			13	63
2002																95	139	107	49		480	158		204		8	5			51	66
2003	7															107	166	85			338			206		11 g	2				230
2004																	170	45			207										
2005					215												96	24		196	329				93						

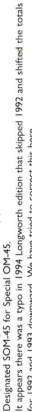

OM-45B Roy Rogers – 2006

OM (Orchestra Model) Production Totals 1929–1933 — Early Models

TOTALS	OM-18	OM-18P	OM-28	OM-42	OM-45	OM-45 Deluxe
	765	95	487	2	40	14
1929	89	30	11	2	19	14
1930	251	65	235		10	
1931	225		166		5	
1932	200		50		6	
1933			25			

Footnotes for OM (Orchestra Models) Production Totals

a Five were made with sunburst finish.
b Three were made with sunburst finish.
c One was made with sunburst finish.
d Designation changed from OM-28VR to simply OM-28V.
e Designated SOM-45 for Special OM-45.
f It appears there was a typo in 1994 Longworth edition that skipped 1992 and shifted the totals for 1992 and 1993 downward. We have tried to correct this here.
g Includes two guitars designated OM-45N with square tube bar in neck, but without scalloped braces.

SIZE 000 PRODUCTION TOTALS — LONG RUNNING MODELS — (PART ONE)

For Classical (C), Nylon String (N) and Gut (G) models, see Classical Chart. 000 "Q" Series models are included in these totals. Switching over to 14-fret (were OM) renamed 000 in 1934. 12- and 14-fret models not separated except where noted. Some early 14-fret guitars marked 000 had the long scale.

000-45 – 1911

Year	000-17	000-17S 12-fret	000-18	000-18P Plectrum	000-18S 12-fret	000-18T Tenor	000-21	000-21 10-String	000-21 Harp Guitar	000-28	000-28-45	000-28F	000-28HX	000-28NY	000-28P Plectrum	000-28S	000-38	000-41	000-42	000-44	000-45	000-45 7-String	000-45H Hawaiian	000-45S 12-fret
TOTALS	26	196	19378	46	3	5	2080	2	4	10257	3	10	2	2	3	31	3	2	450	3	341	3	2	11
1898																								
1899																								
1900																								
1901																								
1902								4 b																
1903								1																
1904								1		2														
1905								2		1														
1906			1 a					1		1 c														
1907								1																
1908																								
1909																								
1910								1	2															
1911	1		3					1		1											1			
1912										4											5			
1913			3							1											1			
1914			3							2											3			
1915			2							4											1			
1916										2														
1917			1						1	4									2	1	2			
1918			4							3										1	1			
1919										2											2			
1920			2																					
1921			3					2		3									5		3			
1922			4					1		5									1		2			
1923			38					1		4											19			
1924			12							3									4		3			
1925			62							20											12			
1926			224					5		8											20			
1927			201							25											25			
1928			50							44											20			
1929			182							48									1		21	1 h		
1930			68				1			82									1 g		1			
1931			178	46			2			2												1 i		
1932										57					3									
1933										1														
1934			326			1				129	1 e								1		14			
1935			176				92			52											24			
1936			280				75			72									27		24			
1937			303		1		223			113	1 f								31		18		2	
1938			277			1	120			97	1								12		19			
1939			152				85			48														
1940			200			1	25			86									24		6			
1941			326				63			36									12		12			
1942			225				48			48									6		6			
1943			400				96			96														
1944			375				120			133														
1945			400				137			147														
1946			500				134			134														
1947			577				223			235 d														
1948			450				120			144														
1949			402				85			122														
1950			416				97			124														
1951			425				122			96														
1952	25		527				109			120														
1953			550				159			134														
1954			601				76			75														
1955			452				50			75														

258 MARTIN GUITARS: A TECHNICAL REFERENCE

SIZE 000 PRODUCTION TOTALS — LONG RUNNING MODELS — (PART TWO)

000 One-of-a-Kinds

The following 18 one-of-a-kind 000 models are not included in 000 production totals

Model	Year
000-18G	1955
000-18H	1938
000-21S	1977
10 String 000-28	1902
Harp 000-28	1906
000-28E	1970
000-28H	1949
000-28K	1921
000-28T	1929
000-30	1919
000-40	1909
000-40H	1933
S-41L	1970
Hays 000-45	1907
Lyre Head 000-45	1914
Vine Fbd. 000-45	1912
000-45G	1939
S-00045	1975

	000-17	000-17S 12-fret	000-18	000-18P Plectrum	000-18S 12-fret	000-18T Tenor	000-21	000-21 10-String	000-21 Harp Guitar	000-28	000-28-45	000-28F (Folk)	000-28HX	000-28NY	000-28P Plectrum	000-28S	000-38	000-41	000-42	000-44	000-45	000-45 7-String	000-45H Hawaiian	000-45S 12-fret
TOTALS	26	196	19378	46	3	5	2080	2	4	10257	3	10	2	2	3	31	3	2	450	3	341	3	2	11
1956			477				75			75														
1957			450				50			75														
1958			401				62			37														
1959			326				25			27														
1960			251							52														
1961			351							13														
1962			300							14														
1963			401																					
1964			276							3														
1965			400				1			176														
1966			550							200														
1967			625							250														
1968			351							102														
1969			327							141														
1970			353							150										7 [j]			
1971			852							232		2				7					1			
1972			650		1					151		1				2					1			
1973			354		2					153		6		2		5					1			
1974			201							221		1	2			17					3			3
1975			206							256											15			2
1976			163							247											3			6
1977			40							50														
1978																								
1979			35							67							3				6			
1980			48				12			43											1			
1981			32							37								2			1			
1982			27							21											1			
1983										9														
1984			10							13														
1985			6							26														
1986			8							29											6			
1987			10							32											4			
1988			16							20											3			
1989			27							48											1			
1990			12							32											6			
1991			6							70											15			
1992			14							76														
1993			45							165														
1994			29							230 [k]														
1995			103							524														
1996			45							209														
1997			91							209														
1998			98							313														
1999			194							335														
2000			160							462														
2001			131							370														
2002		168	129							356														
2003		27	122							394									43					
2004		1	166							440														
2005			131							457									280					

Footnotes for 000 SIZE Production Totals — Long Running Models

a Maple back and sides.
b Noted as "Special."
c Noted as "Special."
d Change to no herringbone.
e Serial # 56496
f Serial # 69054 Marked 000-28S
g 14-fret
h Hawaiian
i Lefthanded
j Seven made with 12-fret necks.
k 000-28 totals from this year and after include sunburst and square rod (Q) models.

APPENDICES 259

SIZE 000 PRODUCTION TOTALS – RECENT MODELS

Year	MX000	000XE Black	000CXE Black	000X1	M000	000CME	000-1 and 000-1E	000-1R	000C-1 and 000C-1E	000-15	000-15S	000C-15E	000-16 (000-16T or M)	000-16GT	000-16R	000-16RGT	000-16SGT	000-16SRGT	000C-16 (000C-16T)	000C-16GTE	000C-16GTE Premium	000C-16RGTE	000C-16RGTE Premium	000C-16RGTE Aura	000-28EC Eric Clapton	000-28H	000-28VS	SP000-16 (SP000-16T)	SP000-16R (SP000-16TR)	SP000C-16	SP000C-16E	SP000C-16R
TOTALS	1102	902	2926	7018	7631	511	6380	2083	2427	7518	1918	1255	2063	2600	507	1183	866	214	1286	2767	986	1702	1823	1586	11194	400	734	768	828	43	179	813
1989													4[l]																			
1990													401						169													
1991													268						169													
1992													298						186													
1993													190						151													
1994							151[a]						286						229													
1995							926[b]						279						169													
1996							618	120					156						110[n]						645[o]							
1997	553				594		793[d]	478[f]					83						62						1159[o]	66						
1998	343				1360		800[e]	208[g]	346[i]				98						41						1091[o]	280						
1999	185				1188		867	265[h]	783[j]	889					24[m]										841	54	76	188	203			114
2000	21			1	1109		623	291	762[k]	1429	307			307	43										804		123	182	182	19	35	229
2001				1094	906		481	217	277	1910	741	198		711	42	282	378			20		104			1268		53	208	193	20	100	240
2002		379		1225	624	12	350	194	258	947	243	496		509	180	183	134			1082		451			1282		176	113	171	4		146
2003		419	1040	1261	637	222	279	276	1	860	183	344		270	113	234	139			755	257	698	272		1316[o]		98	1	57		44	70
2004		87	1035	1500	581	207	235	33		639	219	203		367	83	197	64	196		599	251	447	1192		1399[o]		109	14	6			11
2005		17	851	1937	632	70	257	1		844	225	14		436	22	287	151	18		311	478	2	359	1586	1389[o]		99		16			3

Footnotes for 000 SIZE Production Totals – Recent Models

a. One is designated 000C-1E with pickup.
b. Twenty-eight are designated as 000-1X with Fishman Matrix pickup. Two are designated 000-1E with pickup.
c. Includes three designated 000-1G (Gloss) and thirty-five designated as 000-1X with Fishman Matrix pickup.
d. Includes three designated 000-1G (Gloss) plus fourty-four designated as 000-1X with Fishman Matrix pickup.
e. Fourteen are designated as 000-1X with Fishman Matrix pickup.
f. Four are designated as 000-1RX (Fishman Matrix pickup). Two are designated 000-1RZ with D-1 Sunburst tops.
g. Seven of these are designated 000-1RG (Gloss). Four are designated 000-1RX (Fishman Matrix pickup).
h. One is designated 000-1RZ with D-1 Sunburst tops.
i. Four are designated 000-1RX (Fishman Matrix pickup). Two are designated 000-1RZ with D-1 Sunburst tops.
j. Two are lefthanded. Thirty-five were designated 000C-1 without pickups.
k. Eleven are lefthanded. Eighty were designated 000C-1 without pickups.
l. Eleven are lefthanded. Fifteen were designated 000C-1 without pickups.
m. These four designated 000-16M.
n. Some were designated as 000-16TR (T for Technology). The computer abbreviation was 000TR.
o. Includes two designated 000CTG meaning 000C-16TG (T for Technology, G for gloss).

000-28EC Sunburst totals as follows:

- 7 in 1996
- 23 in 1997
- 11 in 1998
- 15 in 1999
- 14 in 2000
- 9 in 2001
- 24 in 2002
- 7 in 2003
- 7 in 2004
- 43 in 2005

000 One-of-a-Kinds

The following 18 one-of-a-kind 000 models are not included in 000 production totals:

Model	Year
000-18G	1955
000-18H	1938
000-21S	1977
10 String 000-28	1902
Harp 000-28	1906
000-28E	1970
000-28H	1949
000-28K	1921
000-28T	1929
000-30	1919
000-40	1909
000-40H	1933
S-41L	1970
Hays 000-45	1907
Lyre Head 000-45	1914
Vine Fbd. 000-45	1912
000-45G	1939
S-00045	1975

ACOUSTIC BASS
PRODUCTION TOTALS

TOTALS	BM	B-1	B-1E	BC-15E	B-40	BC-40	B-540	B-65	Alt. X Bass	OOC-16GTAE Bass
	331	1602	211	1267	370	72	54	255	81	223
1988					2[a]			3[a]		
1989					92			148		
1990					58			1		
1991					74			40		
1992		145			34	24	24[b]	24	1	
1993		287			29		2	3		
1994	125	268			34	5		18		
1995	101	297			31	20		18		
1996	83	244			12	17	14			
1997	22	231	23	260	4	4	10			
1998		12	47	166		2	4		50	
1999		55	43	148					16	
2000		27	49	124					14	110
2001		36	48	143					1	113
2002			1	141						
2003				139						
2004				146						

Footnotes for ACOUSTIC BASS Production Totals

a Plus one B-40 prototype and one B-65 prototype.
b Plus four B-540 prototypes.

BACKPACKER
TOTALS

TOTALS	Steel String	Nylon String	Mandolin	Ukulele
	142058	13643	4319	4506
1992	623			
1993	5134			
1994	9957	364		
1995	10968	1088		
1996	12792	1366	1452	
1997	12724	1536	1295	
1998	12197	1378	753	128
1999	13625	1285	439	1460
2000	16088	1395	138	810
2001	11875	1348	163	795
2002	11791	1198	77	472
2003	3278	1002	2	450
2004	7935	917		391
2005	8071	766		

SIZE M (0000)[f] PRODUCTION TOTALS

TOTALS	M-16GT	MC-16GTE	MC-16GTE Premium	M-18	M-21	MC-28	M-35	M-36	M-36B (M-36LE)	M-38	MC-37K	M-64	MC-68	X-38	CM00-89	0000-1	0000-28H	0000-38	SWMGT
	224	713	147	106	16	1116	26	1967	20	2114	41	125	217	10	25	377	256	77	84
1975																			
1976						200		200		275									
1977						171		364		200									
1978						20		225		347									
1979				62		42	26	112		182									
1980				18		47		73		98									
1981				5		34		106		48									
1982				17	16	57		46		65									
1983				4		82		56	20	50		11[a]	7[b]						
1984						78		52		29		12	7[c]						
1985						57		48		41	9	21	38						
1986						38		49		44	9	19	53						
1987						64		61		80		12	12						
1988						58		63		63	1	9	28						
1989						92		46		37	1	8	30						
1990						41		78		82	4	4	23						
1991						21		120		122	6	11	17						
1992						14		121		120	2	8	2						
1993								41		110	3	6							
1994								103		75		1							
1995								3		5									
1996																			
1997														10[d]					
1998															25[e]				
1999																104	50		
2000																115	52		
2001	7															67	68	21	
2002	216	392														84	65	56	
2003	1	320	38													7	13		21
2004		1	78														8		63
2005			31																

Footnotes for SIZE M (0000) Production Totals

a All M-64 instruments have adjustable truss rods. The eleven made in 1985 were designated M-64R.
b All MC-68 instruments have adjustable truss rods. The seven made in 1985 were designated MC-68R.
c One of these seven instruments was designated MC-68+. The "+" sign means shaded top.
d Instruments were designated A through J totaling ten instruments.
e These 25 instruments were to be given away as prizes in key USA cities as a promotion for the David Bromberg album *My Own House* on the Fantasy Records label. The serial numbers for these guitars were #408326-408350. The contest instruments were #408326, 330, 331, 332, 334, 336, 337, 338, 346 and 347. The remainder were sold through Martin dealers.
f Between 1997 and 2002, the M size was designated as "0000." After 2002, the M designation was restored.

APPENDICES 261

SIZE D DREADNOUGHT — LONGER RUNNING PRODUCTION TOTALS

Year	D-1 (Original Dreadnought)	D-2 (Original Dreadnought)	D-18 (14-fret)	D-18 (Frap)	D-18E	D-18H Hawaiian	D-18H (Huda)	D-18S (D-18 12-fret)	D-19	D-21	D-25K	D-25K2	D-28 Herringbone 12-fret	D-28 Herringbone 14-fret	D-28 No Herringbone 14-fret	D-28D Frap	D-28E	D-28S	D-28SW Wurlitzer	DC-28	HD-28	D-35	D-35S	D-35SW Wurlitzer	HD-35	D-37K	D-37K2	D-41	D-41S (SD-41S)	D-45	D-45S (SD-45S)	D-76
TOTALS	2	7	71294	176	302	3	2	1669	1715	2933	925	513	41	2054	105916	2	238	1791	30	423	39775	72220	1832	6	6668	414	292	12132	18	6396	24	2074
1931	2	4																														
1932		2																														
1933		1						1 d					1																			
1934			42 a			1		3					4																			
1935			133			2		9					12 e	52 e																		
1936			258					16 e					21 e	81																1		
1937			426										2	61																1		
1938			309										1	148																2		
1939			475											121																2		
1940			377											123																9		
1941			575											134																14		
1942			326											183																19		
1943			425 b											96																24		
1944			407 b											192																19		
1945			475											231 g																		
1946			675											183																			
1947			775											425																			
1948			752											24 h																			
1949			450												426																	
1950			550												506																		
1951			650												427																		
1952			777												475																		
1953			1002												625																		
1954			1151												675																		
1955			1103												804																		
1956			1078							6					806																	
1957			1078							275					702																	
1958			976		1					325					901																	
1959			475		301					200					677			1														
1960			700							25					476		176	2														
1961			675							100					604		1	1														
1962			727							100					507			1														
1963			803							150					680		12	2														
1964			1002						2	200					651		25	1	2													
1965			1133					52	650	125					976		24	4	8			207	1									
1966			2176					150	201	275					1827			2	11			977	35									
1967			2602				2	225		200					2330			20	3			1402	101									
1968			1689					200		351					1959			7				1105	137									
1969			2559					251		300					3161			67	6			1826	175	3								
1970			3037					225		301					3515			125				3334	227	3								
1971			5254					150							5466			163				3597	176									
1972			4224					175							4975			178				4012	150									
1973			4393												5980			251			500	5824	250									
1974			3811					90							5077			225			1486	6184	222		6							
1975			3069					40							4996	2		176			1368	6260	185		464			49		67		
1976			2341	176				10							4056			200		125	1348	5388	12		255			426		162		200
1977			1454												2077			138		1	1044	3522			212			478		81		1874 l
1978			774					23	430		850	501			2250			87		21	844	1975	30		38			502	1	105	1	
1979			1717					9	215 f			1			2316			21		10	526	2750	42		171	175	125	553		110	4	
1980			1093						116						1484			10		26	599	1734	18		95	114	107	506		195	4	
1981			535						17						851			26		7	761	1124			139			452	2	157		
1982			281					4	53 f		35	2			1250			7		21	424	1045	6		172	24	18	511	2	192	2	
1983			400					2	12		24	1 m			743			11		10	560	596	9		162	21	3	2	1	256	1	
1984			224						5						916			3		6	622	622	7		200	7		124		76		
1985			246					1	4		3	6			810			8		8	612	572	11		240	7	3	367	1	40	2	
1986			199					4	6		6	2			825 j			7		16 j	904 j	772	6			7		176		291	1	
1987			258					4	6		5				990			15		7	886	696	10			10	2	122		266	1	
1988			306					4	4		2				952			9		12	1055	800	4				8	78		88		
1989			363					4										4										79	2	45	2	

262 MARTIN GUITARS: A TECHNICAL REFERENCE

SIZE D DREADNOUGHT LONGER-RUNNING PRODUCTION TOTALS (CONTINUED)

TOTALS	D-1 (Original Dreadnought)	D-2 (Original Dreadnought)	D-18 (14-fret)	D-18D (Frap)	D-18E	D-18H Hawaiian	D-18H (Huda)	D-18S (D-18 12-fret)	D-19	D-21	D-25K	D-25K2	D-28 Herringbone 12-fret	D-28 Herringbone 14-fret	D-28 No Herringbone 14-fret	D-28D Frap	D-28E	D-28S	D-28SW Wurlitzer	DC-28	HD-28	D-35	D-35S	D-35SW Wurlitzer	HD-35	D-37K	D-37K2	D-41	D-41S (SD-41S)	D-45	D-45S (SD-45S)	D-76
	2	7	71294	176	302	3	2	1669	1715	2933	925	512	41	2054	105916	2	238	1791	30	423	39773	72220	1832	6	6668	414	292	12132	18	6396	24	2074
1990			293												906					4	1322	742	4		198	4	4	322		111		
1991			312					8							1001			4		24	1106	568	9		168	4	4	286	2	74		
1992			336					5							1213			12		40	1300	688	4		228	14	6	386	2	144		
1993			377					5							1275					26	1284	810			226	7	4	547	4	291		
1994			430 c					3							1639			1		45	1815 k	963	1		320	20	8	611	1	265		
1995			589 c												1856			2		44	1019	917			176			394		215		
1996			335 c												1571					22	1291	740			225			273		288		
1997			445												1962					12	1562	920			246			301		224		
1998			453												1976						1677	947			320			335		195		
1999			558												2165						2113	1060			358			337		197	1	
2000			358												1821						1606	725			355			407		147	1	
2001			582												2788						2356	829			302			581		302		
2002			641												3006						2728	1574			654			564		252		
2003			549												2416						1625	1128			140			543		340		
2004			630												2959						2413	1302			272			674		254		
2005			641												3207						2240	1384			326			443		248		

Footnotes for D SIZE DREADNOUGHT Longer-Running Production Totals

a Total is estimated and includes three guitars designated D-18 Dark Top.
b Three-hundred-eighty-one with old bracing. Twenty-six with new bracing.
c Four with sunburst top in 1994, one with sunburst top in 1995, one with sunburst top in 1996.
d Early 12-fret D-18 models were simply called D-18 12-fret models and not designated D-18S.
e Estimated quantities.
f Twenty-five designated D-19M mahogany top in 1980. One D-19M with a mahogany top in 1982.
g Two-hundred-nineteen with old bracing. Twelve with new bracing.
h Mike Longworth noted a question mark on this entry.
i Two D-28 prototypes (1987) and two HD-28 prototypes (1987) made with cocobolo back and sides.
j Longworth discrepancy. His original edition totals on page 278 showed fifteen vs. sixteen on page 269.
k HD-28 totals include sunburst and "Q" square rod models.
l Ninety-eight were designated as D-76E made as a special offering to Martin employees.
m One made in 1985 is designated D-25K2P, a koa top with low profile (P) neck.

The following one-of-a-kind Dreadnoughts are not included in the above production totals:

DC-1 (Archtop)	2 in 1934	SD8-35 Special	1 in 1969
D-28H Hawaiian	1 in 1934	D-28G (Gut)	1 in 1937, 1 in 1961
D6-20 Special	1 in 1968	D-41E	1 in 1971
D-42S 12-fret	1 in 1934	D-41SE	1 in 1971
D-18M	1 in 1961	SD-41	1 in 1972
D-18T Tenor	1 in 1963	HD-37K2	1 in 1982
D-28T Tenor	1 in 1964	D-45P (Low Profile)	1 in 1987
SD-35S9 Special	1 in 1968	DC-28P (Low Profile)	1 in 1987, 1 in 1988

Note: Model offerings increased significantly after 1986, with even more dramatic increases after 1996. These more recent Dreadnought models are listed in the following charts that cover the years 1986-2005. For 12-String Dreadnoughts, see 12-String Chart. Many Limited and Special Edition Dreadnoughts are listed in the Limited Edition and GOM Charts.

D-100 Fingerboard Detail – 2004

APPENDICES **263**

SIZE D DREADNOUGHT RECENT PRODUCTION TOTALS (PARTS ONE AND TWO)

D SIZE DREADNOUGHT Recent Production Totals (Part One)

TOTALS	DXM (DMX)	DX1	DX1K	DX1R	DXB Black	DXBR Braz.	DXK2	DXME	DCX1E	DCX1RE	DCXE Black	DCXM	DCXME	DM	DCM	DCME	DCRE	DR	D-1	D-1E	D-1R	D-1RE	DC-1	DC-1E	DC-1R	D-2R	D-3R	D-15	D-15S 12-fret	DC-15E	D-16
	15693	25389	1283	3964	245	186	3671	5861	12714	488	724	1267	302	744	56200	1122	6691	25	9006	24008	511	8264	79	1267	5972	48	2433	1098	32459	557	3230	243
1992																				96												
1993																				3588												
1994																				3267 a												
1995																				2762												
1996	43														4260	428	5		771	2100	476	1910 b	73	361 c	260 e		444	87	1276		359	173
1997	49												159		6361	460	786		1771	2561	29	1443	5	178	796		684	221	3179		707	70
1998	760	3757						272				302	405		8091	227	915		1470	2514	1	1089		485 d	1165		490	174	3722		582	
1999	5451	3608			245	186		1678	4				157		8118	7	748	25	845	2165	5	1288	1	208	1309	28	375	167	6437	12	383	
2000	1576	3820		263			1	583	1141				23		6510		806		1188	1316		825		35	625	20	273	145	4625	344	332	
2001	1161	4987		392			1338	703	1269						5337		920		1161	1040		613			454		166	162	4756	48	377	
2002	1502	5203	726	1042			1272	656	2465	49	54				6267		950		791	738		386			385		1	142	3424	70	490	
2003	2787	4014	557	1301			1060	570	4205	439	670	358			4711		782		693	734		384			381				2982	83		
2004	1812			966				791	3630			220			3515		779		316	571		298			324				2058			
2005	552							608				321			3030					556		28			273							

Footnotes for D SIZE DREADNOUGHT Recent Production Totals (Part One)

a Totals below this line include lefthanded and D-1G gloss versions.
b Totals for D-1R include D-1RZ (Sunburst) and D-1RX (Matrix pickup) models.
c Ten listed as DC-1G (Gloss).
d One listed as DC-1G (Gloss).
e 1996–1998 totals include models designated as DC-1X (Matrix pickup installed).

D SIZE DREADNOUGHT Recent Production Totals (Part Two)

TOTALS	D-16GT Gloss Top	D-16T (Satin)	D-16TG (Gloss)	D-16A Ash	D-16H 1991	D-16H 1992	D-16H 1993	D-16K Koa	D-16 Lyptus	D-16M Mahogany	D-16O Oak	D-16R (D-16TR)	D-16R (Gloss)	D-16RGT Gloss Top	D-16W Walnut	DC-16E	DC-16E Premium	DC-16E Koa	DC-16GTE	DC-16GTE Premium	DC-16RE	DC-16RE Aura	DC-16RE Premium	DC-16RGTE	DC-16RGTE Premium	DC-16RGTE Aura	D-17	DC-17E	D-17GT Gloss Top	D-18GE Golden Era	D-18GE Sunburst	D-18V (D-18VM)
	13910	1358	238	818	984	1052	1424	390	156	2120	4	592	636	3731	138	217	3449	79	4145	3043	390	203	2400	1602			1119	133	175	2238	287	2738
1986		10																														
1987		1017																														
1988		96																														
1989		151		7																												
1990		84		751																												
1991				60	980																											
1992			201		4	1052									100																	
1993			35				72								38																	
1994			2				916	390		88																						315 h
1995							436 a			590																						170
1996										660									75													215
1997										782									1329													280 i
1998																			924													253
1999	1475																566		1082								151			230		229
2000	2386																758		735								675			374		242
2001	1873																946										263			376		414
2002	2387										4 b	179 c		651		49	771				121		297					173		424	76 g	167
2003	1517								29			126 d	435	890		168	2				177							132	2	425	78	232
2004	1884								54			140 e	201	742							92	203	1519					1		409	133	221
2005	2388								73			114 f		620		79							584	1602								
												33		828														4				

Footnotes for D SIZE DREADNOUGHT Recent Production Totals (Part Two)

a Three are lefthanded.
b Two with red oak back and sides. Two with white oak back and sides.
c Includes fifty designated D-16TRG made with full gloss.
d Includes forty-three designated D-16TRG made with full gloss.
e Includes two designated D-16TRG made with full gloss.
f Designation simplified from D-16TR (seventy units) to D-16R (forty-four units).
g Sunburst listed as a separate model on price list.
h Includes forty-eight designated D-18VO. "O" is for Vintage Sunburst.
i Simplified from D-18VM to D-18V.

D-45 – 1942

SIZE D DREADNOUGHT
RECENT PRODUCTION TOTALS (PART THREE AND FOUR)

Recent Production Totals (Part Three)

Year	D-18VS (D-18VMS)	D-18VE	D-28GE Golden Era	D-28 Marquis	D-28 Marquis Sunburst	DC-Aura	CHD-28 Cedar Top	LHD-28 Larch Top	HD-28R	HD-28LSV	HD-28V (HD-28VR)	HD-28VE	HD-28VS 12-fret	CHD-35 Cedar Top	LHD-35 Larch Top	D-40	D-40FMG Fig. Mahogany	D-40FW Figured Walnut	D-40QM Quilted Maple	D-41 Special
TOTALS	562	240	600	565	246	821	65	66	830	1218	8534	212	713	19	12	1297	148	148	164	431
1990																				
1991																				
1992																				
1993								2												
1994							40	48	392		1[b]				12					
1995							24	12	225											
1996	82						1	4	121	1	346[b]		56	16		100				
1997	69		103						65	291	689		78	2		160				
1998	88		91						27	127	850		83	1		123				
1999	54		145							138	811[c]		64			92				
2000	46[a]		67							147	767		55			67				
2001	29		48							208	930		58			230				
2002	23		57							81	1252		148			156	146			
2003	116		89							94	786		41			213	2	148	164	378
2004	29	53		19	17	19				131	1078	47	51			156				53
2005	26	187		546	229	802					1024	165	79							

Footnotes for D SIZE DREADNOUGHT Recent Production Totals (Part Three)

a Simplified from D-18VMS to D-18VS.
b One designated as HD-28R in 1994. One designated as HD-28V in 1996.
c Model designation was simplified from HD-28VR to HD-28V.

Recent Production Totals (Part Four)

Year	HPD-41	D-42	D-42K Koa	D-42K2 Koa Top	D-45GE Golden Era	D-45V (D-45VR)	D-60	D-62	SPD16 (SPD-16T)	SPD-16B Black	SPD-16E	SPD-16K	SPD-16K2	SPD-16R (SPD-16TR)	SPD-16M Maple	SPD-16W Walnut	SPDC-16R (SPDC-16TR)	SWD Sustainable Wood	SWDGT (Gloss Top)	SWD Red Birch
TOTALS	109	3675	382	249	167	671	82	142	1698	100	27	563	485	2276	352	254	1020	835	1204	184
1986																				
1987								1												
1988								75												
1989								13												
1990							24	8												
1991							24	5												
1992								16												
1993							13	2												
1994							13	14												
1995		186					8	8												
1996		333																		
1997		297	116			71														
1998		387	19			130														
1999		300	14			47			390					576			75			
2000		266	97	33		74			316			125	138	403			231			
2001		573	44	58		91			299			82	13	507			256		123	
2002	46	373	18	49	71	58			415			95	37	338	144	84	198	267	330	
2003	30	318	37	46	46	77			124	54		106	149	204	74	83	188	328	185	49
2004	25	400	37	30	34	54			102	36		86	78	174	57	37	57	238	195	97
2005	8	242		33	16	69			52	10	27	69	70	74	77	50	15	2	371	38

Willie Nelson and Dick Boak

Willie Nelson N-20 – "Trigger"

Footnotes for CLASSICAL Production Totals

a One 00-44G models made in 1938.
b One 00-45G model made in 1939.
c One 000-18G model made in 1955.
d Collaboration with Thomas S. Humphrey.
e Two prototypes only. Model never issued.

TOTALS	C-1R	CTSH	000C-16SGTNE	000C-16SRNE	N-20WN Willie Nelson	N-20WNB Willie Nelson	Sting CMHS	Sting SWC
	491	268	380	204	59	30	2	45
1995								
1996	d	d						
1997	19	15						
1998	135	144						
1999	85	36			31	24		5
2000	122	16			12	6	2 e	29
2001	115	39			11			5
2002	15	18			5			6
2003			276	107				
2004			22	44				
2005			82	53				

CLASSICAL PRODUCTION TOTALS
GUT (G), NYLON (N) AND CLASSICAL (C)

	00-16C	00-18C	00-18G	00-21G	00-28C	00-28G	00-42G	000-28C	000-28G	N-10 (Short Scale)	N-10 (Long Scale)	N-20 (Short Scale)	N-20 (Long Scale)	N-20B
TOTALS	4235	4351	5138	3	1412	1531	4	560	17	280	555	277	824	2
1936			3			1								
1937			19			4	1		1					
1938			12	1		11	1 a		1					
1939			24	2		19	1 b							
1940			12			18			1					
1941			18			18								
1942			24			24								
1943			6			12			2					
1944			12			12			4					
1945			18			6								
1946			24			30			4					
1947			66			54			3					
1948			36			30								
1949			60			36								
1950			109			66								
1951			158			53								
1952			171			60								
1953			237			48								
1954			350 c			97								
1955			425			108			1 c					
1956			200			74								
1957			375		200	112		178						
1958			375		300	125		175						
1959			725		301	125		100						
1960			703		137	176		100						
1961			900		75	177		6						
1962	302	527	76		125	35		1						
1963	475	475			73									
1964	350	325			59									
1965	375	425			36									
1966	400	400			47									
1967	525	625			15									
1968	700	575			12									
1969	250	225								12	175	12	100	
1970	325	200			1		1			265	100	262	125	
1971	225	175			5					3	48	3	48	
1972	125	75			2						96		98	
1973	50	75			2						84		67	
1974	62	50			3						28		39	
1975	37	36			2						3		37	
1976	3	13			1						5			
1977	2	5			3								24	
1978											2		18	
1979		2			1						6		11	
1980	1	1			5						5		9	
1981	2	5			2								12	
1982					2								17	1
1983		2			3								13	1
1984					2						1		16	
1985	2	2			1								11	
1986					3								11	
1987													18	
1988	1				2								20	
1989		2			4								8	
1990					4								24	
1991					4									
1992	2	2			2						2		12	
1993														
1994					1									

SIZE J (JUMBO) PRODUCTION TOTALS

NOTE: FOR SIZE J 12-STRINGS, SEE 12-STRING CHART.

Year	JM	J-1	JC-1E	J-15	JC-15E	JC-16GTE	JC-16GTE PREMIUM	JC-16RGTE	JC-16RGTE PREMIUM	JC-16RGTE AURA	JC-16WE	JC-16WE PREMIUM	SPJC-16E	SPJC-16RE	J-18 (J-18M)	J-21 (J-21M)	J-21MC	J-40 (J-40M)	J-40BK (J-40MBK)	JC-40 (J-40MC)	J-41 Special	J-65 (J-65M)	HJ-28	SWJGT
TOTALS	1150	1145	247	1662	162	911	558	1087	568	7	105	85	126	244	412	229	57	4861	430	951	126	449	549	156
1985																		259				63		
1986																		275				67		
1987																		332				56		
1988															1		57	397				91		
1989															95	25		388				38		
1990															45[a]	49		344[c]	57	1		8[f]		
1991															48	45		329	36	115		30		
1992															42	32		254	72[d]	76[e]		24		
1993															32	14[b]		307	56	100		18		
1994															49	28		341[g]	64	106		34		
1995															51	8		214[h]	40	132		20		
1996															41	10		96	65	121				
1997		340													3	11		122	21	166			75	
1998		324													5	7		176	17	72			80	
1999		290			27													132	2	54			52	
2000		153			391	153												96		8			104	
2001	301	38	142		316	9								24				91					57	
2002	328		83		317		219		214				10	42				225					95	38
2003	273		20		183		298	35	337	25		13	45	110				157					57	61
2004	234		2		212		227	225	386	241	47	41	55	65				158			35		15	56
2005	14				216		167	298	150	302	7	58	31	16	3			168			91		14	1

Footnotes for SIZE J (JUMBO) Production Totals

- a   Renamed J-18 (previously named J-18M).
- b   Renamed J-21 (previously named J-21M).
- c   Renamed J-40 (previously named J-40M).
- d   Renamed J-40BK (previously named J-40MBK).
- e   Renamed JC-40 (previously named JC-40MC).
- f   Renamed J-65 (previously named J-65M).
- g   Includes one sunburst.
- h   Includes two sunbursts.

J-41 Special – Body Detail

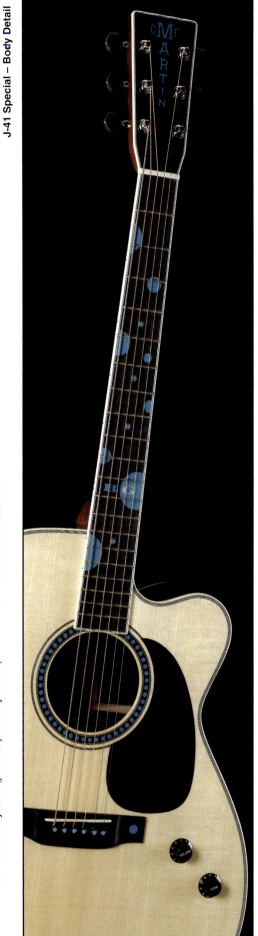

JC Buddy Guy Blues Edition – 2006

MANDOLIN PRODUCTION TOTALS (PART ONE)

Style G Bowl Mandolin – Circa 1895

Year	9 Ribs - Rosewood/Maple	Unidentified Specials	#1 Mandola	#2 Mandola	Mando-Cello	#1 Mandolin	#2 Mandolin	#3 Mandolin	#4 Mandolin	#5 Mandolin	#6 Mandolin	#6a Mandolin	#7 Mandolin	#2 Flat Mandolin	#4 12-String Mandolin	Style 0 Mandolin	Style 00 Mandolin	Style 000 Mandolin	A & AA Mandola	B & BB Mandola	Style R Ditson	Briggs Special	Bitting Special	Bitting Mandola
Totals	5	36	15	1	4	840	949	390	485	280	106	39	32	1	1	726	1258	462	151	43	1	65	40	3
1896	3	2																						
1897	2																							
1898						1	2																	
1899						46	28	2	3															
1900				1		57	53	1	11	1	3													
1901			1			14	89	17	15	11	9													
1902						1	30	37	55	45	8	4	1											
1903						9	141	40	11	17	2	2	1											
1904						22	69	16	67	32	13	6	4											
1905			1			40	45	33	37	14	9	4	5	1 d		6	59 g							
1906						72	39	19	30	21	7	2	3			144	25							
1907		5 a				60	40	24	26	20	3	6	2			95	73	25						
1908		28 b	1		4	22	39	16	42	23	4	1				20 f	25	69						
1909						33	37	25	30	5	3		2			21	72	65						
1910		1 c	3			37	30	33	27	9		4				46	65	148						
1911			7			44	30	3	29	9	3	2	2			40	61	33						
1912						40	45	10	26	15	9		8		1 e	46	96	29			1 j			
1913			2			56	53	19	20	8	7	5	1			48	81	36						
1914						7	32	22	11	12	5	2				17	40 h	30						
1915						12	33	15	9	12	2	2	2			12	30	27	2					
1916						12	6	10	12	6	2	2				7	36			6		24		
1917						29	23	4	4		1	1	1			47	153		7	3		11	10 k	3
1918						41	30	4	5	6	10	1				21	120		19	11		18	27	
1919						52	21	6	2			3				66	135		12	4		12	3	
1920						84	2	5	4	5	1	2				36	133		12					
1921						18	18	2	2	1	1					18	36		12					
1922						12	2	1	5	5							18							
1923						4	3		1							18	37		24					
1924						15	9										12							
1925																	12		12					
1931																			12	3				
1935																				2				
1936																				4				
1937																				3				
1938																				1 i				
1939																			3	3				

Footnotes for MANDOLIN Production Totals (Part One)

- a Four with mahogany joints. One with maple joints.
- b Twenty-six with mahogany joints. Two with maple joints.
- c Maple joints.
- d Mike Longworth designated this instrument as Serial #1492.
- e Mike Longworth designated this instrument as Serial #3732.
- f Some were 3/4 size.
- g Some were 3/4 size.
- h Ten of these had 14 ribs.
- i Serial #16556 has a Style "C" top.
- j This mandolin, Serial #1235 was a bowl back mandolin.
- k Eight were maple.

MANDOLIN PRODUCTION TOTALS (PART TWO)

	A Mandolin	B Mandolin	C Mandolin	D Mandolin	E Mandolin	AK Mandolin	BK Mandolin	A 12-String Mandolin	A Mandola	B Mandola	15 Mandolin	20 Mandolin	30 Mandolin	2-15 Mandolin	2-20 Mandolin	2-30 Mandolin	20S Mandolin	C-2 Mando-Cello	MC-1 Mando-Cello
Totals	13853	1787	394	7	62	1279	57	1	3	3	208	232	2	1906	106	65	30	2	5
1914	46	34	13	5	3														
1915	101	40	16																
1916	80	25	9	2	2														
1917	262	97	16		1	1													
1918	277	82	8		4														
1919	376	157	44		5														
1920	734	391	71		6														
1921	372	93	21			255	51												
1922	413	50	12		6	100													
1923	441	101	24		6	148													
1924	451	88	24		6	175													
1925	400	150	12		12	100													
1926	450	162	50		12	150	6												
1927	350					50													
1928	200	50	12			50													
1929	300	25	39		5														
1930	75	50	10																
1931	275		6																
1932	125	50	6			50		1											
1933	25					50													
1934	125		1 c																
1935	50					25					2	101		18	22	12			
1936	100	6				50					52	25		60	12				
1937	150	9 a				50					15	40	1	24	12	1			
1938	75	12				25					1			24	12	21			3
1939	100	24									12	3			24	12		2	
1940	100	1									36	12		49	24	12			2
1941	175	13 b									27	12				6			
1942	75	24									6	18		60					
1943		12							3	3	6	13	1	48					
1944																			
1945											12	6	1						
1946	200	36									15	1							
1947	475													194					
1948	525													250					
1949	350													125					
1950	375													125			6		
1951	350													75			6		
1952	300													100			6		
1953	450													100			6		
1954	350													150					
1955	200													102			6		
1956	275													100					
1957	350													76					
1958	50													26					
1959	125													50					
1960	200													75					
1961	125													25					1
1962	200													25					
1963	176													25					
1964	175																		

Footnotes for MANDOLIN Production Totals (Part Two)

a Three with #20 headstock.
b Serial #16821 had a blue finish.
c Maple.

MANDOLIN PRODUCTION TOTALS (CONTINUED)

	A Mandolin (Cont.)	B Mandolin (Cont.)	AK2 Mandolin	Custom Shop	Backpacker Mandolin
Totals	13853	1787	394	7	4329
1965	100				
1966	125				
1967	75				
1968	200				
1969	150				
1970	50				
1971	100				
1972	100				
1973	100				
1974	340				
1975	200				
1976	200				
1977	31				
1978					
1979	10				
1980	41				
1981					
1982					
1983	19	1		1	
1984		1	1	3	
1985	4		4	5	
1986	7	1	5		
1987	6		1		
1988	2			1	
1989	2			1	
1990	8	2			
1991	17 d	36 e			
1992	6				
1993	6				
1994					
1995					
1996					1452
1997					1295
1998					753
1999					439
2000					138
2001					163
2002					77
2003					2
2004					
2005					

d Six have mandolin serial numbers. Eleven have guitar serial numbers. In 1991, the separate series of mandolin serial numbers was discontinued. Beginning in that year, the number of mandolins will be available only from the individual production totals in the same manner as any guitar model.

e These forty-one B Mandolins (1983-1987) are constructed with East Indian rosewood.

SIZE 2 1/2 & SIZE 3
PRODUCTION TOTALS

	3-17	2 1/2-17	2 1/2-18	2 1/2-21	2 1/2-28	2 1/2-30	2 1/2-42
TOTALS	1	38	58	29	18	5	1
1898	1						
1899							
1900			2				
1901							
1902							
1903			1				
1904							
1905							
1906					4		
1907						1	1
1908	1			6	2		
1909			1	4		1	
1910		11	1	1			
1911			5	2	2	1	
1912		4	4				
1913		5	5				
1914		4	7				
1915		14				1	
1916			1	1	1		
1917			1	2	1		
1918			2	2	1	1	
1919			2	2			
1920			7	9		1	
1921			15	2	5		
1922			4		2		
1923			3		1		

2 1/2-24 – Circa 1860

2 1/2-24 Peghead Detail – Circa 1860

SIZE 1 (SIZE ONE) PRODUCTION TOTALS

	1-17	1-17P (Plectrum)	1-18	1-18H (Hawaiian)	1-18K (Koa)	1-18T (Tenor - 5-String)	1-18P (Plectrum)	1-21	1-21P (Plectrum)	1-27	1-28	1-28P (Plectrum)	1-30	1-34	1-45
TOTALS	1275	273	964	3	46	3	1	575	1	13	238	19	78	11	6
1898								24		4	9		1	6	
1899	1		19					25		4	16		1	3	1
1900	4		35					29		4	15		7	1	
1901	11		2					31			2		1		
1902			6					24			19		15		1
1903	3		5					28			24		9		
1904	13							36		1	19		11	1	
1905			3					22							
1906			13					18			3		2		1
1907								45			21		5		1
1908	3		7								5				
1909	13		4					16							
1910	10		12					10			6		2		
1911	22		21					10			1		3		
1912	9		9					10			1		2		
1913			17					23			3		2		
1914	10		12		2			55			6				1
1915	23		23	3	18	3		40			23		2		1
1916	25		75		26			44			11		11		
1917	23		117					44			17		4		
1918			236					29			25				
1919			197												1
1920			68				1	6	1		9				
1921								6							
1922															
1923			19												
1924			20												
1925			6												
1926			37												
1927			1												
1928		91										5			
1929		81										8			
1930		50										6			
1931	525	50													
1932	600														
1933															
1934	5														
1935															
1936															
1937															
1938		1 [b]													
1939															
1940															

Footnotes for SIZE 1 Production Totals

a Serial #13582 (Imperial Guitars, Newburgh, NY, Bill Imperial). Incorrectly noted as Serial # 13482.
b This 1-17P was specially made as 5-string.
c This 1-18P was specially made as 5-string.
d This 1-21P was the only one made.

VEGA BANJOS
PRODUCTION TOTALS

Vega Banjo Serial Numbers #1-#1969
Made by C. F. Martin & Co.
For the period 1972-1979.

TOTALS	2022
SS-5 Folklore	95
Folk Ranger-5	3
Ranger-5	3
Ranger-Tenor	3
Folk Wonder-5	124
Wonder-5	561
Wonder-Tenor	70
Wonder-Plectrum	33
Professional-5 a	100
Professional-Tenor	7
Professional-Plectrum	5
Scruggs Mark II-5	1
Scruggs Soloist-5	1
VIP-5	511
VIP-Tenor	55
VIP-Plectrum	45
Folk VIP-5	20
PS-5 Pete Seeger	101
Folk Extra Long	5
Tu-Ba-Phone 2-XL (Extra Long)	25
Tu-Ba-Phone 2-5	29
Whyte Laydie-5	1
V-76 5-string Bicentennial b	92
Vox I-Tenor	46
Vox I-Plectrum	45
Vox IV-Tenor	21
Vox IV-Plectrum	34
Vox V-Tenor	3
Vox V-Plectrum	18
Vox 45-Tenor	1
Vox 45-Plectrum	5
V-41-5	28
V-41-Tenor	2
V-41-Plectrum	1
V-45-5	22
V-45-Tenor	2
V-45-Plectrum	2

Footnotes for
Vega Banjo Production Totals

a Bobby Joe Fenster model (a ficticious endorsee).
b Includes employee models.

SIZE 2 (SIZE TWO) PRODUCTION TOTALS

	TOTALS	2-17 Old	2-17 New	2-17H (Hawaiian)	2-17T (Tenor)	#25	2-18	2-18G	2-18T (Tenor)	2-21	2-21T (Tenor)	2-27	2-28T (Tenor)	2-30	2-34	2-40	2-42	2-44	2-45	2-45T (Tenor)
TOTALS		6100	612	551	45	775	100	1	345	12	1	8	35	7	2	1	2	4	4	2
1898							15													
1899							26			1		3			2					
1900							9			2		1								
1901										1		2								
1902							4													
1903							3											2		
1904										1				1						
1905										1				1						
1906														1						
1907																				
1908		6					2			1		2								
1909																1a				
1910																				
1911																				
1912																				
1913																				
1914																				
1915																				
1916																				
1917																				
1918																				
1919																				
1920																				
1921																				
1922		344																		
1923		798							162	2	1a		6	1					2	1
1924		500							133				29	2					1	1
1925		600					2		50	2				1						
1926		1300		200	15	25				1										
1927		1000		150	30	750	26													
1928		450	50	150																
1929		603	475																	
1930		499	62	51																
1931			9																	
1932			10																	
1933							1											4		
1934			4																	
1935			1																	
1936							12													
1937																				
1938																				
1939																				
1940																				
1941																				
1942																				
1943																				
1944																				
1945																				
1946																				
1947																				
1948																				
1949																				
1950																				
1951																				
1952																				
1953								1a												
1954																				

Footnotes for SIZE 2 Production Totals

a One-of-a-kind Size 2 models included a 2-40 in 1909, a 2-21T (Tenor) in 1928, and a 2-18G in 1954.

APPENDICES 271

SIZE 5 PRODUCTION TOTALS (PART ONE)

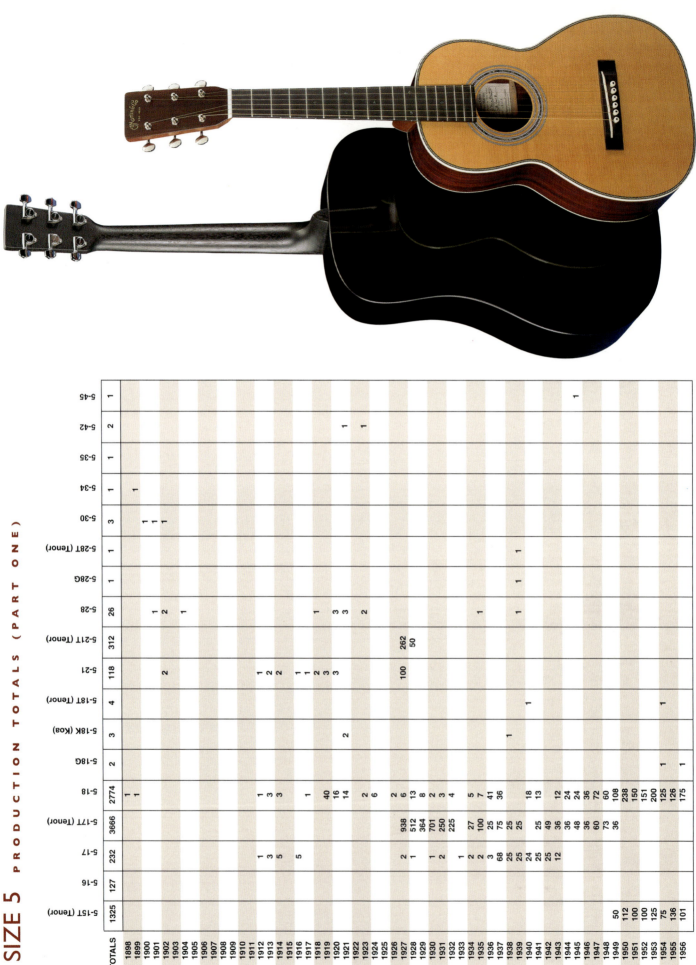

Size 5 "Terz" Mini-Martin – 1999

Year	5-15T (Tenor)	5-16	5-17	5-17T (Tenor)	5-18	5-18G	5-18K (Koa)	5-18T (Tenor)	5-21	5-21T (Tenor)	5-28	5-28G	5-28T (Tenor)	5-30	5-34	5-35	5-42	5-45
TOTALS	1325	127	232	3666	2774	2	3	4	118	312	26	1	1	3	1	1	2	1
1898					1													
1899					1										1			
1900																		
1901																		
1902														1				
1903														1				
1904														1				
1905																		
1906																		
1907																		
1908																		
1909																		
1910																		
1911			1		1						1							
1912			3		3						2							
1913			5		3						1							
1914																		
1915			5															
1916																		
1917					1													
1918									1									
1919									2									
1920									2									
1921							2											
1922																		
1923																		
1924									1									
1925									2		1							
1926			2	938	40				2		3							
1927			1	512	16				3	262	3							
1928				364	14				3	50	2							
1929				701	8													
1930			1	250	2													
1931			2	225	6													
1932					2													
1933			1	27	6													
1934			2	100	13													
1935			2	25	8													
1936			3	75	2													
1937			68	25	3													
1938			25	25	4													
1939			25		5													
1940			24	25	7												1	
1941			25	49	41			1									1	
1942			25	36	36		1				1							
1943			12	48														
1944				36	18													
1945				36	13						1	1	1					1
1946				60	12													
1947				60	24													
1948				73	36													
1949	50			36	60													
1950	112				72													
1951	100				108													
1952	100				238													
1953	125				150													
1954	75				151			1										
1955	136				200	1												
1956	101				125	1												

SIZE 5 PRODUCTION TOTALS (PART TWO)

Claire 2 – 2007

Year	5-15T (Tenor)	5-16	5-17	5-17T (Tenor)	5-18	5-18G	5-18K (Koa)	5-18T (Tenor)	5-21	5-21T (Tenor)	5-28	5-28G	5-28T (Tenor)	5-30	5-34	5-35	5-42
TOTALS	1325	127	232	3666	2774	2	3	4	118	312	26	1	1	3	1	1	2
1957	50				175												
1958	75				175												
1959	50				50												
1960	175	77			126			1									
1961	75	50			77			1									
1962	100				25												
1963	1																
1964																	
1965					3												
1966																	
1967					126												
1968					60												
1969					12						1						
1970					42						1					1	
1971					25												
1972					36												
1973					1												
1974					38												
1975					6												
1976					20												
1977									1		1						
1978					2												
1979					4												
1980					7						3						
1981											4						
1982					2												
1983					4												
1984					4												
1985					3												
1986					1						1						
1987					2												
1988					1												

Year	Mini Martin	5-15	5-16GT	Sting Mini	Claire Brazilian
TOTALS	295	371	199	54	39
1999	10				
2000	94				
2001	45				
2002	43				
2003	36	252	146		
2004	35	51	37	54	
2005	32	68	16		39

Footnotes for SIZE 5 Production Totals

a Longworth originally reported 100 5-21 and 262 5-21T models made in 1927. They were all tenor guitars, but some were designated without the "T" suffix. We have corrected this error to report a total of 362 5-21T models made in 1927.

N, P, Q and R Designation PRODUCTION TOTALS
LOW PROFILE (P), SQUARE NECK ROD (Q AND N) AND ADJUSTABLE TRUSS ROD (R)

Modified Low Oval

Low Profile

Modified V

a

	D-18P	D-25K2P	D-28P	DC-28P	HD-28P	D-35P	HD-35P	D-45P
TOTALS	358	1	1874	2	1959	1485	161	1
1985		1						
1986	18		75		37	33		
1987	135		81		449	375	10	
1988	205		396	1	597	443	86	
1989			594	1	876	634	65	1

b

	D-18Q	D-28Q	HD-28Q	D-35Q	D-41Q	D-45Q	0-18Q	00-18Q	000-18Q	000-28Q	000-28BQ	M-36Q	M-38Q
TOTALS	299	923	96	500	9	36	9	40	48	420	12	6	15
1986	5	8		8					5	5			
1987		21		16	1	4			3	3	12		
1988	5	46		35	1	11		10	15	15			
1989	51	56		70	5	16	2	12		12			
1990	22	62		36					2	28			
1991	20	45		24					7	10			
1992	24	72		32				2		55			
1993	53	107		68	1			12		52			
1994	26	87	19	18		1	7	4		102		6	10
1995	38	141	34	102		3				26			
1996	22	95	28	24		1				46			
1997	16	69	15	42					15	14			5
1998	7	50		7					1	29			
1999	10	47		9	1					16			
2000		11		6						7			
2001		6		3									

	D-41N	D-45N	00-45N	000-45N	OM-45N
TOTALS	112	303	3	16	3
1988	10	21			
1989	20	42			1
1990	21	34	3	1	
1991	28	41		4	2
1992	8	81		11	
1993	13	47			
1994	8	15			
1995	4	17			
1996		3			
1997		2			

c

	D-18R	D-12-18R	D-19R	D-28R	D-12-28R	DC-28R	HD-28R	D-35R	D-37KR	D-37K2R	D-41R	D-45R	J-21MR	J-40MR	J-65MR	J12-65MR	M-18R	MC-28R	M-36R	M-38R	M-64R	MC-68R	0-18R	00-18R	000-18R	000-28R	000-45R	Custom 15R	P
TOTALS	165	5	5	488	27	5	370	361	3	5	42	46	25	147	40	19	10	31	22	27	11	7	2	1	6	17	1	11	
1985	165	5	5	488	27	5	345	336	3	5	42	46	25	147	40	19	10	31	22	27	11	7	2	1	6	17	1	11	
1986							25	25																					

Footnotes for N, P, Q and R Production Totals

a   The P designation, initiated in 1985, differentiated Low Profile from Full Thickness necks.
    The P designation was discontinued in 1990, as it had become superfluous.
b   Q Series (Non-adjustable Square Tube Bar in Neck) and N Series (Non-scalloped bracing with Square Tube Bar in Neck) Production Totals are also included in grand totals for each model.
c   R Series (Adjustable Truss Rod in Neck) Production Totals are also included in grand totals for each model.
d   Eleven of 179 total Custom 15R models made in 1985 had an adjustable truss rod.

12-STRING PRODUCTION TOTALS

Custom OMC-12-String – 1983

Year	DM-12	D12X-1 (DX12-1)	D12XM (DX12M)	D12-1	D12-18	D12-20	D12-20E	D12-28	D12-35	D12-41 (12-fret)	SD12-41 (14-fret)	D12-45 (12-fret)	SD12-45 (14-fret)	SPD12-16R	J12-15	J12-16GT	J12-40 (J12-40M)	J12-65 (J12-65M)	M12-38	0012-35	000012-28H	X-12[d]	X-12-35[e]
TOTALS	4752	2607	523	1416	1743	10340	1	5850	6592	47	6	102	2	181	1092	679	556	163	1	1	79	1	1
1964						152			183													1	1
1965						726			250														
1966						376			625														
1967						1076			802														
1968						1226			803														
1969						1675	1	27	928			3											
1970						1654		408	854	2		24											
1971					277	1026		650	626	16	4	6											
1972					465	1454		602	352	1	1	4	1					1					
1973					326	427		630	378	1		15											
1974					196	352		468	336	3		2											
1975					81	130		392	168	6		6											
1976					62	46		193	115	1		10											
1977					107	4		100	62			4								1			
1978					87	2		196	18														
1979					18	2		195	31	1		1											
1980					7	1		115	10	3		2											
1981					7	2		48	8			1											
1982					14	2		47	7			1									1		
1983					11			48	6	2		1					43	19					
1984					10			38	6	1		1					3	7					
1985					11	3		50	2			2					42	10					
1986					9			55	5	1		2					40	22					
1987					16			97	3								59[b]	20					
1988					11	4		106	2	4		1					79	16[c]					
1989					16			65	6	2							48	44					
1990					8			36	2								72	4					
1991								70	4	1		2					33	6					
1992					4			68	3	1							57	7					
1993								74	2								46	8					
1994								82									30						
1995								82[a]									4						
1996								77															
1997		419		363				81						70	225	92					21		
1998		517	364	202				105						36	233	133					56		
1999		633	144	262				81				13		67	192	125							
2000		664	11	230				66						8	150	124					2		
2001		618	4	182				81							150	124							
2002		555		158				66							138	87							
2003	362	591		19				185							154	118							
2004	710	267						141															
2005	274	351						172															

Footnotes for 12-STRING Production Totals

a One noted as a sunburst.
b Renamed J12-40 (Previously named J12-40M)
c Renamed J12-65 (Previously named J12-65M)
d The X-12 was the prototype for the D12-20 (Ser. #193363).
   Also D12-20A (Ser. #195323) and D12-20B (Ser. #195324) were designated.
e The X-12-35 was the prototype for the D12-35 (Ser. #201943).

The following very early one-of-a-kind 12-String models are not listed in the above totals:

000-18 12-String	–	Made in 1913
000-21 12-String	–	Made in 1921
000-28 12-String	–	Made in 1936
C-1 12-String	–	Made in 1932
C-2 12-String	–	Made in 1932
F-1 12-String	–	Made in 1941

APPENDICES 275

UKULELE Production Totals

TOTALS	Assorted[a]	SO Ukulele	HSO Ukulele	Backpacker Uke
	202588	4347	570	4506[c]
1907	6[b]			
1908				
1909				
1910				
1911				
1912				
1913				
1914				
1915	12			
1916	1371			
1917	1988			
1918	1495			
1919	3541			
1920	3165			
1921	1669			
1922	4793			
1923	4785			
1924	7062			
1925	10870			
1926	14101			
1927	5860			
1928	3605			
1929	3349			
1930	4584			
1931	2718			
1932	987			
1933	737			
1934	917			
1935	985			
1936	1076			
1937	1436			
1938	1144			
1939	862			
1940	917			
1941	1443			
1942	2143			
1943	8163			
1944	3003			
1945	2495			
1946	4231			
1947	1567			
1948	3041			
1949	8076			
1950	11722			
1951	6214			
1952	4532			
1953	4901			
1954	4508			
1955	3848			
1956	4238			
1957	3900			
1958	3691			
1959	5356			
1960	4354			
1961	5126			
1962	4245			
1963	4319			
1964	4488			
1965	2801			
1966	1496			
1967	1425			
1968	75			
1969	111			
1970	311			
1971	512			
1972	525			
1973	375			
1974	126			
1975	286			
1976	232			
1977	95			
1978				
1979	93			
1980	52			
1981	60			
1982	30			
1983	31			
1984	38			
1985	14			
1986	15			
1987	30			
1988	28			
1989	47			
1990	13			
1991	18			
1992	68			
1993	4			
1994	38			
1995				
1996				
1997				
1998				128
1999				1460
2000			54	810
2001		523	250	795
2002		938	118	472
2003		952	57	450
2004		967	59	391
2005		967	32	

Footnotes for UKULELE Production Totals

a Ukulele totals are a combination of production figures and sales totals. These numbers should be sufficient to establish ukulele trends. Included are Soprano, Concert, Tenor, and Baritone ukulele sizes.

b All six were made for Bergstrom Music of Honolulu, Hawaii. These were trail lot samples to calculate pricing. Longworth notes that one was made with a spruce top, though it is likely that all six had spruce.

c Backpacker ukulele totals are also included with the Backpacker

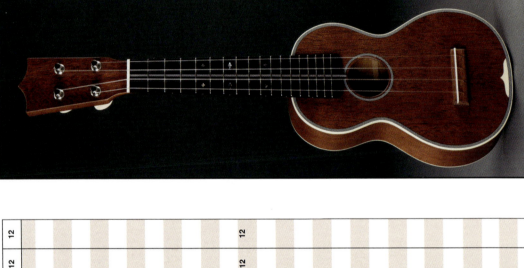

Style 3 Ukulele – 2008

TIPLE Production Totals (Part One)

	Unknown Style	T-15	T-17S (#5 Body)	T-17	T-18	T-28 (Rosewood)	T-28 (Maple)	T-42 (8-String)	T-45	T-Smith	T-Ditson
	213	755	1	1355	2416	489	1	1	1	12	12
1898											
1899											
1900											
1901											
1902											
1903											
1904											
1905											
1906											
1907											
1908											
1909											
1910											
1911											
1912											
1913											
1914											
1915											
1916											
1917	62										
1918	3										
1919	30[a]										
1920	118										
1921				6							
1922					1[b]	2[c]					
1923				25	225	18					
1924				350	375	12					
1925				150	350	6					
1926				50	650	36					
1927				75	100	12					
1928				150							
1929				25							
1930				50							
1931				75		6					
1932				50		6					
1933			1	50		6					
1934				50	25				1	12	12
1935				25	1		1	1[d]			
1936											
1937											
1938					36	6					
1939				25	86	30					
1940				37	36						
1941	[e]			87	48	12					
1942	[e]	62			60	28					
1943	[e]	75			24						
1944		62			12	6					
1945		49			24						
1946		50			12						
1947		50									
1948		50									
1949											
1950											
1951											
1952											
1953											
1954											
1955											
1956											

UNUSUAL SIZES PRODUCTION TOTALS

	Schuyler Model America	Dubtiz Harp Guitar	Harp (No Model)	Extra Large 17" Body	Prototype 00-42 (45)	1/4-18	1/4-28	1/4 12 String	1/2-18	1/2-21	3/4-18	3/4-21	7-28 (7/8 Dreadnought)	7-37K (7/8 Dreadnought)
TOTALS	2	1	1	1	2	24	14	6	18	1	4	1	208	95
1902					2									
1903														
1904														
1905														
1906														
1907	1													
1908														
1909	1													
1910														
1911			1											
1912														
1913		1												
1914														
1915				1		6								
1916						3			3					
1917						5		6	15					
1918						2				1				
1919						3								
1920														
1921														
1922														
1923														
1924														
1925														
1926														
1927														
1928														
1929						1								

No production of these models between 1930 and 1972

	Schuyler Model America	Dubtiz Harp Guitar	Harp (No Model)	Extra Large 17" Body	Prototype 00-42 (45)	1/4-18	1/4-28	1/4 12 String	1/2-18	1/2-21	3/4-18	3/4-21	7-28 (7/8 Dreadnought)	7-37K (7/8 Dreadnought)
1973														
1974						2	2				4	1		
1975						2								
1976														
1977														
1978														
1979							12							
1980														
1981														
1982														
1983														
1984														
1985														
1986														
1987														
1988														
1989														
1990														
1991														
1992														
1993														
1994													112	12
1995													81	76
1996														1
1997													2	2
1998													2	1
1999													1	3
2000														
2001													1	
2002													2	
2003													3	
2004													2	

TIPLE PRODUCTION TOTALS (PART TWO)

	Unknown Style	T-15	T-17S (#5 Body)	T-17	T-18	T-28 (Rosewood)	T-28 (Maple)	T-42 (8-String)	T-45	T-Smith	T-Ditson
TOTALS	213	755	1	1355	2416	489	1	1	1	12	12
1957		50			12	6					
1958		25			12	5					
1959		25			12	6					
1960		50			12	12					
1961		12			24	6					
1962		24			24	18					
1963		48			12	6					
1964		12			24	24					
1965		12			24						
1966		49			24	6					
1967					6	12					
1968					30	18					
1969					18						
1970					12	12					
1971					24	18					
1972					6	12					
1973					18	30					
1974					12	48					
1975					24						
1976					11	4					
1977						17					
1978											
1979					4	5					
1980					2	5					
1981						1					
1982						1					
1983											
1984											
1985											
1986											
1987					1	5					
1988						2					
1989						2					
1990						2					
1991											
1992											
1993					3						
1994											
1995											
1996											
1997											
1998											
1999											
2000											
2001											
2002											
2003											
2004											
2005											

Footnotes for TIPLE Production Totals (Parts One and Two)

a Six instruments were made with eight strings.
b Some were made for Wurlitzer, some were made for Ditson.
c One of these (2) T-28 tiples was an 8-string.
d This T-42 Tiple was an 8-string.
e No Tiples were made from 1941–1945 due to war restrictions.

GUITARS OF THE MONTH (GOM) PRODUCTION TOTALS (PART ONE)

Year	Custom 15B Brazilian	D-18MB	D-18 Special	D-18V	D-18 Vintage	D-21LE	D-28SP 1935	D-28B Brazilian	D-28 Custom	D-28LSH	D3-18	D-35B Brazilian	D-40BLE	D-41B Brazilian	D-41BLE	D-42LE	D-45B Brazilian	D-45 Deluxe	D-45 Gene Autry	D-45KLE	D-45LE	D-45S Deluxe	D-62LE	D-93	HD-18LE	HD-28B Brazilian	HD-28BLE	HD-28BSE (HD-28BLE)	HD-28CTB	HD-28LE	HD-28GM Grand Marquis	HD-28GM LSH Grand Marquis
	1986	1990	1989	1985	1992	1985	1993	1985-6	1984	1991	1991	1985-6	1990	1986	1989	1988	1994	1993	1994	1991	1987	1992	1986	1993	1987	1986	1990	1987	1992	1985	1989	1994
Retail	N/A	$2,300	$1,950	$1,640	$1,998	$1,550	$3,800	$2,100	$2,000	$4,398	$2,398	N/A	$5,598	$2,840	$4,800	$3,300	N/A	$18,200	$22,000	$7,800	$7,500	$9,760	$2,100	$3,000	$2,250	N/A	$3,900	$3,300	$3,800	$2,210	$3,198	$3,900
Export	2	3	13	0	3	0	20	0	0	11	8	0	8	1	8	6	0	10	16	4	6	10	2	17	1	0	8	5	8	0	8	15
USA	10	96	15	56	215	75	224	12	43	200	72	11	50	1	31	69	23	50	50	50	44	50	46	148	50	47	100	88	89	87	112	136
Total	12	99	28	56	218	75	244	12	43	211	80	11	58	1	39	75	23	60	66	54	50	60	48	165	51	47	108	93	97	87	120	151
1984									43																							
1985	10			56		75		1				1																		87		
1986	2							11				10		1									48			47						
1987																					50				51			93[a]				
1988			28													75																
1989															39																	
1990		99											58														108					
1991										211	80									54												
1992					218																	60									120	
1993							244											60						165					97			
1994																	23		66													151[b]

Footnotes for GUITARS OF THE MONTH (GOM) Production Totals (Part One)

a   One of these is designated as an HD-28BLE.
b   Thirty of these were made with sunburst tops.

GUITARS OF THE MONTH (GOM) PRODUCTION TOTALS (PART TWO)

Year	HD-28PSE	HJ-28	HJ-28M	HD-28SE	HOM-35	HD-35B Brazilian	00-18V	00-21B Brazilian	00-21LE	00-45B Brazilian	000-18SOI Sing Out 40th	000-28B Brazilian	000-45B Brazilian	J-21MB Brazilian	J-21MC	J-40MB Brazilian	J-40MBLE Brazilian	J-45M Deluxe	OM-21 Special	OM-28LE	OM-28 Perry Bechtel	OM-28SOI Sing Out 35th	OM-40LE	OMC-28	M-21LE	M-36LE	M-36B Brazilian	M-38B Brazilian	M-45B	M2C-28	N-20B
	1988	1992	1994	1986	1989	1986	1984	1985	1987	1985	1991	1985	1985	1986	1986	1986	1987	1986	1991	1985	1993	1985	1994	1990	1984	1984	1985	1985	1986	1988	1985
Retail	$2,750	$3,050	$3,900	$2,300	$4,000	N/A	$1,520	$2,020	$2,300	N/A	N/A	$2,040	N/A	N/A	$1,750	N/A	$3,000	$6,900	$3,998	$2,180	$4,000	N/A	$7,100	$3,148	$1,600	$2,140	$2,140	$2,508	N/A	$2,700	N/A
Export	3	13	12	8	7	0	0	1	1	0	0	6	0	0	1	0	1	1	4	2	17	0	21	2	0	N/A	0	17	0	2	0
USA	93	56	60	130	53	3	9	1	18	2	40	6	2	1	55	4	16	16	32	39	77	35	69	74	16	N/A	20	17	3	20	1
Total	96	69	72	138	60	3	9	1	19	2	40	6	2	1	56	4	17	17	36	41	94	35	90	76	16	N/A	20	17	3	22	1
1984							9																			N/A					
1985								1		2		6	2							41		35			16		20	17			1
1986						3								1	56	4		17											3		
1987									19								17														
1988	96																													22	
1989					60																										
1990																								76							
1991											40								36												
1992		69																													
1993																					94										
1994			72																				90[a]								

Guitars of the Month, Limited and Special Editions are more fully described in book 2, chapter 3.

Footnotes for GUITARS OF THE MONTH (GOM) Production Totals (Part Two)

a   Thirty-one of these were made with sunburst finish.

278   MARTIN GUITARS: A TECHNICAL REFERENCE

LIMITED and SPECIAL EDITION PRODUCTION TOTALS (PART ONE)

Note: Production totals for Limited and Special Editions are a combination of serial number stamping (which happens when a model is initiated), combined with final inspection records (which occurs after an instrument is completed), so yearly totals listed in the charts below may not correspond with annual serial number records.

YEAR	CEO-1 "CEO's Choice" 1997 $2,600	CEO-1R "CEO's Choice" 2003 $7,999	CEO-2 "CEO's Choice" 1998 $2,900	CEO-3 "CEO's Choice" 1999 $3,500	CEO-4 "CEO's Choice" 2000 $2,500	CEO-4R "CEO's Choice" 2002 $2,699	CEO-5 "CEO's Choice" 2001 $2,649	Cowboy X 2000 $999	Cowboy II 2001 $999	Cowboy III 2001 $1,099	Cowboy IV 2003 $1,199	D-100 Deluxe 2004 Varies	D-16BH Beck 2001 $2,950	D-18 Andy Griffith 2003 $3,699	D-18CW Clarence White 2001 $3,999	D-18DC David Crosby 2002 $3,799	D-21JC Jim Croce 2000 $3,450	D-21JCB Jim Croce 2000 $8,475	D12-42RM Roger McGuinn 1999 $6,900	D-28CW Clarence White 2002 $4,899	D-28CWB Clarence White 2002 $9,999	D-28DM Del McCoury 2002 $4,899	D-28HW Hank Williams 1998 $9,000	D-28KT Kingston Trio 1997 Set of 3	D-28KTBS Bob Shane 2003 $3,799	D-28KTBSDG Bob Shane 2003 $3,999	D-28LF Lester Flatt 1998 $8,500	D-35ET Ernest Tubb 2003 $4,499	D-35 30th Anniversary 1995 $4,000	D-40DM Don McLean 1998 $5,750	D-41DF Dan Fogelberg 2001 $4,750	D-41GJ George Jones 2000 $4,750
TOTALS	135	30	110	56	409	283	366	250	500	750	250	24	99	311	292	250	73	65	65	395	150	115	150	34	19	32	50	90	207	50	141	100
1995																													207			
1996																																
1997	128																							34								
1998	7		110																				150				49			38		
1999				48																							1			12		
2000				8	280			250									72	1														100
2001					83		6		500	5			99		285		35	29	33												141	
2002					44	133	235			745					7	239			14	251	149	115										
2003		30			2	40	69				210			178		11			15	23	1				19	32		90				
2004						40	56				40	18		133					3	121												
2005						70						6																				

LIMITED and SPECIAL EDITION PRODUCTION TOTALS (PART TWO)

YEAR	D-42JC Johnny Cash 1997 $8,200	D-42 Amazon Rosewood 2003 $7,999	D-45 Celtic Knot 2004 $35,000	D-45CFM CFM Sr. 200th 1996 $11,000	D-45CFMB CFM Sr. 200th 1996 $19,500	D-45GA Gene Autry 1994 $22,000	D-45 Mike Longworth 2005 $13,999	D-45SS Stephen Stills 1998 $19,000	D-50 Deluxe 2001 $50,000	D-50K Deluxe 2003 Varies	DC & DCE Trey Anastasio 2005 $5,499	DCRNS Ned Steinberger 2002 $3,649	D Figured Koa Special 2005 $14,999	DM3MD Dave Matthews 1999 $3,250	D Night Dive 2004 $19,999	DSR Sugar Ray 2002 $2,499	DVM Veterans 2002 $3,199	EMP1 Employee Model 1998 $2,450	EMP2 Employee Model 1999 $2,700	EMPNS Employee Model 2000 $2,299	Hawaiian X 2002 $1,099	HD-35SJC Judy Collins 2002 $5,149	HD12-35SJC Judy Collins 2002 $5,349	HD-40 Tom Petty 2004 $4,999	HD12-40 Tom Petty 2004 $5,199	HD-18JB Jimmy Buffett 1998 $3,650	HD-28KM Keb Mo 2001 $3,999	HD-28SO Sing Out! 45th 1996 $4,500	HD-40LSH Tom Paxton 2004 $4,899	HD-40MK Mark Knopfler 2001 $4,999	HD-40MS Marty Stuart 1996 $5,400	HD-7 Roger McGuinn 2005 $5,499
TOTALS	80	30	30	112	91	66ª	91	91	50	22	56	31	25	234	6	57	527	222	30	73	500	50	33	274	90	424	252	45	30	251	250	212
1994						66																										
1995																																
1996				112	91																							45			125	
1997	80																														125	
1998								80										208								216						
1999								11						231				14	13							207						
2000																	343		17	23						1						
2001									40					3			93			50							181			11		
2002									5			31				57	9				389	50	31				71			240		
2003		30								19ᵇ							82				40		2									
2004			10							3					6						15			274	90				30			
2005			20				78				56ᶜ		25								56											212

Footnotes for LIMITED and SPECIAL EDITION Production Totals (Parts One and Two)

a Thirteen have larger name inlaid in fingerboard. Sixteen Gene Autry models were made for the export market, while fifty were for the USA.
b Five are designated D-50K2 Deluxe with koa tops.
c Six of these were DCE with electronics. The remaining eighty-five Trey Anastasio guitars were made in 2006.
d One Marty Stuart model was incorrectly designated HD-28MS.

Guitars of the Month, Limited and Special Editions are more fully described in book 2, chapter 3.

APPENDICES 279

LIMITED and SPECIAL EDITION PRODUCTION TOTALS (PART THREE)

	HDN Negative	HDO Grand Ole Opry 75th	HTA Kitty Wells	JC-16KWS Kenny W. Shepherd	M3M George Martin	JDP Diane Ponzio	M3SC Shawn Colvin	MC-40 Eric Johnson	Meazzi Anniversary (Italy)	MPFF Philly Folk Fest	MTV1 (Satin)	MTV1G (Gloss)	MTV-2 (Satin)	MTV-2G (Gloss)	N-20WN Willie Nelson	N-20WNB Willie Nelson	NWD George Nakashima	0-18TKT Kingston Trio	0-28 Ian Anderson	0-45JB Joan Baez	OM-28 Perry Bechtel	OM-28JM John Mayer	OM-42PS Paul Simon	OM-42 Quilted Maple (I)	OM-42 Quilted Maple (II)	OM-45 Tasmanian Blackwood	OM-40 Rory Block	OMC-18VLJ Laurence Juber	OMC-28 Laurence Juber	OMC-28B Laurence Juber	OM Night Dive	00-16DB Women In Music
YEAR	2002	2000	2002	2001	2005	2003	2002	2003	1996	2002	1996	1996	2003	2003	1998	1998	2000	1997	2004	1998	1993	2003	1997	2003	2004	2005	2004	2002	2004	2004	2004	1997
RETAIL	$3,699	$3,350	$3,299	$3,149	$5,699	$3,999	$3,199	$4,999	N/A	$3,499	$2,200	$2,450	$2,749	$2,999	$5,500	$9,800	$4,750	Set of 3	$5,499	$9,850	$4,000	$4,499	$8,000	$6,999	$7,499	$13,999	$5,199	$4,449	$4,999	$9,999	$19,999	$2,100
TOTALS	135	574	70	198	37	101	120	90	19	85	73	588	15	98	59	30	59	34	87	59	94 b	404	225	30	30	29	38	133	130	50	11	97
1993																					94 b											
1994																																
1995																																
1996												588																				
1997											73							32					225									97
1998															31	24		2		57												
1999									19						12	6				2												
2000		105													11		14															
2001		244		180						84				85	5		41															
2002	135	88	75	18			109			1			14	9			4											128				
2003		63	1			101	11	90					1	4								174		19				5				
2004		49																	87			199		11	10		38		129	50	5	
2005		25			37 a																	31			20	29			1		6	

LIMITED and SPECIAL EDITION PRODUCTION TOTALS (PART FOUR)

	00-16DBR Women In Music	00-17SOI Sing Out 50th	00-18CTN Elizabeth Cotten	00-18SH Steve Howe	00-37KSM Steve Miller	00-37K25M Steve Miller	00-40ST Stauffer	00-45ST Stauffer	00-45S "1902"	000-16RGD Godfrey Daniels	000-18MC Martin Carthy	000-18WG Woody Guthrie	000-28 Norman Blake	000-28B Norman Blake	000-28EC Eric Clapton	000-28S Golden Era 12-fret	000-28LD Lonnie Donegan	000-28LDB Lonnie Donegan	000-40SPR Peter Rowan	000-40QGN Graham Nash	000-42EC Eric Clapton	000-42ECB Eric Clapton	000-45JR Jimmie Rodgers	000-45S Stephen Stills	000C-16RB Babyface	000C Steve Miller	000C-28SMH Merle Haggard	000CBD Dion	000-JBP Jimmy Buffett	000-JBS Jimmy Buffett	000-ECHF Bellezza Nera	000-ECHF Bellezza Bianca
YEAR	1997	2000	2001	1999	2000	2000	1997	1997	2002	2002	2003	1999	2004	2004	2002	1996	2002	2002	2001	2003	1995	2000	1997	2005	2000	2005	2001	2002	2003	2003	2004	2006
RETAIL	$2,400	$2,399	$2,950	$2,950	$5,750	$6,250	$7,900	$20,000	$22,500	$2,849	$3,199	$3,150	$4,999	$9,999	$9,999	$4,000	$4,099	$8,219	$4,999	$4,699	$8,100	$15,000	$25,000	$12,999	$2,850	$4,499	$4,799	$3,299	$3,699	$3,699	$5,999	$5,999
TOTALS	430	50	76	250	68	68	35	25	60	26	67	140	218	52	500	373	72	25	87	147	461	200	52	91	96	383	122	57	304	168	475	10
1993																																
1994																																
1995																					461											
1996																373																
1997	71						34	21															49									
1998	358						1	4															3									
1999	1			195																												
2000		50		55	68	68						117										67			27							
2001			75									23							87			133			67		117					
2002			1						47	21					398		45	25							2		5	57				
2003									2	5	62				26		27			147									301	161		
2004									7		5		146	51	61														3	7	18	
2005													72	1	15									84		376					457	10

Footnotes for LIMITED and SPECIAL EDITION Production Totals (Parts Three and Four)

a A total of 127 George Martin M3M guitars were made. The remaining 90 guitars were completed in 2006.
b In addition to 77 Perry Bechtel models made for the USA, 17 were made for the export market.
c The remaining four guitars in this capped edition of 60 were completed in 2006.
d Twenty-eight were made with sunburst finish.
e Twenty had "THANKS" decal on back.
f The remainder of this edition was made after 2005.

Guitars of the Month, Limited and Special Editions are more fully described in book 2, chapter 3.

ALTERNATIVE, CONCEPT and GRAPHITE
PRODUCTION TOTALS

	Alternative X	Alternative II	Alternative 2 Resonator	Alternative XT Tremolo	Alternative X Midi	Alternative X Bass	Alternative III	Concept J	Concept II	Concept III	Concept IV	Graphite X	Graphite II
YEAR	2001	2002	2004	2003	2003	2004	2002	1998	1999	2003	2004	2003	2003
RETAIL	$1,249	$1,199	$1,499	$1,469	$1,599	$1,549	$1,199	$4,100	$4,100	$3,299	$3,999	$1,349	$1,349
TOTALS	1102	134	195	170	27	66	91	55	35	18	15	63	48
1998								42					
1999								13	35				
2000													
2001	321												
2002	423	96					87						
2003	222	29		111	21		4			18		62	29
2004	63	9	131	37	6	50					14	1	19
2005	73		64	22		16					1		

LIMITED and SPECIAL EDITION
PRODUCTION TOTALS (PART FIVE)

	0000012-28H AG Arlo Guthrie	0000-28H AG Arlo Guthrie	POWMIA	PS2 Paul Simon	SP-NAMM 100th Anniversary	SWB Sting Acoustic Bass	SWC Sting Nylon String	Tattoo
YEAR	1997	1997	2006	2002	2001	1999	1999	2004
RETAIL	$4,950	$4,750	$5,699	$3,499	$2,499	$3,200	$3,500	$1,299
TOTALS	30	30	8	200	100	26	46	100
1998	30	30						
1999						19	21	
2000						7	19	
2001					95		6	
2002				200	5			
2003								
2004								24
2005			8[a]					76

Footnotes for LIMITED and SPECIAL EDITION Production Totals (Part Five)

a The POWMIA model was introduced in 2006, but the first batch noted here was made in 2005.

SHENANDOAH and SIGMA MARTIN
PRODUCTION TOTALS

Sigma Martin

	DR-28N	DR-35N
TOTALS	1611	1098
1981	125	125
1982	1486	973

Shenandoah

	CS-18	CS-28	CS-35	CS-28H	D-1832	D-1932	D-2832	D-3532	D-4132	D-4532B	D-6032	D-6732	D12-1932	D12-2832	HD-2832	HD-2832B	000-2832	Misc. Prototypes	SE-2832	SE-6032	Violins
TOTALS	25	25	25	25	2166	158	7240	5827	60	24	36	60	12	1519	4054	25	967	34	72	60	52
1983					101		836	589													
1984					325		2155	1225						51	156		56				
1985	25	25	25	25	244		771	999						150	731		307	7			52
1986					314		747	846						187	607	1	216				
1987					200		850	784						396	746		54	20			
1988					205		302	295						60	359		82	7			
1989					191		451	427						203	411						
1990					202		528	348						154	540	24	96				
1991					228	156	324	168	60	24	36	60	12	168	276		72		72	60	
1992					156	2	276	144						48	228		84				
1993								2						102							

Footnotes for SHENANDOAH and SIGMA MARTIN Production Totals

a Sigma Martin Serial Numbers started with Martin Serial #900001 and totaled 2709 units. These numbers affect Martin production totals in the year 2002.

Shenandoah Catalog Cover – 1989

Footnotes for GOM, SPECIAL and LIMITED Quick Reference Chart (Part One)

a The following Brazilian rosewood guitars were made in 1983 but these preceded the formal Guitar of the Month program:

D-28V Brazilian	128
000-28V Brazilian	15
D-45V Brazilian	39

b One marked "HD-28BLE."
c This edition was never issued beyond prototype stage.

GOM, SPECIAL and LIMITED EDITION QUICK REFERENCE CHART (PART ONE)

YEAR	MODEL	LIST PRICE	# SOLD	Foreign or Protos
1984	00-18V	$1520.00	9	
	D-28 Custom	$2000.00	43	
	M-21LE	$1600.00	16	
	M-36LE	$2140.00	N/A	
	D-28V Brazilian a	N/A	25	
	D-35V Brazilian	N/A	10	
1985	D-18V	$1640.00	56	
	D-21LE	$1550.00	75	
	HD-28BLE	$2210.00	87	
	OM28LE	$2180.00	39	(+ 2 foreign*)
	00-21B Brazilian	$2020.00	1	
	00-45B Brazilian	N/A	2	
	000-28B Brazilian	N/A	6	
	000-45B Brazilian	$2040.00	2	
	D-28B Brazilian	$2100.00	1	
	D-35B Brazilian	$2100.00	1	
	M-36B Brazilian	$2140.00	20	
	M-38B Brazilian	$2508.00	17	
	N-20B Brazilian	N/A	1	
	OM-28SOI SingOut! 35th	N/A	35	None
1986	J-45M Deluxe	$6900.00	16	(+ 1 foreign)
	J-21MC	$1750.00	55	(+ 1 foreign)
	D-62LE	$2100.00	46	(+ 2 foreign)
	HD-28SE	$2300.00	130	(+8 foreign)
	D-28B Brazilian	N/A	11	
	D-28B Brazilian	N/A	47	
	D-35B Brazilian	N/A	10	
	HD-28B Brazilian	N/A	3	
	D-41B Brazilian	$2840.00	1	
	Custom 15B Brazilian	N/A	10	
	M-45B Brazilian	N/A	3	
1987	D-45LE	$7500.00	44	(+ 6 foreign)
	HD-18LE	$2250.00	50	(+ 1 foreign)
	D-21LE	$2350.00	18	(+ 1 foreign)
	J-40MBLE	$3000.00	16	(+ 1 foreign)
	HD-28BSE b	$3300.00	88	(+ 5 foreign)
	Cust. 15B	N/A	2	
1988	M2C-28	$2700.00	20	(+ 2 foreign)
	HD-28M	$2170.00	77	(+ 4 foreign)
	HD-42PSE	$2750.00	93	(+ 3 foreign)
	D-42LE	$3300.00	69	(+ 6 foreign)
	D-41BLE	$4800.00	31	(+ 8 foreign)
1989	HD-28GM Grand Marquis	$3198.00	112	(+ 8 foreign)
	HOM-35	$4000.00	53	(+ 7 foreign)
	D-18 Special	$1950.00	15	(+13 foreign)
	D-40BLE	$5598.00	50	(+ 8 foreign)
1990	HD-28BLE	$3900.00	100	(+ 8 foreign)
	OMC-28	$3148.00	74	(+ 2 foreign)
	D-18MB	$2300.00	96	(+ 3 foreign)
	D3-18	$2398.00	72	(+ 8 foreign)
1991	D-28LSH	$4398.00	200	(+ 11 foreign)
	D-45KLE	$7800.00	50	(+ 4 foreign)
	OM-21 Special	$3998.00	32	(+ 4 foreign)
	000-18SO! SingOut! 40th	N/A	40	
1992	D-18 Vintage	$1998.00	215	(+ 3 foreign*)
	HJ-28	$3050.00	56	(+ 13 foreign)
	HD-28 C.T.B.	$3800.00	89	(+ 10 foreign)
	D-45S Deluxe	$9760.00	50	(+ 10 foreign)
1993	D-93	$3000.00	148	(+ 17 foreign)
	D-28SP 1935 Special	$3800.00	224	(+ 20 foreign)
	OM-28 Perry Bechtel	$4000.00	77	(+ 17 foreign)
	D-45 Deluxe	$18200.00	50	(+ 17 foreign)
1994	D-45 Gene Autry	$22000.00	50	(+ 16 foreign)
	OM-40LE (natural)	$7100.00	45	(+ 12 foreign)
	OM-40LE (sunburst)	$7430.00	20	(+ 12 foreign)
	HD-28 GM LSH	$4500.00	106	(+ 9 foreign)
	HD-28 GM LSH (sunburst)	$4830.00	30	(+ 6 foreign)
	HJ-28M	$3900.00	60	(+ 12 foreign)

YEAR	MODEL	LIST PRICE	# SOLD	Foreign or Protos
1995	000-42EC Clapton (natural)	$8100.00	433	2 Protos
	000-42EC Clapton (sunburst)	$8320.00	28	1 Proto
	D-35 30th Anniversary Model	$4000.00	207	2 Protos
	D-18 Golden Era® (natural)	$3100.00	272	2 Protos
	D-18 Golden Era® (sunburst)	$3320.00	48	1 Protos
	HD-40MS Marty Stuart Model	$5400.00	250	2 Protos
1996	D-45 Deluxe CFM Sr. (Brazilian)	$19,500.00	91	2 Protos
	D-45 CFM Sr. (East Indian)	$11,000.00	114	2 Protos
	000-28 12-fret Golden Era®	$4,000.00	367	2 Protos
	MTV-1 Satin Finish	$2,200.00	73	2 Protos
	MTV-1 Gloss Finish	$2,450.00	588	2 Protos
	HD-28SO! 45th (12-fret)	$4,500.00	45	1 Proto
	Meazzi Anniversary	N/A	19	
	Paul Simon OM-42PS	$3,499.00	223	4 Protos
1997	Jimmie Rodgers 000-45JR	$25,000.00	52	2 Protos
	Kingston Trio Set Of 3	$12,500.00	34	2 Protos
	CEO-1 "CEO's Choice"	$2,600.00	128	2 Protos
	CEO-1R "CEO's Choice'	$2,800.00	191	2 Protos
	Martin/Stauffer 00-40	$7,900.00	35	2 Protos
	Martin/Stauffer 00-45	$20,000.00	25	2 Protos
	00-16DB Women In Music	$2,100.00	97	2 Protos
	Arlo Guthrie 0000-28H AG	$4,750.00	30	2 Protos
	Johnny Cash D-42JC (Black)	$8,200.00	80	2 Protos
	00-16DBR Women In Music	$3,650.00	430	2 Protos
1998	HD-18JB Jimmy Buffett Model	$4,450.00	424	2 Protos
	CMSH Sting Classical c	N/A	0	2 Protos
	D-28HW Hank Williams Sr.	$9,000.00	150	2 Protos
	0-45JB Joan Baez	$9,850.00	59	2 Protos
	EMP-1 Employee Model	$2,450.00	222	2 Protos
	00-21GE Golden Era	$3,950.00	163	2 Protos
	CEO-2 CEO's Choice	$2,900.00	110	2 Protos
	Concept J	$4,100.00	53	2 Protos
	SWD Certified Wood Model	$1,399.00	575	2 Protos
	D-45SS Stephen Stills	$19,000.00	91	2 Protos
	D-40DM Don McLean	$5,750.00	50	2 Protos
	D-28LF Lester Flatt	$8,500.00	59	2 Protos
	N-20WN Willie Nelson (East Indian)	$5,500.00	30	2 Protos
1999	N-20WNB Willie Nelson (Brazilian)	$9,800.00	14	2 Protos
	OM-45 Deluxe Golden Era	$27,500.00	65	2 Protos
	Roger McGuinn D12-42RM	$6,900.00	250	2 Protos
	Steve Howe 00-18SH	$2,950.00	26	2 Protos
	Sting SWB Certified Wood Ac. Bass	$3,200.00	46	2 Protos
	Sting SWC Certified Wood Classic	$3,500.00	346	2 Protos
	D-28GE Special Edition	$9,000.00	30	2 Protos
	EMP-2 Employees Model	$2,700.00	56	2 Protos
	CEO-3 "CEO's Choice"	$3,500.00	open	2 Protos
	Size 5 "Mini-Martin" (dick boak)	$3,250.00	140	2 Protos
	Woody Guthrie 000-18WG	$3,150.00	234	2 Protos
	Dave Matthews DM3MD	$3,250.00	35	2 Protos
	Concept II	$4,100.00	575	2 Protos
2000	D-18GE Golden Era	$3,500.00	200	3 Protos
	Eric Clapton 000-42ECB	$15,000.00	574	3 Protos
	Grand Ole Opry HDO	$3,350.00	73	2 Protos
	Jim Croce D-21JC Indian	$3,450.00	65	2 Protos
	Jim Croce D-21JC Brazilian	$8,475.00	110	3 Protos
	Jonny Lang JLJCR Jumbo	$2,750.00	59	3 Protos
	Nakashima NWD Walnut	$4,750.00	50	3 Protos
	00-17SO! 50th	$2,399.00	96	4 Protos
	Babyface OOOC-16RB	$2,850.00	73	1 Proto
	EMP-NS Employee Model	$2,299.00	100	3 Protos
	George Jones D-41GJ	$4,750.00	61	3 Protos
	Gordon Lightfoot D-18GL	$3,500.00	68	3 Protos
	Steve Miller 00-37K SM	$5,750.00	68	3 Protos
	Steve Miller 00-37K2 SM	$6,250.00	409	2 Protos
	CEO-4 Special "CEO's Choice"	$2,500.00	250	3 Protos
	Cowboy X Limited Edition	$999.00		
2001	Merle Haggard 000C-28SMH	$4,799.00	122	3 Protos

Footnotes for GOM, SPECIAL and LIMITED Quick Reference Chart (Part Two)

- a   Capped at this number due to short supply of Brazilian rosewood.
- b   Supplied with standard pickguard.
- c   Supplied with double pickguard.
- d   This edition was never issued beyond prototype stage.
- e   NAMM Show Special
  (Orders accepted from dealers in attendance only).

GOM, SPECIAL and LIMITED EDITION QUICK REFERENCE CHART (PART TWO)

YEAR	MODEL	LIST PRICE	# SOLD	Foreign or Protos
2001	Keb Mo HD-28KM	$3,999.00	252	3 Protos
	Clarence White D-18CW	$3,999.00	292	3 Protos
	Kenny Wayne Shepherd JC-16KWS	$3,149.00	198	3 Protos
	Elizabeth Cotten 00-18CTN	$3,299.00	76	3 Protos
	D-50 Deluxe First Edition	$50,000.00	50	2 Protos
	Cowboy II Limited Edition	$999.00	500	1 Proto
	SP-NAMM100 NAMM 100th	$2,499.00	100	None
	Peter Rowan 000-40MPR	$4,999.00	87	3 Protos
	Beck D-16BH	$2,950.00	99	3 Protos
	Mark Knopfler HD-40MK	$4,999.00	251	3 Protos
	Dan Fogelberg D-41DF	$4,750.00	141	3 Protos
	Cowboy III	$1099.00	750	2 Protos
2002	CEO-5 "CEO's Choice"	$2,649.00	60	2 Protos
	Eric Clapton 000-28ECB	$9,999.00	500	3 Protos
	Judy Collins HD-35SJC 6-String	$5,149.00	50	3 Protos
	Judy Collins HD12-35SJC 12-Str.	$5,349.00	33	3 Protos
	David Crosby D-18DC	$3,799.00	250	3 Protos
	Shawn Colvin M3SC	$3,199.00	120	3 Protos
	Dion 000CBD "The Wanderer"	$3,299.00	57	3 Protos
	Lonnie Donegan 000-28LD	$4,099.00	72	3 Protos
	Lonnie Donegan 000-28LDB	$8,219.00	25	3 Protos
	Laurence Juber OMC-18VLJ	$4,449.00	133	3 Protos
	00-45S "1902" a	$22,500.00	60	2 Protos
	DCRNS Steinberger TransAction™	$3,649.00	31	2 Protos
	MPFF Philadelphia Folk Festival	$3,449.00	85	2 Protos
	Godfrey Daniels 000-16RGD 25th	$2,849.00	26	2 Protos
	Hawaiian X	$1,099.00	Pending/500	2 Protos
	Alternative II	$1,199.00	134	2 Protos
	CEO-4R "CEO's Choice"	$1,199.00	91	2 Protos
	DVM Veterans' Special	$2,699.00	Open	2 Protos
	Del McCoury D-28DM	$3,199.00	597	2 Protos
	Bob Shane D-28KTBS b	$3,799.00	115	2 Protos
	Bob Shane D-28KTBSDG c	$3,999.00	32	2 Protos
	Kitty Wells HTA Honky Tonk Angel	$3,299.00	70	3 Protos
	Paul Simon PS2	$3,499.00	200	3 Protos
	HDN Negative	$3,699.00	135	3 Protos
	Sugar Ray DSR	$2,499.0.0	57	2 Protos
	Clarence White D-28CW	$4,899.00	Open	3 Protos
	Clarence White D-28CWB	$9,999.00	150	2 Protos
2003	Martin Carthy 000-18MC	$3,199.00	84	3 Protos
	Graham Nash 000-40Q2GN	$4,699.00	147	4 Protos
	Cowboy IV	$1,199.00	250	2 Protos
	HS-0 Ukulele	$699.00	Open	2 Protos
	OM-28 John Mayer	$4499.00	404	4 Protos
	D-18 Andy Griffith	$3699.00	311	4 Protos
	D-37W Lucinda Williams d	$4999.00	0	4 Protos
	MC-40 Eric Johnson	$4999.00	90	4 Protos
	D-35 Ernest Tubb	$4499.00	90	4 Protos
	OM-42 Quilted Maple e	$6,999.00	Pending/50	2 Protos
	Felix The Cat	$549.00	30	3 Protos
	HD-40 Tom Petty 6-String	$4999.00	756	4 Protos
	HD12-40 Tom Petty 12-String	$5199.00	274	4 Protos
	OMC-28 Laurence Juber	$4999.00	90	4 Protos
	OMC-28B Laurence Juber a	$9999.00	133	4 Protos
	0-28 Ian Anderson "Chameleon"	$5499.00	87	4 Protos
2004	000-28 Norman Blake	$4999.00	Open	4 Protos

YEAR	MODEL	LIST PRICE	# SOLD	Foreign or Protos
2004	000-28B Norman Blake a	$9999.00	52	4 Protos
	OM Night Dive	$19999.00	13	1 Proto
	D Night Dive	$19999.00	7	None
	D-45 Celtic Knot (pre-50) a	$35000.00	15	None
	D-100 (post 50) a	$100,000.00	50	None
	Concept IV	$3999.00	15	3 Protos
	HD-40LSH Tom Paxton	$4899.00	30	4 Protos
	OM-40 Rory Block	$5199.00	38	4 Protos
	000-ECHF "Bellezza Nera"	$5999.00	476	4 Protos
	Tattoo	$1299.00	100	2 Protos
	OM-42QM2 e	$7499.00	30	2 Protos
	DC Aura	$3399.00	Open	3 Protos
2005	OMC Aura	$3399.00	Open	4 Protos
	D-45 Mike Longworth	$13999.00	91	4 Protos
	000-45S Stephen Stills	$12999.00	91	4 Protos
	000C Steve Miller	$4499.00	383	4 Protos
	HD-7 Roger McGuinn e	$5499.00	Open	4 Protos
	D Figured Koa e	$14999.00	25	2 Proto
	DC Trey Anastasio	$5199.00	141 Comb.	None
	DCE Trey Anastasio	$5499.00	141 Comb.	None
	M3M George Martin	$5699.00	127	4 Protos
	Sting: Mini	$3999.00	100	3 Protos
	Claire's Guitar	$6999.00	100	3 Protos
	OMC Fingerstyle 1	$3799.00	Open	3 Protos
	LX Realtree	$649.00	Open	10 Protos
	OM-45 Tasmanian Blackwood	$13999.00	29	1 Proto
2006	Arts & Crafts	$5799.00	100	4 Protos
	OMC-41 Richie Sambura	$6999.00	200 Comb.	4 Protos
	MC12-41 Richie Sambura	$7199.00	200 Comb.	4 Protos
	000-ECHF Bellezza Bianca	$5999.00	410	4 Protos
	000C-28 Andy Summers	$5999.00	87	4 Protos
	OM-45 Roy Rogers	$4399.00	84	4 Protos
	OM-45B Roy Rogers	$14999.00	14	4 Protos
	FeLiX II	$599.00	625	10 Protos
	POW/MIA	$5699.00	Open	4 Protos
	OMJM John Mayer	$3999.00	Open	4 Protos
	XC1T Ellipse	$1199.00	Open	4 Protos
	5-K Ukulele	$5199.00	Open	4 Protos
	D-42 Flamed Mahogany e	$9999.00	30	2 Protos
	D-42 Peter Frampton	$7799.00	76	4 Protos
	HD-35 Nancy Wilson	$4399.00	101	4 Protos
	JC Buddy Guy	$6399.00	36	4 Protos
	000-40S Mark Knopfler	$6999.00	155	4 Protos
	Cowboy V	$599.00	500	4 Protos
	M-42 David Bromberg	$6999.00	83	4 Protos
	SW00DB Machiche	$2999.00	125	4 Protos
	D-35 Johnny Cash	$5499.00	Open	None
	OM-42 Flamed Mahogany e	$9999.00	30	2 Protos
2007	Doobie-42 Tom Johnston	$8499.00	35	4 Protos
	FeLiX III	$649.00	Open/1000	5 Protos
	Claire 2	$6799.00	Open/100	4 Protos
	Ditson Dreadaught 111	$6499.00	Open	4 Protos
	CSN Gerry Tolman Tribute	$4999.00	Open	7 Protos
	D-7 Roger McGuinn	$2999.00	Open	4 Protos
	OMC Artinger 1	$4499.00	Open	4 Protos
	Daisy Uke	$5449.00	Open/100	3 Protos
	D-28 Authentic	$39999.00	50	4 Protos
	OMC Red Birch	$2999.00	175	3 Protos
	D-42 Amazon Rosewood	$9999.00	35	4 Protos
	OM Negative	$5599.00	60	4 Protos
	HDC-40 Travis Tritt	$8999.00	40	4 Protos
	D-42 Cambodian Rosewood a	$1249.00	19	4 Protos
	000-X Hippie	$4599.00	200	4 Protos
	000-18 Norman Blake	$15999.00	Open	4 Protos
	0-45S Stephen Stills	$6299.00	91	4 Protos
	00-21 Kingston Trio (Dave Guard)	$4499.00	100	4 Protos
	00-42K Robbie Robertson	$8799.00	100	4 Protos
	00-42K2 Robbie Robertson	$8999.00	100	4 Protos

APPENDICES 283

CUSTOM SHOP
PRODUCTION TOTALS

	Custom Shop Totals[a]	Custom Breakdown[a]				Test Model	Prototypes & Misc.[c]
		Custom X Series	Custom Satin	Custom Gloss[b]	Custom Artist Edition		
Totals	**38434**	**4717**	**8231**	**20240**	**502**	**118**	**2507**
1979	257			257			
1980	433			433			
1981	351			351			
1982	219			219			
1983	502			502			
1984	281			281			
1985	247			247			
1986	334			334			
1987	313			313			
1988	250			250			
1989	192			192			
1990	231			231			
1991	271			271			
1992	427			427			
1993	436			436			48
1994	557		38	519			126
1995	712			712			132
1996	573			573			101
1997	624			624			192
1998	772			772			379
1999	864			864		2	250
2000	1340			1340		12	245
2001	3442			3442		10	297
2002	1260			1260		23	229
2003	1249	1		1248		14	
2004	2594	23	97	2474			95
2005	5102	305	3111	1614	72	15	121
2006	8710	2732	2915	2836	227	9	232
2007	5891	1656	2070	1962	203	33	60

Footnotes for CUSTOM SHOP Production Totals

a Custom Shop Totals include the breakdown totals from the four Custom Shop columns to the right of the Totals column.

b Custom Gloss includes Dovetail Full Gloss guitars as well as mortise-and-tenon Gloss Top models.

c These totals include prototypes, sales samples and miscellaneous instruments not otherwise designated.

ELECTRIC GUITAR and BASS
PRODUCTION TOTALS

	E-18	EM-18	EB-18 Bass	EMB-18 Bass	E-28	EB-28 Bass	Solidbody Unidentified	F-50	F-55	F-65	XTE-70	XTE-75	GT-70	GT-75	GT-75R	GT-75-12 12-String	XGT-85	X-12
Totals	**341**	**1375**	**874**	**2**	**194**	**217**	**98**	**519**	**665**	**566**	**3**	**3**	**453**	**750**	**1**	**2**	**1**	**1**
1961																		
1962																		
1963																		
1964																		
1965								15	15	15								
1966								201	325	250	3	3	126	75	1	1	1	1
1967								125	150	101			327	576		1		
1968								177	125	125				99				
1969								1	50	75								
1970																		
1971																		
1972																		
1973																		
1974																		
1975																		
1976																		
1977																		
1978																		
1979	341	a	a	a														
1980		a	a	a														
1981		1375	874	2														
1982		a	a	a	194	217	98											
1983		a	a	a	a	a	a											

Footnotes for ELECTRIC GUITAR and BASS Production Totals

a Annual tallies for production of 18 and 28 Series electric guitars and basses were not accurately kept forcing us to provide total production numbers for the five-year period from 1979-1983.

Note: All electric guitar and bass production was suspended after 1983. Acoustic basses are not covered in this section.

PRICE CHARTS AND OTHER APPENDICES

The original Longworth editions contained price charts for most models and years. We suppose that this information was interesting to owners of vintage guitars who could reference the price of their instrument and compare it with current prices or escalated vintage values. Again, the problem was that this information was presented inefficiently and took up more space than it deserved. In preparing this revised edition, we made a conscious decision to reduce the vast number of pages allocated to pricing information. This is accomplished by reducing the number of models for which prices are listed. Naturally, in choosing which guitars to include, we tried to focus upon models that had the highest production totals and the greatest longevity. If you are looking for the price of a specific model and you don't find it, we suggest that you look for a similar one in a particular time range and this should provide the approximate price range. We apologize to those that feel this information is crucial, but frankly, we saw more importance in reporting the production totals than we did in reporting historical prices. In the coming years, as we immerse ourselves in the archiving process, we hope to publish accurate reprints of historic Martin catalogs to satisfy customer desire for model descriptions, product offerings, pricing, and general style of conducting business.

Please note in the price charts that if a year is mentioned twice or even three times, it is because there was one or more price increases during that year.

Mike Longworth made a few interesting observations concerning pricing in the original text that deserve repeating. He notes that for a short time, beginning in April of 1973, Martin did not issue retail price lists and that the prices listed for that short period are estimated (and thought to be accurate) based upon the dealer net prices. Perhaps Martin management at the time felt that the absence of a retail price list would somehow level the playing field among competing Martin dealerships. Furthermore, beginning in 1972, most Martin guitars were sold as packaged units with cases included and that prices reflect this change in marketing practices. This change was most likely done to help minimize shipping damage of instruments purchased without a case, but increased revenue from case sales would also have been a factor.

OTHER APPENDICES

In addition to Production Totals and Price Charts in the Appendix section, you will find Serial Number Charts for both guitar and mandolin that enable the precise yearly dating of Martin instruments. The Martin Instrument Dimensions chart lists the important dimensions of virtually all Martin models. This information can be useful when ordering cases or when trying to identify historic models. A Quick Reference Chart (by date) related to Guitars of the Month, Limited Editions, and Special Editions contains both edition totals and pricing information. This information is also shown in the Guitars of the Month Production Totals or the Limited and Special Editions Production Totals Charts, but these charts are presented alphabetically by model. If you need a quick primer on Martin model designations, go to the Understanding the Series and Styles of Martin Nomenclature chart. For those interested in knowing what cases fit specific sizes of guitars, we have provided a chart of Martin Case Designations. Lastly, we have provided a page depicting several Special and Limited Edition Picks, created primarily in 12 or 24 gross quantities to promote specific guitars or events.

Price List of Martin Guitars – circa 1870

PRICE CHARTS AND OTHER APPENDICES

0, 00, 000 Size Prices (Selected Models) 286–288
1 Series Prices 291
12-String Model Prices 293
15 and 17 Series Prices 291
Acoustic Bass Prices 294
Archtop Model Prices 288
Backpacker Prices 295
Classical Prices 289
Dreadnought Prices (Selected Models) 286–288
Electric Guitar Prices 288
Guitar of the Month Prices* 278
GOM, Limited and Special Edition Quick Reference* 282–283
J Size Jumbo Prices 291
Limited and Special Edition Prices* 279–281
M Size (0000) Prices 290
Mandolin Prices 292–293
Martin Case Designations 297
Martin Guitar and Mandolin Serial Numbers 296
Martin Instrument Dimensions 298–299
OM Orchestra Model Prices 286–288
Road Series Prices 290
Special and Limited Edition Picks 302–303
Ukulele and Tiple Prices 294–295
Understanding the Series and Styles of Martin Nomenclature 300–302
X Series Prices 290

*These prices are included on the production charts in the previous section.

APPENDICES **285**

0, 00, 000, OM and DREADNOUGHT PRICES

SELECTED REPRESENTATIVE (POPULAR) MODELS — (PART ONE)

Year	0-15	0-16NY	0-17	00-17	0-18	0-18K	00-18	000-18	D-18	D-18S	0-21	00-21	D-21	0-28	0-28K	00-28	000-28	D-28	D-28S	HD-28	D-35	HD-35	D-41	0-42	00-42	0-45	00-45	000-45	OM-45	D-45
1870														60																
1897					30		32.5				48.5	51.5		61.5		67								92.5	98					
1898					30		32.5				32.5	35		45		50								75	80					
1899					35		32.5				32.5	35		45		50								75	80					
1900					35		37.5				37.5	40		45		50								75	80					
1901					35		37.5				37.5	40		45		50								75	80					
1902					35		37.5				37.5	40		45		50								75	80					
1903					35		37.5				37.5	40		45		50								75	80					
1904			20	25	35		37.5				37.5	40		45		50								75	80	105	110	120		
1905			20	25	35		37.5				37.5	40		45		50								75	80	105	110	120		
1906			20	25	35		37.5				37.5	40		45		50								75	80	105	110	120		
1907			20	25	35		37.5				37.5	40		45		50								75	80	105	110	120		
1908			20	25	25		30				35	40		45		50								75	80	105	110	120		
1909			20	25	25		30				35	40		45		50								75	80	105	110	120		
1910			20	25	25		30				35	40		45		50								75	80	110	115	125		
1911			20	25	25		30				35	40		45		50								75	80	110	115	125		
1912			20	25	25		30				35	40		45		50								75	80	110	115	125		
1913			20	25	25		30				35	40		45		50								75	80	110	115	125		
1914			20	25	25		30				35	40		45		50								75	80	110	115	120		
1915			20	25	25		30				35	40		45		50								75	80	110	115	125		
1916			20	25	30		30				35	40		45		50	55							75	85	110	120	125		
1917			20	25	30		35	40			35	40		45		55	55							80	85	115	132	150		
1918			20	25	33		35	40			40	45		50		55	55							80	93.5	115	126.5	150		
1919			20	25	36	36	38.5	40			44	49.5		55	60	60.5	55							88	102	138	144	150		
1920			20	25	36	36	42	48			48	54		60	60	66	60							96	102	138	144	150		
1921			20	25	36	39.6	42	48			48	54		60	66	66	60							96	100	135	140	150		
1922			20	25	30	40	35	40			45	50		60	70	65	70							95	110	135	140	150		
1923			20	25	33	40	38.5	40			49.5	55		60	66	71.5	77							104.5	110	148.5	154	165		
1924			20	25	35	40	40	45			50	55		70	70	75	80							105	110	150	155	165		
1925			20	25	35	40	40	45			50	55		70	70	75	80							105	110	150	155	165		
1926			20	25	40	45	40	50			55	60		75	75	80	85								110	155	160	170		
1927			20	25	40	45	40	50			55	60		75	75	80	85								110	155	160	170		
1928			30	30	40	45	45	50			55	60		75	75	80	85								110	155	160	170		
1929			30	30	40	45	45	50			55	60		75	75	80	85								110	155	160	170		
1930			30	30	40	45	45	50			55	60		75	75	80	85								110	155	160	170		
1931			30	35	40	45	45	50			55	60		75	75	80	85								110	155	160	170		
1932			30	35	40	45	45	50			55	60		75	75	80	85								110	155	160	170		
1933			30	35	40	45	45	50			55	60		75	75	80	85								110	155	160	170	180	
1934			30	35	40	45	45	50			55	60		75	75	80	90	100							110	155	160	170	180	200
1935			30	35	40		45	55	65		55	60		75		80	90	100							110	155	160	175	170	200
1936			30	35	40		45	55	65		55	60		75		80	90	100							110	155	160	175	170	200
1937			30	35	40		45	55	65		55	60				80	90	100							110	155	160	175	175	200
1938			35	35	40		50	60	65		55	60					100	115									185			
1939			35	40	45		50	67	75		60	65					110	125									185			
1940			30	40	45		50	67	83		70	70					110	125												
1941			35	40	45		55	67	83		70	80					110	125												
1942			35	40	45		55	67	83		70	80					110	125												
1943			35	40	45		55	77	95		70	80					127	144												
1944			35	46	52		64	77	95		80	80					127	144												
1945			40	46	52		64	85	105		80	92					140	160												
1947		25		46	58		70	85	100			105					140	160												225
1948		28		50	60		70	95	115			105					160	180												
1949		45		55	70		80	105	125			120					160	180												
1950	60			70	80		90	105	125			130					175	200										225		250

0, 00, 000, OM and DREADNOUGHT PRICES
SELECTED REPRESENTATIVE (POPULAR) MODELS — (PART TWO)

Year	0-15	0-16NY	0-17	00-17	0-18	0-18K	00-18	000-18	D-18	D-18S	0-21	00-21	D-21	0-28	0-28K	00-28	000-28	D-28	D-28S	HD-28	D-35	HD-35	D-41	0-42	00-42	0-45	00-45	000-45	OM-45	D-45
1951	60		70	70	80		90	105	125			130					175	200												
1952	60		70	70	80		90	105	125			130					175	200												
1953	65		75	75	85		95	110	130			140					185	210												
1954	65		75	75	85		95	110	130			140					185	210												
1955	70		85	85	95		105	120	140			150					200	225												
1956	80		95	95	105		115	135	155			165					220	250												
1957	87		100	100	115		125	145	170			175					235	270												
1958	87		100	100	115		125	145	170			175					235	270												
1959	92		105	105	125		135	150	180			185					250	285												
1960	99.5				135		145	160	195			198					270	310												
1961		139.5			135		145	160	195			215					270	310												
1962		139.5			145		155	175	210			229.5	200				370	369.5												
1963		149.5			154.5		164.5	189.5	229			229.5	220				360	369.5												
1964		149.5			154.5		164.5	189.5	229			245	220				330	390				425								
1965		150			160		175	200	250			280	230				350	375				390								
1965		195			220		230	240	250			255	250				375	345				410								
1966		180			200		210	220	230			285	275				375	375				440								
1967		190			210		225	240	230	320		310	315				375	400				440								
1968		210			210		250	270	295	320		310	345				385	400	425			440								
1969		210			230		250	270	295	320		310	345				410	425	425			465		800			1650				1200
1970		225			240		260	285	325	320		330	375				410	425	465			465		850			1800				1200
1970		240			250		275	300	325	350		350	400				440	465	465			495		850			1800				1200
1971		250			295		295	295	350	375		395					475	495	495			535		925			1800				1650
1972		250			310		310	310	375	375		395					475	495	495			535		1080			1950				1800
1973		325			385		385	385	450	450		470					550	570	570			610		1190			1950				1950
1974		480			480		480	530	530	530		630					660	660	660			680		1220			2010				2010
1974		490			530		530	610	580	580		680					740	740	740			760		1190			2010				2010
1975		510			560		560	610	650	650		710					770	770	770			790		1220			2200				2200
1976		510			560		560	610	650	650		710					770	770	770			790		1400			2270				2270
1976		550			590		590	640	675	700		760					840	840	830			860		1450			2400				2400
1977		570			630		660	700	700	750		790					870	870	920			890		1500			2500				2500
1978		700			700		750	750	800	850		850					900	900	1000	1100		950		1500			2500				2500
1978		800			800		850	850	850	950		950					1000	1000	1100	1100		1050	1300	1600			2500		3000	2500	2600
1979		1000			1000		1050	1050	900	950		950					1000	1000	1100	1200		1100	1310	1610			3000		3010	2600	2610
1979		1010			1010		1060	1060	910	1100		1180					1200	1050	1250	1200		1110	1410	1740			3010		3210	2810	2810
1979		1080			1010		1130	1130	980	1180		1190					1210	1060	1260	1260		1200	1410	1740			3010		3210	2810	2810
1980		1080			1080		1130	1130	980	1180		1270					1290	1140	1340	1340	1360	1200	1410	1740			3210		3210	2810	2810
1980		1090			1080		1130	1130	980	1180		1270					1290	1140	1340	1340	1360	1200	1410	1740			3210		3210	2810	2810
1980		1090			1090		1140	1140	990	1190		1280					1300	1150	1350	1350	1370	1210	1420	1750			3220		3220	2820	2820
1980		1090			1090		1140	1140	990	1190		1280					1300	1150	1350	1350	1370	1210	1420	1750			3220		3220	2820	2820
1981		1138			1138		1191	1191	1033	1243		1338					1359	1201	1411	1432	1485	1264	1485	1831			3375		3375	2955	2955
1981		1189			1189		1244	1244	1078	1299		1399					1421	1255	1475	1507	1553	1321	1553	1916			3537		3537	3096	3056
1982		1307			1307		1368	1368	1185	1428		1538					1563	1380	1622	1657	1708	1453	1708	2107			3890		3890	3405	3405
1982		1125			1225		1245	1165	1185	1185		1340					1360	1380	1380	1657	1708	1453	1708	2107			3505		3505	3405	3405
1983		1125			1225		1245	1165	1185	1185		1340					1360	1380	1380	1657	1708	1453	1708	2107			3505		3505	3405	3405
1984		1175			1275		1295	1215	1235	1235		1390					1410	1430	1430	1707	1758	1503	1758	2207			3605		3604	3505	3505
1985		1235		1060	1335		1355	1275	1295	1295		1450					1470	1490	1490	1767	1818	1563	1818	2267			3665		3665	3565	3565
1985		1235		1060	1335		1355	1275	1295	1295		1450					1470	1490	1490	1767	1818	1563	1818	2267			3665		3665	3565	3565
1986		1235		1060	1335		1355	1275	1295	1295		1450					1470	1490	1490	1767	1818	1563	1818	2267			3755		3755	3655	3655
1986		1235		1060	1335		1355	1275	1295	1295		1450					1470	1490	1490	1767	1818	1563	1818	2267			3755		3755	3655	3655
1987		1346		1156	1456		1478	1334	1354	1354		1582					1538	1558	1558	1866	1920	1636	1920	2438			4046		4046	4046	3938
1987		1500		1250	1600		1600	1600	1600	1600		1700					1800	1568	1800	1850	1930	1646	1930	2600			4600		4600	4600	4500
1988		1500		1250	1600		1600	1600	1600	1600		1700					1800	1568	1800	1850	1930	1646	1930	2600			4600		4600	4600	4500
1988		1576		1314	1680		1680	1680	1680	1680		1786					1890	1648	1890	1944	2028	1730	2028	2600			5000		5000	4600	4500
1988		1640			1748		1748	1748	1748	1748		1858					1966	1714	1966	2022	2320	1800	2230	2704			5200		5200	5200	5056
1989		1640			1748		1748	1748	1492	1748		1858					1966	1714	1966	2022	2320	1800	2320	2704			5200		5200	5200	5056

APPENDICES 287

0, 00, 000, OM and DREADNOUGHT PRICES
SELECTED REPRESENTATIVE (POPULAR) MODELS — (PART THREE)

	00-15	0-16NY	0-17	00-17	0-18K	0-18	00-18	000-18	D-18	D-18S	0-21	00-21	D-21 Special	0-28K	00-28	000-28	D-28	D-28S	HD-28	D-35	HD-35	D-41	D-42	000-42	OM-42	00-45	000-45	OM-45	D-45
1990	80	1810				1930	1930	1830	1560			2050				2060	1790	2170	2140	1880	2430	2820				5720	5440	5440	5330
1991	80	1900				2030	2030	1920	1640	1930		2160				2170	1880	2280	2250	1980	2550	2960				6000	5710	5710	5600
1991	75	1900				2030	2030	1920	1640	2030		2160				2170	1880	2280	2250	1980	2550	2960				6000	5710	5710	5600
1992	80	1980				2120	2120	2000	1710	2120		2250				2260	1960	2380	2340	2060	2660	3080				6240	5940	5940	5830
1993	80	2180				2330	2330	2200	1800	2330		2480				2490	2060	2620	2460	21060	2790	3390				6860	6530	6530	6410
1994	80	2400						2420	1910			2730				2740	2190		2610	2290	2960	3730							7050
1995	80							2130	2030							2430	2330		2770	2430	3140	3960							7480
1996	75							2130	2030							2430	2330		2770	2430	3140	3960							7480
1997	75							2130	2030							2430	2330		2770	2430	3140	3960	4850						7480
1998	75							2130	2030							2430	2330		2770	2430	3140	3960	4850						7480
1999	75							2130	2030							2430	2330		2770	2430	3140	3960	4850						7480
2000	75							2190	2099							2499	2399		2850	2499	3225	4050	4975		4975				7680
2001	75							2199	2099							2499	2399		2850	2499	3225	4050	4975		4975				7680
2002	75							2289	2159							2599	2469		2959	2599	3349	4199	5179	5449	5179				7979
2002	75							2289	2159							2599	2469		2959	2599	3349	4199	5179	5449	5179				7979
2003	75							2399	2249							2749	2599		3099	2749	3499	4399	5449	5449	5449				8299
2004	75							2399	2249							2749	2599		3099	2749	3499	4399	5449	5449	5449				8299
2005	75							2549	2399							2949	2749		3199	2849	3499	4549	5649	5649	5649				8849
2005	75							2549	2399							2949	2749		3199	2849	3499	4549	5649	5649	5649				8849
2006	75							2649	2499							2999	2849		3299	2949	3549	4699	5849	5849	5849				9299
2007	75							2649	2499							2999	2849		3299	2949	3549	4699	5849	5849	5849				9299
2008								2649	2499							2999	2849		3299	2949	3549	4699	5849	5849	5849				9299

ARCHTOP PRICES — HISTORIC

	C-1	C-2	C-3	F-1	F-2	F-7	F-9	R-17	R-18
1931	80	120	200						
1932	80	120	200						
1933	75	120	200						50
1933	80	125	210						55
1934	80	125							55
1935	80	125		85	135	175	250	40	55
1936	80	125		90	135	175	250	40	55
1937	75	125		100	150	175	250	35	55
1938	75	125				175	250	35	55
1939	75	125				175	250	35	55
1940	75	125				175	250	40	55
1941	83	140				195	275	45	60

ELECTRIC GUITAR PRICES

	E-18	EM-18	EB-18 Bass	E-28	EB-28 Bass	F-50	F-55	F-65	GT-70	GT-75	GT-75 12-String
1962						225	275	300			
1963						235	290	310			
1964						235	290	310			
1965						235	290	310			
1966						235	290	310	340	370	
1967							265	285	370	395	
1968									370	395	425
1969									370	395	
1970											
1971											
1972											
1973											
1974											
1975											
1976											
1976											
1977											
1978											
1979	660	700	650								
1980	660	700	650	1200	1200						
1981	660	700	650	1200	1200						
1982	687	729	676	1254	1254						

ARCHTOP PRICES — AMERICAN ARCHTOP

	CF-1	CF-1 Sunburst	CF-1 Black	CF-2	CF-2 Sunburst	CF-2 Black
2004	4499	4999		4999	5499	
2005	4499	4999	5249	4999	5499	5749
2005	4499	4999	5249	4999	5499	5749
2006	4499	4999	5399	4999	5499	5899
2006	4699	5199	5399	5149	5649	5899
2007	4649	5149	5399	5149	5649	5899
2008	4649	5149		5149	5649	5899

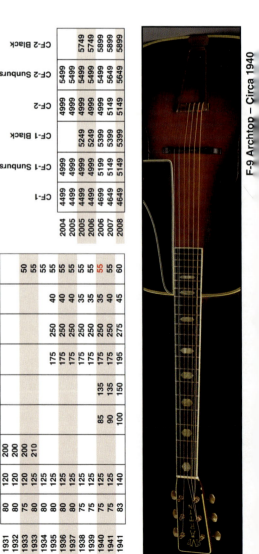

F-9 Archtop – Circa 1940

CLASSICAL PRICES (PART TWO)

Year	00-16C	00-18C	00-18G	00-21G	00-28G	000-28G	N-10	N-20	C-1R	C-TSH	000C-16SGTNE	000C-16SRNE
1983	1325	1400			1540		1450	1620				
1984	1375	1450			1590		1500	1670				
1985	1435	1510			1650		1560	1730				
1986	1435	1510			1650		1560	1730				
1987	1566	1648			1802		1702	1890				
1988	1600	1700			1900		1800	2000				
1989	1680	1786			1996		1890	2100				
1990	1748	1858			2076		1966	2196				
1991	1930	2050			2290		2170	2410				
1992	2030	2160			2410		2280	2530				
1993	2120	2250			2510		2380	2640				
1994	2330	2480			2760		2620	2900				
1995								3190				
1996												
1997												
1998									1500	3750		
1999									1500	3750		
2000									1500	3750		
2001									1500	3750		
2002									1575	3850		
2003									1575	3850	1899	2399
2004									1575	3850	1899	2399
2005											1899	2499
2005											1949	2499
2006											1949	2499
2006											2049	2699
2007											2049	
2008											2299	

CTSH – Thomas S. Humphrey – 1998

In Memory Of
Tom Humphrey
1948-2008

000C-16SRNE – 2003

CLASSICAL PRICES (PART ONE)

Year	00-16C	00-18C	00-18G	00-21G	00-28C	00-28G	000-28C	N-10	N-20
1937			50			85			
1938			50			85			
1939			50			85			
1940			50			85			
1941			50			90			
1942			55			100			
1943			55			100			
1944			55			100			
1945			55			100			
1946			55			115			
1947			65			115			
1948			65			130			
1949			65			130			
1950			75			150			
1950			75			165			
1951			85			165			
1952		185	95			165			
1953	154.5	199.5	95			175			
1954	164.5	199.5	100			175			
1955	164.5	225	115			190			
1956	175	215	130			215			
1957	210	205	140		340	230	325		
1958	190	230	150		370	230	349.5		
1959	200	230	165		370	245	349.5		
1960	225	260	165			270	350		
1961	225	260				270	365		
1962	235	260					320		
1963	235	285					320		
1964	250	285					320		
1965	275	300					320		
1966	275	325					370		
1967	350	325					395	375	475
1968	480	400					395	375	475
1969	530	530					425	400	500
1970	560	580					450	400	500
1971	560	610					450	475	575
1972	600	610					525	475	680
1973	650	650					730	580	760
1974	670	670					760	630	790
1975	750	850					790	660	790
1976	850	850					850	660	850
1977	850	950					940	710	890
1978	1050	950					1050	790	950
1979	1060	1140					1150	900	1050
1979	1150	1150					1150	900	1050
1980	1130	1220			1370		1280	1130	1350
1980	1140	1220			1380		1290	1140	1360
1981	1140	1230			1443		1290	1210	1430
1981	1191	1285			1509		1370	1210	1440
1982	1244	1343			1659			1275	1506
1982	1368	1477			1732			1332	1575
1982	1325	1400			1540			1450	1620
1982								1465	1732

MC-45 – 1983

M (0000) MODEL PRICES
SELECTED REPRESENTATIVE MODELS

Year	M-18	M-21	MC-28	M-36	M-38	MC-37K	M-64	MC-68	0000-28H	0000-38	0000-1	M-16GT
1976					1200							
1977					1200							
1977					1200							
1978				1100	1400							
1979				1110	1410							
1979				1200	1510							
1980				1200	1510							
1980				1210	1520							
1981				1210	1520							
1981				1264	1590							
1982				1321	1663							
1983			1559	1453	1829							
1984	1290	1600	1559	1453	1829							
1985	1350		1609	1503	1879							
1986	1350		1669	1563	1939		1640					
1986	1350		1669	1563	1939		1640					
1987	1424		1762	1563	1939		1640	2170				
1987	1550		1900	1650	2048		1732	2170				
1988	1628		1996	1660	2058	2100	1742	2170				
1989			2076	1744	2162	2184	1830					
1990			2170	1814	2250	2290	1904	2300				
1991			2280	1890	2350	2410	1990	2400				
1992			2380	1990	2470	2510	2090	2520				
1993			2500	2070	2570	2760	2180	2630				
1994			2650	2170	2700		2290	2760				
1995				2390	2970		2520	2930				
1996												
1997									2770			
1998									2770	3150	1099	
1999									2770		1099	
2000									2770		1099	
2001											1099	
2002												
2003												
2004												
2005												
2006				2999	4199							1225
2007				2999	4199							1225
2008												1279

X SERIES PRICES
SELECTED REPRESENTATIVE MODELS

Year	DXM	DX1	DXME	DCXME	DCX1E	DXBR	D12XM	D12X1	DXR	MX000	000X1	00CXRAE	00CXMAE	00CXAEBLACK	00CXAENAVYX	00CXAERED
1998	599		749													
1999	599		749													
2000	599	649	749	849												
2001	599	649	749	849	899											
2002	599	649	749	849	899		699	749								
2002	599	649	769		919	749		749	649	599	649					
2003	619	669	789		949			769		599	649	799	799	799	799	799
2004	619	669	789		949			769			649	799	799	799	799	799
2005	619	669	789		949			769			669	799	799	819	799	799
2006	619	669	789		949			769			669			849		
2006	669	719	839		999			819			669			849		
2007	669	719	839		999			819			719			899		
2008	669	719	839		999			819			719			999		

ROAD SERIES PRICES
SELECTED REPRESENTATIVE MODELS

Year	DM	DR	DCM	DCME	DCRE	DM12	JM	M000	000R	000CME	OMM	00M	00CME	00CMAE	BM
1996	899	1099													
1997	899	1099	1150			1150	899	899	1099						
1998	899	1099	1150	1300		1150	899	899	1099		899		1399	1399	1249
1999	899	1099	1150	1300		1150	899	899	1099	1300	925		1399	1399	1249
2000	899	1125		1300	1500	1199	925	925	1125	1350	925	925	1399	1425	1249
2001	925	1125		1350		1199	925	925			925	925			1299
2001	925	1125		1379		1199	925	925			925				1299
2002	925	1125		1379		1199	925	925			949				
2003	949	1149		1379		1199	949	949							
2004	949	1199		1419		1199	949	949							
2005	999	1249		1499		1249	999	999							
2006	1049	1249		1599		1299	1049	1049							
2006	1049	1299		1599		1349	1049	1049							
2007	1099	1399		1649		1349	1099	1099							
2007	1199	1399		1799		1449	1199	1199							
2008	1199	1399		1799		1449	1199	1199							

J (JUMBO) MODEL PRICES
SELECTED REPRESENTATIVE MODELS

Year	J-18 (J-18M)	J-21 (J-21M)	J-21MC	J-40 (J-40M)	J-40BK (J-40MBK)	JC-40 (J-40MC)	J12-40 (J12-40M)	J-65 (J-65M)	J-65M	J-65M (with MEQ)	J12-65 (J12-65M)	HJ-28
1985												
1986		1570		1750			1825					
1986		1570		1750			1825					
1987		1656	1750	1750			1825					
1987		1666		1848			1910					
1988	1634	1750		1858			1920					
1988	1710			1952			2016					
1989	1800	1820		2030	2184		2098	1972				
1990	1880	1900		2120	2280		2190	2060				
1991		2000		2230	2400		2300	2170				
1992	1970	2080		2320	2500	2340	2400	2260				
1993	2170	2290		2440	2630	2440	2520	2370	2730		2042	
1994	2300	2520		2590	2790	2560	2680	2520			2140	
1995	2300			2750	2970	2720	2850	2680			2250	
1996				3250	3470	2890	3350				2340	
1997				3250		3390				2895	2460	2770
1998				3250							2610	2770
1999				3350								2770
2000				3350								2770
2000				3350								
2001				3350								
2002				3489								
2002				3489								
2003				3489								
2004				3489								
2004				3699								
2005				3699								
2005				3899								
2006				4049								
2007				4049								
2008				4049								

J-41 Special – 2007

1 SERIES PRICES
SELECTED REPRESENTATIVE MODELS

Year	D-1	DC-1	DC1E	D-1R	D12-1	D-2R	D-3R	J-1	0000-1	000-1	000-1R	0000-1E	OM-1	00-1	B-1	C-1R
1994	1099															
1995	1099															
1996	1099	1300		1300												
1997	1099	1300		1300												
1998	1099	1300	1499	1300		1850	1950								1449	1500
1999	1099	1300	1499	1300		1349	1425	1099	1099	1099	1300			1250	1449	1500
2000	1099	1300	1499	1300	1300	1349	1425	1099	1099	1099	1300	1499		1250	1449	1500
2000	1099	1300	1499	1300	1300	1349	1425	1099	1099	1099	1300	1499		1250	1449	1500
2001	1099		1499	1300	1300	1349	1425	1099	1099	1099	1300	1499	1099	1250	1499	1575
2002	1099		1499	1300	1300	1349	1425	1099	1099	1099	1300	1499	1099		1499	1575
2002	1099		1499	1300	1300	1349	1425			1099	1300		1099		1499	1575
2003	1129		1529	1300	1300	1349	1425			1099	1300		1099		1499	1575
2003	1129		1529	1300		1349	1425			1099	1300				1749	
2004	1129		1569	1329		1399	1425			1129	1329				1499	
2005	1199		1569				1479			1129					1599	
2006	1199		1649							1199					1699	
2006	1299		1749							1299					1699	
2007	1299		1749												1699	

15 & 17 SERIES PRICES
SELECTED REPRESENTATIVE MODELS

Year	D-15	DC-15E	D-17	D-15S	J12-15	J-15	JC-15E	000-15	0000C-15E	000-15S	OM-15	OMC-15E	00-15	000C-15AE	00-17	BC-15E
1997	849															
1998	849							849					849			
1999	849			1179				849					849			1499
2000	849	1249	1650		999	1099		849	1249	999			849			1499
2000	949	1249	1650		1099	1099	1349	949	1249	1099			949	1249	1650	1599
2001	949	1249			1099	949	1349	949	1349	1099	949	1459	949	1349	1650	1599
2002	949	1349			1139	949		949	1349	1099	949		949	1489	1650	1659
2002	979	1459			1139	949		979	1459	1219	949		979		1650	1699
2003	979	1499			1139	979		979	1495	1219	979		979		1650	1699
2004	979	1499			1199	979		979		1299	979		979			1699
2004	1029	1599			1249	1029		1029		1399			1029			1799
2005	1099	1699			1249	1099		1099		1399			1099			1899
2006	1099	1699			1299	1099		1099		1499			1099			1899
2007	1149	1749			1299	1149		1149		1499			1149			1949
2007	1249	1899			1399	1249		1249		1629			1249			2099
2008	1249	1899			1399	1249		1249		1629			1249			2099

000-15 Detail – 2003

Mandolin Prices (Part One)

Model	1896	1897	1898	1899	1900	1901	1902	1903	1904	1905	1906	1907	1908	1909	1910	1911	1912	1913	1914	1915	1916	1917	1918	1919	1920	1921	1922	1923	1924	1925	1926	1927	1928	1929	1930	1931	1932	1933	1934	1935	1936	1937	1938	1939	1940	1941	1942	1944	1945	1946	1947
G1 Bowl Mandolin	28																																																		
G2 Bowl Mandolin	33																																																		
G3 Bowl Mandolin	40																																																		
G5 Bowl Mandolin	80																																																		
#00 Bowl Mandolin										15	15	15	15	15	15	15	15	15	15	20	20	20	20	24	24	26.4	30	30																							
#0 Bowl Mandolin													20	20	20	20	20	20	20	20	20	20	30	30	30	33	35	35																							
#1 Bowl Mandolin	20	20	20	20	20	25	25	25	25	25	25	25	25	25	25	30	30	36	36	36	36	36	39.6	40																											
#2 Bowl Mandolin	25	25	30	30	30	30	30	30	30	30	30	30	30	30																																					
#3 Bowl Mandolin	30	30	35	35	35	35	35	35	35	35	35	35	35	35	40																																				
#4 Bowl Mandolin	40	40	40	40	40	40	40	40	40	40	40	40	40	45	50																																				
#5 Bowl Mandolin	50	50	50	50	50	50	50	50	50	50	50	50	50	50																																					
#6 Bowl Mandolin	75	75	75	75	75	75	75	75	75	75	75	75	75	75	75	75	80																																		
#7 Bowl Mandolin							100	100	100	100	100	100	100	100	100	100	100																																		
#A Bowl Mandola																		27.5	30	30	30	25	25	27.5	30	30	30	30	35	35	35	35	30	30	30	30	30	30	30	30	30	30	30	30	30	30	30	35	35		
#B Bowl Mandola																		38.5	42	42	40	40	40	44	50	50	50	55	55	55	55	55	50	50	50	50	50	50	50	50	50	50	50	50	50	55	55				
A Flat Back Mandolin																		15	15	15	20	22	24	24	24	20	20	22	25	25	25	25	27.5	27.5	27.5	25	25	25	20	22.5	22.5	25	25	25	28	28	28	32.5	32.5	Cont.	
B Flat Back Mandolin																		25	25	25	30	33	36	36	36	35	38.5	40	40	40	40	45	45	45	45	40	40	40	35	35	35	40	40	40	40	40	45	45			
C Flat Back Mandolin																		40	40	55	60	60	60	50	50	50	55	55	55	55	55	55	60	60	60	55	55	50	50												
D Flat Back Mandolin																		60	60																																
E Flat Back Mandolin																		100	100	100	110	120	120	100	100	110	110	110	115	115	115	110	110	110																	
AK Flat Back Mandolin																							25	25	25	30	30	30	27.5	35	35	35	30	30	30	25	25														
B Flat Back Mandolin																																																		Cont.	
AK2 Flat Back Mandolin																																																		Cont.	
15 Carved Mandolin																																			50	50	40	40	45	45	45	45	45	45	50	50	50	50			
20 Carved Mandolin																																			75	75	75	75	75	75	75	75	75	75							
2-15 Carved Mandolin																																								50	50	50	50	50	50	55	55	55	55	65	65 Cont.
2-20 Carved Mandolin																																									85	85	85	85	85	85	85	95	95	95	95
2-30 Carved Mandolin																																													135	135	135	135	150	150	150 150
MC-1 Mando Cello																																											80	80	85	85	85	85	80	80	80

12-STRING PRICES
SELECTED REPRESENTATIVE MODELS

Year	D12XM	D12X1	DM-12	D12-1	J12-15	J12-16GT	SPD12-16R	D12-18	D12-20	D12-28	D12-35	D12-41	D12-45	J12-40 (J12-40M)	J12-65 (J12-65M)	D12-2832 Shenandoah
1965									290		410					
1966									295		435					
1966									325		460					
1967									325		460					
1968									325		460					
1969									350		485					
1970									350		485					
1970									375		525					
1971									375		565					
1972									425		595					
1973									500	625	670		1200			
1974								580	580	680	730		1650			
1974								630	630	790	810		1650			
1975								700	700	820	840		1800			
1976								750	700	820	840	1400	1950			
1977								750	750	880	900	1500	2010			
1978								800	830	920	940	1600	2200			
1979								900	900	950	1000	1600	2320			
1979								950	1000	1050	1000	1600	2500			
1979								950	1100	1100	1000	1900	2700			
1979								960	1100	1100	1240	1910	2700			
1980								1030	1110	1110	1250	2040	3210			
1980								1030	1180	1200	1340	2040	3410			
1981								1040	1180	1200	1340	2040	3410			
1982								1086	1180	1210	1350	2050	3410			
1982								1134	1190	1264	1350	2146	3420			
1983								1134	1243	1321	1411	2247	3585			
1983								1134	1299	1453	1475	2471	3758			
1984								1134	1428	1453	1622	2340	4133			
1985								1297	1347	1453	1626	2340	3660			
1986								1357	1347	1503	1676	2440	3660			
1986								1357	1397	1563	1736	2500	3760			
1987								1357	1457	1563	1736	2500	3820	1825	1775	810
1988								1420	1457	1563	1736	2500	3820	1825	1775	840
1988						1398		1550	1700	1636	1816	2690	4116	1825	1775	840
1989					999	1450		1628	1786	1646	1900	2800	4700	1910	1858	900
1990					1099	1450		1628	1786	1730	1996	2800	4700	1920	1868	950
1991					1099	1499		1694	1858	1730	1996	2800	5100	2016	1962	950
1992					1099	1499		1770	2050	1800	2076	2912	5304	2098	1962	998
1993			1150		1139	1499		1860	2160	1880	2290	3210	5840	2190	2042	1038
1994			1150		1139	1499		1940	2250	1980	2410	3370	6130	2250	2140	1130
1995			1199		1199	1599		2130	2480	2060	2510	3510	6380	2340	2250	1200
1996			1199		1199	1599	2200	2350		2160	2760	3860	7020	2400	2340	1200
1997			1199		1199	1599	2200			2380				2520	2460	(Disc)
1998			1249	1300	1249	1699	2250			2530				2680	2610	
1999	699	749	1299	1300	1199	1699				2530				2850	2770	
2000	699	749	1299	1300	1199	1699				2530				3350		
2000		749	1299	1300	1349	1699				2530						
2001		769	1299	1300	1399	1699				2530						
2002		769	1199	1300						2599						
2002		769	1199							2599						
2003		769	1199							2689						
2004		769	1199							2689						
2004		769	1249							2799						
2005		769	1299							2799						
2005		769	1299							2949						
2006		769	1299							2949						
2007		819	1449							3049						
2008		819	1449							3049						

Style 7 Bowl Mandolin – 1902

J12-16GT – 2000

MANDOLIN PRICES
(PART TWO)

Year	A Flat Back Mandolin	AK Flat Back Mandolin	B Flat Back Mandolin	AK2 Flat Back Mandolin	2-15 Carved Mandolin
1948	36				
1949	40				
1950	45				75
1950	50				85
1951	50				90
1952	50				100
1953	53				100
1954	53				100
1955	56				110
1956	62				110
1957	68				125
1958	68				140
1959	72				150
1960	78.5				150
1961	78.5				160
1962	82.5				175
1963	82.5				175
1963	89.5				195
1964	89.5				195
1965	97.5				214.5
1965	115				214.5
1966	130				230
1966	150				
1967	150				
1968	160				
1969	225				
1970	225				
1970	240				
1971	240				
1972	240				
1972	240				
1973	290				
1974	330				
1974	340				
1975	340				
1976	370				
1976	380				
1977	600				
1978	700				
1978	700				
1979	500				
1980	540	675	650	690	
1981	540	709	683	725	
1981	567	744	717	761	
1982	595	818	789	837	
1982	655	818	789	837	
1983	655	818	789	837	
1984	655	818	789	837	
1985	715	878	849	897	
1986	715	878	849	897	
1986	715	878	849	897	
1987	788	966	936		
1988	1116	1516	1516		
1989	1288				
1990	1340				
1990	1480				
1991	1560				
1992	1630				
1993	1790				
	Disc.				

ACOUSTIC BASS PRICES

Year	BM	B-1	B-1E	BC-15E	B-40[a]	BC-40[a]	B-540[a]	B-65[a]	Alt. X Bass	00C-16GTAE Bass
1989					2150			2050		
1990					2150			2050		
1991					2240			2140		
1992					2350			2250		
1993					2570	2630	2630	2460		
1994					2730	2770	2790	2610		
1995					2730	2940	2790	2610		
1996		1449			2900	2940				
1997		1449			2900	3120				
1998	1229	1449				3120				
1999	1299	1499		1499						
2000	1299	1499		1599						
2001		1499		1599						
2002		1499	1819	1659						
2003		1499	1819	1659						
2004		1599	1899	1699						
2005		1599	1899	1699					1499	
2006		1699	1899	1799					1499	
2007		1749	2049	1899						
2008				1949						2099
				2099						2099

Footnotes for ACOUSTIC BASS Pricing

a Bass thinline pickups and active preamps with volume and tone controls were shown on the price list as an option for an additional charge from 1989 to 1994.

B-40 and B-65 Acoustic Basses – 1989

UKULELE and TIPLE PRICES
REPRESENTATIVE MODELS — (PART ONE)

Year	#0	#1	#2	#3	#5	1-C Concert	1-T Tenor	B-51 Baritone	#1K	#2K	#3K	#5K	T-18 Tiple	T-28 Tiple
1918		10	15	25										
1919		13.2	17.6	27.5										
1920	10	14	18	30							27	50	30	
1921	10	14	18	30					14	17	27	50	33	70
1922	10	12	15	25					14	17	27	55	35	70
1923	10	12	15	25					14	17	27	55	35	70
1924	11	13.2	16.5	27.5		18			15.4	18.7	29.7	60	35	75
1925	11	13.5	17.5	27.5		18			16	20	30	55	35	75
1926	12	14	17.5	27.5		20	25		16	20	30	55	40	75
1927	12	14	17.5	27.5		20	25		16	20	30	60	40	75
1928	12	15	20	30		20	25		18	24	35	60	40	75
1929	11	13.5	17.5	27.5		18	25		18	24	35	55	40	75
1930	11	13.5	17.5	27.5		18	25		16	20	30	55	40	75
1931	10	12.5	17.5	27.5		16	20		16	20	30	50	30	50
1932	10	12.5	17.5	27.5		15	20		15	17.5	27.5	50	30	50
1933	10	12.5	15	25		15	20		14		27.5	50	30	50
1934	10	12.5	15	25		15	20		12.5		27.5	50	35	50
1935	10	12.5	15	25		15	20		12.5		27.5	50	35	50
1936	10	12.5	15	25		15	20		12.5		27.5	50	35	50
1937	10	12.5	15	25		15	20		12.5			50	35	50
1938	10	12.5	15	25		15	20		12.5			50	35	50
1939	10	12.5	15	25		15	20		12.5			50	35	60
1940	10	12.5	15	25	50	15	20		14				35	60
1941	12	14	17	28	55	17	22.5		14				40	70
1942	12	14	17	28	55	17	22.5						40	78
1943	12	14	17	28		17	22.5						40	78
1944	12	14	17	28		17	22.5						40	78
1945	12	14	20	28		20	26						46	80
1946	13	16	20	32		20	26						46	80
1947	13	18	20	32		22	30						50	84
1948	15	18	22	35		24	32						50	80
1949	16	20	22.5	40		27.5	35						55	90
1950	18	22.5	22.5	45		27.5	35						55	90
1950	20	25	30	47.5		32.5	40						60	90
1951	20	25	30	47.5		32.5	40						60	90
1952	20	25	30	47.5		32.5	40						60	90
1953	20	27	32	50		35	42						65	95
1954	20	27	32	50		35	42						65	95
1955	22	30	35	55		38	45						70	100
1956	25	35	40	60		42	50						80	110
1957	27	37	43	65		45	55						87	120
1958	27	37	45	68		45	55						87	120
1959	28	40	45	68		48	58						92	125
1960	29.5	42.5	48.5	72.5		52.5	63.5	75					99.5	135
1961	29.5	42.5	48.5	72.5		52.5	63.5	75					99.5	135
1962	32.5	45	50	75		55	67.5	79.5					109.5	145
1963	32.5	45	50	75		55	67.5	79.5					109.5	145
1963	34.5	47.5	53.5	79.5		59.5	72.5	84.5					117.5	154.5
1964	34.5	47.5	53.5	79.5		59.5	72.5	84.5					117.5	154.5
1965	35	47.5	55	82.5		60	77.5	87.5					125	170
1965	35	47.5	55	82.5		60	77.5	87.5					125	170
1966	45			85			90	100					140	185
1966	65			100			115	125					150	185
1967	65			100			115	125					165	210

BACKPACKER PRICES (WITH BAG)

Year	Steel String	Nylon String	Steel w/ Electronics	Nylon w/ Electronics	Mandolin	Ukulele
1992	239					
1993	254					
1994	254					
1995	254	254				
1996	254	254	364	379		
1997	254	254	379	379		
1998	254	254	379	379		
1999	254	254	379	379	289	
2000	254	254	379	379	289	
2001	274	274	379	379	306	
2002	274	274	409	409	306	
2003	274	274	409	409	306	209
2004	274	274	409	409	306	209
2004	289	289	409	409	349	209
2005	289	289	429	429	349	209
2006	299	299	429	429	349	225
2007	299	299	449	449	349	225

Footnotes for BACKPACKER Prices

a Price shown is with Thinline 332® Electronics. Extra charge for enhanced System I Electronics.

Backpacker Family – 2000

UKULELE and TIPLE PRICES
REPRESENTATIVE MODELS — (PART TWO)

Year	0#	#1	#2	#3	#5	1-C Concert	1-T Tenor	B-51 Baritone	#1K	#2K	#3K	#5K	T-18 Tiple	T-28 Tiple
1968	70												165	210
1968	70												175	220
1969	70												175	220
1970	70			110									175	220
1971	80			110			125	135					185	220
1972	80			125			125	135					185	220
1973	80			125			125	135					185	220
1973	160			220			180	150					300	350
1974	180			240			190	150					330	350
1974	190			250			200	220					330	380
1975	190			250			200	240					340	380
1976	200			260			220	250					340	400
1976	210			280			230	250					370	400
1977	500			650			650	270					380	430
1977	500			650			650	280					800	450
1978	500			650			650	700					800	850
1979	350			450			450	700					800	850
1979	350			450			450	500					600	850
1979	350			450			450	500					600	650
1980	380			490			490	540					600	650
1980	380			490			490	540					650	650
1981	399			515			490	540					650	710
1981	419			541			515	567					683	710
1982	461			595			541	595					717	746
1982	461			595			595	655					789	783
1983	461			595			595	655					789	861
1984	461			595			595	655					789	861
1985	521			655			655	655					789	861
1986	521			655			655	715					849	921
1986	521			655			655	715					849	921
1987	574			720			720	715					849	921
1988	916			1016			1016	788					936	1014
1988	1010			1228			1228	1116					1216	1316
1989	1052			1278			1278	1348					1278	1382
1990	1160			1410			1410	1402					1330	1438
1991	1220			1480			1480	1550					1470	1590
1992	1270			1540			1540	1630					1550	1670
1993	1570			1860			1860	1700					1620	1740
1994	1810			2050			2050	2040					1950	2080
1995								2250						
1996														
1997														
1998														
1999														
2000														
2001														
2002														
2003				2249										
2004														
2005														
2006												5199		
2007												5199		
2008											2449	5199		

MARTIN GUITAR and MANDOLIN SERIAL NUMBERS

Martin Guitar Serial Numbers

YEAR	LAST NUMBER	YEARLY TOTALS
1898	8348	348
1899	8716	368
1900	9128	412
1901	9310	182
1902	9528	218
1903	9810	282
1904	9988	178
1905	10120	132
1906	10329	209
1907	10727	398
1908	10883	156
1909	11018	135
1910	11203	185
1911	11413	210
1912	11565	152
1913	11821	256
1914	12047	226
1915	12209	162
1916	12390	181
1917	12988	598
1918	13450	462
1919	14512	1062
1920	15848	1336
1921	16758	910
1922	17839	1081
1923	19891	2052
1924	22008	2117
1925	24116	2108
1926	28689	4573
1927	34435	5746
1928	37568	3133
1929	40843	3275
1930	45317	4474
1931	49589	4272
1932	52590	3001
1933	55084	2494
1934	58679	3595
1935	61947	3268
1936	65176	3229
1937	68865	3689
1938	71866	3001
1939	74061	2195
1940	76734	2673
1941	80013	3279
1942	83107	3094
1943	86724	3617
1944	90149	3425
1945	93623	3474
1946	98158	4535
1947	103468	5310
1948	108269	4801
1949	112961	4692
1950	117961	5000
1951	122799	4838
1952	128436	5637
1953	134501	6065
1954	141345	6844
1955	147328	5983
1956	152775	5447
1957	159061	6286
1958	165576	6515
1959	171047	5471
1960	175689	4642
1961	181297	5608
1962	187384	6087
1963	193327	5943
1964	199626	6299
1965	207030	7404
1966	217215	10185
1967	230095	12880
1968	241925	11830
1969	256003	14078
1970	271633	15630
1971	294270	22637
1972	313302	19032
1973	333873	20571
1974	353387	19514
1975	371828	18441
1976	388800	16972
1977	399625	10825
1978	407800	8175
1979	419900	12100
1980	430300	10400
1981	436474	6174
1982	439627	3153
1983	446101	6474
1984	453300	7199
1985	460575	7275
1986	468175	7600
1987	476216	8041
1988	483952	7736
1989	493279	9327
1990	503309	10030
1991	512487	9178
1992	522655	10168
1993	535223	12568
1994	551696	16473
1995	570434	18738
1996	592930	22496
1997	624799	31869
1998	668796	43997
1999	724077	55281
2000	780500	56423
2001	845644	65144
2002	916759	71115 [a]
2003	978706	61947
2004	1042558	63852
2005	1115862	73304
2006	1197799	81937
2007	1268091	70292

Footnotes for Martin Guitar Serial Numbers

[a] Sigma Martin Serial Numbers are 900001 through 902908 (2907 units). These numbers affect Martin production totals in the year 2002.

Martin Mandolin Serial Numbers

YEAR	LAST NUMBER	YEARLY TOTALS
1895	23	23
1896	112	89
1897	155	43
1898	359	204
1899	577	218
1900	800	223
1901	881	81
1902	1171	290
1903	1348	177
1904	1507	159
1905	1669	162
1906	2026	357
1907	2357	331
1908	2510	153
1909	2786	276
1910	3098	312
1911	3431	333
1912	3847	416
1913	4162	315
1914	4462	300
1915	4767	305
1916	5007	240
1917	5752	745
1918	6370	618
1919	7237	867
1920	8761	1524
1921	9627	866
1922	10196	569
1923	11020	824
1924	11809	789
1925	12520	711
1926	13359	839
1927	13833	474
1928	14170	337
1929	14630	460
1930	14892	262
1931	15290	398
1932	15476	186
1933	15528	52
1934	15729	201
1935	15887	158
1936	16156	269
1937	16437	281
1938	16580	143
1939	16747	167
1940	16957	210
1941	17263	306
1942	17405	142
1943	NONE	0
1944	NONE	0
1945	NONE	0
1946	17641	236
1947	18303	662
1948	19078	775
1949	19559	481
1950	20065	506
1951	20496	431
1952	20902	406
1953	21452	550
1954	21952	500
1955	22254	302
1956	22629	375
1957	22985	356
1958	23111	126
1959	23262	151
1960	23512	250
1961	23663	151
1962	23938	275
1963	24139	201
1964	24339	200
1965	24439	100
1966	24564	125
1967	24639	75
1968	24839	200
1969	24989	150
1970	25039	50
1971	25139	100
1972	25289	150
1973	25339	50
1974	25679	340
1975	25895	216
1976	26045	150
1977	26101	56
1978	26101	0
1979	26112	11
1980	26156	44
1981	26215	59
1982	26225	10
1983	26247	22
1984	26254	7
1985	26263	9
1986	26273	10
1987	26279	6
1988	26281	2
1989	26283	2
1990	26291	8
1991	26297	6
1991	509122 [b]	(11)
1992	509122	(0) [c]
1993	533213	(6)

Footnotes for Martin Mandolin Serial Numbers

[b] As of 1991, mandolins started receiving guitar serial numbers.
[c] Mike Longworth's records show a duplicated reference for 1992.

MARTIN CASE DESIGNATIONS [a]

GUITAR SIZE or MODEL	300 SERIES	400 SERIES	500 SERIES	600 SERIES	Gig Bag	Other Designations (See Footnotes) [b]
D Dreadnought 14 Fret	345		545	640	#52BGB	640B, 545A, 545AF, 545BD, 545DL, 545DLB, 545E, 545EC, 545EXL, 545T, 545TT
D Dreadnought 12 Fret	341		540			540C, 540CMC (for CEO4, CEO4R), 540V
Dreadnought 14 Fret (Thin Body)	344					Used for David Gray, Beck and Travis Tritt Signature Editions
J Jumbo 14 Fret	380		580	640		580C. 580J & 580J2 used for "Concept" Model
M (0000) Grand Auditorium 14 Fret	370		570	640		570C, 570D, #Z70BU
OM Orchestra Model 14 Fret	330		533	630	#52BGB	533 Artinger, 533C, 533EC, 533EW, 533ENEG, 533EJM, #Z30BU
000 Auditorium 14 Fret	330	430	533	630	#52BGB	533 designations as above, 330BL, 330BR, 330SS, 533C
000 Auditorium 12 Fret	320, 331		535, 532			532 for Norman Blake – 12 fret neck, 14 fret body; 535AC, 535C
00 Grand Concert 14 Fret	350		534	620	#52BGB	534C
00 Grand Concert 12 Fret			525	610		900 Series (Replica Stauffer Coffin Case)
00 Grand Concert 14 Fret (Deep Body)	334			620D, 620DB		"D" or "DB" for Deeper Body Depth
00 Grand Concert (Thin Body AE)	310CE					310SS (Alternative X)
0 Concert 14 Fret				610*		* Padding Required
0 Concert 12-Fret			515			
7/8 Size Dreadnought				610		
N Classical	320		520H			
Thomas Humphrey Classical	320					
0 Tenor			500, 515	600, 610		
CF American Archtop	348BGT					
Size 5 Terz or Mini Martin	314, 318DB					318C. "DB" for Dick Boak's Miri Martin Edition.
Little Martin					#52BTG	12BTGX, plus Felix and Realtree Edition Gig Bags
Tiple		414				
Soprano Ukulele – Styles 0, 3 & 5		412	505		#52BBPU	#52BBPU also used for Backpacker Ukulele
Concert Ukulele		413				
T Tenor Ukulele		414				
B-51 Baritone Ukulele		416				
A Mandolin		425				
Acoustic Bass	310BN, 360		560			
Backpacker Guitar					#52BBP	#52BBPU used for Backpacker Ukulele

Key for Case Suffixes:

A	Alligator
AC	Arts and Crafts
AF	American Flag
B	Black
BD	Black Denim
BL	Black
BR	Brown
BU	Slate Blue ABS
C	Cabernet Interior
C	Claire
CMC	Chris Martin CEO Case
D	Deep Body
DB	Dick Boak Mini Martin
DB	Beep Body
DL	Brown Leather
DLB	Black Leather
E	Electronics Compatible
EC	Electronic Cabernet
EJM	John Mayer
EW	Electric White
EXL	Extra Wide (Elvis case)
J & J2	Concept J Guitars
NEG	White Ext./Blk Int.
SS	Silver Snakeskin
T	Tweed
TT	Taupe Tweed
Z30BU	Slate Blue ABS
Z70BU	Slate Blue ABS
V	Vintage (Ditson)

Footnotes for Martin Guitar Case Designations

a Martin case part numbers are typically preceeded with "12C," so a Style 640 case would carry the full designation of 12C640.

b Cases listed under Other Designations typically have special coverings as noted in the "Key for Case Suffixes" at above right. We have attempted to cover the primary case offerings with this chart, but there are historic sizes and styles that may have been omitted.

MARTIN INSTRUMENT DIMENSIONS (PAGE ONE)

GUITAR SIZE or MODEL	Total Length	Body Length	Body Width Upper Bout	Body Width Lower Bout	Body Depth At Neck	Body Depth At End Piece	Fingerboard Width At Nut	Fingerboard Width 12th Fret	Soundhole Diameter	Scale Length
12-FRET NECK MODELS										
Size 1/4	26 7/8"	12 1/16"	6 5/8"	8 15/16"	3 1/16"	3 9/16"	1 5/8"	1 15/16"	2 5/8"	17"
Size 1/2 a	31 1/2"	15 1/16"	7 3/8"	10 1/8"	2 7/8"	3 3/8"	1 3/4"	2 1/4"	3 1/8"	20 7/8"
Size 5 (Mini Martin or Terz)	33"	16"	8 1/4"	11 1/4"	3 1/8"	3 7/8"	1 5/8"	2 1/16"	3 1/4"	21.4" or 22"
Size 4	33"	16"	8 15/16"	11 1/2"	3 1/4"	3 3/4"	1 3/4"	2 3/16"	3 1/4"	22"
Size 3 1/2 b	33 1/2"	16 7/8"	8"	10 11/16"	3 1/8"	3 7/8"	1 3/4"	2 1/8"	3 7/16"	22"
Size 3	36"	17 3/8"	8 1/8"	11 1/4"	3 1/8"	3 13/16"	1 3/4"	2 3/16"	3 11/32"	23 7/8"
Size 2 1/2	36 1/2"	17 7/8"	8 1/4"	11 5/8"	3 1/8"	3 7/8"	1 13/16"	2 3/16"	3 1/2"	24.5"
Size 2	37"	18 1/4"	8 1/2"	12"	3 3/4"	4"	1 13/16"	2 1/4"	3 1/2"	24.5"
Size 1	37 3/4"	18 7/8"	9 1/4"	12 3/4"	3 3/8"	4 3/16"	1 7/8"	2 5/16"	3 9/16"	24.9"
Size 0	37 3/4"	19 1/8"	9 1/2"	13 1/2"	3 3/8"	4 3/16"	1 7/8"	2 5/16"	3 5/8"	24.9" c
Size 00	39 3/4"	19 5/8"	9 3/4"	14 1/8"	3 1/4"	4 1/16"	1 7/8"	2 5/16"	3 3/4"	25.4" d
Size 000 (Norman Blake – 14 Fret Body)	38 1/8"	20 7/16"	11 13/32"	15"	3 1/4"	4 1/16"	1 13/16"	2 5/16"	3 7/8"	24.9"
Size D (Dreadnought)	39 9/16"	20 15/16"	11 1/2"	15 5/8"	3 15/16"	4 3/4"	1 7/8"	2 5/16"	4"	25.4"
14-FRET NECK MODELS										
Size LX Little Martin	34"	15 3/4"	8 3/16"	12 17/32"	3 5/64"	3 13/16"	1 11/16"	2 1/16"	3 1/4"	23"
Size 0	38 3/8"	18 3/8"	10"	13 1/2"	3 13/32"	4 1/4"	1 11/16"	2 1/8"	3 5/8"	24.9"
Size 0 Tenor	35 1/4"	17 3/16"	9 7/8"	13 1/2"	3 1/4"	4"	1 1/4"	1 1/2"	3 5/8"	23"
Size 00	38 5/8"	18 7/8"	10 7/8"	13 5/16"	3 11/32"	4 1/8"	1 11/16"	2 1/8"	3 3/4"	24.9"
Size 00DB (Deep Body)	38 5/8"	18 7/8"	10 7/8"	13 5/16"	3 27/32"	4 5/8"	1 11/16"	2 1/8"	3 3/4"	24.9"
Size 000	39 3/8"	19 3/8"	11 13/32"	15 1/4"	3 1/4"	4 1/8"	1 11/16"	2 1/4"	3 7/8"	24.9"
Size OM	39 3/8"	19 3/8"	11 13/32"	15 1/4"	3 1/4"	4 1/8"	1 3/4"	2 1/8"	4"	25.4"
Size D (Dreadnought)	40 1/4"	20"	11 1/2"	15 5/8"	3 15/16"	4 7/8"	1 11/16"	2 1/8"	4"	25.4"
Size D (Dreadnought – 000 Depth) e	40 1/4"	20"	11 11/16"	16"	3 11/32"	4 1/8"	1 11/16"	2 1/8"	4"	25.4"
Size M (0000)	40 3/8"	20 1/8"	11 11/16"	16"	3 5/16"	4 1/8"	1 11/16"	2 1/8"	4"	25.4"
Size J (M Shape – Dreadnought Depth)	40 3/8"	20 1/8"	11 11/16"	16"	3 15/16"	4 7/8"	1 11/16"	2 1/8"	4"	25.4"
Size 7 (7/8 Dreadnought)	36 1/16"	17 1/2"	10"	13 11/16"	3 31/64"	4 3/8"	1 5/8"	2"	3 3/4"	23"
ACOUSTIC BASS										
B and BC Models	47 3/8"	20 1/8"	11 11/16"	16"	3 15/16"	4 7/8"	1.58"	2.18"	4"	34.15"
00 Thin Body Models	46 3/8"	18 7/8"	10 7/8"	13 5/16"	3 11/32"	4 1/8"	1.58"	2.18"	3 3/4"	34.15"
ARCHTOPS AND CARVED TOPS										
Size C (Carved)	39 1/8"	19 3/8"	11 1/4"	15"	3 3/8"	4 3/16"	1 11/16"	2 1/4"	N/A	24.9"
Size F (Carved)	39 7/8"	20 1/8"	11 9/16"	16"	3 1/4"	4 1/8"	1 5/8"	2 1/8"	N/A	24.9"
Size R (Arched or Carved)	38 3/8"	18 7/8"	10 13/16"	14 5/8"	3 11/32"	4 1/4"	1 11/16"	2 1/4"	N/A	24.9"
CF-1 American Archtop (Deep Body)	43 1/2"	20 7/8"	12 7/8"	17"	3"	3"	1 3/4"	2 1/8"	N/A	25"
CF-2 American Archtop (Thin Body)	43 1/2"	20 7/8"	12 7/8"	17"	2 1/2"	2 1/2"	1 3/4"	2 1/8"	N/A	25"
CLASSICAL, NYLON, GUT STRING										
Size N	38 1/2"	19 1/8"	10 3/4"	14 7/16"	3 21/32"	4 1/8"	2 1/8 or 1 7/8"	2 3/8 or 2 5/16"	3 9/16"	26 3/8 or 25.4"
Size 00C Classical	37 3/4"	19 5/8"	9 3/4"	14 1/8"	3 1/4"	4 1/16"	1 15/16"	2 5/16"	3 3/4"	25.25" or 25.4"
Size 00G Classical	37 5/8"	18 7/8"	10 7/8"	13 5/16"	3 1/4"	4 1/16"	1 15/16"	2 3/8"	3 3/4"	25.25" or 25.4"
Size 000C Classical	39 3/8"	20 3/8"	10 3/4"	15 1/16"	3 1/4"	4 3/32"	1 15/16"	2 5/16"	3 7/8"	25.4"
Size 000G Classical	38 1/8"	19 3/8"	11 1/4"	15"	3 11/32"	4 1/8"	1 13/16"	2 5/16"	3 7/8"	25.4"
Thomas Humphrey Classical	38 5/8"	19 3/8"	11 1/2"	14 7/8"	3 1/8"	4 1/2"	2 1/16"	2 7/16"	3 7/16"	64.85 cm

MARTIN INSTRUMENT DIMENSIONS (PART TWO)

GUITAR SIZE or MODEL	Total Length	Body Length	Body Width Upper Bout	Body Width Lower Bout	Body Depth At Neck	Body Depth At End Piece	Fingerboard Width At Nut	Fingerboard Width 12th Fret	Soundhole Diameter	Scale Length
ELECTRIC GUITARS and BASSES										
F Models	40 1/8"	20 1/8"	11 1/2"	16"	2"	2"	1 5/8"	2"	None	24.9"
GT-70 Models	40 3/16"	19 3/4"	11 3/4"	16"	2"	2"	1 11/16"	2"	None	24.9"
GT-75 Models	40 3/16"	16 7/8"	11 3/4"	16"	2"	2"	1 11/16"	2"	None	24.9"
E-18 and EM-18 Models	39 3/16"	17 5/8"	Asymmetrical	12 13/16"	1 11/16 or 17/16"	1 11/16 or 17/16"	1 5/8"	2 1/8"	None	25.4"
EB-18 Electric Basses	45 9/32"	17 5/8"	Asymmetrical	12 13/16"	1 11/16 or 17/16"	1 11/16 or 17/16"	1 9/16"	2 1/8"	None	34" (33.825")
E-28	39 1/4"	17"	Asymmetrical	12 13/16"	1 1/4" at rim	1 3/4" at center	1 5/8"	2 1/16"	None	24.9"
EB-28 Electric Basses	45 5/16"	17"	Asymmetrical	12 13/16"	1 1/4" at rim	1 3/4" at center	1 9/16"	2 1/8"	None	33.1625"
MANDOLINS										
Bowl Back Models	23 1/2"	12"	No Upper Bout	7 3/4"	5 3/16" at center	N/A	1 3/16"	1 9/16"	1 3/4" x 2 3/4"	13"
Flat Back Models	23 3/4"	12 1/8"	No Upper Bout	9 1/2" f	2 3/16"	2 5/8"	1 3/16"	1 9/16"	1 3/4" x 2 11/16"	13"
Carved Oval Hole	24 3/4"	13"	No Upper Bout	10"	3" at center	1 7/8" at edge	1 3/16"	1 9/16"	1 1/8" x 2 3/8"	13"
Carved F Scrolls	26"	13"	No Upper Bout	10"	3"	1 7/8" at edge	1 3/16"	1 9/16"	F-holes	13 3/4"
UKULELE, TAROPATCH, TIPLE										
Soprano Ukulele – Styles 0, 3 and 5	21"	9 7/16"	5"	6 3/8"	2"	2 5/16"	1 13/32"	1 13/16"	1 3/4"	13 5/8"
Concert Ukulele	23 1/4"	11"	5 3/4"	7 5/8"	2 1/4"	2 3/4"	1 13/32"	1 13/16"	2 1/8"	14 3/4"
Tenor Ukulele	26 1/4"	12 1/16"	6 5/8"	8 15/16"	2 3/8"	2 7/8"	1 11/32"	1 23/32"	2 5/8"	17"
Baritone Ukulele	30 11/16"	14"	7 1/2"	10"	2 11/16"	3 3/8"	1 3/8"	1 11/16"	2 13/16"	20 1/8"
Taropatch	25"	11"	5 5/8"	7 5/8"	2 1/4"	2 3/4"	1 9/16"	2 1/8"	2 1/16"	14 7/8"
Tiple	27 1/4"	12 1/16"	6 5/8"	8 15/16"	3 1/16"	3 9/16"	1 1/2"	1 3/4"	2 5/8"	17"

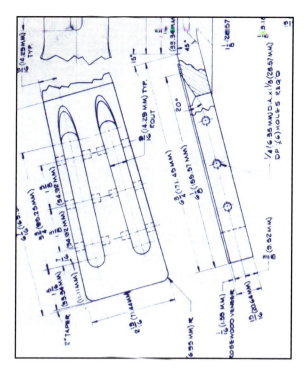

Footnotes for Martin Instrument Measurements

Note: Due to wood shrinkage over time, variations in production methods, different methods of measurement, and general hand craftsmanship, dimensions may vary slightly.

a   Size 1/2 measurements courtesy of R. C. Snoddy.
b   Size 3 1/2 measurements courtesy of Jeff Tripp.
c   Some 00 12-fret models were made with 25.4" scale. Mike Longworth makes note of new 00-45 models.
d   Some 000 12-fret models were 24.9" scale.
e   Thinner body depth used on Beck, EMP-2 Employee, and Kitty Wells editions.
f   Early flat-back mandolins had 9" body widths until sometime in 1917. The wider 9 1/2" models were gradually introduced, beginning with Serial Numbers #5555 through #5566.

UNDERSTANDING THE SERIES AND STYLES OF MARTIN NOMENCLATURE

Through the years, Martin's great success has been predicated upon the company's ability to adapt to the ever-changing marketplace. In recent years, Martin has expanded its offering from the traditional Martin instruments (often referred to as the Standard models) into several new lines. Without abandoning models associated with Martin's rich heritage, the company built upon that heritage and fortified its high end with Special/Limited Edition and Vintage inspired models. In developing a more affordable "lower" end, Martin embraced new technology and delivered the resulting cost savings to guitar buyers in the form of lower-priced models.

In the process, however, it has become increasingly more difficult to understand the differences between guitar models. Because Martin began introducing so many new models and series after 1990, it became especially important to categorize the guitars into a sensible model grid or matrix of sizes and styles. Such a matrix has been used for the format of the Martin Retail Price List since January 1997. In general, the different Series offerings (e.g., Standard Series, Vintage Series, 16 Series, etc.) are shown as columns left to right, while the various sizes offered (e.g., Dreadnought, OM, Jumbo, etc.) are shown in horizontal rows. The generalized descriptions of Series Attributes and a Glossary of Alphabetic Coding are provided below:

BASIC SERIES DESCRIPTIONS (CURRENT)

- Little Martin (LX)
    - Small 14-fret body based loosely upon 0-18T size
    - High pressure laminate back and sides
    - High pressure laminate or spruce top options
    - Stratabond® neck
- X Series (DXM, 000XM, etc)
    - High pressure laminate back and sides
    - High pressure laminate or spruce top options
    - Patented neck mortise and unique bracing
    - Stratabond® neck
- Road Series (DM, 000M, etc.)
    - Solid top, laminate back and sides
    - Satin finish only
    - Single band herringbone wood rosette
    - Patented neck mortise and A-frame bracing
- 1 Series (D-1, 000-1, etc.)
    - Solid top
    - Laminated wood sides
    - Solid mahogany back or laminated rosewood back
    - Satin finish only
    - Patented neck mortise and A-frame bracing
- 15 Series (D-15, 000-15, etc.)
    - Solid mahogany or sapele top, back and sides
    - No bindings, decal rosette
    - Satin finish only
    - Patented neck mortise and A-frame bracing
- 16 Series (D-16, 000-16GT, etc.)
    - Solid wood body construction
    - Patented neck mortise and hybrid bracing
- 17 Series (D-17, 000-17, etc.)
    - Solid mahogany top, back and sides
    - Tortoise color bindings, inlaid rosette
    - Gloss or gloss top finish
    - Patented neck Mortise, Assorted Bracing Patterns
- Standard Series (D-28, OM-21, 000-18, etc.)
    - Solid woods utilized throughout
    - Gloss lacquered bodies
    - Hand fit dovetail neck attachment
- Vintage Series (HD-28V, 000-28EC, OM-28V, etc.)
    - Pre-war appointments (with adjustable truss rods)
    - Gloss lacquered bodies
    - Solid woods utilized throughout
    - Hand fit dovetail neck attachment
- Golden Era® Series (D-18 Golden Era, etc.)
    - Faithfully replicated pre-war appointments (With adjustable truss rods)
    - Adirondack spruce tops
    - Gloss lacquered bodies
    - Solid woods utilized throughout
    - Hand fit dovetail neck attachment
- Marquis Series (D-28 Marquis, OM-28 Marquis, etc.)
    - Golden Era® specifications with the exception of East Indian rosewood replacing Brazilian rosewood
    - Adirondack spruce tops
- Authentic Series (D-18 Authentic, 000-18 Authentic, etc.)
    - Exact reproductions of historic instruments
    - Hide glue construction
    - Period accurate hand carved bracing
    - Period accurate tonewoods
- Special & Limited Editions (e.g., D-28 Elvis Presley, etc.)
    - Generally high-end instruments, but specific models can borrow design features from any series.

Note: Some of the letters listed on the following pages appear as both prefixes and suffixes in model codes, sometimes indicating the same feature. The "H" prefix in HD-28, for instance, indicates a herringbone top border, while the "H" suffix in 000-28H indicates the same feature (and both models ran concurrently).

Confusion can also result from combinations of letters as suffixes, especially when one of the letters was later deleted or moved, but the model's appointments remained the same: A 1989 J-40MBK and a 1990 J-40BK are identical models, while a J-40MC from 1989 is the same as the JC-40 from the following year. (The M was dropped, and the C for "cutaway" was changed to a prefix.)

Some letters have been used to indicate several different features. This is especially true of the letters "M" and "S." If you find a Martin instrument with letters following the style number that are not listed on the following pages, check the Limited and Special Editions charts (in this appendix section) and also chapter 3 of this Technical Reference, which has descriptions of most Guitars of the Month and Limited Editions. Many of these models have the artist's initials as a suffix code (e.g., 0-45JB for Joan Baez). Some short-lived guitar models with unique codes, especially suffix letters, are not included here.

BASIC PREFIXES (CURRENT)

- 0 = Concert size guitar
- 0 = 0 (soprano) ukulele
- 00 = Grand Concert size guitar
- 000 = Auditorium size guitar
- 5 = Size 5 "Terz" guitar
- 7 = 7/8 Size Dreadnought
- ALT = Alternative (aluminum top)
- B = Acoustic Bass (exception black)
- CEO = CEO's Choice (Chris Martin designed)
- CF = American Archtop (Dale Unger collaboration)
- C = Cutaway ("C" follows body code, precedes dash)
- D = Dreadnought guitar
- EMP = Employee designed model or edition
- H = Herringbone top inlay (as in HD-28)
- HP = Herringbone Pearl
- HSO = Hybrid soprano ukulele, 0 size
- J = Jumbo guitar
- M = Grand Auditorium (0000) size guitar
- Mini = Mini (size 5)
- N = Martin Classical Shape, as in N-10, N-20
- OM = Orchestra Model (Long scale 000, 1 3/4" at Nut)
- SO = Soprano ukulele, 0 size
- SW = SmartWood℠ Certified Wood Model or "Sustainable Wood" Series
- 12 = 12-string (follows body code, precedes dash)

HISTORICAL PREFIXES

- 0000 = Grand auditorium "M" size guitar
- 1 = Size 1 guitar
- 1 Uke = Style 1 ukulele (as in 1-C Concert ukulele)
- 1-T = Style 1 tenor ukulele
- 2 = Size 2 guitar
- 2 1/2 = Size 2 1/2 guitar
- 3 = Size 3 guitar
- 3 Uke = Style 3 ukulele
- 4 = Size 4 guitar
- 4 = Also quarter size (tiple sized 6-String guitar)
- 5 = Size 5 "Terz" Guitar
- 5 = Style 5 ukulele (as in 5K ukulele)
- 7 = 7/8 size Dreadnought
- A = A mandolin (mahogany)
- B = B mandolin (rosewood)
- C = Archtop (historical, 000 Shape)
- CM = Custom Shop prefix (Also "CUST")
- CUST = Custom Shop prefix (Also "CM")
- E = Electric solidbody
- F = Archtop or thinbody electric (historical, 0000 shape)
- G = Style G bowlback mandolins
- GT = Thin hollowbody electric
- Mini = Mini-Martin (Size 5–Terz Guitar)
- R = Archtop (Historical, 00 Shape)
- S = Special (usually a custom order)
- SO = Soprano Uke, 0 Style (recent)
- T = Tiple
- SP = Special Appointments

BASIC SUFFIXES (CURRENT)

- AE = Thinbody acoustic/electric
- B = Brazilian rosewood or black finish
- BK = Black finish
- C = Cutaway (now usually a prefix)
- DB = Deep body
- E = Electronics installed
- GE = Golden Era®
- GT = Gloss top
- K = Hawaiian koa back & sides
- K2 = Koa back & sides w/koa top
- LE = Limited edition
- LS = Large soundhole
- M = Mahogany (exception maple)
- M = Suffix on early J models (does not indicate wood)
- N = Nylon strings
- NY = New Yorker model
- QM = Quilted mahogany or quilted maple
- R = Rosewood (typically East Indian rosewood)
- S = 12-Fret w/ slotted headstock
- V = Vintage appointments/Vintage Series
- W = Walnut
- X = Indicates X Series

HISTORICAL SUFFIXES

- A = Ash back & sides (model D-16A)
- BLE = Brazilian limited edition
- BR = Brazilian rosewood
- BSE = Brazilian signature edition
- C = Classical
- C = Concert ukulele
- C = Cutaway (before -)
- E = Electronics installed
- FMG = Figured mahogany
- FW = Figured walnut
- G = Classical (gut or nylon strings)
- GE = Golden Era®
- GM = Grand Marquis
- GOM = Guitar of the month
- GT = Gloss top
- H = Herringbone (wood)
- H = Also Hawaiian (high nut made for slide)
- HP = Herringbone pearl
- K = Koa, Hawaiian
- LE = Limited edition
- LS = Large soundhole
- M = Mahogany (exception maple)
- MB = Maple binding
- MP = Morado rosewood, low profile neck
- N = Nylon strings
- P = Plectrum neck (4-string, long scale)
- P = Low profile neck (with adjustable truss rod) (during 1985 transition, dropped in 1986)
- Q = Non-adjustable rod (primarily made for Japan)
- QM = Quilted mahogany or quilted maple
- R = Adjustable rod (during 1985 transition, dropped in 1986)

R	=	Rosewood (typically East Indian rosewood)
S	=	"Standard" body: 12-fret w/ slotted headstock
S	=	Special order or with special features
SE	=	Signature edition
SW	=	Special Wurlitzer
T	=	Tenor (as in 0-18T)
TSH	=	Thomas S. Humphrey (model CTSH classical)
V	=	Vintage appointments/Vintage Series
VM	=	Vintage mahogany model ("M" subsequently dropped)
VR	=	Vintage rosewood model ("R" subsequently dropped)
W	=	Walnut (back & sides)

64	=	Style 64, maple back and sides, dark binding
65	=	Style 65, as above with binding also on neck
68	=	Style 68, maple back and sides, white bindings
76	=	Style 76, 1976 D-76 & V-76 Bicentennial models
100	=	Style 100 Deluxe, Brazilian rosewood back and sides based upon one millionth guitar design

NUMERIC STYLES OF APPOINTMENT

Since it is impossible to fully describe Martin numeric suffixes and styles in this quick reference format, please see chapter 2 of this Technical Reference for more complete details about individual styles. The descriptions below usually match only the styles as found post-1930, when the model code was added to the neck block just above the serial number. For descriptions of the earlier versions of these styles previous to that date, see chapter 2.

15	=	Style 15, mahogany top, back and sides, unbound
16	=	Style 16, varies, typically simple appointments
17	=	Style 17, mahogany top, back and sides, simple bindings
18	=	Style 18, mahogany back and sides, spruce top
19	=	Style 19, mahogany back and sides, top stained brown
20	=	Style 20, two distinctly different versions. See chapter 2
21	=	Style 21, rosewood back and sides, dark bindings
22	=	Style 22, early style, see chapter 2
23	=	Style 23, early style, based on wholesale price
24	=	Style 24, early style, based on wholesale price
25	=	Style 25K, koa back and sides, dark binding
26	=	Style 26, similar to Style 28 but in size 1
27	=	Style 27, similar to Style 30, slightly plainer
28	=	Style 28, rosewood back and sides, white bindings
30	=	Style 30, pearl rosette, colored marquetry, bound neck
34		Style 34, same as Style 30 with ivory bridge
35	=	Style 35, Rosewood back and sides, three-piece back
36	=	Style 36, Similar to Style 35 with tinted top
37		Style 37K, flamed koa back and sides, white binding
38		Style 38, rosewood back and sides, bound neck and headstock
40	=	Style 40, different appts depending on year See chapter 2
41	=	Style 41 top pearl bordered, no pearl around fingerboard
42	=	Style 42 top pearl Including perimeter of fingerboard
44	=	Style 44, deluxe binding but no pearl bordering
45	=	Style 45 top, sides and back pearl bordered
50	=	Style 50, Style 45 with lots of additional inlay
62	=	Style 62, maple back and sides, dark binding

OTHER PREFIXES AND SUFFIXES

Although we have attempted to provide a thorough and useful list, there may be some additional infrequent prefixes and suffixes noted in the production charts or in the text that are not listed here.

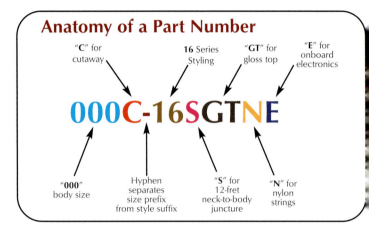

ANATOMY OF A PART NUMBER

As more and more models were added to the Martin price list in the 1980s and '90s, the consistency and ease of understanding of Martin's elegant nomenclature system became a bit strained, necessitating the "Anatomy of a Part Number" key. This appeared in Sounding Board Volume 13 and dissects the eleven digit 000C-16SGTNE model – a 16 Series 000 Auditorium- sized Venetian cutaway with a 12-fret neck and a gloss lacquered top made for nylon strings with onboard electronics! It's a far cry from the simplicity of a D-18 or Style 18 Dreadnought.

Nevertheless, an educated Martin aficionado can make sense out of just about any combination of Martin numbers and letters, especially with the help of this appendix.

SPECIAL AND LIMITED EDITION PICKS

The following page shows a sampling of some of the specially imprinted guitar picks that were issued primarily in the late 1990s in 12- or 24-gross limited quantities to promote specific artist signature model guitar projects or special Martin related events.

Jim Croce D-21JC 2000 (Back)	Steve Miller 1993 "Pegasus"	Steve Howe 00-18SH 1999	Gordon Lightfoot D-18GL 2000 (Back)			
Jim Croce D-21JC 2000 (Front)	Johnny Cash D-42JC 1997	Sting CMHS (Never Issued) 1998	Gordon Lightfoot D-18GL 2000 (Front)	Martin Guitar Masterpieces Book Tour 2003		
Dave Matthews DM3MD 1999 (Back)	Paul Simon OM-42PS 1997	Eric Clapton 000-42EC 1995 (Back)	Jimmie Rodgers 000-45JR 1997 (Back)	Steve Miller 00-37K – 00-37K2 2000 (Back)		
Dave Matthews DM3MD 1999 (Front)	Joan Baez 0-45JB 1998	Eric Clapton 000-42EC 1995 (Front)	Jimmie Rodgers 000-45JR 1997 (Front)			
Mark Knopfler HD-40MK 2001 (Back)	George Jones D-41GJ 2000	Eric Clapton 000-28EC 1996 (Front)	Jimmy Buffett HD-18JB 1998 (Back)	Steve Miller 00-37K – 00-37K2 2000 (Front)		
Mark Knopfler HD-40MK 2001 (Front)	Roger McGuinn D12-42RM 1999	Eric Clapton 000-28EC 1996 (Front)	Jimmy Buffett HD-18JB 1998 (Front)	Japan Trade Shows 2000 (Back)		
PA Council of the Arts 2000 (Front)	Kingston Trio 40th Anniversary 1997	Eric Clapton 000-42ECB 2000 (Back)	Woody Guthrie 000-18WG 1999 (Back)			
PA Council of the Arts 2000 (Back)	MTV-1 Unplugged 1996	Eric Clapton 000-42ECB 2000 (Front)	Woody Guthrie 000-18WG 1999 (Front)	Japan Trade Shows 2000 (Front)		

Glossary

A-brace. Top bracing pattern generally shaped in the form of an A.

Abalone. A colorful shell material commonly used for instrument inlays, including the pearl borders at the edges of the body.

Action. A term generally used to describe the string height above the frets.

Backstrip, or **Backstripe.** A decorative inlay in the center of the back of a guitar.

Bar Fret. A nickel silver fret with a rectangular cross section rather than T shaped.

Bearclaw. A "figure," or distortion in the grain, of spruce top wood that's supposed to look like bear claws (but rarely does).

Belly bridge. The modern steel-string guitar bridge that has a bulge toward the rear adding stability to the guitar top.

Binding. An inlaid corner trim, sometimes multi-layered, along the edges of the body and neck. It serves both a decorative and protective function.

Bird's-eye. A naturally occurring spotted pattern of a small circular figure in some maple wood.

Body. The main portion of the guitar consisting of a top, back, and sides.

Bookmatched. Two successive cuts from a piece of wood glued together to form one larger panel with symmetrical grain patterns on the left and right sides.

Bout. An outward bend or curve in the body of a guitar. Usually referred to as upper or lower bout. Between these two is the waist.

Brace. Wood reinforcements glued inside the top and back of the guitar body to add strength and improve tone.

Bridge. Conducts the vibration of the strings to the soundboard. The strings first make contact with a separate saddle, which is part of the bridge.

Bridge plate. Flat, hardwood top brace located directly underneath the bridge area of the top.

Bridge pins. Tapered pins that fit into the bridge, used to anchor the strings to the top of the guitar.

Center strip. The interior reinforcement of the joint between the two halves of the guitar's back. In Martin guitars it is made of spruce.

Cross brace. The major braces under a guitar top that cross just below the soundhole, forming an X pattern. Sometimes written as "X brace."

Dart or headstock diamond. A triangular-shaped volute carved into the back of a guitar neck at the base of the headstock.

Dovetail. A classic woodworking joint and the traditional method of neck attachment for fine steel-string guitars and mandolins.

End block. Structural block of wood at the opposite end of the body from the neck block. The top, back, and sides are glued to the end block at the bottom end of the guitar.

Endpiece. The decorative wedge-shaped piece at the bottom of the guitar where the two sides come together over the end block.

Fan bracing. Top bracing pattern generally shaped in the form of a fan, now associated with Spanish guitars.

Fingerboard. Surface of the neck that contains the frets, also called the fretboard. This is usually a piece of wood that is harder than the neck itself.

Finish. The protective coating covering the guitar.

Flame. Sometimes called figure, refers to parallel horizontal curls in the wood grain, resembling flames, also called "fiddleback."

French polish. An oil polishing technique that allows very thin layers of shellac to be applied as a finish upon wood, or to the top of an existing finish.

Fretboard. See fingerboard.

Frets. Metal bars inlayed at specific intervals along the fingerboard to define the individual notes of the chromatic scale.

Frets clear. Acoustic guitars are generally described by the number of frets that are clear of the body, rather than the total number of frets on the fretboard.

Friction peg. Violin-style wood or ivory tapered pins mounted in the headstock, perpendicular to the plane of the fingerboard, used to adjust string tension.

Hawaiian guitar. A steel-string guitar with the strings elevated high above the fretboard, played with the instrument held horizontally on the lap. The strings are "fretted" with a steel bar held in the left hand.

Headstock. The flattened area at the end of the neck where the tuners are mounted. Sometimes called a peghead.

Headplate. The wood veneer covering the face of the headstock or peghead.

Heel. Portion of the neck that joins the body. The heel is roughly perpendicular to the fretboard surface.

Heelcap. A decorative cap (wood, ivory, or plastic) on the end of the neck heel, roughly parallel to the back of the guitar.

Inlay. Decorative material that is embedded into a recess cut into the body, neck, or headstock of a guitar.

Ivoroid. Off-white celluloid with darker lines that simulate the grain found in genuine ivory, widely used as binding or other trim.

Kerfed lining. Wedge-shaped wood strips, with saw kerfs to allow bending, used to reinforce the joint between top or back and the sides.

Ladder brace. Top bracing pattern using parallel horizontal braces.

Lining. See kerfed lining.

Machine heads. See patent heads.

Marquetry. A repetitive pattern of different colored woods arranged in a band that is used as a decorative inlay.

Mother-of pearl. A white iridescent shell material commonly used for instrument inlays.

Neck block. Structural block of wood found inside the body at the base of the neck.

Nut. Rectangular bar located at the upper end of the fingerboard (below the peghead), grooved to provide proper string height and spacing.

Onboard electronics. A preamp mounted in an acoustic guitar that has been fitted with a pickup, and usually including tone and volume controls.

Patent heads or **machines** (archaic). A set of worm gears mounted in a headstock, usually three on each side, used to adjust the tension of the strings. Now usually called "tuning machines" or simply "tuners."

Pearl. A generic term for the material from a variety of mollusk shells. "Pearl bordering" is usually made of abalone, but "pearl position markers" (on a guitar neck) are usually white mother-of-pearl.

Peghead. The flat portion at the upper end of the neck where the tuners are located. Sometimes called a headstock.

Pickguard. A thin plate of plastic, or other material, that protects an instrument's top from scratches.

Piezo. Shorthand for "piezoelectric," referring to the crystal or ceramic substances that generate a minute electric signal when mechanically stressed. Piezo elements are used in under-the-saddle pickups and in soundboard-mounted transducers that amplify the sound of acoustic instruments.

Pin bridge. A bridge with vertical holes that allow the strings to be anchored to the top using tapered pins.

Purfling. Decorative wooden or plastic inlay, usually found along the edge of the top and back but often identical to the material found around the soundhole.

Pyramid bridge. A rectangular bridge with peaks that resemble pyramids at both ends.

Quilted. The repeating figure in the grain of maple or mahogany that resembles stitched or puckered cloth.

Radius. The horizontal arc of a fretboard, measured parallel to the frets. Generally stated as a measurement of the radius of a circle.

Ribs. The sides of the guitar.

Rosette. The decorative rings or inlay work found around the soundhole in the guitar's top.

Saddle. The removable part of the bridge that the strings pass over, so the saddle defines the end of the vibrating strings' length.

Scale length. Free length of the vibrating string from nut to saddle. Because of compensation and saddle angle, the most accurate measurement is to double the distance from the nut to the center of the 12th fret.

Scalloped brace. A top brace with a concave relief cut in its profile.

Screw neck. A neck with a mechanical angle adjustment in the heel, activated by a key or screw.

Side dots. Small position markers that are inlaid into the edge of the fretboard, facing the player.

Spanish foot. A section of wood that extends from the bottom of the neck block and is glued to the guitar's back.

Sunburst. A colored finish or wood stain that is darker at the edges and lighter in the center.

Tailpiece. A wood or metal device that is mounted at the lower end of the body, above the end block, and anchors the strings.

T-bar. A non-adjustable steel neck reinforcement, embedded beneath the fretboard, that has a T-shaped cross section. See truss rod.

T- frets. Refers to the cross sectional shape of modern metal frets.

Terz. A short scale length guitar tuned a musical third higher than classical tuning.

Tie block. The rectangular portion of a guitar bridge with small horizontal holes that allow the strings to be anchored (tied) to the top without using tapered pins. Usually associated with Spanish guitars.

Truss rod. A reinforcing rod in the neck that counters the tension of the strings to keep the neck straight.

Veneer. A thin wood laminate used in the construction of some guitar bodies or to cover the face of the headstock.

Vienna headstock. Scroll shaped headstock with six tuning machines mounted on the same side. Often referred to as a "Stauffer" headstock.

Volute. A raised area carved into the back of an instrument neck at the base of the headstock. On Martin guitars, it is triangular in shape.

Waist. The narrow portion of the guitar's body between the upper and lower bout.

Wings. Laminations to the sides of the headstock that allow the neck to be constructed from a narrower piece of wood. Sometimes called "ears."

X Brace. A top bracing pattern generally shaped in the form of an X. See cross brace.

Indices

General Index

Note: Page numbers in *italics* refer to illustrations and captions.
For specific models/styles, please consult the Models and Styles Index.

0 size
   prices for, 286–88, *286–88*
   production totals of, 252–53, *252–53*
00 size
   prices for, 286–88, *286–88*
   production totals for, 254–56, *254–56*
000 size
   prices for, 286–88, *286–88*
   production totals for, 258–60, *258–60*
1 size, 270, *270*
3 size, 270, *270*
5 size, 272–73, *272–73*
15/17 Series, 118
16 Series, 120–21
17 Series, 291, *291*
60 Series, 84, *84*

acoustic bass guitars, 114
   prices for, 294, *294*
   production totals for, 261, *261*
A.D. Grover, 220
adjustable truss rod neck, 23
   in Jumbos, 97
   in Limited Edition models, 130
aging toner, 131
Allen Organ Company, 184
alternative guitars, 281, *281*
American Guitar Society, 227
amplifiers, 184
Anderson, Ian, 156, *156*
animal-hide glue, 126
Appleply laminated neck block, 7
appointments, 11
archtop models, 9, *9*, 12, 54, *54*, 166, *166*
   acoustic, 167–78
   carved tops on, 177
   CF Series, 187, *187*
   colored finishes on, 43
   influence on later Martin guitar models, 168
   mando cellos made from, 207
   prices for, 288, *288*
   production totals for, 256, *256*
   in rosewood, 171, *171*
"Arkie," 92

Artinger, Matt, 164, *164*
Ashborn, James, 223
Authentic Series, 126
Autry, Gene, 41, 82, 92, 95

backpacker guitars, 295, *295*
   prices for, 295, *295*
   production totals for, 261, *261*
back purfling. *See* backstrip
backstrip, 13, *13–14*, 132, 176
Bacon Banjo Company, 220, 226
Bacon & Day, 220
Baez, Joan, 143, *143*
banjos, 220
bar frets, 32, *32*
baritone ukuleles, 217, *217*
bass guitars, 185, *185*, 186, *186*
Bechtel, Perry, 88
Belltone guitars, 226
belly bridges, 39, *39*, 102
bindings
   Ivoroid, 131
   ivory-grained celluloid on 0-28K, 100, *100*
Bird of Paradise, 208
Bitting Specials, 227, 231
   guitars, 233
   mandolins, 233
Blake, Norman, 157, *157*
Boak, Dick, *114*, 129, 142, *142*, 266, *266*
Bourgeois, Dana, 244
bowl-back mandolins, 189–98, 240
bracing. *See also* scalloped top bracing
   back, 23
   fan pattern bracing, 21, 107
   high X, 131
   internal, 20, *20*
   ladder, 179
   lattice-bracing in classical guitars, 108
   patterns, 22
   top, 21
   X-bracing on cutaway acoustic-electrics, 109, *109*
   X-bracing on early Ditson guitars, 238

Brazilian (wood), 132
bridges, 38–39, *38–39*
   belly bridges, 39, *39*, 102
   classical, 39, *39*
   pyramid bridge, 38, *38*
   straight line, 39, *39*
Briggs Special guitars, 227, 234
Briggs Special mandolins, 234
Bromberg, David, 74, *74*, 96
Bruno, Charles, 228
Buffet, Jimmy, 153, *153*
Byrd, Commander, 209, *209*

Cable Piano Company, 228
Carl Fischer Company, 102, 229
carved top guitars, 177
carved-top mandolins, 204–6, *204–6*
Cash, Johnny, 87, *87*, 142, *142*, 174, *174*
catalogs
   1896, 191, *191*
   1927, 210
   1935, 176, *176*
   for ukuleles, 212, *212*, 213
C. A. Zoebisch, 189
cedar necks, 25
cedar tops, 72, *72*
celluloid binding, 11, 12
CF Series, 187, *187*
"chain link" pattern, 14, *14*
"checkered" pattern, 14, *14*
C.H. Gaskins & Co., 199, *199*
Chicago Musical Instrument Company, 228
Clapton, Eric, 79, 154, *154*
classical guitars, 47, 104–8
   bridges, 39, *39*
   prices for, 289, *289*
   production totals for, 266, *266*
   Spanish shape, 107
"coffin" cases, 5
coloring, 43
computer numeric control (CNC), 30, 116
concept guitars, 281, *281*
"concert" models, 15
concert ukulele, 216, *216*
Coolidge, Calvin, 209, *209*

Croce, Jim, 146, *146*
Crosby, David, 163, *163*
C Series, 12, 106
    archtop 12-string guitars in, 110
    flyer for, 169, *169*
    mando-cellos in, 170
    tenor/plectrum guitars in, 172
custom branding, 223–25
    Bacon Banjo Company, 220, 226
    Belltone guitars, 226
    Bitting Special, 227, 231, 233
    Briggs Special, 227, 234
    Bruno, 228
    Cable Piano Company, 228
    Carl Fischer Company, 102, 229
    Chicago Musical Instrument Company, 228
    Ditson Company, 93, *93*, 223–24, 226, 234–40, *236, 238–40*
    E.U. Wurlitzer, 94, 224, 226
    Foden Special Guitars, 241–42
    Grinnell Brothers, 229
    Handley, J.A., 229
    H&A Selmer, Inc., 231
    H.A. Weymann & Son, 233
    Jenkins, 229
    John Wanamaker, 233
    Kealakai, 230
    Montgomery Ward, 230
    Olcott-Bickford, Vahdah, 79, 227
    Paramount Banjo Company, 220, 230, 243, *243*
    Rudick's Music Store, 225, *225*, 231
    Rudolph Wurlitzer, 233, 248–49, *248–49*
    Schoenberg Guitars, 231, 244, *244*
    Southern California Music Co., 223–24, 226, 232, 238, 245–46, *245–46*
    S.S. Stewart, 232
    Stetson, 232
    William J. Smith & Co., 217, 232
Custom Shop, 28, 44, 89
    Dreadnoughts made by, 94
    first order by Boak, 129
    as impetus for Vintage Series, 123
    production totals for, 284, *284*
cutaway guitars
    acoustic-electric, 109, 121
    bodies, 10
    electric, 181, *181*, 183, *183*

D-100 fingerboard, 263, *263*
decals, 6

DeFelipis, Carlos, 204
de Goni, Delores Nevares, 64
"de Goni" model, 64
Deichman, John, 3, 21
diamond. *See* volute
dimensions. *See* instrument dimensions
The Ditson Company, instruments made for, 234–35, 236–39, *236–39*
    1-45, 236, *236*
    Charles Ditson Company, 223–24, 226, 234
    darker finish on guitars, 42
    Dreadnought, 93, *93*, 239, *239*
    mandolins, 240
    Martin's relationship with, 92
    Octa-Chorda, 239, *239*
    Oliver Ditson Company, 228, 234
    stamps on, 235
    ukuleles, 240, *240*
    X-bracing, 238
documentation, 3
"double bound," 58
dovetail neck joint, 7
Dreadnoughts (D Series), 8–9, *9*, 54, *54*, 69, 71, 85, *85*, 87, *87*, 92–95, 262, *262*
    archtops and, 167
    as bass guitars, 114
    Chicago Musical Instrument Company selling, 228
    Ditson 111 Dreadnought, 93, *93*, 239, *239*
    evolution of, 95
    14-fret fingerboards on, 93
    herringbone pattern on, 12
    history of, 92
    Hunt's Hawaiian guitar resulting in, 224, 235
    Jumbos as alternative to, 97, *97*
    most lightly braced, 72
    OM versions, 93–94
    prices for, 286–88, *286–88*
    production totals for, 262–65, *262–65*
    promotion of, 93
    scale length of, 31
    size 7, 10
    in tenor/plectrum guitars, 103
    12-string, 111
Dresdner, Mike, 116
D Series. *See* Dreadnoughts
D shape necks, 30, *30*

ebony rod, 36, *36*
Edison, Thomas, 209, *209*

18-fret fingerboard, 101
electric guitars, 179–87
    prices for, 288, *288*
    production totals for, 284, *284*
Epiphone guitars, 167, 168
E Series, 184–86, *184–86*
E.U. Wurlitzer, 226
    custom branding for, 224
    original Dreadnoughts sold at, 94

fan pattern bracing, 21, 107
Fender, Leo, 98
finishes, 42–43
    aging toner, 131
    sunburst, 86, *86*
    top, 44
Fischl, Dennis, 20
flat-back mandolins, 199–203
    A, 200, *200*
    AK, 200, *200*
    B, 201, *201*
    BK, 201
    C, 202, *202*
    D, 203
    E, 203, *203*
Flat Response Audio Pickups (FRAP pickups), 46
Flatt, Lester, 144, *144*
flattop guitar, 20
Fletcher, Tex, 82
Foden Special Guitars, 241–42
Foden, William, 229, 241, *241*
foreign editions, 130
4-string guitars. *See* tenor/ plectrum guitars
14-fret necks, 88–89, 90, *90*, 93
French polish, 42, *42*
fretboard position markers, 32, 33, *33*, 242, *242*
    on F-series, 34
    snowflakes, in D-45, 83
    Style 45 guitar/Style D mandolin, 203
fretboard scale length, 31, 88–89
frets, 31
    T frets, 32, *32*
    20-fret fingerboard introduced, 67
Frets, 129
F Series, 10, 168, 174–76
    fretboard position markers on, 34
    M-Series originating from, 96
F Series Electric Guitars, 181
f-shape soundholes, 16

Gibson guitars, 167–68
Gibson mandolins, 190, 204
Golden Era Series, 125

GOM (Guitars of the Month), 129–30
    production totals for, 278, *278*
    quick reference chart for, 282–83, *282–83*
    retirement of, 130
"Grand Auditorium" model, 96
graphite guitars, 281, *281*
Great Depression, 225
Griffith, Andy, 155, *155*
Grinnell Brothers, 229
G Series, 105
GT Series, 182–83, *182–83*
guitar cases, 297, *297*
Guitar Player, 129
guitar shapes. *See also* nomenclature
    archtop, 9, *9,* 12
    early, 8, *8*
    modern, 9, *9*
    20th century, 88
guitar sizes, *8,* 8–9. *See also specific guitar sizes*
Guitars of the Month. *See* GOM
gut-string guitars. *See* classical guitars
Guy, Buddy, 162, *162*

Handley, J.A., 229
"harp guitars," 9, *9*
harp style mandolins, 199, *199*
H&A Selmer, Inc., 231
Hawaiian guitars, 21, 41, *41,* 47, 58, 75, *75,* 98, *98,* 98–102, 223, 224
Hawaiian music, 208
H.A. Weymann & Son, 233
headstock
    decals on, 6
    inlay, 27–28, *27–28*
    serial numbers on, 5, *5*
    shape evolution, 26, *26*
    slotted, 25–26
    Stauffer, 17, *17*
    volute (diamond), 29, *29*
Henry, Frank, 166, *166*
herringbone, 12, *12,* 64, 72
"herringbone D-28," 94
"herringbone Martin," 93, *93*
High Pressure Laminate. *See* HPL
high X, 131
Horton, Roy, 82
HPL (High Pressure Laminate), 119
Humphrey, Thomas, 108
Hunt, Harry, 224, 235, 237, *237,* 238

inlays, 27–28, *27–28,* 34, *34–35,* 242, *242*
instrument dimensions, 298–99, *298–99*
internal bracing, 20, *20*
I Series, 116, 291, *291*
Ivoroid binding, 131, 205
    in archtop guitars, 171
ivory, 40
ivory binding, 11, 65, *65*
ivory-grained celluloid binding, 100, *100*

Jenkins, 229
John Wanamaker, 233
J Series (Jumbo), 10, 58, 97
    as Dreadnought alternative, 97, *97*
    J12-40M, 113
    prices for, 291, *291*
J size, 267, *267*
Juber, Laurence, 151, *151*
Jumbo. *See* J Series (Jumbo)

Kealakai, 230
Keaton, Buster, 208, *208*
Keb Mo, 148, *148*
Kingston Trio, 103
Knopfler, Mark, 149, *149*
koa
    mandolins made from, 199
    Southern California Music procuring, 224
    taropatch in, 215
    for ukuleles, 209, 212, *212,* 214, *214*
koa guitars, 43, 63, 73, *73,* 98–102, 246, *246*
    Southern California Music Co. specializing in, 245, *245*
Konter, Richard, 209, *209*
Konter uke, 209, *209*
K Series, 99

ladder bracing, 179
"ladies' models," 8, 15
Lange, William, 243
Larson Brothers, 223
lattice-braced soundboard, 108
Laurence Juber models, 89, 91, *91*
Lightfoot, Gordon, *147*
Lilly, Russell, 83
Limited Edition, 130
    production totals for, 279–81, *279–81*
    quick reference charts for, 282–83, *282–83*

Limited Production Martin Guitars, 133–65
    Concept models, 146, *146*
    custom signature editions, 160, 162–63, 165
    Guitars of the Month, 129–30
    mahogany ID plate on, 7
    1984, 133
    1985, 133
    1986, 133–34
    1987, 134
    1988, 134–35
    1989, 135
    1990, 135
    1991, 136
    1992, 136
    1993, 136
    1993 OM-28 Perry Bechtel, 137, *137*
    1994, 137–38
    1994 D-45 Gene Autry, 137, *137*
    1995, 138–39
    1996, 140
    1997, 140–42
    1998, 142–44
    1999, 144–45
    production guidelines for, 130
    Signature Series, 129–30
    The Sounding Board to inform about, 139, *139*
    2000, 145–48
    2001, 148–50
    2002, 150–52
    2003, 152–55
    2004, 156–58
    2005, 158–60
    2006, 160–62
    2007, 163–65
Lindbergh, Charles, 209, *209*
logo, 6
long saddle, 131
Longworth, Mike, 3, 77, 82
    on pricing, 285
    production records kept by, 251
    on Shenandoah models, 115
low profile (LP), 131, 274, *274*
LP. *See* low profile
L.R. Baggs, 46
Lundberg, Jon, 96
Lyon & Healy, 204

mahogany, 25
    neck on M-38, 74
    stains on, 43
    ukuleles made from, 209

mahogany guitars, 44–45, 58, 118, *118*, 186, *186*
  in R Series, 177
  12-string, 112
mando-cellos, 193, 207
  C-2 archtop bodies to make, 207
  in C Series, 170, 172
mandolas, 193, 201, 206, *206*, 207
  bowl-back/flat-back, 207
mandolins, 4, 40, *41*, 167, 189–206
  Bitting Specials, 233
  bowl-back, 189–98, 240
  Briggs Special, 234
  building of, 190, *190*
  carved tops on, 204–6
  for The Ditson Company, 240
  flat back styles, 199–203
  by Gibson, 190, 204
  harp style, 199, *199*
  koa used for, 199
  oval soundholes on, 16
  pickguard styles of, 190
  popularity of, at turn of century, 189
  prices for, 292–93, *292–93*
  production totals for, 268–69, *268–69*
  in rosewood/koa, 199
  sales declining in 1930s, 204
  serial numbers for, 296, *296*
  Style D position markers similar to D-45 guitar style, 203
manufacturing methods, recorded changes in, 48–50
maple, 202, *202*
maple guitars, 45, 84, *84,* 85, *85,* 113, *113,* 175, *175,* 184, *184*
marquetry
  backstrip, 13, *13–14*
  colored, on Style 24, 62, *62*
  herringbone, 12, *12*
Marquis Series, 125
Martin/American archtop, 256, *256*
Martin, C. F., III, 3, 164, *164,* 167, 187, *187,* 227
Martin, Chris, 114
Martin foremen, 3
Martin, Frank Henry, 3, 44–45
  custom branding started by, 223
  Hunt consulting with, 235
  mandolin line developed by, 189
  mandolin research by, 191, *191*
  reduction of number of models by, 18
Martin, George, 159, *159*

Martin Guitar Series, 1993-2007, 116–26
  Authentic Series, 126
  15/17 Series, 118
  Golden Era Series, 125
  I Series, 116
  Marquis Series, 125
  Road Series, 117
  16 Series, 120–21
  Standard Series, 122
  Vintage Series, 123–24
  X Series, 119
Martin, Herbert Keller, 210
Martin/Humphrey models, 108
Martin Museum, 225
Mayer, John, 154, *154*
McFadden, Matt, 114
metal extender nuts, 98
Micarta, 40
M models, 96
M. Nunes & Sons, 247, *247*
model codes. *See* nomenclature
modified low oval neck, 274, *274*
modified V neck, 274, *274*
Montgomery Ward, 230
Moore, Jackie "Kid," 82
mortise-and-tenon neck joint (M&T neck joint), 7, 120
"mosaic" pattern, 14, *14*
M Series, 10, 290, *290*
M size, 261, *261*
M&T neck joint. *See* mortise-and-tenon neck joint

NAMM trade shows, 129
Nazareth, Pa., 4
neck joint
  dovetail, 7, 37, *37*
  mortise-and-tenon, 7, 120
  neck-to-body joints, 36
necks
  adjustable truss rod, 23, 97, 130
  cedar, 25
  D shape, 30, *30*
  early styles/materials, 23–24, *24*
  14-fret necks, 88–89, 90, *90,* 93
  inlays, 34, *34–35*
  low profile, 131, 274, *274*
  mahogany, 74
  modified low oval, 274, *274*
  modified V, 274, *274*
  neck block, 5, 7
  reinforcement, 36, *36*
  "screw neck," in Style 42, 78
  12-frets on 12-string guitars, 111
  12-fret v. 14-fret, 25–26
  twentieth century styles, 25

V shape, 30, *30,* 131
  widths/shape, 30, *30*
Nelson, Willie, *107,* 266, *266*
1999, 144–45
nomenclature, 300–302
N, P, Q, R sizes, 274, *274*
N Series, 47, 107
nut adjusters, 245
nylon string guitars. *See* classical guitars

Octa-Chorda, 239, *239*
Olcott-Bickford, Vahdah, 79, 227
OM (Orchestra Models), 9, 88–89
  modern day, 91, *91*
  original styles, 90, *90*
  prices for, 286–88, *286–88*
  production totals for, 257, *257*
  scale length of, 31
orange-top finish, 42, *42*
Orchestra Model. *See* OM
Oriolo, Don, 156, *156*
oval soundholes, 16

paper labels, 4–5, *4–5*
Paramount Banjo Company, 220, 230, 243, *243*
"parlor" guitars, 66
part numbers, 302
Patent pegs, 24
pearl bordering, 15, *15,* 80, *80,* 132, 202, *202*
  in Dreadnoughts, 95
pearl inlays, 27–28
peg head, 24
Perlburg and Halpin, 226
pickguards, 40–41, *41,* 131
pickguard styles, 190
picks, 302–3
pickups, 46
plaques, 27, *27*
prices
  for 0 size models, 286–88, *286–88*
  for 00 size models, 286–88, *286–88*
  for 000 size models, 286–88, *286–88*
  for 12-string guitars, 293, *293*
  for 15 Series, 291, *291*
  for 17 Series, 291, *291*
  for acoustic bass guitars, 294, *294*
  for archtop models, 288, *288*
  for backpacker guitars, 295, *295*
  for classical guitars, 289, *289*
  for Dreadnoughts, 286–88, *286–88*

for electric guitars, 288, *288*
for I Series, 291, *291*
for J Series, 291, *291*
for mandolins, 292–93, *292–93*
for M Series, 290, *290*
for OM models, 286–88, *286–88*
for Road Series, 290, *290*
for tiples, 294–95, *294–95*
for ukuleles, 294–95, *294–95*
for X Series, 290, *290*
pricing system, 53, 285, *285*
production totals
    for 0 size, 252–53, *252–53*
    for 00 size, 254–56, *254–56*
    for 000 size, 258–60, *258–60*
    for 1 size, 270, *270*
    for 2 1/2 size, 270, *270*
    for 3 size, 270, *270*
    for 5 size, 272–73, *272–73*
    for 12-string guitars, 275, *275*
    for acoustic bass, 261, *261*
    for alternative guitars, 281, *281*
    for archtop models, 256, *256*
    for backpacker guitars, 261, *261*
    Boak researching, 251
    for classical guitars, 266, *266*
    for concept guitars, 281, *281*
    for Custom Shop, 284, *284*
    for D size Dreadnought, 262–65, *262–65*
    for electric guitars, 284, *284*
    for GOM, 278, *278*
    for graphite guitars, 281, *281*
    for Limited and Special Edition, 279, *279*
    Longworth consolidating records of, 251
    for mandolins, 268–69, *268–69*
    for Martin/American archtop, 256, *256*
    methodology for tracking, 251
    for M size, 261, *261*
    1916 to 1921, 237, *237*, 238, *238*
    for N, P, Q, R sizes, 274, *274*
    for OM, 257, *257*
    for Shenandoah models, 281, *281*
    for Sigma Martin models, 281, *281*
    for tiples, 276–77, *276–77*
    for ukuleles, 276, *276*
    for unusual sizes, 277, *277*
    for Vega banjos, 271, *271*
P suffix, 36
purfling, 19, *19*
pyramid bridge, 38, *38*

recorded changes in manufacturing methods, 48–50

rectangular bridge, 38, *38*
reference charts, 282–83, *282–83*
Remaley, Earl, 179, *179*
Road Series, 117, 290, *290*
Robertson, Robbie, 165, *165*
Robinson, Larry, 87
Rolando label, 230, 246, *246*
rosettes, 16, *16–17*
    on pre-WWII guitars, 19, *19*
    on styles after 1900, 18
rosewood, 132, 199
rosewood binding, 11
rosewood guitars, 44–45, 60, 77
    in archtop style, 171, *171*
R Series, 177–78
Rudick's Music Store, 225, *225*, 231
Rudolph Wurlitzer, 233
    advertising for, 248, *248*
    model 2092, 249, *249*
    model codes for Martin guitars made for, 248

saddle materials, 40
saddles, 38–39, *38–39*, 131
sales catalogs, 3
sapele (African hardwood), 118
scalloped top bracing, 22, *22*, 84
    in Dreadnoughts, 95
    in HD-35, 72, *72*
    in J-40, 76, *76*
Schoenberg, Eric, 244
Schoenberg Guitars, 231, 244
    Soloist, 244, *244*
    20-fret fingerboards on, 244, *244*
"screw neck," 78
Scruggs, Earl, 144, *144*
serial numbers, 53
    for guitars/mandolins, 296, *296*
    on headstock, 5, *5*
Shenandoah models
    Longworth on, 115
    production totals for, 281, *281*
Sigma Martin models, 281, *281*
Signature Series, 129–30, *130*
Simon, Paul, 140, *140*
slotted headstock, 25–26
Smith, William J., 217
snowflake fingerboards, 83, 91
soundholes, 5, 16
The Sounding Board, 139, *139*
Southern California Music Co., 223–24, 226, 232, 238, 245–46, *245–46*
    koa guitars specialty of, 245, *245*
    Rolando label in, 230, 246, *246*
"Spanish" bracing. *See* fan pattern bracing
Spanish classical guitar shape, 107

Spanish models, 98
Special Edition
    production totals for, 279–81, *279–81*
    quick reference charts for, 282–83, *282–83*
specific playing style guitars, 98–114
    acoustic bass, 114
    classical, 104–8
    cutaway acoustic-electric, 109
    Hawaiian, 98–102
    tenor/plectrum, 102–4
    12-string, 110–13
spruce, 132
spruce-top guitars, 45
    in C Series, 170
    in F Series, 174–76
    in J-40, 76, *76*
    in M-38, 74, *74*
    in Road Series, 117
    in R Series, 177
square steel tubing, 36, *36*
S.S. Stewart, 232
stains, 43
stamps, 4, *4*
    Ditson/Martin, on Ditson guitars, 235
    internal, 6
Standard Series, 122
Stauffer headstock, 17, *17*, 23
steel guitars. *See* Hawaiian guitars
steel strings, 47
Stetson, 232
Stills, Stephen, 163, *163*
straight-line bridges, 39, *39*
string guage, 6
strings, 47
Stuart, Marty, 155, *155*
Summers, Andy, 161, *161*
sunburst finish, 86, *86*

taropatch, 215, *215*, 216
    for B. Keaton, 208, *208*
T-bar, 36, *36*
tenor/plectrum guitars, 102–4
    in C Series, 172
    Dreadnoughts in, 103
tenor ukulele, 216, *216*
"Terz" guitars, 8, 16, 272, *272*
T frets, 32, *32*
Thinline pickups, 46
Thompson, T.J., 244
Tolman, Gerry, 163, *163*
top finishes, 44
tortoise, 131
tuners, 132

Tusq, 40
12-fret necks, 111
12-string guitars, 110–13
   in C Series, 170, 172, *172*
   in Dreadnought shape, 111
   electric, 183, *183*
   prices for, 293, *293*
   production totals for, 275, *275*
20-fret fingerboard, 67, 80
   on D-45, 82
   Foden suggesting, 241
   on Schoenberg Guitars, 244, *244*
"two side screw," 24

ukuleles, 6, 99, 167, 208, *208, 208–14*, 210–11, *210–11*, 213–14, *213–14*, 216–17, *216–17*, 217, *217*
   baritone, 217, *217*
   in *Bird of Paradise*, 208
   catalogs for, *212,* 212–13
   concert, 216, *216*
   for The Ditson Company, 240, *240*
   Hawaiian music stimulating sales of, 208
   koa for, 209, 212, *212,* 214, *214*
   mahogany for, 209
   prices for, 294–95, *294–95*
   production totals for, 276, *276*
   revival of, in 2006, 210
   taropatch, 216
   tenor, 216, *216*
Umanov, Matt, 96
Unger, Dale, 167, 187, *187*
unusual sizes, 277, *277*

Vega banjos, 271, *271*
Vega of Boston, 220, *220*
"Vienna head." *See* Stauffer headstock
Vintage Series, 95, 123–24
Vintage toner, 44
volute (diamond), 29, *29*
V shape necks, 30, *30,* 131

White, Clarence, 148, *148*
William J. Smith & Co., 217, 232
Willie Nelson N-20, 266, *266*
Wolverine. *See* Grinnell Brothers
women, 8
   "ladies' models," 8
   Women & Music models, 10, 120
Women & Music models, 10, 120

woods, 44–46, 132, 199
   cedar, 25, 72, *72*
   koa, 199, 209, 212, *212,* 214, *214,* 215, 224
   mahogany, 25, 43, 74, 209
   maple, 202, *202*
   rosewood, 132
   spruce, 132

X-bracing pattern, 21, 22, *22*
   on cutaway acoustic-electrics, 109, *109*
   on Ditson guitars, 238
X Series, 22, *22,* 119, 290, *290*

Young, Neil, 163, *163*

"zigzag" pattern (zipper), 13, *14*
"zipper" pattern. *See* "zigzag" pattern

Models and Styles Index

All model and style numbers are for guitars unless otherwise indicated.

0 (mandolins), 198
0 (ukuleles), 211, *211*, 217, *217*
0-15, *54*
0-16NY, 55, 123
0-17H, 101, *101*
0-18K, 99, *99*
0-18T, 103, *103*
0-21, 61, *61*
0-28, 42, *42*, 66
0-28 Ian Anderson, 156, *156*
0-28K, 100, *100*
0-30, 70, *70*
0-34, 70, *70*
0-44, 253, *253*
0-45, 80, *80*, 81, *81*
0-45JB, 143, *143*
00 (mandolins), 198, *198*
00-16C, 106
00-16DBM, 120, *120*
00-17, 57, *57*, 118, *118*
00-18C, 106
00-18G, 105, *105*
00-18H, 101, *101*
00-25K, 63, *63*
00-25K2, 63, *63*
00-28, 66, *66*
00-28C, 106
00-28G, 105, *105*
00-40H, 102, *102*, 256, *256*
00-42, 78, *78*, 80
00-42K Robbie Robertson, 165, *165*
00-45, 81, *81*
00-55, 225
00CXAE, 119, *119*
000 (mandolins), 198
000-16SGTNE, 109, *109*
000-16SRNE, 109, *109*
000-18, 59, *59*
000-18 Authentic 1937, 126, *126*
000-18 Authentic Sunburst, 126, *126*
000-18GE, 125, *125*
000-21, 61, *61*
000-28, 68, *68*
000-28C, 106, *106*
000-28EC, 124, *124*, 154, *154*
000-28 Norman Blake, 157, *157*

000-42 (Eric Clapton's 1939 version), 79, *79*
000-42EC, 138, *138*
000-45, 258, *258*
000C-16SRNE-2003, 289, *289*
000C-28 Andy Summers, 161, *161*
000-JBS, 153, *153*
000-OM, 117, *117*
1 (Ditson), 237, 239, *239*
1 (taropatch), 215, *215*
1 (ukuleles), 210, 211
1-45 (Ditson), 236, *236*
1-C (ukuleles), 216, *216*
1-T (ukuleles), 216, *216*, 217, *217*
1K (ukuleles), 211, *211*
2 (Ditson), 237
2 (mandolins), 194, *194*
2 (ukuleles), 212, *212*
2 1/2-24 (circa 1860), 270, *270*
2 1/2-24 peghead detail, 270, *270*
2-15 (mandolins), 205, *205*
2-17H, 101
2-20 (mandolins), 206, *206*
2-27, 65, *65*
2-28T, 103, *103*
2-30 (mandolins), 206, *206*
2-40, 75, *75*
2-44, 79, *79*
2K (ukuleles), 212
3 (Ditson), 237
3 (mandolins), 194, *194*
3 (ukuleles), 208, *208*, 213, *213*, 217, *217*, 276, *276*
3K (ukuleles), 213, *213*
4 (mandolins), 195, *195*
5 (mandolins), 195, *195*
5 (ukuleles), 214, *214*
5-15, 118, *118*
5-15T, 103, *103*
5K (ukuleles), 214, *214*
5 size "Terz" Mini-Martin, 272, *272*
6 (mandolins), 196, *196*
6-A (mandolins), 196
7 (mandolins), 197, *197*, 293, *293*
10, 53
10-100, 53

11 (Ditson), 237
15, 54, *54*
15 (mandolins), 204, *204*
16, 55–56, *55–56*
17, 18, 25, 42, 57
18, 18, 19, *19*, 58, 59
18K, 99, 245
19, 60
20, 60
20 (mandolins), 205, *205*
21, 11–12, 13, *14*, 18, 19, *19*, 60
21K, 100
22, 62
22 (Ditson), 237
23, 62
24, 62, *62*
25, 63, *63*
26, 64, *64*
27, 65, *65*
28, 11–12, 66, *66*, 68
 backstrip, 13, *14*
 fretboard position markers on, 33, *33*
 headstock volute on, 29, *29*
 history of, 67
 rosette style on, 18, 19, *19*
28K, 100, *100*, 245
30, 70, *70*
30 (mandolins), 205
33, 62
33 (Ditson), 237, *237*, 238, *238*
34, 70, *70*
35, 71
36, 73, *73*
37, 73, *73*
38, 74, *74*
40, 15, 75, *75*
40, modern era, 76, *76*
41, 77, *77*
42, 13, 15, 78–79, *78–79*, 241, *241*
 fretboard position markers on, 33, *33*
 pearl bordering on, 15, *15*
 rosette style on, 19, *19*
44, 79, *79*
44 Soloist, 227

MODELS AND STYLES INDEX 313

45, 13, 27, 80, *80,* 81, *81*
   fretboard position markers on, 33, *33*
   headstock inlay on, 28
   pearl bordering on, 15
   rosette style on, 19, *19*
45 headplate, 132
50, 84, *84*
51 (ukuleles), 217, *217*
60, 84, *84*
62, 85, *85*
64, 85, *85*
65, 86, *86*
68, 86, *86*
76, 87, *87*
100, 87, *87*
111 (Ditson), 237, 239, *239*
222 (Ditson), 237
333 (Ditson), 237, *237*
1350 (Southern California Music Co.), 246
1400 (Southern California Music Co.), 246
1500 (Southern California Music Co.), 246
2092 (Wurlitzer), 249

A (Foden), 241
A (mandolins), 200, *200,* 219, *219*
AK (mandolins), 200, *200*

B (Foden), 241
B (mandolas), 201
B (mandolins), 201, *201*
B-40 bass, 294, *294*
B-65 bass, 294, *294*
B-540 bass, 114, *114*
BB (mandolas), 201
BC-15E, 114, *114*
BK (mandolins), 201

C (Foden), 242
C (mandolins), 202, *202*
C-1 archtop, 170, *170*
C-2, 168, 171, *171*
C-2, 12-string version, 172, *172*
C-2 archtop guitars, 207
C-3, 173, *173*
CF-1, 187, *187*
CF-1 American Archtop, 256, *256*
CF-2, 187, *187*

C-IR, 108
CSN Gerry Tolman Tribute, 163, *163*
CTSH-Humphrey model, 108, *108*
CTSH-Thomas S. Humphrey, 289, *289*
Custom 8, 69
Custom 15, 69
Custom OMC-12-string, 275, *275*

D (Foden), 242
D (mandolins), 203
D-1, 37, *37,* 116, *116*
D-3R, 116, *116*
D12-18, 112, *112*
D12-20, 110, *110,* 111, *111*
D12-28, 112, *112*
D12-35, 110, *110,* 111, *111*
D12-41, 112
D12-45, 110, *110,* 112
D12XI, 119, *119*
D-15S, 118, *118*
D-16, 120, *120*
D-16A, 56
D-16H, 56, *56*
D-16K, 56
D-16M, 56
D-16T, 56
D-16W, 56
D-18, 59, *59*
D-18 Andy Griffith, 155, *155*
D-18CW, 148, *148*
D-18GL, 147, *147*
D-19, 60
D-21, 61
D-21JC, 146, *146*
D-28, 67, 68*,* 93, *93*
D-28 LF, 144, *144*
D-28S, 68, *68*
D-35, 29, 71, *71*
D-37K2, 73, *73*
D-41, 77, *77*
D-42JC, 142, *142*
D-42K2, 79, *79*
D-45, 82–83, *82–83,* 94*,* 95, 203, 210, 265, *265*
D-45 Gene Autry, 137, *137*
D-45 Marquis, 125, *125*
D-45 Mike Longworth, 83, *83*
D-45SS Stephen Stills, 83, *83*
D-62, 85, *85*

D-76, 87, *87*
D-100, 87, *87,* 197, *197*
D-100 fingerboard, 263, *263*
DC-28E, 122, *122*
DCM, 117, *117*

E (Foden), 242, *242*
E (mandolins), 203, *203*
E-18, 184, *184*
E-28, 186, *186*
EB-18, 185, *185*
EB-28, 186, *186*
EM-18, 185, *185*

F-1, 174
F-2, 174, *174*
F-5, 175, *175*
F-7, 174, *174,* 175, *175*
F-9, 176, *176*
F-50, 179, *179,* 181
F-55, 179, *179,* 181, *181*
F-65, 181, *181*
FeLiX LX, 156, *156*

G (mandolins), 191, 268, *268*
G-1 (mandolin), 192, *192*
G-5 (mandolin), 192, *192*
"Grand Auditorium" model, 96
GT-70, 182
GT-75, 183, *183*

HD-28, 69, *69*
HD-28KM, 148, *148*
HD-28V, 69, 124, *124*
HD-35, 72
HD-40, 34–35
HD-40MK, 149, *149*
"herringbone D-28," 94
"herringbone Martin," 93, *93*
HPD-41, 77, *77*

I (mandolin), 193, *193*
I-17P, 104, *104*
I-18, 59, *59*
I-26, 64, *64*

J12-15, 113, *113*
J12-16GT, 293, *293*
J12-40M, 113
J12-65M, 113, *113*
J-40, 23, 76, *76*

J-40M, 76, *76*
J-41 Special, 267, *267*
J-65M, 86, *86*
JC-16MC, 120, *120*
JC Buddy Guy, 162, *162*, 267, *267*

L (Paramount), 243, *243*

M2C 28, 134, *134*
M3M George Martin, 159, *159*
M-36, 73, *73*
M-38, 23, 44, 74, *74*
M-64, 85, *85*
MC-1 (mando-cello), 207, *207*
MC-40, 34–35, *34–35*
MC-45, 290, *290*
MC-68, 86, *86*
MTV-2, 153, *153*

N-10 classic, 53, 107
N-20 classic, 107, *107*

Octa-Chorda, 239, *239*
OM-18, 90, *90*
OM-18P, 104
OM-21, 61, *61*
OM-21 Special, 122, *122*
OM-28, 89, *89*
OM-28JM, 154, *154*
OM-28 Marquis Madagascar, 125, *125*
OM-28 Perry Bechtel, 137, *137*
OM-35, 71, *71*
OM-40, 34–35, *34–35*
OM-45, 81, *81*
OM-45B Roy Rogers, 257, *257*
OM-45 Deluxe, 90
OMC-18VLJ, 151, *151*
OMC-28LJ, 91, *91*
OMC Artinger I, 164, *164*
OMCXK2, 119, *119*

Prototype E-18 Electric, 284, *284*

R-15, 177
R-17, 16, 177, *177*
R-18, 16, 178, *178*

S-0028-H, 115, *115*
SC-20E, 115, *115*
SD-28H, 115, *115*
SOM-45, 91

T-15 (tiples), 218, *218*
T-17 (tiples), 218, *218*
T-18 (tiples), 219, *219*
T-28 (tiples), 219, *219*

Willie Nelson N-20, 266, *266*

X-35, 71